NAVLIPI

A NEW UNIVERSAL SCRIPT ("ALPHABET") ACCOMMODATING THE PHONEMIC IDIOSYNCRASIES OF ALL THE WORLD'S LANGUAGES.
VOLUME II, NAVLIPI COMPANION: A PRIMER IN LINGUISTICS, PHONETICS, PHONEMICS AND WRITING SYSTEMS WITH A DIFFERENCE

By Prasanna Chandrasekhar

with *FOREWORD/APPRECIATION*
by NICHOLAS OSTLER

and additional *FOREWORD*
by CHRISTOPHER MOSELEY

© Copyright 2013, Alternative Book Press

Library of Congress Cataloging-in-Publication Data

Chandrasekhar, Prasanna.

    NAVLIPI. A New Universal Script ("Alphabet") Accommodating The Phonemic Idiosyncrasies of All The World's Languages.
Volume II, Navlipi Companion: A Primer in Linguistics, Phonetics, Phonemics and Writing Systems with a Difference.

with Foreword/Appreciation by Nicholas Ostler and additional Foreword by Christopher Moseley.

    p. cm.
 Includes bibliographical references and index.
 1. Language and languages--Phonetic transcriptions. 2. Phonetic alphabet. I. Title.

P226.C43 2012
411 –dc23
    2013939516

Volume II:
Print Edition ISBN 978-1-940122-02-1
E-Book Edition ISBN 978-1-940122-03-8

              Alternative Book Press
    2 Timber Lane, #301, Marlboro, NJ 07733, USA.
           www.alternativebookpress.com

with **FOREWORD/APPRECIATION**
by
Nicholas Ostler
[Author, most recently, of *The Last Lingua Franca: English Until the Return of Babel* (Walker & Company, 2010);
of *Empires of the Word: A Language History of the World* (HarperCollins, 2005);
and of several other works in the fields of language and linguistics.]

and additional **FOREWORD**
by
Christopher Moseley
[Editor-in-chief of *UNESCO Atlas of the World's Languages in Danger* (UNESCO Press, 3rd Edition, Paris, 2010- includes online interactive version);
Editor of *Encyclopedia of the World's Endangered Languages* (Routledge, 2007);
Co-Editor of *Atlas of the World's Languages* (Routledge, 1994); of *Foundation for Endangered Languages*, London, U.K., http://www.ogmios.org/ .]

Dedicated to Yaaska,

Paanini and the

predecessors they reference, among the world's first linguists; and to the endangered languages of the world.

Yadbhaawi, tadbhaawi, yadabhaawi, na tad anyathaa

Copyright © 2010, 2011, 2012, 2013, Prasanna Chandrasekhar, all rights reserved

TABLE OF CONTENTS

FOREWORD/APPRECIATION TO VOLUME I

by *Nicholas Ostler*

[Author, most recently, of *The Last Lingua Franca: English Until the Return of Babel* (Walker & Company, 2010); Author of *Empires of the Word: A Language History of the World* (Harper Collins, 2005); and of several other works in the fields of language and linguistics.]

....*xv*

FOREWORD TO VOLUME I

by *Christopher Moseley*

[Editor-in-chief of *UNESCO Atlas of the World's Languages in Danger* (UNESCO Press, 3rd Edition, Paris, 2010- includes online interactive version); Editor of *Encyclopedia of the World's Endangered Languages* (Routledge, 2007); Co-Editor of *Atlas of the World's Languages* (Routledge, 1994); of *Foundation for Endangered Languages*, London, U.K., http://www.ogmios.org/ .]

....*xvii*

PREFACE AND OBJECTIVES OF THIS SECOND VOLUME

[PROVIDING A GOOD OVERVIEW OF THE ENTIRE BOOK- READ THIS FIRST!]

..........................*xxiii*

CHAPTER 1.
ORIGINS OF LANGUAGE; POINTS OF ARTICULATION; BASIC CLASSIFICATION OF VOWELS, NONVOWELS, TONES
.....1

TABLE OF CONTENTS

1.1 PURPOSE OF THIS SECOND VOLUME IN THE NAVLIPI SERIES 3

1.2 THEORIES OF LANGUAGE AS A MERE EXPRESSION AND OUTWARD MANIFESTATION OF HUMAN INTELLIGENCE, WITH THE SPEECH APPARATUS BEING MERELY THE MOST CONVENIENT, BUT BY NO MEANS ONLY, MEDIUM FOR ITS EXPRESSION 4

1.3 POINTS OF ARTICULATION IN THE SPEECH APPARATUS: THE TERMS PHONE, PHONOLOGY AND ARTITION (ARTICULATION POSITION, POINT OF ARTICULATION) 10

1.4 BASIC CLASSIFICATION OF PHONES (SOUNDS): THE TERMS VOWEL AND NON-VOWEL 17

1.5 BASIC CLASSIFICATION OF VOWELS 19

    1.5.1 JAW, LIP AND TONGUE POSITION, AND LENGTH, AS KEY VARIABLES IN VOWEL CLASSIFICATION 19
    1.5.2 COMBINATIONS OF JAW, LIP, TONGUE POSITION AND LENGTH, TO GENERATE INDIVIDUAL VOWELS... 26
    1.5.3 VOWEL EQUATIONS: FUNDAMENTAL, DERIVATIVE AND "CARDINAL" VOWELS AND DIPHTHONGS 29
    1.5.4 JAW, LIP, AND TONGUE POSITION, AND LENGTH, AS BASIS OF SYSTEMATIC CLASSIFICATION OF VOWELS................................. 31

1.6 SEMIVOWELS AS DERIVATIVES OF VOWELS.. 32

1.7 BASIC CLASSIFICATION OF NON-VOWELS 35

    1.7.1 THE TERMS *VOICING (VOICED* AND *UNVOICED* OR *DEVOICED)*, CLOSURE, PLOSIVE, STOP, NASALIZATION, ASPIRATION 35
    1.7.2 THE TERMS *FRICATIVE, FRICATIZATION, SIBILANT, FLAP, TAP AND TRILL* 38
    1.7.3 OTHER, LESS COMMON NON-VOWEL PHONES: 40
    CLICKS, EJECTIVES, IMPLOSIVES 40
    1.7.4 *ARTITION, VOICING* AND *"COLOR"* OF THE PHONE *(PHONOCHROMATICITY)* AS KEY VARIABLES IN PHONOLOGICAL CLASSIFICATION OF NON-VOWELS 41

1.8 TONES, TONAL ACCENT, PITCH AND STRESS (ICTUS) ACCENT: FUNDAMENTAL vs. SIGNIFICANT TONES 43

1.9 PARTING NOTE ON THE EXTANT PRIMER AND MID-LEVEL LITERATURE IN PHONOLOGY, LINGUISTICS, AND RELATED FIELDS 47

1.10 EXERCISES 52

CHAPTER 2.
WRITING: METHODS OF TRANSCRIPTION AND "ALPHABETS"

.....53

TABLE OF CONTENTS

2.1 PURPOSE OF THIS CHAPTER 54

2.2 SOME BASIC TERMINOLOGY ESSENTIAL FOR FURTHER DISCUSSION 55

2.3 BRIEF DISCUSSION OF ORIGINS OF WRITING AND SOME STANDARD TERMS USED IN THE CURRENT STATE OF THE ART: 56

2.4 THE REBUS PRINCIPLE, ADDITIONAL STANDARD ORTHOGRAPHIC TERMS (*DETERMINATIVE, LOGOSYLLABIC, LOGOPHONETIC, ABJAD, ALPHABETIC, ABUGIDA, FEATURAL*) AND SOME NEW TERMS (*MAATRAIC, PHONOGRAPHIC*) 63

2.5 MORE SPECIFIC CHARACTERISTICS OF SCRIPTS AND THE NEW TERMS *COMPLETENESS, VAIGYAANIC, EMPIRICITY, UNIPHONOGRAPHIC, UNIPHONEMOGRAPHIC, QUASI-PHONETIC* AND *PHONEMO-IDIOSYNCRATIC* 67

2.6 TOOLS AVAILABLE FOR THE MODERN ORTHOGRAPHER: 77

2.7 EXERCISES 85

CHAPTER 3.
PHONOLOGICAL CLASSIFICATION AND SOME NEW PHONOLOGICAL TERMS

.....87

TABLE OF CONTENTS

3.1 NOTE ON IMPORTANCE OF THIS CHAPTER 88

3.2 THE TERM *PHONOLOGICAL VARIABLE* AND THE NEW TERMS *ARTITION*, *PHONOCHROMATICITY*, *PHONOCHROME*, *FORWARD FRICATIVE* 89

    3.2.1 The *Phonological Variable* as Applied to Vowels, and its Discretization and Limitation 89
    3.2.2 The Phonological Variable as Applied to Nonvowels: *Artition* and *Phonochromaticity* and the 15 Artitions and 35 Phonochromes 92
    3.2.3 The *Forward Fricative* 96
    3.2.4 Linguistic Significance of the Forward Fricative 97

3.3 THE TERMS *PHONEME*, *TONEME*, *CHRONEME* AND THE NEW TERM *GALATOPHONE* 99

    3.3.1 The *Phoneme* and the *Allophone* 99
    3.3.2 The *Toneme*, the "*Allotone*" and the *Chroneme* 101
    3.3.3 The *Galatophone* 102

3.4 THE ALL-IMPORTANT *PHONEMIC CONDENSATE* 106

3.5 OTHER, MISCELLANEOUS PHONOLOGICAL TERMINOLOGY 110

3.6 EXERCISES 112

CHAPTER 4.
THE WORLD'S MAJOR LANGUAGE FAMILIES- A PRIMER
.....113

TABLE OF CONTENTS

4.1 OBJECTIVES OF THIS CHAPTER 116

4.2 SUMMARY OF WORLD LANGUAGE FAMILIES AND THE SEVEN PREDOMINANT LANGUAGE FAMILIES 117

4.3 LANGUAGE vs. DIALECT: A MORE EXACT DEFINITION 147

4.4 THE INDO-EUROPEAN (INDO-GERMANIC) FAMILY 150

    4.4.1 EXTENT AND NUMBER OF SPEAKERS 150
    4.4.2 INDIAN ("INDIC") BRANCH 152
    4.4.3 IRANIAN (PERSIAN) BRANCH 157
    4.4.4 GREEK BRANCH 158
    4.4.5 BALTO-SLAVIC BRANCH 159
    4.4.6 ARMENIAN BRANCH 160
    4.4.7 ALBANIAN BRANCH 161
    4.4.8 GERMANIC BRANCH 161
    4.4.9 ROMANCE (ALSO CALLED *ITALIC*) BRANCH 162
    4.4.10 KELTIC (*CELTIC*) BRANCH 162
    4.4.11 EXTINCT INDO-EUROPEAN LANGUAGES 163

4.5 THE SINO-TIBETAN FAMILY 164

    4.5.1 EXTENT AND NUMBER OF SPEAKERS 164
    4.5.2 THE CHINESE LANGUAGES 165
    4.5.3 THE TIBETO-BURMAN LANGUAGES 168

4.6 THE NIGER-CONGO FAMILY 169

4.7 THE AFRO-ASIATIC (FORMERLY CALLED HAMITO-SEMITIC) FAMILY 172

4.8 AUSTRONESIAN (FORMERLY MALAYO-POLYNESIAN) FAMILY 174

4.9 ALTAIC FAMILY AND JAPANESE 178

4.9.1 URALIC, ALTAIC, "URAL-ALTAIC", "FINNO-UGRIC" AND JAPANESE 178
4.9.2 EXTENT AND NUMBER OF SPEAKERS 179
4.9.3 TURKIC BRANCH 179
4.9.4 TUNGUSIC (SIBERIAN) AND MONGOLIC (MONGOLIAN) BRANCHES 179
4.9.5 SCRIPTS OF THE ALTAIC FAMILY AND JAPANESE 180

4.10 DRAVIDIAN FAMILY 181

4.10.1 DRAVIDIANS AND THEIR ORIGINS IN THE INDIAN AND WORLD CONTEXTS . 181
    4.10.1.1 Are Dravidians Native to India or Were They Migrants from the Iran/Iraq Region? 181
    4.10.1.2 Dravidians, Aaryans (Aryans), Haplogroups and The Last Ice Age. 185
    4.10.1.3 Tamil, Elamite and "Proto-Dravidian" 188
    4.10.1.4 Recent DNA Studies and Archaeological Excavations Shedding Some Light on Dravidian Origins 192
    4.10.1.5 The Likely Dravidian/Aaryan (Aryan) Tapestry in the Indian Geographical Context From About 10 000 BCE 193
4.10.2 EXTENT AND NUMBER OF SPEAKERS 201

4.11 AUSTRO-ASIATIC FAMILY 203

4.12 DAIC FAMILY 205

4.13 NILO-SAHARAN FAMILY 207

4.14 URALIC FAMILY 208

4.15 HMONG-MIEN (ALSO CALLED MIAO-YAO) FAMILY 209

4.16 KHOISAN (!XHOSAN) FAMILY (*THE "CLICK" LANGUAGES)* 210

4.17 ORIGINAL LANGUAGE FAMILIES OF NORTH AND CENTRAL AMERICA, THE CARIBBEAN AND EASTERNMOST SIBERIA 211

TABLE OF CONTENTS

4.18 ORIGINAL LANGUAGE FAMILIES OF SOUTH AMERICA 216

4.19 OTHER LANGUAGE FAMILIES 218

4.20 EXTINCT, MORIBUND OR INACTIVE LANGUAGES *OF SIGNIFICANCE* OF THE ANCIENT WORLD 219

4.21 LIVING LANGUAGE ISOLATES 228

4.22 "SUPRA" OR "MACRO" LANGUAGE FAMILIES 232

4.23 LANGUAGES WITH AN "ENGLISH-LIKE" ("*ANGRAMAYA*", A NEW TERM) STRUCTURE (WITH BASE FROM ONE LANGUAGE FAMILY, ALL 'HIGHER' VOCABULARY FROM OTHER FAMILIES) 233

    4.23.1 THE STRUCTURE OF ENGLISH 233
    4.23.2 SOME OTHER "*ANGRAMAYA*" LANGUAGES BESIDES ENGLISH: HINDI/URDU, INDONESIAN/MALAYSIAN LANGUAGES, KHMER, THAI, MYANMARI (BURMESE), SWAAHILI (SWAHILI), OTHERS 236

4.24 BRIEF SYNOPSIS OF PHONETIC SHIFTS BETWEEN LANGUAGES IN FAMILIES 241

4.25 LANGUAGE, ETHNICITY, "RACE" AND COLOR 248

4.26 EXERCISES 258

CHAPTER 5.
GRAMMAR AND GRAMMATICAL TERMS, THE *FORM* OF LANGUAGE, ORDER IN LANGUAGE, AND POSSIBLE STRUCTURE OF A SINGLE, PARENT HUMAN LANGUAGE, THE *"ANTI-NOSTRATIC"*

.....261

TABLE OF CONTENTS

5.1 SYNOPSIS OF GRAMMATICAL TERMS FOUND EXTENSIVELY IN THE LINGUISTICS LITERATURE AND THEIR UNDERLYING BASES 263

5.1.1 PREMISE OF THIS CHAPTER AND WHAT IS COVERED AND NOT COVERED IN THIS CHAPTER.. 263
5.1.2 THE VERB AS FUNDAMENT OF LANGUAGE 264
5.1.3 ATTRIBUTES OF THE VERB: NUMBERS, GENDERS, TENSES, MOODS, VOICES AND OTHERS... 264
5.1.4 SUMMARY OF VERB ATTRIBUTES (PROPERTIES) AND FORMS 271
5.1.5 ATTRIBUTES OF THE SUBSTANTIVE: NUMBERS, GENDERS, CASES AND OTHER ATTRIBUTES... 272

5.2 THE *FORM* OF LANGUAGE: TYPOLOGY, MORPHEMES AND MORPHOLOGY 273

5.2.1 TYPOLOGY 273
5.2.2. DESCRIPTION OF THE VARIOUS TYPOLOGIES 275
5.2.3 DIFFERENCES IN INFLECTION IN AGGLUTINATIVE VS. NON-AGGLUTINATIVE LANGUAGES: SYNTHETIC LANGUAGES 280
5.2.4 POLYSYNTHETIC LANGUAGES 281
5.2.5 OTHER CLASSIFICATION METHODS FOR TYPOLOGY.. 286
5.2.6 COMBINATIONS OF TYPOLOGIES 286

5.3 TRANSFORMATION BETWEEN TYPOLOGIES 287

5.3.1 SOME EVIDENT PRINCIPLES REGARDING TRANSFORMATION BETWEEN TYPOLOGIES 287
5.3.2 CAVEAT REGARDING TYPOLOGICAL CLASSIFICATION 288

5.4 FORM AND ORDER IN LANGUAGE 290

5.5 FAINT HINTS OF THE ORIGINS OF LANGUAGE: 297

5.5.1 INFANT PHONEMES AND WHAT THEY MAY TELL US OF THE STRUCTURE OF EARLY HUMAN LANGUAGE; THE CONCEPT OF SELF AND NOT-SELF, TERMS BORROWED FROM IMMUNOLOGY 297
5.5.2 OTHER FEATURES OF HYPOTHETICAL EARLY HUMAN LANGUAGES 303
5.5.3 POSSIBLE FORM OF EARLY HUMAN PROTO-LANGUAGES 305
5.5.4 CONCOMITANT MONOSYLLABIC AND HIGHLY INFLECTIONAL CHARACTER: IS IT POSSIBLE? 308

5.6 EXERCISES 310

CHAPTER 5 APPENDIX (TABLE 5-8). ILLUSTRATION OF EXTREME INFLECTIONAL CHARACTER IN A LANGUAGE: PARADIGMS FOR CONJUGATION OF THE SANSKRIT VERBAL ROOT -wid- (-vid-) IN THE 2nd, 4th, 6th, 7th and 10th CONJUGATIONS, IN ACTIVE AND MIDDLE VOICES

[*Table 5-8* (appended here due to its length)]

.....311

TABLE OF CONTENTS

5.A.1 OVERVIEW OF THESE FIVE CONJUGATIONS 313

5.A.2 Conjugation of *wid (vid)* in 2nd conjugation, meaning "to know, to understand, to discoVer" (stem: *wed*) (Cognates English *wit*, German *wissen*, Latin *video*, etc.) 314

5.A.3 CONJUGATION OF *WID (VID)*, IN 4TH CONJUGATION, MEANING "TO BE, TO EXIST, TO DISCOVER OR UNDERSTAND ONESELF" 331

5.A.4 CONJUGATION OF *wid (vid)*, IN 6TH CONJUGATION, MEANING TO "FIND, TO COME TO KNOW, RECOGNIZE, COME TO DISCOVER" 333

5.A.5. CONJUGATION OF *wid*, IN 7TH CONJUGATION, MEANING "TO UNDERSTAND" 338

TABLE OF CONTENTS

xii

5.A.6 CONJUGATION OF *wid*, **IN 10TH CONJUGATION, MEANING " TO TELL, TO COMMUNICATE, TO FEEL"** **340**

GLOSSARY
....343

LITERATURE CITED

[INCLUDING 624 REFERENCES, CITED IN ORDER OF THEIR APPEARANCE IN THE TEXT, BUT WITH ADDITIONAL GROUPING AND SUB-GROUPING TO FACILITATE EASY REFERENCE. INCLUDES EDITORIAL NOTE ON METHOD OF LITERATURE CITATION USED.]

....355

INDEX
....413

ABOUT THE AUTHOR
.... 429

FOREWORD/APPRECIATION TO VOLUME I

by
Nicholas Ostler

[Author, most recently, of *The Last Lingua Franca: English Until the Return of Babel* (Walker & Company, 2010);
Author of *Empires of the Word: A Language History of the World* (Harper Collins, 2005);
and of several other works in the fields of language and linguistics.]

Navlipi (despite its Sanskritic name, which means "new-script") is a systematic extension of Roman script, with a number of aims in view: To be a practical (legible and writable) script for all the world's languages, but at the same time to represent the languages' sounds exactly and consistently, making no compromises on the phonemic principle. In this ambitious goal, it goes beyond existing scripts: Beyond ordinary Roman scripts, because it requires that its symbols are interpreted the same way everywhere; beyond phonetic scripts such as the International Phonetic Alphabet, by representing phonemes singly, rather than as a set of phones; and beyond all the other scripts, by attempting to replace every single one of them without loss of significant phonetic detail. (Chandrasekhar resigns himself to the loss of any historical and etymological traces that may survive in some languages' writing systems.) As such, it aims to be a technical tool for the analysis of languages (for linguists), at the same time as it serves as a practical orthography for every language in the world.

This is a stupendous aim for a single system created by a single scholar, and its author, Prasanna Chandrasekhar, realizes that his chances of success are slim. Nevertheless, the fact that a single human vocal tract is capable - with the right exposure in youth - to articulate any one of the world's languages perhaps encourages us to believe that it would be possible for a single written script - with enough of the right diacritics - to encompass every language, all without compromise in showing all the significant distinctions to be made in the language.

The main obstacle to Chandrasekhar's achievement is the phenomenon of "phonemic idiosyncrasy", whereby the actual speech sounds are organized into different, and cross-cutting, significant sets in various languages: For example, *p*, whether

FOREWORDS

aspirated or unaspirated, is the same phoneme in English, but the two versions belong to contrasting phonemes in Hindi, where (however) *f* is heard as the same sound as aspirated-*p*. By juxtaposing letters, Chandrasekhar conjures up new symbols that represent directly the complex phonemic reality. As a result, no language can be successfully written in *Navlipi* unless its phonemic system has been structurally analysed, which is perhaps no bad thing. Unfortunately, though, phonemic analyses tend to be controversial. This could put a brake on implementation.

The world may well be "too much with us" for *Navlipi* to stand very much chance of widespread adoption as a practical script: One is reminded of the very short-lived success of even Khubilai (Kublai) Khan when he commissioned the brilliant scholar 'Phagspa to create a common script for all the languages of his empire, from Persian and Tibetan to Mongolian and Mandarin. The world tends to set its communication standards for historical reasons, and to suit the powers that be, rather than any academic ideal. But the script is also a dramatic object lesson in the constraints of phonemic analysis, and so may enjoy some popularity among linguists for its technical aims.

The attempt to have all the possible virtues of a phonetic writing system at once - on the basis of single man's ideal - is what makes this a heroic endeavour.

Nicholas Ostler
Bath, England

FOREWORD TO VOLUME I

by
Christopher Moseley
[of *Foundation for Endangered Languages*, London, U.K.,
http://www.ogmios.org/;
Editor-in-chief of *UNESCO Atlas of the World's Languages in Danger* (UNESCO Press, 3rd Edition, Paris, 2010- includes online interactive version);
Editor of *Encyclopedia of the World's Endangered Languages* (Routledge, 2007);
Co-Editor of *Atlas of the World's Languages* (Routledge, 1994)]

The name *Navlipi* is one of a number of new terms which are introduced in this unique volume. In it, Dr. Prasanna Chandrasekhar proposes a most ambitious scheme, one which has eluded linguistic science for centuries: A method of reducing all the world's major languages to writing in a uniform way. The name itself derives from Sanskrit, and means 'new script'. It is nothing less than a new script that Dr. Chandrasekhar is offering the world in the pages that follow.

Dr. Chandrasekhar has made a study of all the world's more commonly used scripts and compared their efficiency in rendering the languages they represent. His project was originally a unified script for the languages of India, but he soon extended its mandate to cover all the languages of the world. *Navlipi,* however, is not based on Devanagari or any Indian script, but on Roman, the most widely adapted script in the world. Furthermore, he has devised a scheme where the 26 standard Roman letters are supplemented by only five more. Tones and other supraphonemic features are also catered for, by a system of 'post-ops' (postpositional operators). In other words, it differs from the International Phonetic Alphabet (which aims at the same comprehensive universality) in not attempting to greatly extend the range of distinct graphemes, but rather, aims at the most economic use of the existing inventory, very modestly extended. What is more, its inventor claims and demonstrates that it can be used in a cursive version in handwriting, in addition to the inventory of letters for printing.

Dr. Chandrasekhar's academic background is in chemistry, and his current work is in the defense contracting industry, but his ethnic background places him in a multilingual, multiscriptal society. An idea like *Navlipi* was most likely to arise in India, where numerous scripts compete for the eye's attention in everyday life, and an inquiring mind such as the author's was moved to try to distil them into a single uniform writing system.

The author sets out his alphabet in the form of tables which clearly show the phonemes represented by each letter, grouped by place and manner of articulation, rather like a phonetic chart, He does not comment in the tables on the frequency of each phoneme in the world's languages, except to state where it is negligible. There have been many claims of a perfect fit between the written script and the spoken form of some of the world's languages (such as Hangul and Korean), but so far no claim has been made for a perfect fit of a single script for all the world's languages.

The *Navlipi* script has been put extensively to the test on a wide range of languages, and the test transcriptions make up a large part of the original text of the volumes presented here. Its accuracy in rendering the phonemic distinctions in each language will be weighed, by a native-speaker audience, against the possible sacrifices of etymological transparency. However, it is one of the objects of Dr. Chandrasekhar's project that phonological consistency outweighs etymological or phonemic 'idiosyncrasy', as the author calls it. In terms of phoneme-grapheme correspondence, *Navlipi* is demonstrated to be faithful to the sounds of a language while not being over-complex to write. Dr. Chandrasekhar has made exhaustive comparisons even with scripts which are confined to use with one language (Cherokee, Varang Kshiti and many others).

And what is remarkable about the author's researches is that he has given each of these scripts a rigorous test for universalising it – applying it to the full range (as he sees it) of the world's contrastive phonemes – and in each case he finds them wanting. Their lack of adaptability lies not merely in the impossibility of reassigning redundant graphemes (in other words, a restricted range of possible written signs), but also in less quantifiable, or more 'relative' ways, such as *recognisability* and *intuitiveness*. The primacy of the alphabet in its traditional guise – that is, with upper and lower case letters, and cursive variants – is clearly evident to Dr. Chandrasekhar. However, it is to his credit that he adopts this option only after thoroughly testing the alternatives. What is also attractive to him, one can't help feeling (and this relates to his concept of 'intuitiveness') is the perfectly-balanced degree of contrast between letter-shapes in an alphabet like the Roman one. Perfectly balanced, that is, in terms of visual perception, brain-to-eye co-ordination.

This brings the user of *Navlipi* to the issue of variant letters *vs.* diacritics. Dr. Chandrasekhar has deliberately avoided diacritical marks of the accepted type (cedilla, acute, &c.) above and below the base-letters to indicate a change of phonemic quality from the base. Rather, each letter is to be considered as a complete, separate and organic unit. But that is not to say that the new symbols are not clearly derived from older ones, or that they bear no organic relationship to letters without these extensions. The extensions are of two main types – bars within the letter, and the so-called 'post-ops', which are actually adjuncts written to the right of the base letters. These indicate non-segmental features such as tone, nasalization and the like. This may be taken to be the minimal distinctive variation in an alphabet consisting only of primary symbols, with no secondary or optional members of the inventory. Yet of course these newly created symbols will in some cases be optional – for those languages that do not possess the phonemes in question.

The author's coverage of the range of possible 'post-ops' will give an indication of how comprehensive a range of languages and their contrastive phonemes can be accommodated by this scheme. The 'post-ops' are the simplest and readiest solution to the problem of adapting what is essentially a 31-letter alphabet to all possible phonemic environments. It is interesting to speculate on the effect on literacy in many rarely-written languages that this scheme would have. What looks at first like an attempt at an accurate transcription system for linguists could, the author suggests, be a useful vehicle for everyday writing in any conceivable language.

The author's guiding principle in creating the alphabet and its attendant 'post-ops', then, has been to take note of the frequency of phonemes, in the major languages of the world with which he is familiar, in assigning, reassigning or creating the distinct letters, while allowing for the less frequently occurring ones in his maximally economic system of 'post-ops'. It is, in this sense, primarily an alphabet for practical everyday use with any language. The forms of the new letters themselves have been created bearing in mind their associations with already existing letters.

In dealing with tone, the author has had to be especially thorough. Each language where tone is contrastive (Chinese, Vietnamese, Igbo, to take some obvious examples) has its own set of contrastive oppositions. Dr. Chandrasekhar demonstrates exhaustively the unwieldy nature of the renderings of these contrastive tones (ranging from the mandatory system, in Vietnamese, through the semi-optional marking system of Igbo, to the official and semi-official transcription systems of Mandarin and Cantonese) and posits his own uniform system for showing tone. He goes further, and shows how tone could be marked in *Navlipi* even for languages where tone is predictable but not completely phonemic, such as Swedish. The number of speakers of tone-languages in the world is formidable, and *Navlipi* is presented as lending itself especially well to the rendering on these languages consistently.

Who, then, is the potential 'user of *Navlipi*'? The author contends that his original aim was to bridge the gap, using a Romanized system, between the discrete scripts of India – the Devanagari and its variants that emanate from Braahmi, including the scripts of the Dravidian languages of south India, as well as the smaller scripts such as those for the Munda languages. He soon realised, however, that his invention had potential use, with easy adaptation, to many other non-Roman, or at least non-alphabetic, scripts – Arabic and Chinese for instance – as well as those national alphabets that are still wavering between systems, such as some of the languages of former Soviet Central Asia. Thus he looks forward to adaptation on a national, indeed a multinational, scale, if not a fully international one. He does not use the term 'auxiliary' and does not entertain the notion of a traditional script continuing alongside the use of *Navlipi* for teaching purposes.

Persuading the world to adopt *Navlipi* presents quite a challenge, of course, and the author is well aware of the difficulties he will meet. He presents, in one chapter, both the arguments for and the arguments against its adoption. Who are the actual decision-makers in such cases? The national Academies, where they exist? Governments? Common popular usage? The press? There is no single answer, and the author addresses himself to both the linguistic scientist and the lay reader, and rests his case.

The author's vision stretches both backward and forward in time, as concerns the implications of this script: It can be used to transcribe ancient languages; and on the other hand, it can be adapted to voice recognition technology.

It is refreshing to find this basic issue in linguistics tackled from the point of view of someone versed in the physical sciences. What you find in the following pages and the ensuing volumes is a comprehensive exposition of a theory which is put to rigorous testing. The author does create his own terminology, which might meet with some resistance from those used to the terminological conventions of linguistic science – but he is internally consistent. Some of his terms – such as *phonochromaticity* – are directly analogous with terms in the physical sciences. Where a new term is introduced, it is explained fully.

I commend this book to any reader who is interested in the age-old problem of rendering all languages uniformly in writing. It has been tried before, by Lepsius in the nineteenth century and several others, but the present volume may prove to be the most comprehensive attempt yet made.

Christopher Moseley
Reading, England

FOREWORDS

xxii

PREFACE AND OBJECTIVES OF THIS SECOND VOLUME

This book, the second volume in the *NAVLIPI* series, comprises a companion volume to the main and first *NAVLIPI* book, which was entitled *NAVLIPI, A New, Universal, Script ("Alphabet") Accommodating The Phonemic Idiosyncrasies of All The World's Languages. Volume I: Another Look at Phonic and Phonemic Classification: NAVLIPI.*

This, second volume is, firstly, intended for *completeness*: It attempts to provide a wider foundation for the subjects that a new phonic and phonemic classification and script, as presented in the first *NAVLIPI* volume, must deal with. It attempts to keep the reader as thoroughly informed as possible in discussions which may touch upon these subjects. Without this completeness, this author felt that the *NAVLIPI* script might not be fully appreciated by a lay reader, and its impact thus lessened.

One of the primary objectives of this second volume is *pedagogical*, attempting to educate a *layman* in such closely related yet diverse fields as phonetics, phonemics, basic linguistic concepts and language families of the world.

To the best of this author's knowledge, this has heretofore not been done before "**under one roof**", as it were, i.e. in a single volume; such a single source at an introductory level is still direly lacking, in any language. Furthermore, even the separate sources that do provide such introductions, such as some of the references cited in this volume (see Chapter 1), frequently do so, in this author's opinion, in a somewhat cursory and superficial fashion. The present volume presents these subjects in a unique fashion, from first principles, as it were; this is an approach not found, again to the best of the author's knowledge, in any primer or elementary volume in the English-language and West-European-languages world. It thus attempts to present, again to the best of the author's knowledge, the most *complete* linguistics, phonetics and phonemics primer in a single work to date.

However, this volume does not just attempt a compilation of existing knowledge. It also presents some **new and unique concepts** and introduces **new terminology**. Hence the qualification in its title, ...A PRIMER..........*WITH A DIFFERENCE*.

PREFACE

Examples of entirely new concepts presented for the first time that are also associated with new terminology are *galatophone, forward fricative, phonemic condensate, maatraic* and *vaigyaanic*. Examples of terminology or concepts resuscitated from ancient texts are the terms *phonochromaticity* and *phonochrome,* or the concept that the *verb* rather than the substantive (i.e. noun, pronoun, etc.) may be the fundament of language, i.e. the grammatical form first invented when language developed (as always insisted upon by the ancient Indian grammarians); this may appear counter-intuitive to a layman or even an experienced linguist, who may favor the substantive as the first form, perhaps visualizing a caveperson first calling out and naming objects that he or she saw!

Among other entirely new concepts presented for the first time are derivation of a putative, pre-historic parent language, dubbed the *Anti-Nostratic*, from infant phonemes in progressively older infants which appear to be common across *all* the world's language families. In the context of this discussion of a putative parent language derived from infant phonemes, another important concept, that of *self* and *not-self* (terms borrowed from immunology), is introduced.

Another new concept presented in detail for the first time is the concept that language is simply the outward manifestation of an increased human intelligence and that the vocal apparatus and genes associated with it (e.g. the FOXP2) are merely incidental to language: In their absence, some other form of linguistic expression, such as thigh slapping, may have evolved, with all the grammatical complexity of the most complex inflected language of today; the very recent development of the children's Nicaraguan Sign Language and the adults' Arabic Sign Language are discussed in this context. The tendency of languages to naturally develop greater order, and, ultimately, highly inflectional character, when left in linguistic isolation, is also discussed in the context of its relation to concepts, borrowed from thermodynamics, of increased or decreased entropy in isolated and un-isolated systems.

Chapter 1 commences by attempting to give the lay reader an extremely thorough grounding in phonetics and phonological classification. Chapter 2 attempts to lucidly discuss methods and systems of writing in great detail, attempting to condense what may be found in several hundred pages in extant texts into a single chapter. It also introduces some new concepts and terminology, and has a detailed discussion on the tools available for the modern orthographer attempting to devise a new script (such as *NAVLIPI*), e.g. transformed letters, diacritics, multigraphs, line position, post-ops and pre-ops. Chapter 3 further develops phonological classification and again introduces a few new concepts and terms. Chapter 4 discusses language families in great detail. Chapter 5 discusses grammar, order and structure in language, again in great detail.

The book also attempts to present *much more depth and detail than found in extant primers and elementary texts*. For example, in the chapter on the world's major language families, along with the usual detailed discussion, it also depicts languages and language families in a unique, graphical way that clearly relates the temporal (time-based) relationship of the languages and their parents, their relative affinity or cognacy, and the extent of influences from *unrelated* languages and language families; this is done all in one 2-d graph. As another example from this chapter, the controversy of whether to consider Japanese as a language isolate or to group it with the Altaic family, and, going beyond this, whether the old appellation "Ural-Altaic" still has significance, is dealt with in great depth, yet in just a few paragraphs. Again in this chapter on language families, the subject of the original provenance of the Dravidians and their language family (i.e. whether native to northern and central India or migrants from the Iran-Iraq region), on which so much light has been shed by very recent (last 10 years) DNA studies, is again dealt with in a short space but in great depth. In this regard, maps of possible Aaryan (Aryan) - Dravidian interactions in the context of the end of the last Ice Age are also presented.

The chapter on grammar will give the lay reader a very clear understanding of such concepts as all possible attributes of verbs (number, gender, tense, mood, voice, animation, etc.) and of substantives (three numbers, three genders, 10 cases, etc.), and the forms and typologies of languages. Clear understanding of these is otherwise very difficult to acquire, even from perusal of multiple texts in these subjects.

A final caveat is to be noted in the context of what this second volume in the *NAVLIPI* series seeks to achieve: While it attempts to treat diverse but closely related subjects such as phonology, linguistics and language families *"under one roof"* as it were, that is to say in a *single* source, it cannot be expected to be as detailed as single texts dealing with each of these fields or their sub-fields individually. As noted at the outset of Chapter 1 herein, many such texts may be recommended. To cite just a few in the English language only: The widely circulated books by O'Connor (PHo-1], Aronoff / Rees-Miller [LN-1], Daniels/Bright [SCr-1] and others; the general and specialized works by prominent authors in the linguistics, phonetics, orthography, and related fields, from Panini (Paaninii) to Sapir, Bloomfield, Jespersen, Malmberg, Misra, and Chomsky [LN-31 to 41]; and several detailed monographs, textbooks and reference works which may be hard for the lay reader to peruse [LN-1 to 30, PHo-1 to 20, SCr-1 to 20].

PREFACE

ACKNOWLEDGEMENTS: The author wishes to express his gratitude to the following for invaluable assistance: April Zay (graphics), Katharine Stanley (editorial), Sarah Murray (some literature search), Carrie Mowbray (Greek/Latin/IE paradigms), Meghana Joshi (language transcriptions) and Ashwin Chandrasekhar (cover design).

Prasanna Chandrasekhar
Holmdel, New Jersey, USA

CHAPTER 1.
ORIGINS OF LANGUAGE; POINTS OF ARTICULATION; BASIC CLASSIFICATION OF VOWELS, NONVOWELS, TONES

TABLE OF CONTENTS

1.1 PURPOSE OF THIS SECOND VOLUME IN THE NAVLIPI SERIES 3

1.2 THEORIES OF LANGUAGE AS A MERE EXPRESSION AND OUTWARD MANIFESTATION OF HUMAN INTELLIGENCE, WITH THE SPEECH APPARATUS BEING MERELY THE MOST CONVENIENT, BUT BY NO MEANS ONLY, MEDIUM FOR ITS EXPRESSION 4

1.3 POINTS OF ARTICULATION IN THE SPEECH APPARATUS: THE TERMS PHONE, PHONOLOGY AND ARTITION (ARTICULATION POSITION, POINT OF ARTICULATION) 10

1.4 BASIC CLASSIFICATION OF PHONES (SOUNDS): THE TERMS VOWEL AND NON-VOWEL 17

1.5 BASIC CLASSIFICATION OF VOWELS 19

    1.5.1 JAW, LIP AND TONGUE POSITION, AND LENGTH, AS KEY VARIABLES IN VOWEL CLASSIFICATION 19
    1.5.2 COMBINATIONS OF JAW, LIP, TONGUE POSITION AND LENGTH, TO GENERATE INDIVIDUAL VOWELS 26
    1.5.3 VOWEL EQUATIONS: FUNDAMENTAL, DERIVATIVE AND "CARDINAL" VOWELS AND DIPHTHONGS 29
    1.5.4 JAW, LIP, AND TONGUE POSITION, AND LENGTH, AS BASIS OF SYSTEMATIC CLASSIFICATION OF VOWELS 31

1.6 SEMIVOWELS AS DERIVATIVES OF VOWELS 32

Chapter 1: Origins of Language, Points of Articulation; Basic Classification of Vowels, Nonvowels, Tones

1.7 BASIC CLASSIFICATION OF NON-VOWELS 35

    1.7.1 THE TERMS *VOICING (VOICED* AND *UNVOICED* OR *DEVOICED)*, CLOSURE, PLOSIVE, STOP, NASALIZATION, ASPIRATION 35
    1.7.2 THE TERMS *FRICATIVE, FRICATIZATION, SIBILANT, FLAP, TAP AND TRILL* 38
    1.7.3 OTHER, LESS COMMON NON-VOWEL PHONES: 40
    CLICKS, EJECTIVES, IMPLOSIVES 40
    1.7.4 *ARTITION, VOICING* AND *"COLOR"* OF THE PHONE (*PHONOCHROMATICITY*) AS KEY VARIABLES IN PHONOLOGICAL CLASSIFICATION OF NON-VOWELS 41

1.8 TONES, TONAL ACCENT, PITCH AND STRESS (ICTUS) ACCENT: FUNDAMENTAL vs. SIGNIFICANT TONES 43

1.9 PARTING NOTE ON THE EXTANT PRIMER AND MID-LEVEL LITERATURE IN PHONOLOGY, LINGUISTICS, AND RELATED FIELDS 47

1.10 EXERCISES 52

Chapter 1: Origins of Language, Points of Articulation; Basic Classification of Vowels, Nonvowels, Tones

1.1 PURPOSE OF THIS SECOND VOLUME IN THE NAVLIPI SERIES

The purpose of this second volume in the *NAVLIPI* series has been outlined at some length in the PREFACE AND OBJECTIVES OF THIS VOLUME, to which reference is made. As noted therein, it attempts to treat diverse but closely related subjects such as phonology, linguistics and language families *"under one roof"* as it were, that is to say in a *single* source. Such a single source at an introductory level is still direly lacking, in any language. Furthermore, even the separate sources that do provide such introductions, such as some of the references cited above, frequently do so, in this author's opinion, in a somewhat cursory and superficial fashion.

Nevertheless, it cannot be expected to be as detailed as single texts dealing with each of these fields or their sub-fields individually. Many such texts may be recommended. To cite just a few in the English language only: The widely circulated books by O'Connor (PHo-1], Aronoff / Rees-Miller [LN-1], Daniels/Bright [SCr-1] and others; the general and specialized works by prominent authors in the linguistics, phonetics, orthography, and related fields, from Panini (Paaninii) to Sapir, Bloomfield, Jespersen, Malmberg, Misra, and Chomsky [LN-31 to 41]; and several detailed monographs, textbooks and reference works which may be hard for the lay reader to peruse [LN-1 to 30, PHo-1 to 20, SCr-1 to 20].

Although this volume is written for the layman, *it also contain **many new concepts, terms and treatments** essential for the subsequent discussions and treatments in this book.*

For example, new terms, such as **phonemic condensate, phonochromaticity, artition** (articulation position)**, and *forward-fricative*,** are introduced in this volume. For that reason, **the experienced linguist or phoneticist is respectfully urged to review it as well**.

Chapter 1: Origins of Language, Points of Articulation; Basic Classification of Vowels, Nonvowels, Tones

1.2 THEORIES OF LANGUAGE AS A MERE EXPRESSION AND OUTWARD MANIFESTATION OF HUMAN INTELLIGENCE, WITH THE SPEECH APPARATUS BEING MERELY THE MOST CONVENIENT, BUT BY NO MEANS ONLY, MEDIUM FOR ITS EXPRESSION

It is this author's very considered view that language, as expressed by speech produced by the human speech apparatus or by other means such as sign language, *is simply an outward manifestation and <u>outlet</u> for the innate human intelligence residing in our brains*.

Over the course of the last million years or so of human evolution, the speech apparatus, embodied in our oral cavities, pulmonary system, vocal chords, etc., was present as just *one of the many other possible outlets available for language* [LN-42, 43, GDn-1 to 16, LN-56 to 72]. It may be fair to say that it was undoubtedly the most convenient. It subsequently evolved with us [GDn-1 to 23, LN-44]. It is thus, today, the most widely used medium for expression of human language. However, it is certainly and by no means the only one. We can summarize these concepts by the following statement:

> **If the present human speech apparatus had not been available for language,** *then another form of expression*, **perhaps** *thigh slapping, facial gestures or hand sign language, or combinations thereof,* **would have developed** *to the same degree of complexity and variation* **as our present speech-based languages.** [LN-45]

.....(1.1)

Chapter 1: Origins of Language, Points of Articulation; Basic Classification of Vowels, Nonvowels, Tones

Or, to put it another way:

> **The key factor that caused the development of language in humans was *the crossing of a certain threshold of intelligence*. Other factors had a far smaller, if any, influence.**

.....(1.2)

What this statement implies is that, if *speech* or *gestures* (sign language) were unavailable [LN-56 to 72, LN-95 to 111, GDn-11 to 16], *human intelligence would have burst out in some other form of expression*, such as the above-cited thigh-slapping.

The genetic, evolutionary basis of language would thus appear to be the overall evolution of increased intelligence in *Homo*, rather than specific genes relating to or appropriated for speech or gesture production (such as the FOXP2 gene, see below).

Although the above statement was made by this author in 1982 [LN-45], and implied obliquely, though not directly, by authors such as Sapir much earlier [LN-34 to 36], it is only within the last 10 years (as of this writing, 2006-8) that *strong, almost irrefutable evidence* in support of it has come about. We may now briefly recount some of this evidence.

The first of this evidence is two remarkable, completely independent studies of the *spontaneous development of a new language,* specifically a *sign* language, with astoundingly similar results. In the first, a new language, not a speech language but rather a *sign* language, arose *spontaneously* in deaf children in a school for the deaf in Nicaragua [LN-56, 57]. This was followed attentively over decades since the 1970's, by Ann Senghas of Columbia University (New York, NY, USA) and others [LN-56-57], and finally given the name **Nicaraguan Sign Language (NSL)**. *No one taught the children how to sign*. They appeared to have simply worked it out for themselves. Over time, the language became more sophisticated. What is even more astounding is that, as it got more sophisticated over two or three decades (but the blink of an eye in terms of human evolution, even language evolution), *NSL acquired the signed equivalents of case endings almost as complex as those of Classical Greek or Sanskrit!* An obvious conclusion of this (still ongoing) work was that, for such *spontaneous* emergence of sign language, the

Chapter 1: Origins of Language, Points of Articulation; Basic Classification of Vowels, Nonvowels, Tones

children must have had *some inherent tendency to correlate their gestures to meaning* (i.e. semantics). That is to say, *the new, complex language they developed was simply the bursting out of their innate, human intelligence, which <u>had</u> to find some such outlet, and thus did*.

Had this spontaneous evolution of NSL been an isolated development, it might have been taken with a degree of circumspection. However, remarkably, exactly such an independent, *spontaneous* development of sign language was observed recently in another group, halfway across the world. This is now called the **Al-Sayyid Bedouin Sign Language (ASBSL)** [LN-58]. This is "spoken" in a village of less than 4 000 people in the Negev desert of present-day Israel, founded by an Egyptian who married a local woman 200 years ago. Two of the five sons the couple had were deaf, but only 150 residents of the village are deaf today. This sign language developed *spontaneously and independently*. Remarkably, this sign language is now used by both deaf and hearing members of the community to communicate with each other. This language developed in just the last three generations of the community, i.e. over less than about 80 years. More remarkably, the word order of the language, subject-object-verb, is different from that of Arabic and Hebrew, and *ASBSL* is also not related in any way to the Jordanian and Israeli Sign Languages used in the region among deaf people. And as for *NSL*, *ASBSL* is also getting increasingly sophisticated over time periods of decades. For example, the current generation is said to sign twice as fast as the previous one. Unlike NSL, however, ASBSL has not yet developed case endings. This actually appears to show that, just as for vocal language, sign languages can develop different grammatical structures in different parts of the world. Wendy Sandler of the University of Haifa (Haifa, Israel), intends to follow the ASBSL's development in the future [LN-58]. A problem may however be that the community is dispersing and the language is thus under the influence of Jordanian and Israeli Sign Language used by the larger deaf community in the region.

The second bit of evidence in support of the above statement, is studies of *bonobo* (mountain chimpanzee) and chimpanzee *gesture* (as differentiated from *expression*) language over several decades [LN-59 to 62]. These studies culminated in recently published work by Pollick, de Waal and others [LN-59 to 62, GDn-24]. Now, *expressions* are found in most primates and are believed to be "hard-wired" by evolution. On the other hand, *gestures* are learnt, can vary in meaning among different groups, and are thought to be present only in humans and immediate relatives such as bonobos and chimpanzees. Gestures develop as a language - with different connotations for the same gesture in different populations – to a degree of sophistication and a level of development in concordance with the intelligence of the species: Thus, in bonobos, one achieves a

Chapter 1: Origins of Language, Points of Articulation; Basic Classification of Vowels, Nonvowels, Tones

limit of just about 200 gestures. On the other hand, among deaf Nicaraguan children, a complete, fully inflectional language is achieved. Thus, these studies lend strong credence to the hypothesis that language first manifested itself in the means of expression most conveniently available to evolving humans at first, i.e. *gestures* [LN-59 to 72]. As the intelligence of the human species articulating it increased, it became increasingly complex, eventually developing into language as we know it today. The pleasantry one might make about overtly gesticulating and talkative people, that the best way to shut them up is to tie up their hands, apparently has some basis in the first outward manifestation of developing human intelligence as language, in gestures.

The third bit of evidence in support of the above statement, which was at first turned on its head by many researches as evidence *against* the statement, relates to the findings regarding the FOXP2 gene [GDn-12 to 16]. This gene was "discovered" through study of a London, England family, called the "KE family", most of whose members were unable to properly control the facial and vocal tract muscle motions necessary for *vocal* speech. Studies initially implicated a gene, labeled the FOXP2 [GDn-12 to 16]. This gene was apparently traced genetically to be older than the 70 million-year-old juncture of commonality of the mouse and human species. Affecting certain types of muscular control, it was apparently appropriated (usurped) by evolution in humans for facial and vocal tract control, and thus, ultimately, vocal speech. When this gene was first implicated, during the infancy of modern evolutionary biology and DNA techniques a generation ago from this writing (2005-7), it was trumpeted as evidence of a "speech gene" or even a "language gene" that was the root of human language.

A small fact was however glossed over during this initial enthusiasm: That the members of the KE family, who could not produce vocal speech, *nevertheless got along fine via other modes of expression and communication as sophisticated as any human language.* That is to say, they were *speech* impaired, not *language* impaired!

Subsequent studies, such as those with NSL, ASBSL and with bonobo/chimpanzee gestures (see above), have confirmed that this FOXP2 "speech gene" is precisely that, a gene affecting muscle control for production of *vocal speech* that really has little effect on *language*.

A converse argument can also be cited as evidence in support of the above statement: Parrot speech is phonologically as complex as human speech, but semantically it is meaningless. This may be ascribed to the fact that parrots' overall intelligence does not come close to that of humans, so the outward expression of that intelligence, even if in

Chapter 1: Origins of Language, Points of Articulation; Basic Classification of Vowels, Nonvowels, Tones

phonologically perfect speech, is meaningless in terms of *language*.

Further support of the above statement is found in the relative ease with which modern humans who are denied access to the speech apparatus from birth (i.e. congenitally deaf people) take to other forms of expression, e.g. *sign language*. Today, those who work with *sign* language in any capacity know that it has the same degree of complexity as language expressed by *vocal* speech [LN-62 to 72]. And as has been well established, deaf babies start "babbling" immediately in sign language, i.e. with their fingers and hands [LN-72, LN-95 to 111].

Thus, modern sign language for the hearing impaired, frequently adapted to a particular language or even region (e.g. "American Sign Language" vs. "British Sign Language" for English), provides proof that an alternative form of expression, other than speech, is perfectly adequate for the expression of modern languages of very different linguistic origins and for today's level of human intelligence.

There is of course another argument, sometimes propounded with respect to speech-based language as it relates to human evolution: That the development of speech itself spurred the evolutionary increase in human intelligence as it relates to language interactively. It is this author's unflinching view that, while this may be very true, another form of language expression, such as the thigh slapping, facial expression or sign language cited above, would have developed equally well. And *it* would have *also interactively spurred the evolutionary increase in human intelligence to the same degree*. In other words, *human intelligence "had no way to go but up"*, and if the speech apparatus were unavailable, something else would have provided the evolutionary vehicle for language. Indeed, it is quite possible that, in that event, perhaps, our facial expressions and facial muscles (if facial expressions were the preferred embodiment of language) would then have evolved to a degree of complexity, suitable for the outward expression of language, which is unthinkable today.

The extrapolation of the above argument relating the present-day level of human intelligence to speech may also be valid *in the other direction*: That is to say, we may posit that, if humans possessed overall intelligence that was, say, *three times that of present-day humans*, then the outward expression of that intelligence, i.e. language, would be much, much more complex than our present-day languages. In that case, if (vocal) speech were then still the embodiment of that language, then, for starters, the number of phonemes (sound units with linguistic value defined later in this book) would be much more than the 20 to 40 typically found in your average language today. And

Chapter 1: Origins of Language, Points of Articulation; Basic Classification of Vowels, Nonvowels, Tones

quite possibly, the speech apparatus may not then have been able to handle such a complex language alone, and may have had to be combined with another expression of sound (we're back to thigh slapping or facial expressions again!) or visual communication. Or, even more fantastically, it could have led to the evolution of some other sensory organ. The field of language origins has remained in flux for the past 60 years, with many very divergent viewpoints even among eminent authorities (LN-4, 62 to 63, 70]

Chapter 1: Origins of Language, Points of Articulation; Basic Classification of Vowels, Nonvowels, Tones

1.3 POINTS OF ARTICULATION IN THE SPEECH APPARATUS: THE TERMS PHONE, PHONOLOGY AND ARTITION (ARTICULATION POSITION, POINT OF ARTICULATION)

Any *sound* emitted by the human speech apparatus can technically be given the appellation ***phone*** (Greek noun .·''◁▭ (*phone*), "sound, voice", Sanskrit verb *bhan*, "to speak, to sound"). Such human speech sounds are generally made by modulation of lung, pharynx (a part of the air passage above the lungs) or mouth air in various ways. ***Phonology*** is then, quite obviously, the study of phones or human speech sounds. Going further, ***phonological classification*** is then the systematic classification of these sounds or phones.

The great majority of speech phones are uttered or articulated with some element of the speech apparatus being in a particular ***articulation position*** (abbreviated as ***ARTITION*** in later parts of this book). For example, in uttering the *p* in English *put*, the lips, one element of the speech apparatus, are closed. This is then, quite obviously, called the *bilabial* articulation position, and the *p* is called a bilabial sound. Articulation position can refer to the lips, or to the location of contact of the tip of the tongue (as in the *t* of *tip*), or to the location of contact of the base of the tongue in the throat (as in the *k* of *king*). Articulation position is one of the fundamental elements of phone (i.e., speech) production, and it is very important to have a thorough understanding of it. As a first step in our understanding of human phonology then, it is most important to have an appreciation of the *various articulation positions of the human speech apparatus*, which are now discussed.

The designations of the main parts of the human speech apparatus, and the most common articulation positions, are shown in **Figs. 1-1a,b** below. Many of the labels therein, e.g. *palate* and *pharynx*, are well known to the layman from school anatomy.

Chapter 1: Origins of Language, Points of Articulation; Basic Classification of Vowels, Nonvowels, Tones

Fig. 1-1a: Organs for human speech.

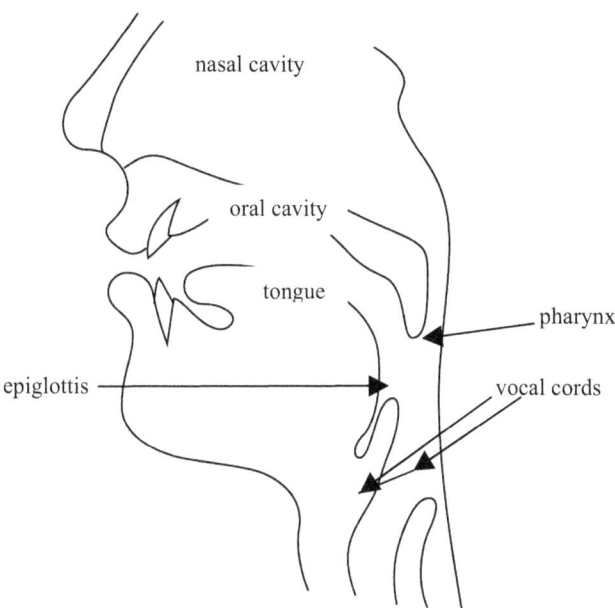

Fig. 1-1b: The articulation positions. Note that some positions are not applicable to certain ethnic groups. For example, the alveolar ridge has been observed to not exist in speakers of Xo! Bushman in south west Africa [PHo-21, 23, 25]; thus alveolar plosives such as the English/German [t] are not applicable to them.

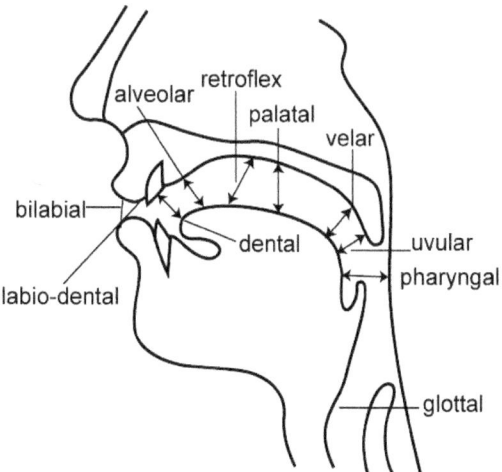

Chapter 1: Origins of Language, Points of Articulation; Basic Classification of Vowels, Nonvowels, Tones

Fig. 1-2: An example of an *actual* articulation position, here showing the tongue in the *velar* (also known as *guttural*) articulation position.

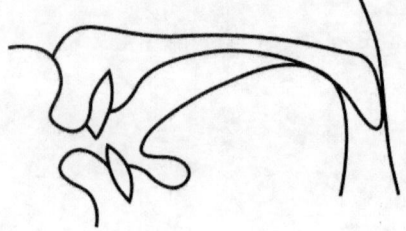

VELAR ARTITION

With particular regard to the parts of the Figure above showing the speech anatomy, it is important to note that *Homo sapiens* is a varied species, and some parts of the speech apparatus shown in the figure may be different or not exist at all for some of our species. For example, Traill [PHo-21], in his presentation of !Xo Bushman (a language of South Africa that includes many click sounds), showed X-ray photos which showed that, in many speakers of this language, the alveolar ridge does not exist at all! Rather the palate appears to blend in directly with the dental ridge. This was supported by work of the dentist van Reenen [PHo-23]. Thus, to characterize an articulation position as "alveolar" (where the tongue contacts the alveolar ridge during articulation, like the *t* in English *tin*) for such speakers would be meaningless. Similarly, it has been postulated that some persons of native Northern European, Amerindian and West African descent are anatomically incapable of articulating the uvular nasal phone of Japanese [LAs-59, 60] (the terms "uvular" and "nasal" will become clearer to the layman from the sequel).

Thus, we must remember the important caveat that, for a species as varied as *Homo sapiens*, descriptions of articulation positions and other phonological variables, such as those in the figures above, should be taken as a general guide only.

Chapter 1: Origins of Language, Points of Articulation; Basic Classification of Vowels, Nonvowels, Tones

Referring to **Figs. 1-1a-b** it is most easy to visualize the articulation positions *as a progression starting from the back of the speech apparatus and going towards the front*. In **Fig. 1-1b**, this would be:

BACK OF SPEECH APPARATUS
glottal →
pharyngeal →
uvular →
velar →
palatal →
retroflex →
alveolar →
dental →
bilabial;
FRONT OF SPEECH APPARATUS
etc.. etc.

...(1.3)

The *articulation position* most commonly refer to the point at which the *tongue* makes contact with the anatomical part in question, e.g. the palate for the palatal articulation position. However, in some positions, e.g. the *bilabial* or the *pharyngeal*, the tongue quite obviously does not play a part. In our discussions, we can conveniently abbreviate **articulation position** as ***ARTITION***, which then becomes a new term.

It is perhaps easiest to visualize what the artitions represent by giving word examples for some of them, as in the Table below:

Chapter 1: Origins of Language, Points of Articulation; Basic Classification of Vowels, Nonvowels, Tones

Table 1-1: Some examples of major ***artitions*** *(articulation positions)* (cf. **Fig. 1-1**), from the back to the front of the mouth, and word examples illustrating them.

ARTITION	DESCRIPTION	WORD EXAMPLE
Uvular	Base of tongue/front of throat contacts the uvula	The French *r* of Parisian *rouler* ("to roll)
Velar	Base of tongue contacts the velum; sometimes called *guttural* in older literature	The *c* of English *cat*. Also the *g* of English *goat*
Palatal	Tip and below-tip portion of tongue contacts palate, *mouth nearly closed*	The *ch* of Spanish *chica* ("girl") and, approximately, the *ch* of English *check*
Retroflex	Tip of tongue "curled back" and touching palate; sometimes called *cerebral* in older literature	The *t* in Hindi *tiikaa* ("commentary, exegesis"), *d* of Hindi *daantnaa* ("to scold")
Alveolar	Tip and below-tip portion of tongue contacts alveolar ridge	The *t* of English *talk*. Also the *d* of English *do*
Dental	Tip and below-tip portion of tongue contacts base of upper teeth	The *t* of Spanish *tu*, Hindi *tuu* ("you", singular)
Bilabial	Two lips used in closed or nearly closed position	The *p* of English *put*. Also the *b* of English *book*
Labiodental (more correctly, ***infralabio-supradental*** reflecting the lower-lip/upper-teeth contact):	Upper teeth contact the lower lip	The *f* of English *feel*. Also the *v* of English *veal*

Chapter 1: Origins of Language, Points of Articulation; Basic Classification of Vowels, Nonvowels, Tones

For the beginner in phonetics, it is best to try to "get a feel" for the contact, i.e. the contacting organs, for each artition. Start with the bilabial, which is easiest to visualize. Say English *put,* and notice how the lips first close and then part with the out-breath as the *p* is articulated. Now try the same for the *c* in English *cat*. Notice how the base of the tongue seems to contact the upper throat as the *c* is being articulated. Now try the same with the *t* in English *talk*. So far, these artitions are relatively easy to follow. The uvular and palatal may be a little more difficult for the layman, but articulation of the sounds in the word examples above two to three times should be more than enough for even the layman to grasp these artitions easily.

Two other artitions are of note. The *retroflex* position is mostly unknown to persons of non-Indian origin, as it is found mostly in Indian languages. Try pronouncing the *t* in English *top,* but with the tip of the tongue curled back in the mouth, touching the roof of the mouth (the palate). The palatal position, e.g. for the *j* of English *joke,* is unique among the tongue artitions listed above in that the jaw is normally in a nearly closed position, with the upper and lower front teeth frequently contacting each other. This is in contrast to most of the other artitions (e.g. the alveolar), where the jaw is in a "mid" or "close-mid" position, i.e. slightly open.

Several things now become apparent from this visualization of artitions:

Firstly, we see that there can be many **intermediate positions**, e.g. *alveolo-dental*, not covered by our limited classification. Indeed, if we tried to cover all the artitions found in the world's languages, we would have too many, and our task would be very complex. We must thus set forth some limit, some criteria by which to select only the most relevant artitions, i.e. to *discretize*. This **discretization** of artitions (as opposed to the potentially infinite **continuous** positions available, the terms *discrete* and *continuous* somewhat mirroring their use in quantum vs. classical mechanics), is a subject dealt with later in this book.

Secondly, it is apparent that the tongue itself can make contact in variable positions, e.g. at its tip (*apex*), or just below the tip, or in the middle of its body. These tongue contact positions are then, in quite evident nomenclature, called, respectively, **apico-, apico-medio-** and **medio-**. Thus, **apico-dental**, indicates contact of the apex of the tongue with the dental ridge, whilst **medio-dental**, indicates contact of the middle of the tongue with the dental ridge both being subsets of the *dental* position. In some cases, the tongue makes contact predominantly or exclusively in one position only: For example, in velar sounds, a certain part of the back (*dorsum*) of the tongue makes contact with the velum.

Thus, when we say *velar*, we do not need to say *dorso-velar* since *dorso-velar* is implied for most world languages.

Thirdly, we can immediately see, from glancing at the above Figures and Tables, that *artition*, logically going from the back to the front of the speech apparatus *can be one of the fundamental bases for a system of classification of phones*, i.e. a phonological classification system. This is in fact precisely what was done in the world's first, scientific, phonological classification system, the ancient Indian system. This system is still used today in the scripts of all of the Indian and most of the South-East Asian languages. It is also used in the most recent script inventions, e.g. those of the **International Phonetic Association** ((hereinafter referred to as the ***IPA***).

We also respectfully emphasize to the reader that *it is very important to have a thorough appreciation of the above terminology for artitions*, even perhaps to the point of memorizing the artitions shown in the above Figures and Tables. This would make further reading in this book much, much easier.

Chapter 1: Origins of Language, Points of Articulation; Basic Classification of Vowels, Nonvowels, Tones

1.4 BASIC CLASSIFICATION OF PHONES (SOUNDS): THE TERMS VOWEL AND NON-VOWEL

Most of us who have been educated in the English-speaking or in the Western European world are familiar with the most basic bifurcation in the classification among phones that we are taught in elementary (primary) school: That of *vowels* ("a, e, i, o, u") and *"consonants"*.

Unfortunately, we have to say to those taught in this fashion, *toss these classifications that you learned out the window*, for they are inaccurate (to put it mildly) from a phonological point of view! The reason for this will become apparent in the next few paragraphs. A myriad of other phonologically inaccurate terms, such as "hard vs. soft *c* or *g*" taught to the reader educated in English, will also have to be chucked out the window, as the reader will see from the discussion below!

For our purposes, we distinguish two basic classes of phones, **VOWELS** and **NON-VOWELS**. We first give a definition of vowels:

> **VOWELS** *represent any phone during the articulation of which* **the breath is entirely unimpeded**.

.....(1.4)

Thus, quite obviously, the *a, e, i, o, u* of English *father, they, hit, go,* and *put*, corresponding to the list of "vowels" taught in English-language instruction, are indeed vowels by this definition (some are components of *diphthongs* in the above words, but that term, introduced later, can be ignored for now). So far, there is no surprise for us.

However, what may come as a surprise for the person educated in the English-language or Western European world is that the *r* in the American pronunciation of English *hitter* and *doer,* or the *l* in both the American and British pronunciations of *able*, are also *vowels*! Phoneticists call these *vocalic-r* and *vocalic-l*. (These terms are used to distinguish these vowels from the semivowel *r* and *l*, but these terms will be introduced later to avoid confusing the reader.)

Chapter 1: Origins of Language, Points of Articulation; Basic Classification of Vowels, Nonvowels, Tones

The layman can more clearly visualize such "new" vowels if he/she tries repeating the *r* sound of the words above alone, as a continuous sound, *rrrrrrrrr* (American pronunciation only, i.e. with the tongue curled back as in American hitt*er*). This articulation, in terms of impediment to the breath, is hardly different from the *ee* (*ii*) of English *weed*. In both these cases, the tongue makes contact with some element of the speech apparatus: The sides of the tongue contact the teeth in the case of *weed* or b*ee*t, and the tip of the tongue contacts the alveolar ridge in the case of *able* whilst it contacts the palate in the case of *hitter*. Thus, according to the above definition, in *hitter*, the *r* is truly a vowel. This is also true for the *l* of *able*. Again, we can see this by articulating the sound continuously as *lllllllll*. In terms of impediment to the breath, the sound has very little difference from the *ee* of *beet*. It's just that the articulating organs seem to be a bit more "scrunched up" in the case of *able*.

We can also see that, by this definition of a vowel as having *no impediment to the breath*, the hissing sound, *sssssssss*, is *not* a vowel. For in this, we clearly see that the breath is impeded at the contacting point of the tongue with the alveolar ridge, producing the hissing. Conversely, in a more lose definition, the continuous *mmmmmmmm* sound, used in English to indicate the good taste of food, and distinctly in many African languages (e.g. in the current (2007) South African President's surname, *Mbeki*), can also be considered to be a **nasal vowel**. So as not to confuse the reader further, we will deal with such "nasal vowels" later in this book.

This very specific, above definition of vowels was used by some of the world's first phonologists, the ancient Indian phonologists. It is to this day still used in all the Indian and South-East Asian scripts.

We can now turn to defining non-vowels, as below:

> **NON-VOWELS** *in our definition are then, quite obviously,* **all phones that are not vowels**. *Non-vowels and vowels are thus used in binary, oppositional classification.*

.....(**1.5**)

1.5 BASIC CLASSIFICATION OF VOWELS

1.5.1 JAW, LIP AND TONGUE POSITION, AND LENGTH, AS KEY VARIABLES IN VOWEL CLASSIFICATION

Let us now turn to how we may *classify* vowels. We find we can do this by considering just five variables, only four of which are of significance: jaw, lip and tongue, position, and length.

JAW POSITION: Let us carefully observe the position of the jaw in the utterance of the highlighted vowel in the English words *creature, about, but* and *father*. It can be seen that in the utterance of the *a* sound in these four words, the jaw progressively goes from a near closed position to a fully open position.

These four positions of the jaw are loosely called **close, close-mid, open-mid** and **open**. The *mid* position is, in most Western phonetics literature as well as the terminology of the IPA, further broken down into **close-mid** and **open-mid**.

It should be immediately apparent to the reader however that the description of the human jaw position is not as discrete and simplistic as that above: For example, in addition to just *open* and *closed* positions, the jaw can also move **sideways** and **forward**, as well as back, i.e. **retracted**; the resultant sounds produced are quite different. As it turns out, the *sideways and retracted movements are phonemically significant in almost none of the world's languages*. However, the *forward movement unfortunately is significant*, in two important Indian languages, Maraathii and Tamil, the latter being the most important living representative of the Dravidian family of languages.

The phones this *jaw-forward* position applies to in Tamil are the retroflex lateral and central semivowels, for which the *jaw-normal* and *jaw-forward* positions are phonemically distinct. For example, we have the Tamil words *pal.l.am*, "hole" (with the *l.* used to represent the retroflex lateral articulated in the "jaw-normal" position) and *pazham* "fruit" (with the *zh* used to represent the retroflex central, articulated in the *jaw-forward* position). (All these terms are explained in the sequel in this chapter.) Needless to say, such forward jaw movement is another parameter *not given consideration at all in the IPA treatment*.

Chapter 1: Origins of Language, Points of Articulation; Basic Classification of Vowels, Nonvowels, Tones

Technically, then, each of the above four jaw positions, i.e. *close, close-mid, open-mid,* and *open,* can have a *jaw-forward* variant, leading to *eight* positions in total. However, since the jaw-forward position is phonemically significant only in Maraathii and Tamil among widely used languages of the world, and in these the distinction is only between (*close-mid, jaw-normal*) and (*close-mid, jaw-forward*), we can, conveniently, limit our treatment of jaw position to just these additional ones only.

To summarize then, based on the above discussion, we have arrived at, in the most common usage, <u>*five*</u> jaw positions used for vowels: **Close/jaw-normal, close-mid/jaw-normal, close-mid/jaw-forward, open-mid/jaw-normal**, and **open/jaw-normal**. We can omit the "*jaw-normal*" designations except where they are needed to distinguish against "jaw-forward" positions, to then arrive at the following *five* designations for jaw position, as shown in the Table below; the ***jaw-retracted*** position is included in the *Navlipi* vowel classification for completeness only:

Table 1-2: The five (5) jaw positions used by *Navlipi* for vowels.

JAW POSITION	WORD EXAMPLE
close	English *creature*
close-mid/jaw-normal	English *about*; Maraathi *padaaitsa* ("to fall"); Tamil *pal.am*
close-mid/jaw-forward	Maraathi *palaaitsa* ("to run") (vocalic –*l*); Tamil *pal.am* ("fruit") (vocalic –*l*)
open-mid	English *but*
open	English *father*

LIP POSITION: Let us say the English words *but, beet* and *boot,* while carefully observing the position of the lips. We will see that the lips are, respectively in these words, ***flat*** (neither stretched nor rounded, in *but*), ***stretched*** (in *beet*) and ***rounded*** (in *boot*). In most phonetic treatments, including the ancient Indian, lip position is assigned these three variables. The IPA treatment however unfortunately does not consider the stretched position of the lips at all. The IPA thus considers only two positions, "normal"

Chapter 1: Origins of Language, Points of Articulation; Basic Classification of Vowels, Nonvowels, Tones

and "rounded". And the rounded position is considered in a very cursory manner, almost as an aside, in its "vowel charts".

It should be apparent to the reader that there can be many intermediate positions between the above three. In the interest of manageability, however, it behooves us *to limit the positions to the three above,* ***flat****,* ***stretched****,* and ***rounded****,* using the principle of *discretization*. This principle was presented earlier and is discussed again, in reference to vowel classification, immediately below. To summarize then, we have the following basic lip positions, as shown in the Table below:

Table 1-3: The three (3) lip positions used by *Navlipi* for vowels.

- *flat* as in English *but*
- *stretched* as in English *beet*
- *rounded* as in English *boot*

TONGUE (ARTICULATION) POSITION: Let us carefully observe the tongue's successive position in the mouth in the articulation of the highlighted vowels and semivowels in the English words *but, beet, boot, doer* (in American pronunciation), and *able*, and the original, medieval pronunciation (but not modern) of the Serbo-Croat place name *Srbrnca,* or the current pronunciations of the Sanskrit words *Rg* or *Rta*.

In *but, beet, boot*, we will note that the tongue is, respectively, in the **mid *(normal)*, *front (forward)*** and **back *(retracted)*** positions. These are three distinctive positions assigned to vowels in most phonetic treatments. We may also note that in the *mid* position, the tongue is close to its artition for *velar* non-vowels. Similarly, in the *front (forward)* position, the tongue is close to the palate, and in the *back (retracted)* position, the lips tend automatically towards some rounding. For these reasons, the three positions *mid, front (forward)* and *back (retracted)* positions are also sometimes also denoted as **velar, palatal** and **bilabial**. *This secondary terminology for the tongue position in vowels* will become more apparent in the treatment of the derivation of semivowels from vowels further below. This secondary terminology was incidentally used in the ancient Indian phonological classification, to classify vowels, semivowels and non-vowels under the same umbrella, in terms of tongue position.

In many Western phonetic treatments, the tongue position is further given the classification *high* and *low*, depending upon whether it is high or low in the mouth. Thus, the *uu* sound in English *boot* is said to have the tongue in a "high, back" position. However, this treatment appears to conflate and confound the presence of the *jaw* position as an independent variable: Whether the tongue is "high" or "low" while also being "back" is dependent to an appreciable degree on whether the jaw position is fully open, mid or closed. It will be seen that the jaw position as an independent variable, as used in our treatment, is sufficient to account for such "high, low" positions of the tongue. And we note that the highly scientific ancient Indian phonological treatments did not further classify the tongue position in this, "high, low" fashion, although they *did* mention it [LN-31 to 33].

The Terms "Lateral" and "Central": Before being able to discuss the other word examples we have chosen above, i.e. *doer* (in American pronunciation), *print* (in British pronunciation) and *able*, and the Serbo-Croat place name *Srbrnca*, we need to introduce and understand two additional terms, **lateral** and **central**.

Let us first take the take the tongue to the position for the *l* sound of English *able*, and just hold it there. Now, while holding the tongue in this position, let us breathe forcefully in and out through the mouth. We will see that the sides of the tongue feel cool - the breath appears to be going in and out around the sides, i.e. the *lateral* part, of the tongue, while the central portion of the tongue appears to be held firmly in place (touching the alveolar ridge). For this reason, such *l* sounds are termed **laterals** in phonetic terminology.

Now let us take the take the tongue to the *r* sound in the British pronunciation of *print*, and again just hold it there. Let us then again breathe forcefully in and out through the mouth. while holding the tongue in this position. We will now see that the breath appears to be going out through the *central* portion of the tongue (this should be feeling cool), whilst the lateral portions are firmly anchored. For this reason, such *r* sounds are termed **central** sounds in phonetic terminology.

We may thus briefly summarize what we have learned about centrals and laterals:

> In general, all *"r-sounds"* are considered ***centrals*** and all *"l-sounds"* are considered ***laterals***.

...(**1.6**)

We may also note that, in the articulation of the *l* of English *able*, in addition to the tongue being *lateral*, it is also in the *alveolar* articulation position. Thus, the *l* of English *able* is denoted by us as an ***alveolar lateral vowel***. (It is a vowel according to the definition given by us earlier).

In a similar fashion, the *r* in the British pronunciation of *print* is denoted as an ***alveolar central semivowel***. (The term *semivowel* is defined further below). The *r* in the Serbo-Croat place name *Srbrnca*, was originally a true vowel, an ***alveolar central vowel***, corresponding to vocalic-*r* of Old Church Slavonic. However, today, it is pronounced as an alveolar trill. But the word retains the original spelling, hence its use of the letter *r* without any other following vowel. Similarly, the vowels in Sanskrit ***R****g* and ***R****ta* are also alveolar central vowels. On the other hand, in the American pronunciation, the *r* of *doer* is a ***retroflex central vowel***, since the tongue is curled back and touching the palate in its articulation. It is not nearly as curled back as in Indian renditions of the same retroflex vowel, but it is nevertheless very distinct from the alveolar contact of the *r* of British *print*.

So far, we have identified the following among centrals and laterals: ***alveolar lateral, alveolar central*** and ***retroflex central***. The ***retroflex lateral***, i.e. the "*l* sound" articulated with the tongue curled back, is common in Indian languages, though rare just about everywhere else.

Tongue (Articulation) Position, continued: We can then summarize the ***tongue artitions*** of relevance as being those in the **Table** below:

Table 1-4: The tongue artitions (articulation positions) used by *Navlipi* for vowels.

ARTITION	EXAMPLE
mid (normal)	as in English *but*
forward (front, palatal)	as in English *beet*
retracted, (back, bilabial)	as in English *boot*
alveolar lateral	as in English *able*
alveolar central	as in Sanskrit **R***shi*, **R***ta*
retroflex lateral	as in Tamil *palam*, "fruit"
retroflex central	as in American pronunciation of English *doer*

VOWEL LENGTH: This is perhaps the vowel property that is easiest to understand for the layman. We can see the contrast of short/long vowels in the English word pairs *bit/beet, put/boot*, etc.. English does not have a phonemic distinction between the short/long [aa]. For example, in American pronunciation, *hot* has a short [aa], whereas *father* has a long [aa], but the meaning of the words is not changed if one changes the short to long and long to short. On the other hand, Tamil *does* have such a phonemic distinction. Thus we have (using [*d.*] to designate a retroflex voiced flap) ***aad.upu***, with a short [aa] vowel, meaning "coal-stove" and ***aad.a***, with a long [aa] vowel, meaning "goat".

Although we have presented only two lengths, *short* and *long*, some languages have a phonemic distinction between several lengths, e.g. *short, intermediate* and *long*. One such example is Mixteco, a language still spoken widely in the rural, mountainous regions of the Oaxaca province of Mexico.

Chapter 1: Origins of Language, Points of Articulation; Basic Classification of Vowels, Nonvowels, Tones

Three vowel lengths are however more than sufficient to account for all of the world's major languages. We thus treat of the following three lengths in our work:

short
long
extra long (rare)

....(**1.7**)

When three lengths, *short, intermediate* and *long*, are present in a language, our *"long"* above will correspond to the *intermediate*.

As will be seen later in this book, ***Navlipi*** has a simple, intuitive and very easy to read transcription method of short/long vowels: For the long vowel, the vowel symbol is simply reduplicated. For the *extra long* vowel, the vowel can be reproduced in triplicate; alternatively, a vowel lengthening symbol, the ubiquitous "subscripted little circle" of ***Navlipi***, is added to the long vowel. Thus, *i*, *ii*, and *iii* (or *ii*) would represent, respectively, the short, intermediate, and long [i] vowels, as in English h*i*t, h*ea*t, and wh*eeee*.

DISCRETIZATION OF PHONOLOGICAL VARIABLES: As already discussed briefly above, and as should be apparent to any reader from our "continuous" discussions, each variable we have dealt with, e.g. *tongue position, lip position* and *jaw position* is in theory continuous; it can have many additional positions intermediate between those we have assigned. For example, the jaw can have positions intermediate between the *close* and the *close-mid*, the lips can of course have innumerable positions between fully *stretched* and fully *rounded*, and even the *length* of vowels can have more than the three values we have assigned, *short, intermediate* and *long*.

Thus, as has been emphasized many times in this book, *some discretization* of variables is absolutely necessary if one is to avoid making the problem of classification completely unmanageable. That is why we limit our variables, as described in the previous paragraph.

In this respect, it helps us tremendously that, in most of the world's languages, fine differences in the variables, for example, fully-stretched-lips vs. almost-fully-stretched-lips, are *not* phonemically distinct, and thus not practically significant. As noted in an

Chapter 1: Origins of Language, Points of Articulation; Basic Classification of Vowels, Nonvowels, Tones

earlier paragraph, perhaps if humans had three times the intelligence we do now, we would need 200 phonemes to express ourselves instead of the average 20 to 40 in a typical language, and in that case we *would* need to take into account such fine differences in articulation positions. Fortunately, we do not need to do that yet.

1.5.2 COMBINATIONS OF JAW, LIP, TONGUE POSITION AND LENGTH, TO GENERATE INDIVIDUAL VOWELS

Combinations of jaw, lip, tongue position and length: Summing up our limited, discretized treatment above, we now have the following basic variables available to us in our classification of vowels:

Table 1-5: The *jaw position, lip position, tongue position* and *length* variables used by *Navlipi*.

VARIABLE TYPE	VARIABLES	NUMBER
Jaw position	close; close-mid/jaw-normal; close-mid/jaw-forward ; open-mid; and open; (close-mid/jaw-retracted listed for completeness only, but not used practically.)	5
Lip position	flat; stretched; rounded	3
Tongue position	mid (normal); forward (front, palatal); retracted (back, bilabial); alveolar lateral; alveolar central; retroflex lateral; retroflex central	7
Length	short; long (or intermediate); extra long (or long)	3

We can immediately see that **combinations** of the above variables permit us to not only describe virtually all vowels that are encountered in the world's languages, but also the *transitions* between the vowels.

For example, the *a* of English *father* is articulated with the jaw in the fully *open* position,

Chapter 1: Origins of Language, Points of Articulation; Basic Classification of Vowels, Nonvowels, Tones

the lips *flat* and the tongue in the *mid* position. If we were now to articulate this with the lips *stretched* and the tongue *front (forward)*, we would get the *a* of English *back*. Similarly, the *ee* of English is articulated with the jaw *close*, the lips *stretched* and the tongue *forward*. If we were to try to articulate this sound with the jaw *close-mid* but the lips and tongue the same (except for any normal compensation that may occur), we would get the sound of *ai* of English *fair*. If we were to now to open the jaw further to the *open-mid* position, we would get the sound of *e* of English *they*. Again, if we were now to open the jaw yet further, to the completely *open* position, we would get the sound of *a* of English *that* or *back* again. Thus, in this case, we have a steady transition of the sounds of English *beet, fair, they,* and *that* by simply progressively opening the jaw. **As** yet another example, the *oo* of English *boot* is normally articulated with the lips *rounded* and tongue *back (retracted)*. If we were to articulate this with the lips *stretched* (the tongue would then automatically come *forward* a bit), we would get the "French/German *u*" of French br*u*ler or German m*ü*tter.

The concept of "compensation" and "practical" phonetics: The sharp reader will immediately see that the above descriptions are somewhat simplistic and not entirely accurate. For example, we can articulate the *a* of English *father* with the lips *stretched* and the tongue *front (forward)*, and still manage, if we try hard enough, to get something close to the original sound of *father* rather than the *a* of English *back*. This is because we are able to make the tongue *compensate* somewhat, for being moved forward and for the lips being stretched, by moving the middle portion of the tongue high up in the mouth. The resulting sound is not exactly the *a* of *father*, but close.

It is important to realize, in this respect, that ***in our treatments throughout this book, we do not consider such <u>compensatory</u> mechanisms***, i.e. we do *not* consider ***compensation***. Rather we rely on a "practical" model of phonetics, with only phonemically significant articulations considered.

Fundamental and "Cardinal" Vowels: In most ancient as well as modern phonological treatments, including the ancient Indian and the modern IPA, *three "fundamental" vowels* are given a fundamental position in any treatment of vowels. These vowels and their connotation are summarized below.

One of the reasons these vowels are considered "fundamental" is that all other pure vowels and diphthongs can be derived from them, using simple equations such as those presented further below. Other reasons will become apparent in the sequel in this book.

Chapter 1: Origins of Language, Points of Articulation; Basic Classification of Vowels, Nonvowels, Tones

Perhaps the best analogy for these three fundamental vowels is the three **primary colors**. We are all aware how the three primary colors can be "mixed" to generate *all* the colors known in the visible spectral region. In a similar fashion, *all the other (derivative) vowels can be derived through a simple "combination" of the fundamental vowels*. Recognizing this, the ancient Indian phoneticians [LN-31 to 33, LAi-3] gave a set of vowel "equations", as described further below, which are a subset of the rules of *Sandhi* (euphonic combination of phones, defined in more detail in a later chapter).

Table 1-6: The Fundamental Vowels, analogous to the "primary colors".

[a] = (*u* of English b*u*t)
[i] = *(i* of English b*i*t)
[u] = *(u* of English p*u*t)

The Western phonetic treatments also use the term **cardinal** vowels. This author feels that the term *fundamental* vowels, as described above, is more appropriate than *cardinal* vowel. For a discussion of the latter term, the reader is referred to excellent introductory phonetics texts written in the Western pedagogical tradition [PHo-1, PHo- 2 to 20].

How fundamental these vowels truly are can be seen in a quick glance at the *formant frequencies* for these vowels, illustrated in the Figure below.

Chapter 1: Origins of Language, Points of Articulation; Basic Classification of Vowels, Nonvowels, Tones

Fig. 1-3: *Formant frequencies* for the fundamental vowels, showing the latter's truly "fundamental" nature: Nearly all other vowels lie within the solid lines shown.

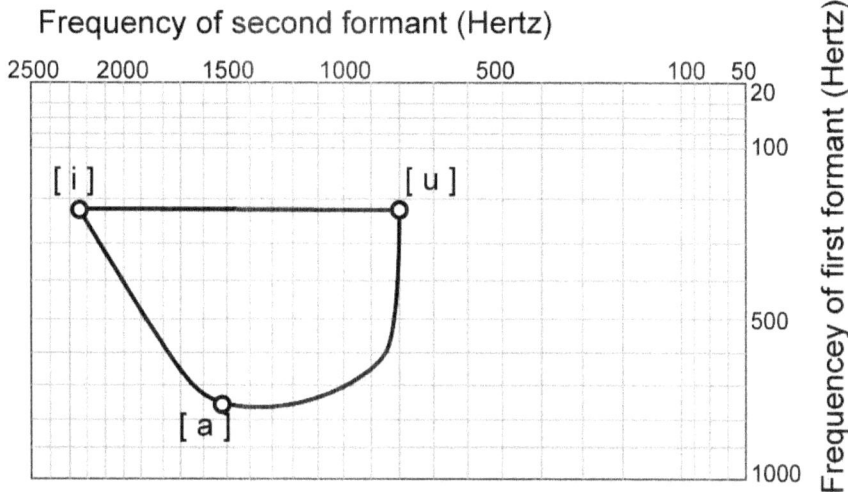

1.5.3 VOWEL EQUATIONS: FUNDAMENTAL, DERIVATIVE AND "CARDINAL" VOWELS AND DIPHTHONGS

Vowel equations: The ancient Indian phonologists realized the relationships expressed at the beginning of this section, and set up a number of ***vowel equations*** to express them, part of their overall ***Sandhi*** (euphonic combination) system [LN-31 to 33, LAi-3]. Let us quickly look at this system of vowel equations. They are summarized in the Figure below.

Chapter 1: Origins of Language, Points of Articulation; Basic Classification of Vowels, Nonvowels, Tones

Fig. 1-4: Summary of *vowel equations* first used by the ancient Indian phoneticians in their system of *Sandhi* (euphonic combination).

Using, for the moment, the following temporary transcription:

> *u* of English *but* = **[a]**
> *a* of English *father* = **[aa]**
> *i* of English *bit* = **[i]**
> *ee* of English *beet* = **[ii]**
> *u* of English *put* = **[u]**
> *oo* of English *boot* = **[uu]**
>
> *e* of English *they* = **[E]**
> *a* of English *back* = **[c]**
> *o* of English *boat* = **[o]**
> *o* of English *bought* = **[Ω]**

We then have, as the major vowel equations (example words given in parentheses for convenience):

- [a] (*but*) + [a] (*but*) = [aa] (*father*)
- [i] (*bit*) + [i] (*bit*) = [ii] (*beet*)
- [u] (*put*) + [u] (*put*) = [uu] (*boot*)

- [a] (*but*) + i (*bit*) = E (*they*)
- [a] (*but*) + [u] (*put*) = [o] (*boat*)

- [aa] (*father*) + [i] (*bit*) = [c] *back*
- [aa] (*father*) + [u] (*put*) = [Ω] (*bought*)

These equations describe in mathematical form exactly those relationships discussed in the previous section.

For instance, taking the first example cited in that section, the *a* of English *father*, i.e. [aa] in our temporary transcription, if we articulate this with the lips *stretched* and the tongue *front (forward)*, i.e. exactly as for the vowel [i], we would get the *a* of English *back*, i.e. [c] in our temporary transcription. Thus, we have, [aa] + [i] = [c].

Another way of describing these equations is to say that the right hand side represents an intermediate position between the left hand side elements. For example, the [o] represents the intermediate position between the positions for the articulation of [a] and [u], i.e. : **[a] + [u] = [o]**. The reader may want to take a few of the other equations and work them out using the other examples of the previous paragraph.

Diphthongs: Most readers must have encountered the term "dipthong" in primary school. *Diphthongs* are, quite obviously, combinations of vowels. Thus, e.g., the *ey* in English *they* is actually a diphthong, a *sequential* (one after another) combination of the vowels [E] and [i], i.e. [Ei]. Similarly, the diphthong *ou* in English *though* represents a sequential combination of [o] and [u]. Some common English diphthongs are:

[Ei] (*they*)
[ou] (*though*)
[aai] (*high*)
[ΩE] (*boy*)

....(1.8)

1.5.4 JAW, LIP, AND TONGUE POSITION, AND LENGTH, AS BASIS OF SYSTEMATIC CLASSIFICATION OF VOWELS

We can easily see from the above discussion that the ***four variables*** of ***(jaw, lip, tongue) position*** and ***length***, as expressed in the various Tables and Figures above, provide a convenient method of classification of vowels, ***as a 4-dimensional matrix***. In fact, this is exactly what was done in the ancient Indian phonological classification. This classification was discussed in more detail in the first volume of this *NAVLIPI* series.

Chapter 1: Origins of Language, Points of Articulation; Basic Classification of Vowels, Nonvowels, Tones

1.6 SEMIVOWELS AS DERIVATIVES OF VOWELS

We now turn to a subject dealt with in older Western phonetics texts, but abandoned in more recent texts, that of the relation of "semivowels" and vowels. Semi-vowels are today covered (in Western texts) by a newer, and in this author's opinion, less accurate term, "approximants."

To visualize the relationship between semivowels and their "parent" vowels, let us look at the orthography (spelling) of the common English word *yes*. Let us now substitute this spelling by *ies*. If we say the initial sound in *ies* rapidly enough, the word sounds identical to *yes*. Similarly, if we pronounce *uell* rapidly enough, it sounds exactly like *well*. The *y* and *w* sounds are called **semivowels**, and are directly related to and derived *from their corresponding vowels* (here [i] and [u]). As another English example, say *uit* or *iu* rapidly; they sound exactly like *wit* and *you*.

This fundamental relationship of vowels to semivowels was recognized in many other phonological treatments and ancient scripts, not just the Indian. As an example, the old Latin orthography for semivowels simply used the corresponding vowels - there were no separate letters for semivowels in the "alphabet". For example, the later Latin word *justicia* ("justice") was originally spelled *iusticia*, the letter *j* ("*jod*", our English "*j*") being a later invention and even today absent in nearly all Latin dictionaries. Indeed, as is well know, the letter *u* (our English "*yu*") was a recent invention: we have all seen Latin inscriptions from 100 or more years ago where the *v* is used in place of the *u*, which does not appear to exist. Thus, the Latin *venio* ("I come") was originally written *uenio*, and pronounced like *wenio*, with the initial sound a semivowel [w] rather than a fricative [v]. Some *common* semivowels and their parent vowels are listed in **Table 1-7** below.

Chapter 1: Origins of Language, Points of Articulation; Basic Classification of Vowels, Nonvowels, Tones

Table 1-7: Common semivowels and corresponding parent vowels, with English word examples.

SEMIVOWEL	CORRESPONDING PARENT VOWEL
[j] (as in *yes*)	[i] (as in *hit*)
[w] (as in *well*)	[u] (as in *put*)
[r]## (as in American pronunciation of *print*)	[rrr]** (as in American *doer*)
[l] (as in *let*)	[lll]** (as in *able*)

(for simplicity, *alveolar* -r only is considered here)
** *(This crude transcription will have to do until* **Navlipi** *is introduced!)*

The specific rule for generating a semivowel from a vowel can be expressed in simple form as:

[*vowel*] + [any *fundamental vowel*] =
[corresponding *semivowel*]

...(1.9)

Applying the above rule to each *fundamental* vowel in turn, we have:

- ❖ [i] + ([a] or [i] or [u]) = [ja] or [ji] or [ju]
- ❖ [u] + ([a] or [i] or [u]) = [wa] or [wi] or [wu]
- ❖ [lll] + ([a] or [i] or [u]) = [la] or [li] or [lu]
- ❖ [rrr] + ([a] or [i] or [u]) = [ra] or [ri] or [ru]

...(1.10)

Once again, in the above, we are following exactly the treatment of vowels and semivowels of the ancient Indian phonologists. This author feels that this treatment is far

Chapter 1: Origins of Language, Points of Articulation; Basic Classification of Vowels, Nonvowels, Tones

more accurate than that of the IPA. For example, the IPA does not even recognize the fundamental *r* sounds as vowels (i.e. *vocalic-r*). It then runs into problems when such vowels are actually articulated as vowels in languages as common as English and Irish. It tackles this problem by giving these vowels the curious appellation **rhoticity**, whatever that is meant to imply! The IPA then considers an *r* vowel, i.e. a central vowel, as a non-central vowel to which this property of "rhoticity" has been added!

Before we end our discussion of semivowels, another note on terminology commonly found in many Western phonological works is pertinent. Some of these works [LN-73 to 76] use the term **liquid** for semivowel. Thus, the common [l] (alveolar, lateral) semivowel of English is denoted in this terminology as an *alveolar, lateral liquid*. This terminology however *misses the fundamental relationship of the semivowels to their parent vowels*. Furthermore, this term, *liquid* then does *not* differentiate between the semivowel and the vowel. Thus, vocalic-*r* and semivowel-*r* are both given the same term, *liquid*! Some books then try to use qualifiers to differentiate the vowel from the semivowel. For example, one prominent book used in American linguistics courses notes "Nasals and liquids are classified as consonants. However, they sometimes act like vowels....." [LN-74]. Furthermore, the central (*r*-sound) and lateral (*l*-sound) semivowels on the one hand, and the bilabial ([w]) and palatal ([y] or [j]) semivowels on the other, are not treated together as semivowels, all with a relationship to parent vowels. Rather, the latter, ([w] and [y]/[j]) are called **glides**. These *glides* in turn are then given such qualifiers as "..if the vocal tract were any more open, the result would be a vowel...", etc. [LN-74].

1.7 BASIC CLASSIFICATION OF NON-VOWELS

1.7.1 THE TERMS *VOICING (VOICED* AND *UNVOICED* OR *DEVOICED)*, CLOSURE, PLOSIVE, STOP, NASALIZATION, ASPIRATION

Voiced, Unvoiced, Voicing: Another most important binary opposition in phones (sounds) is that of **voiced** and **unvoiced (or de-voiced)**. The associated term is **voicing**.

In **voiced** sounds, **the vocal chords vibrate**. In unvoiced sounds, they do not. We say that this is another binary classification because all phones (sounds) *must* fall into one of these two classes.

Voicing can be visualized by the layman in two relatively simple ways [PHo-1]. In the first, gently grasp the "Adam's apple" of the throat between the thumb and forefinger while articulating a sound, such as *aaaaaaaa* (as when the doctor asks you to say "Ah"). You can feel the vocal chords vibrate. Now do the same while saying English *back* and monitor carefully if the vocal chords vibrate at the *b* sound. They do. Now do the same thing with English *pack*, and you will see that the vocal chords do *not* vibrate at the *p* sound. Try the same with the unvoiced/voiced English word pairs *feel/veal, sap/zap* (if you find it hard, try the phones only, i.e. *ffffffffff* vs. *vvvvvvvvv*, *sssssssss* vs. *zzzzzzzz*, etc.) A second way of visualizing voicing is to close the ears by putting one's hands over them. One can then clearly hear whether the voice box, i.e. the vocal chords, are vibrating or not.

Other examples of unvoiced/voiced word pairs in English, with points of articulation corresponding to **Fig. 1-1** also indicated, are as in the **Table** below:

Table 1-8: Examples of unvoiced/voiced word pair examples and their artitions.

UNVOICED/VOICED WORD PAIR	ARTITION (ARTICULATION POSITION)
*c*ot/*g*ot	(velar)
*ch*at/*j*et	(palatal)
*t*ip/*d*ip	(alveolar)
*p*at/*b*at	(bilabial)
*th*ought/*th*at	(interdental)
*f*at/*v*at	(infralabio-supradental)

In older European literature, *unvoiced* phones were also denoted as **surd**, and *voiced* sounds as **sonant**; these are Latin-based terms adapted into English from the usage of 18th-century French linguists (surd, e.g. is from Latin *surdus*, "deaf"). These terms are sometimes used interchangeably with *voiced/unvoiced* in this book.

It is very important to understand the voiced/unvoiced opposition *conceptually* as well as physically: The *c* (unvoiced) and *g* (voiced) of *cot, got*, as an example, *are really the same phone*, in fact the *identical* sound, except that in one case (the *g*) the vocal chords vibrate and in the other they don't. The *artition* is the same for both phones (velar in this case) and that is really the key feature of distinction. In an ideal "alphabet", we would (or ought to) have very similar symbols for these two phones, placed next to each other in the "alphabet".

Closure, Plosive, Stop: We can now turn to two related terms, **closure** and **plosive**. If the reader practiced the sounds in the examples in the Table above, he/she may have noticed that, in articulation of many of them, a *closure* or contact of the articulating organs occurs *prior to* actual utterance of the sound. Thus, e.g., prior to utterance of the *p* of English *put*, the lips are closed. This is called *closure*. Then, when the sound is actually uttered, there is a small explosion of the *p* in breath. This explosion is the basis of calling this sound a *plosive*. Try visualizing this with the utterance of English *put*. Hold your lips in the position you use to say this word, but hold them without uttering anything for a few seconds. Then utter the word. You will see that there is an explosion of the breath as it is let out from the lips.

In a similar fashion, in articulation of the *c* in English *cat*, there is a brief but firm closure

Chapter 1: Origins of Language, Points of Articulation; Basic Classification of Vowels, Nonvowels, Tones

of the base of the tongue with the velum, and thus the *c* is a plosive. It is important to recognize that the term plosive has nothing to do with whether a sound is voiced or unvoiced. A plosive can be either. Thus, the *p* in English *put* is an unvoiced plosive and the *b* in English *but* is a voiced plosive. Similarly, the *c* and *g* of English *cat, got* are, respectively, unvoiced and voiced plosives.

The hissing sounds *s* and *z* as in English *sat* or *zebra* are *not* plosives, since *no closure* of the articulating organs followed by an explosion of breath occurs. (They are called *fricatives*, see later in this chapter.)

Plosives are what many schooled in the English-speaking world may have learned as "hard consonants", sounds such as the *c, g, t, d, p, b* in the English examples above (*cot, got, tip, dip, pat, bat*).

It is important to recognize that the terms *closure* and *plosive* are of far greater phonological accuracy than the term "consonant" that many of us in the English-speaking world learned in primary school. All examples cited in the Table above except the last two (*thought/that, fat/vat*) are unvoiced/voiced plosive pairs.

Another phonological term used in the literature of phonetics and linguistics is ***stop***. A *stop*, as the name implies, is *any phone (sound) in which the breath from the mouth is stopped, even momentarily, before uttering the sound*. Thus, quite obviously, vowels are *not* stops. The *mouth* distinction is important, because nasals such as the *n* of English *new* are considered stops, even though breath is continually being let out through the nose before, during and after articulation of the sound. Thus, quite obviously, *plosives are, necessarily, always stops, but all stops are not plosives*: The nasal stops are *not* plosives. The qualifier "even momentarily" in the italicized definition at the beginning of this paragraph is also important: Trilled sounds, such as the "rolled-*r*", are also considered stops since there is a stopping of the breath, however fleeting, in their utterance. On the other hand, hissing sounds, such as *s* and *z* as in English *sat* or *zebra,* are *not* stops, since, although there is impediment to the breath, there is not a complete *stopping* of the breath. Unfortunately in the contemporary linguistics and phonology literature, the two terms *stop* and *plosive* are frequently interchanged and conflated, even by learned authors.

Aspiration, Nasalization: These terms denote other, important characteristics of phones. *Aspiration*, an "extra puff of air", so to speak, uttered with a phone, is a differentiation given to *plosives* that may be somewhat unfamiliar to the European. It is today found as a phonemic distinction (a term which is, unfortunately for the layman, defined only later in this chapter!) most prominently in the North Indian languages, in Cantonese, and in Korean. That is to say, it has significance only in these major languages. Although it is not phonemically distinct in English, it is nevertheless used quite routinely in the articulation of important plosives in the English language. Thus, if a small, lighted match were held in front of the lips during the British, American or Australian articulation of the *p* in *pin* or *put*, the flame would be put out. (In Indian or Irish articulation, it would not!) But the flame would continue to burn during the articulation of the *p* in English *spy* or *spit*, since these plosives are *not* aspirated. Aspiration is usually transliterated in Roman script by the addition of a post-positional ***h***. Thus aspirated *p, t, k* are written *ph, th, kh*, etc..

Nasalization is much easier and more straightforward to understand for the layman. The *n* and *m* in English *no*, *me*, are, quite obviously, nasals. That is to say, during their articulation, *breath passes through the nose*. During the articulation of the *n* in *no*, an alveolar closure occurs, i.e., the tongue contacts the alveolar ridge. This is thus called an *alveolar nasal*. On the other hand, in the utterance of the *m* in *me*, a bilabial closure occurs; this is thus a *bilabial nasal*. The *n* and *m* in the above examples are *not* plosives, since no explosion of air occurs during their articulation. Thus, the above *n* and *m* are *nasal stops*. Vowels such as the *a* of English *father* can also of course be nasalized. As is widely known, French uses many nasalized vowels (although English rarely does), as does Hindi/Urdu, e.g. French *en* ("in") is a purely *nasalized vowel*.

1.7.2 THE TERMS *FRICATIVE, FRICATIZATION, SIBILANT, FLAP, TAP AND TRILL*

Fricatives, Fricatization, Sibilants, Shibilants, Spirants: We were introduced to the hissing sounds *ssssss* and *zzzzzz* as in English *sat* or *zebra*, above. These are clearly not plosives, i.e. there is no closure of articulating organs followed by a sudden explosion of breath. However, there *is* an impediment to the breath, specifically a ***frictional impediment to the breath***. Such phones are known as ***fricatives***.

Other examples of fricatives are the *f* and *v* sounds of English *fit* and *veal*, the *th* sounds in American/British/Australian (but *not* Indian or Irish!) articulation of *think, that*, the *sh* in English *shoot*, the *s* in English *leisure* (a sort of *zh* sound), the *ch* in German *doch*, Scottish *Loch*. In all of these, there is a frictional or rubbing sound. The reader can visualize this frictional sound clearly by articulating the root sound only, in each of these words examples, i.e. the sounds *fffff, vvvvvv, thhhhh, shhhhhh, chhhhhhh* etc.

Chapter 1: Origins of Language, Points of Articulation; Basic Classification of Vowels, Nonvowels, Tones

The fricatives *ssssss*, *zzzzzz* and *shhhhh* have a unique hissing sound, and are frequently given the appellation **sibilants** (sometimes in the older literature, the sounds *shhhh* and *zhhhh* are further sub-classified as **shibilants**). Perhaps the most common fricative, found in almost every major language, is the common *h* sound, as in English *his*; this is a "glottal" fricative, with the articulation position being deep down in the throat, at the glottis.

The process of making a frictionalized sound out of what would normally not be a fricative is then called *fricatization*. Thus, the *ch* sound of Scottish *Loch* is the *fricatized* version of the *ck* sound of *lock*, i.e. the velar unvoiced stop. Similarly, the *sh* of English *shoot* is the fricatized version of the *ch* of English *check* (in the Irish and Indian, but not American or British pronunciation!). In the older or archaic literature, *fricatives* were also denoted sometimes as **spirants** (Latin *spirare*, "to breathe").

Flaps, Taps: We have thus far encountered two important overall classes of non-vowels: *plosives* and *fricatives*. Both are *stops*. In the plosive, for example the *t* in English *take*, there is a definite, complete closure of the articulating organs, *followed by* explosion of the breath during articulation of the sound.

However, in some articulations of the *t* sound, the sound is articulated so fast that *there isn't time to effect a complete, firm closure of the organs prior to articulation*. This is seen, for example, in the American (but not British) pronunciation of *matter* or *hitter*: The *t* is never fully articulated here, just *"lightly hit"*. The *r* sound in languages such as Spanish or Hindi or Arabic (e.g. in Spanish *seguro*, "secure", Hindi *rehenaa*, "to stay", Arabic and Hindi/Urdu *haraam*, "forbidden"), also have a "light hit" of the articulating organ, in this case the tongue against the alveolar ridge, rather than a full closure followed by an explosion of breath.

Such sounds are denoted as ***flaps*** or the nearly synonymous ***taps***. The terminology *tap* quite obviously has its origins in the connotation of a light "tap" of the tongue against the articulation point in such sounds as the common *r*. The most common "*r* sound" of most languages is in fact the most common example of the flap/tap.

Flaps/taps are important in nearly all major Indian languages, where they have phonemic distinction as compared to their corresponding plosives. (They are expressed in common Indian scripts such as Naagari, as well as in Roman transcription, with a dot underneath the corresponding plosive.) Examples are the highlighted phones in the Hindi words *ka***d**ak* ("hard, stiff"), *ga***dh***, ("fort").

Trills: When a *tap* or *flap* is uttered *in repeated fashion*, for example the well-known "rolled *r*" articulated in many languages, this is known as a ***trill***. Thus, the *r* in the South American Spanish pronunciation of *burro* ("donkey") is a "trilled *r*". The common *r* sound of many languages is a trilled *r* rather than a simple tap.

Quite evidently, the terms ***Fricative, Fricatization, Sibilant, Flap, Tap*** and ***Trill*** are applicable to *non-vowels* only.

1.7.3 OTHER, LESS COMMON NON-VOWEL PHONES: CLICKS, EJECTIVES, IMPLOSIVES

Clicks: In English, we are familiar with the sound transcribed as *tsk tsk,* frequently used to convey regret or sadness. This is a *click*. More specifically, it is an ingressive, dental click. The sound is made with the tongue in the same artition as the dental, "Spanish" [t], or, sometimes as the English [s], but the breath is then sucked *in* (rather than let out) at the tongue. The breath used is not from the pulmonary (lungs etc.) apparatus; the velum is closed, preventing this. Rather, it is with what is known as the *mouth-air system*.

The click transcribed in English as *tut tut* is very similar, but at a different artition, the alveolar: It is thus an ingressive, alveolar click. Another click that may be familiar to the reader is the *"giddyap"* click, used, e.g., by drivers in goading a horse or mule. This has a slightly different type of articulation. The tongue is held as if one were going to utter the alveolar lateral phone, i.e. the [l]-sound, but then, instead of pulmonary air being expelled, the side of the tongue is dragged and "sucked" along the roof of the mouth, either on the left side or the right side (but not both). This sound nevertheless fulfils the criterion for an ingressive click: Ingress of air and no pulmonary mechanism (velic closure).

Another odd click is the ingressive bilabial click. This has vulgar connotations, as, e.g., in its use by eunuchs in India in days of yore.

Clicks are of linguistic importance [PHo-21 to 27] primarily in South African and South West African languages, e.g. Zulu and !Xo Bushman.

In addition to artition as in the English examples above, clicks can be further varied by such properties as nasalization and aspiration. For example, Zulu possesses the above two

English clicks (alveolar, lateral) and a third (retroflex artition), each with aspirated and nasal variants, yielding nine (9) click phonemes. There are also *egressive* clicks in some languages, but these are extremely rare.

Ejectives: Another type of phone that does not use a pulmonary mechanism is the ejective [PHo-1, 24]. In this, the vocal chords (glottis) are *closed* (just as in utterance of the glottal stop). An additional closure is then effected at another location in the oral apparatus, e.g. the lips (for bilabial ejectives) or the tongue + upper teeth (for dental ejectives). The breath in the oral cavity is then compressed by raising the tongue, and the closure in the oral cavity opened abruptly, yielding a sound. The air flow is *egressive*. When the closure is at the lips, for a bilabial ejective, a sound like a cork popping is audible. The closure may not be complete, but can be fricatized, yielding [s] and [f] ejectives, among others. Ejectives are found in such languages as Amharic (the major language of Ethiopia), and Georgian (a language of the Caucasus region thought by some to be related distantly to Basque), which have bilabial, velar, dental and affricative ejectives which are distinct phonemes.

Implosives: Implosives [PHo-1, 24] are in a sense the opposite of ejectives. The mechanism of air transfer is the same, but its direction is *ingressive* rather than egressive. For the bilabial implosive, the sound is more "hollow" than that of the bilabial ejective. Implosives are in general much rarer than ejectives. They are frequently found in languages of the Malay (Austronesian) family in Indonesia. For example, many Indonesian languages in the Sulawesi region possess voiced bilabial and dental implosives as distinct phonemes.

1.7.4 *ARTITION, VOICING* AND *"COLOR"* OF THE PHONE (*PHONOCHROMATICITY*) AS KEY VARIABLES IN PHONOLOGICAL CLASSIFICATION OF NON-VOWELS

If the reader has now been able to absorb the definitions and explanations presented in the sections above with some success, he/she should be able to immediately see that *artition* can be used as one, important parameter in the *phonological classification of non-vowels*.

To identify another, major parameter, then, we can, for practical purposes, simply lump the other important characteristics of a non-vowel, such as *voicing, aspiration, fricatization* and *clicking*, into a single parameter. We can call this parameter the **color of the phone**, a term borrowed from the ancient Indian phoneticians (from *warna(varna)-maalaa*). We can then coin the term **PHONOCHROMATICITY** to denote this "color of the phone". The Table below illustrates this two-parameter classification for a very limited set of variables: Just five variables for *artition* and seven variables for *phonochromaticity*.

Table 1-9: Illustration of the use of the two parameters ***artition*** and ***phonochromaticity*** for the phonological classification of ***non-vowels***. For simplicity, just three (3) variables are shown for phonochromaticity and four (4) for artition. (As a reference point, the ancient Indian phonological classification of non-vowels used five (5) variables for artition and seven (7) variables for phonochromaticity.)

Phonochromaticity (x-axis) →

Artition (y-axis) ↓

	Unvoiced Unaspirated	Voiced Unaspirated	Nasal
Velar	English *sky*	English *go*	English *king*
Palatal	Spanish *chico*	English *gender*	English *inch*
Alveolar	English *stop*	English *do*	English *not*
Bilabial	English *spy*	English *but*	English *me*

1.8 TONES, TONAL ACCENT, PITCH AND STRESS (ICTUS) ACCENT: FUNDAMENTAL vs. SIGNIFICANT TONES

We are all familiar with the fact that the Chinese languages have the property of **tone** or **tonal accent** (sometimes referred to as *musical* accent), and that two identical words uttered in different tones, i.e. different **pitch**, may mean two entirely different things: In linguistic jargon, we would say that different tones are phonemically distinct.

We are also familiar, from non-tonal languages like English or Hindi/Urdu or French, that they have the property of **stress accent**. What we may not be familiar with however is the fact that these two phenomena are in fact related, and that in some languages, *tone* accents eventually degenerated into *stress* accents. (Stress accents were, in the older phonetics literature, also called **ictus** accents, a term borrowed from poetry.) We may also be surprised to learn that tonal accent still exists in a subdued way in common contemporary languages such as Italian and, to a lesser extent, Maraathi, though it may not be officially recognized.

Let us first quickly look at some common examples of tone variation. As a first example, let us look at the common speech (*Putonghua*) of the Beijing dialect of Mandarin Chinese. Here, we have four tones. These are depicted in the Table below. For now, the simple description and method of transcription in the Table is adequate. As Mandarin word examples, we have: *yi (1st tone)*, "one"; *yi (4th tone)*, "hundred million"; *shi (2nd tone)*, "ten"; *xao (3rd tone)*, "good". Thus, we can see that *yi* has an entirely different meaning depending on whether it is articulated in the 1st or 4th tone.

As a second example, we can now look at tones of the Hong Kong dialect of Yue (Cantonese), summarized in the Table. Here we have *six* tones. We can look at some example words in Cantonese, where the extreme significance of tone is even more apparent: *si (1st tone)*, "silk", *si (2nd tone)*, "to try"; *si (3rd tone)*, "matter"; *si (4th tone)*, "time"; *si (5th tone)*, "history", *si (6th tone)*, "city". What to non-Chinese may appear to be the same word, *si*, has radically different meanings in the six different tones it can be uttered in.

Chapter 1: Origins of Language, Points of Articulation; Basic Classification of Vowels, Nonvowels, Tones

Table 1-10: Summary of tones found in Mandarin Chinese, Cantonese (Yue) Chinese and Yoruba.

TONE	PROPERTIES
MANDARIN	
1st	high and level
2nd	rising
3rd	falling-rising
4th	falling
CANTONESE (YUE)	
1st	high
2nd	mid and level and level
3rd	low-mid and level
4th	falling, low-mid to low
5th	rising, low-mid to high
6th	rising, low-mid to mid
YORUBA	
1st	high and level
2nd	mid and level
3rd	low and level
4th	rising, low to high
5th	falling, high to low

As a final example, we can look at the tones of Yoruba (the major Bantu-family language of Nigeria), also summarized in the above Table. This language has five tones. Some word examples are: *ba (1st tone)*, "to meet"; *ba (2nd tone)*, "to hide"; *ba (3rd tone)*, "to perch"; *yi (4th tone)*, "this", *na (5th tone)*, "the".

In the above three language examples, the tones make a fundamental difference in meaning for the same "word". We can say then that these languages have ***FUNDAMENTAL tones***.

There are other examples of languages where the tone is not so fundamental, but is nevertheless *significant*. We can say these languages have ***SIGNIFICANT tones***.

Chapter 1: Origins of Language, Points of Articulation; Basic Classification of Vowels, Nonvowels, Tones

Let us look at some examples of language with *significant tones*. The major examples of these languages are mostly non-living languages of the Indo-European group. For instance, the older variety of Sanskrit, called Vedic Sanskrit, had three tones: *acute* or raised (high pitch) (called *ud-daata* in Sanskrit); *grave* or low and unraised (called *an-ud-daata*) and *circumflex,* originally a combination of *acute* and *grave*, but later simply used as a mid (called *swarita*). The older Greek, called Homeric Greek, also had the identical three accents in active use: *acute, grave and circumflex*, as did the older Latin. In fact, the "acute, grave, circumflex" accents of our French courses (*aigu, grave, circomflex)* are defunct remnants from Latin and Greek.

The tones in these ancient languages were not *fundamental,* in the sense that one did not normally find a series of words which had radically different meaning depending upon which tone they were uttered in. They were however *significant*, in the sense that particular syllables in words had particular accents, and were to be pronounced in those accents only. If pronounced in other accents, they may not have been understood, and *could* alter the meaning.

Remnants of such *significant* tones are found, among living European languages, in Italian. For example, when one says *non fumare,* "don't smoke" or "no smoking", one normally articulates the four syllables in an (*acute, acute, grave, grave*) pitch. If one were to say *non fumare* in a (*grave, grave, acute, acute*) pitch, one would definitely get funny looks from native Italian speakers, although one might perhaps still ultimately be understood. As is well known, among European languages Swedish also has significant tones, rather more significant than Italian. Among Indian languages, Maraathi has some significant tones.

Languages such as Hindi/Urdu, Spanish, English or French of course possess **stress accent**. And these stress accents are frequently *significant*, i.e. the meaning of the word changes if the accent is put in a different place. For example, the following English homophones (words that sound the same) are verb or noun depending on whether the stress (accent) is on the 2nd syllable (verb) or 1st syllable (noun):

object/object; import/import; incite/insight; pervert/pervert.
$$\ldots (1.11)$$

With respect to these English examples, the reader may immediately remark that, at least in one of them (*object*), the pronunciation of the first syllable is different enough that the words are not homophones. However, in all the other examples, the words are

Chapter 1: Origins of Language, Points of Articulation; Basic Classification of Vowels, Nonvowels, Tones

pronounced identically, and are thus true homophones, except for the location of the stress accent.

As another example from a different language family, the Navajo word *tadigis* with the accent on the second syllable means "you wash yourself", whereas with the accent on the first syllable it means "he washes himself" [LN-36]. Spanish orthography, as we all know, frequently specifies accent, and sometimes this accent falls on a syllable we may not expect it to fall on, for example in the word *lexicógrafo*, "lexicographer" and the place name *Bógota*, the accent falls on, to English-speakers, odd places. In these Spanish examples, the stress accent is not truly *significant*, just desirable.

We may also note one important feature about the *stress* accents in all these example words: The stressed syllable almost always has a higher *pitch*. I.e., we have a de facto *acute* accent. *What we perceive as a stress accent is in fact also a pitch or tone accent*, specifically an acute accent. In fact, this is the mechanism by which the musical or pitch (or tone) accents of the old Indo-European languages, such as Sanskrit or Greek or Latin, degenerated into *stress* or *ictus* accents. And conversely, the relatively few tonal accents in a language such as Swedish can be easily expressed in terms of a stress accent [LAs-18], dispensing completely with the concept of tones for such languages.

The major tonal languages are concentrated in the Sino-Tibetan family (e.g. Mandarin or Yue), Baantu family (now called Niger-Congo family, example language Yoruba) and some South American language families.

Chapter 1: Origins of Language, Points of Articulation; Basic Classification of Vowels, Nonvowels, Tones

1.9 PARTING NOTE ON THE EXTANT PRIMER AND MID-LEVEL LITERATURE IN PHONOLOGY, LINGUISTICS, AND RELATED FIELDS

As noted at the beginning of this chapter, an additional objective of this book is to provide an introduction to diverse but closely related subjects such as *phonology, linguistics* and *language families* "**under one roof**", as it were, i.e. in a single source. In this respect then, the author feels that a parting note on *the extent and quality of the primer and more specialized literature in these fields* is in order here. We confine our discussion for the moment to the English language literature.

On expert reading, much of the pedagogical literature in the above fields reveals some deficiencies. These can be varied, ranging from the relatively innocuous- e.g. a too cursory or too superficial treatment of the subject - to more serious inaccuracies, to, in rare cases, astounding errors. Part of the reason for this of course may be the nature of the beast: These fields, when combined, are so vast that no single person can be expected to have a complete command of all areas of them. We will leave further comment on the causes and remedies of the situation to another time and place. Rather, here we will simply cite some examples illustrating our point from the literature.

As one example of serious deficiencies, a book published by Ohio State University and, unfortunately, widely used in American linguistics courses [LN-73], has glaring errors which have as yet still not been corrected in multiple printings! For example, a comparative table in this book, which purports to list "Indic" and Maraathi (Marathi) words in side-by-side columns does not in fact use Maraathi words at all, but rather words from a Raajasthaani (Rajasthani) dialect of Hindi! [LN-73] This would be the equivalent of showing a comparative table of words with columns labeled "Latin" and "French", but then using Romanian words in place of the French words! On another page, this book gives erroneous Dewanaagari transcriptions of Sanskrit and misidentified Sumerian hieroglyphs [LN-73, 74]. This leads one to wonder if the book was proofread at all before publication.

Other books [LN-76] do not have such glaring errors, but impart little essential information, or treat subjects in a very cursory manner. For example, the chapter on language families in the wide-ranging Aronoff/Rees-Miller handbook [LN-1], again widely used in elementary linguistics courses in many American universities, is a rather

Chapter 1: Origins of Language, Points of Articulation; Basic Classification of Vowels, Nonvowels, Tones

superficial treatment of this subject; it would impart not much more additional information to a reader than that available in the lay literature such as newspapers and magazines, or even, today, on Wikipedia. In this respect, it may be compared with Chapter 4 later in our book, on language families, which treats the same subject: The reader can make his/her own judgment in this regard.

As an example of a publication with lesser but still notable errors, the otherwise excellent book on the world's writing systems edited by Daniels and Bright [SCr-1] contains small errors, e.g. the blanket, casual and erroneous statements of Parpola in his chapter on the decipherment of the Harappan script regarding Indian scripts; these statements appear to betray some ignorance of Indian phonological and grammatical tradition (which may be understandable, since very few non-Indian-origin Indologists may be familiar with this tradition). This is in spite of Parpola having carried out extremely eminent work on the Harappan script and having assistance from eminent Indian-origin scholars (Mahadevan and others) [LAi-13 to 18]; indeed, together, Mahadevan and Parpola are the world's foremost scholars on the Harappan script.

There are however also quite excellent pedagogical books with no such errors. One such example is the book by O'Connor on *phonology* [PHo-1], which gives a thorough and excellent treatment of phonology, easily understood by an educated layman. This book is comprehensive, and remains up to date, in spite of a 1973 publication date. This is in contrast to other, even newer books in this field [PHo-2 to 20], which appear outdated. It is respectfully noted, however, that none of these otherwise excellent books treat of as wide a range of fields as our book attempts in its primer chapters.

As another note on the extant linguistics literature, many scientists coming from a physical sciences background, such as this author, are surprised to see that a lot of what would appear to be pure hypothecation and conjecture, with little or no evidentiary backing such as from archaeological or philological sources, appears to pass for valid theory in linguistics. Such conjecture would be immediately shot down in the physical sciences without adequate experimental (i.e., evidentiary) proof. Frequently, this conjecture appears to fulfill a particular viewpoint originally propounded by eminences whom other workers do not want to refute.

Again, we may cite just a few examples of these: **(1)** The hypothesis that writing was first brought to Egypt from Sumer has no archaeological, philological or other evidentiary backing. Indeed, the great differences in the type of writing would indicate independent origins. The fact that Sumerian writing was on preserved substrates such as clay whereas

Chapter 1: Origins of Language, Points of Articulation; Basic Classification of Vowels, Nonvowels, Tones

Egyptian writing was on perishable ones such as papyrus would negate any attempt at drawing temporal inferences. Yet this hypothesis persists in all the linguistics literature even in otherwise eminent books [SCr-1]! **(2)** The hypothesis that the first human languages were click languages or had a strong click element. This is supposedly based on the fact that certain ethnic groups, which have retained their distinct ethnic identities in spite of the encroachment of other ethnic groups and which are traceable, via mitochondrial DNA, to very early in the hominid family tree, possess click languages. These groups include, in particular the Ju!huansi of Southwestern Africa and the Hadzabe of East Africa [LAs-7]. Yet proponents of this theory refuse to look at the glaring contrary evidence: That the Hadzabe and Ju!huansi languages are totally unrelated, even in the nature of their clicks. On the other hand, they are closely related to regional languages which do *not* possess clicks. This would appear to indicate that they might either have acquired clicks recently, or that the related non-click languages *lost* clicks recently. The first human languages may indeed have been click languages, but the Ju!huansi/Hadzabe evidence cited certainly neither supports nor detracts from this conclusion!

Also in the general linguistics literature, there are innumerable primers that, in the view of this author, present a very superficial and sometimes erroneous overview of linguistics [LN-73 to 76, LN-3 to LN-30]. Unfortunately, many of these are widely used in courses, especially in the English-language world.

Turning now to the more the more specialized literature, as examples of deficiencies therein, we may cite the examples of the following two paragraphs:

As a first example, McAlpin [LAi-24], in his commendable (and ultimately, accurate) attempt to relate Elamite and Tamil as Dravidian languages, erroneously uses many Tamil words of obvious Sanskrit (i.e. Indo-European) borrowing. Some examples are *kutiira* ("hut, settlement"), *shava* ("corpse") and *channa* ("beauty"). He apparently believes these are of Dravidian provenance! He need merely have asked just about any Tamil-speaker to proofread this part of his work before publishing, and would have immediately been told that these were non-Dravidian words of Sanskrit origin! McAlpin's conclusion that Elamite and Tamil are both Dravidian and are related appears to be eminently correct, and his work is thus seminal in this respect; one need only look at more mundane, definitely Dravidian cognates as presented in a table later in this book (e.g., *Nii*, "you", *ulh*, "home, inside"). Nevertheless, his work could have done without these errors. (Our present book contains, in a later chapter, a short table of cognate Tamil and Elamite words.)

Chapter 1: Origins of Language, Points of Articulation; Basic Classification of Vowels, Nonvowels, Tones

As a second example, the book on Indo-European linguistics by Szemerenyi [IEu-6] reveals, to an experienced Sanskritist such as this author, a startling ignorance of the Sanskrit language. This is striking because one would expect that Sanskrit would be one of the most important languages required to be mastered for an appreciation of Indo-European linguistics.

Turning now to recent forays by non-linguists into linguistic and language matters, we note that these have unfortunately bared even less qualification on the part of many of these authors. Examples are recent (2003 and later) publications attempting to apply the techniques of evolutionary biology to tracing language origins [LN-77(a)], attempted in spite of caveats on applications of mathematical and statistical techniques to linguistics issues propounded as early as 1965 [LN-78]. For example, one such recent publication in a pre-eminent journal [LN-77(a)] used nonexistent appellations such as "Afghani" and "Waziristani" for languages; did the authors mean Pushtu/Pukhto, the language of NWFP and eastern Afghanistan, and Dari, the language of Kabul? It also showed incorrect provenances in a language tree, and betrayed a complete ignorance of the languages addressed by the authors' study. Thus, the credibility of the authors in addressing issues of languages and linguistics may be called into question, even if their credibility in statistical evolutionary biology techniques may be unquestionable. Most importantly, then, their work completely ignored the fact that language origin is a highly subjective field and thus *may not yield accurately to statistical analyses* [LN-78]: Consideration must also be given to *semantic* and *grammatical-form* relationships between words, not just how word roots play out in a DNA- or gene-tracing computer program! Unfortunately, the same authors repeated their application of such evolutionary biology techniques some years later ([LN-77(b)]) to come to an even more profound conclusion solely based on some sort of statistical phonemic analysis spanning all the world's languages: That language originated in southwestern Africa. In this author's humble opinion, this conclusion may or may not be true; however, to arrive at it using statistical techniques applied to phonemes across essentially all the world's languages is fraught! To reiterate, it is difficult to apply such sweeping statistical methods to language, which has nuances of etymology and semantics that do not lend themselves to statistical analysis. And this especially from an author who has a poor grounding in the fundamentals of phonemes and of linguistics. In this respect, reference is respectfully made to the application of phonemic analysis - in particular infant phonemes - to the reconstruction of a parent language, as done at the end of Chapter 5 in this book.

Finally, in a lighter vein, many books also have errors of a sort that betray (an understandable) lack of familiarity with non-linguistics subjects, but which one would, nevertheless, reasonably not expect in proof-read works. For example, the otherwise excellent Aronoff/Rees-Miller handbook [LN-1], mentioned above, repeatedly cites the human species as *homo sapiens* (*sic*, i.e. without an initial capital (upper case) *H*, as in *Homo sapiens*). If the various authors of each independent chapter had all momentarily forgotten their Linnaean nomenclature from high school biology, then one would think that the proverbial graduate student assigned to proof-read the manuscript would at least have picked this up!

1.10 EXERCISES

(1) In one paragraph, discuss the relation of human intelligence and its development to the development of human language as proposed in this book.

(2) Enumerate all the points of articulation in the speech apparatus.

(3) Classify vowels in detail with the variables of *jaw, lip* and *tongue* position. Which variables and/or vowels are not treated of or treated incompletely in extant classifications such as that of the International Phonetic Association (IPA)?

(4) Define the terms *phone, artition, vowel, non-vowel, diphthong, triphthong, voicing, plosive, stop, aspiration, fricative, sibilant, tap, flap, trill.*

(5) Define the terms *artition* and *phonochromaticity*.

(6) Discuss *tone* in terms of point of origin and subsequent transition. In this context, compare tones in Mandarin, Cantonese, Yoruba and Cashinahua. Discuss *significant* vs. *fundamental* tones as defined in this book. In this context, compare and contrast the tones of Swedish and the ancient Indo-European languages with those of Mandarin.

CHAPTER 2.
WRITING: METHODS OF TRANSCRIPTION AND "ALPHABETS"

TABLE OF CONTENTS

2.1 PURPOSE OF THIS CHAPTER 54

2.2 SOME BASIC TERMINOLOGY ESSENTIAL FOR FURTHER DISCUSSION 55

2.3 BRIEF DISCUSSION OF ORIGINS OF WRITING AND SOME STANDARD TERMS USED IN THE CURRENT STATE OF THE ART: 56

2.4 THE REBUS PRINCIPLE, ADDITIONAL STANDARD ORTHOGRAPHIC TERMS (*DETERMINATIVE, LOGOSYLLABIC, LOGOPHONETIC, ABJAD, ALPHABETIC, ABUGIDA, FEATURAL*) AND SOME NEW TERMS (*MAATRAIC, PHONOGRAPHIC*) 63

2.5 MORE SPECIFIC CHARACTERISTICS OF SCRIPTS AND THE NEW TERMS *COMPLETENESS, VAIGYAANIC, EMPIRICITY, UNIPHONOGRAPHIC, UNIPHONEMOGRAPHIC, QUASI-PHONETIC* AND *PHONEMO-IDIOSYNCRATIC* 67

2.6 TOOLS AVAILABLE FOR THE MODERN ORTHOGRAPHER: 77

2.7 EXERCISES 85

Chapter 2: Writing: Methods of Transcription and "Alphabets"

2.1 PURPOSE OF THIS CHAPTER

This chapter seeks to discuss writing systems *specifically from the point of view of* **Navlipi**. It is thus by no means a general primer in writing systems of the world. Excellent such primers are available and have been cited in Chapter 1 [SCr-1 to SCr-20], e.g. the excellent English language book edited by Daniels and Bright [SCr-1].

This chapter rather seeks to introduce terminology for writing systems *specifically relevant to **NAVLIPI**,* including *new terminology, e.g.* such terms as **completeness**, **empiricity**, **uniphonographic**, **vaigyaanic** and **maatraic**, which are defined further below. Thus, once again, as for Chapter 1, *the linguistics or orthography expert as well as the layman are both respectfully encouraged to review this chapter well.*

2.2 SOME BASIC TERMINOLOGY ESSENTIAL FOR FURTHER DISCUSSION

To commence our brief review of terminology, let us first quickly look at the following terms:

1) *Transcription*
2) *Orthography*
3) *Script*
4) *Alphabet*
5) *Symbol*
6) *Letter*
7) *Character*
8) *Glyph*

Writing, i.e. the **transcription of phones or ideas**, is sometimes also denoted as **orthography.** Orthography literally means "spelling", but is freely used today to indicate transcription or a writing system. A writing system is called a **script** in the most generalized sense. In very basic layman's terms, *script* is synonymous with **alphabet**.

Each individual *element* of the writing system or transcription may be designated variously as a **symbol**, a **letter** or a **character**. Thus the *letter "a"* of the Roman "alphabet" is a *symbol*, as is a "*character*" in Chinese writing. A more scientific and more specific term for a symbol, letter or character is **GLYPH**. We shall use *glyph* in preference to the other designations in this book.

The term "*alphabet*" has been used by linguists schooled in the Western tradition to denote an orthography which differentiates and distinguishes between vowels and non-vowels (termed "consonants" in the Western linguistic tradition). Thus, there is typically a glyph for each vowel and non-vowel in an alphabet. An alphabet also strives (though rarely succeeds) to assign a single glyph to a single phone. As we will discuss later in this section, the term "*alphabet*" starts to become nebulous, and in some cases, nonsensical, once the characteristics and specific properties of orthographies are analyzed in a more detailed and scientific way. For this reason, this book strives to use the term "*alphabet*" as little as possible. We shall prefer *script* or, occasionally, *orthography*.

2.3 BRIEF DISCUSSION OF ORIGINS OF WRITING AND SOME STANDARD TERMS USED IN THE CURRENT STATE OF THE ART: *IDEOGRAPHIC, LOGOGRAPHIC AND SYLLABIC*

As should be evident even to a layman, the first orthographies were ***ideographic*** [SCr-1, SCr-8 to SCr-21, SCr-37, SCr-40]. That is to say, humans first started to write by drawing pictures to represent objects, ideas or words. In a purely *ideographic* orthography, each picture represents a single word. Thus, in a purely ideographic orthography, one would need a separate picture for each word in a language. In some ways, the modern Chinese script, a descendant of an ancient ideographic script, is a living example of this: The number of Chinese characters nearly equals the number of words in a typical Chinese language such as Mandarin. Quite evidently, *ideographic* is synonymous in a general way with ***pictographic*** [SCr-25 to 28].

The Chinese symbol (character) for "three" (Mandarin Putonghua pronunciation *saan*, 1st tone) still looks like three horizontal lines, even in its reduced/simplified form [SCr-29]. As is also well known, the Greek and Roman alphabets are descended from Phoenician and other Semitic "alphabets" that started from ideographic representations [SCr-38 to SCr-44]: The first four letters of the Semitic "alphabets", *'alef, beth* (beit), *gimmel, daleth*, whence Greek *alpha, beta, gamma, delta* and Roman *a, b, d*, were originally ideograms: *'Alef* represented the head of an ox (capital *A* still looks like the head of an ox with horns), *beth* (beit) a house, etc. etc... Later, these letters started to represent anything with the initial sound [a], [b] etc.. Finally, the letters developed into what we know today as the Greek and Roman alphabets.

Ideographic and *pictographic* are also synonymous, in a general sense, with ***logographic***, which implies that each glyph represents a *word* (Cl. Greek *logos*). An ideographic, pictographic or logographic script would then be termed, respectively, an ***ideography, pictography*** or ***logography***.

Nearly all the ancient writing systems had ideographic origins. We can still see the ideographic origin in many ancient orthographies and their descendants or survivors [SCr-1, SCr-38 to SCr-44, SCr-25 to SCr-32]. The Chinese example of the glyph for "three" and the Greek example of *alpha* and *beta* and have already been given above.

Chapter 2: Writing: Methods of Transcription and "Alphabets"

57

Some other examples are given in **Figs. 2-1** and **2-2** below. In these figures, **Sumerian, Chinese and Indian scripts** are given for representative purposes only. Their choice does not by any means imply that other orthographies, e.g. the Egyptian or Maayan-Olmec [SCr-23 to SCr-24, SCr-32 to SCr-38], are less important.

> **Fig. 2-1** *(cont. overleaf)*: Some of the world's first *ideographs*, which clearly show resemblances to the objects they describe, (or, in the case of undeciphered glyphs, are presumed to describe). *These three scripts (Sumerian, Chinese, Indian) are shown here for representative purposes only. Their choice does not by any means imply that other orthographies, e.g. the Egyptian or Maayan-Olmec are less important.* [After references SCr-1, SCr-21 to SCr-24, SCr-33 to SCr-38, LAi-13 to LAi-16, reproduced with permission.]
>
> ***Below, left***, Sumerian, ca. 3200 BCE, related to the later, refined Sumerian (see next Figure).
> ***Below, right,*** Chinese, ca. 2000 BCE (?), related to the later, refined Chinese (see next Figure).
> ***Overleaf***: Indian, ca. 3500 BCE, also *possibly* related to the later Braahmi (ca. 1300 BCE?). (*The numbers given for the correlation with the standardized glyphs are from the Mahadevan Concordance.*)

Sumerian, "stalk of grain"

Chinese, "Sun"

Chapter 2: Writing: Methods of Transcription and "Alphabets"

(Fig. 2-1, cont.):

> *Indian (Harappan), possibly originally representing stalks of grain, and/or a farm implement or human figure, although undeciphered.*
>
> *(The inset figures show the corresponding Harappan glyphs with Mahadevan Concordance numbers.)*

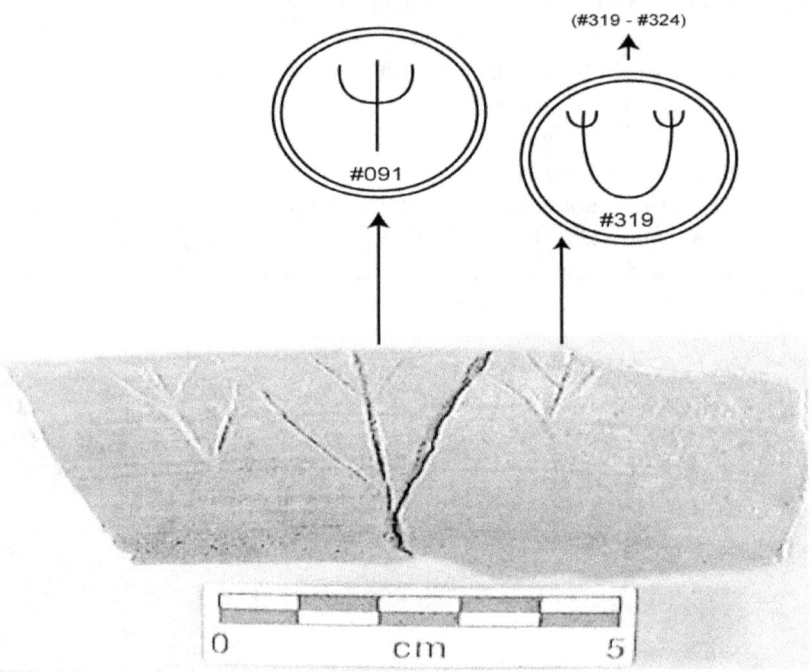

Chapter 2: Writing: Methods of Transcription and "Alphabets"

59

Fig. 2-2 (***cont. overleaf***): Further to **Fig. 2-1**, illustration of the ideographic origin and depiction of the further evolution of some glyphs found in Sumerian, Chinese and Indian (Harappan) scripts.

The steady evolution and refinement are shown from left to right in each case. The still-undeciphered Indian glyphs are believed to be logophonetic rather than purely ideographic, but their ideographic origin is clearly evident, e.g. in the "man" glyph. The cross-resemblance between the scripts of these presumably independently evolved civilizations may also be noted, e.g. that between the Sumerian and Chinese for "Sun" and that between Chinese and Indian for "person". In the later (ca. 1300 BCE ?) Indian (Braahmi) glyphs, also shown, the derivations for the letters "wa", "ta" from the "wiina" and the "tala" tree, as shown, are according to the traditions handed down by the ancient Indian grammarians. Their possible relations to the earlier Harappan letters also shown. Additional glyphs showing the possible Harappan-Braahmi relation are presented and discussed in the first NAVLIPI volume. (The numbers given for the Indian glyphs are from the Mahadevan Concordance.) (After Refs. [SCr-1, SCr-21 to SCr-24, SCr-33 to SCr-38, LAi-13 to LAi-16], reproduced with permission.).

SUMERIAN

(Steady refinement shown from left to right)

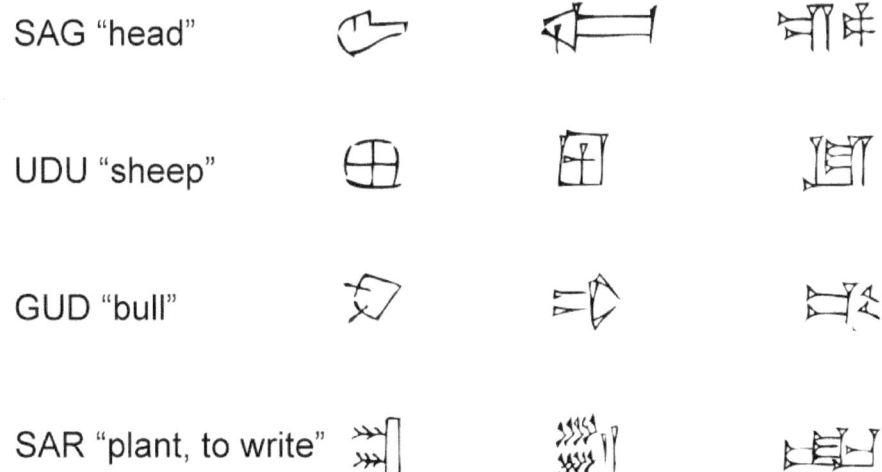

Chapter 2: Writing: Methods of Transcription and "Alphabets"

(Fig. 2-2, cont.)

CHINESE

(Steady refinement shown from left to right)

sun (ri)	☉	⊖	⊖	日
moon (yué)	☽	☽	☽	月
person (rén)				人
tree (mú)				木
up (sháng)		⊥		上
down (xia)	⌒	T		下

Chapter 2: Writing: Methods of Transcription and "Alphabets"

(Fig. 2-2, cont.)
INDIAN (HARAPPAN)

<u>TOP</u>: *Glyphs clearly betraying ideographic origins.*
<u>BOTTOM</u>: *Harappan and hypothetical Braahmi refinements of selected ideographs. Interpretation of the Harappan glyphs and their hypothetical Braahmi cognates remains somewhat speculative, since this script remains undeciphered, but again, their ideographic origin is clearly evident to most scholars.*
(All glyph numbers are from the Mahadevan Concordance.)

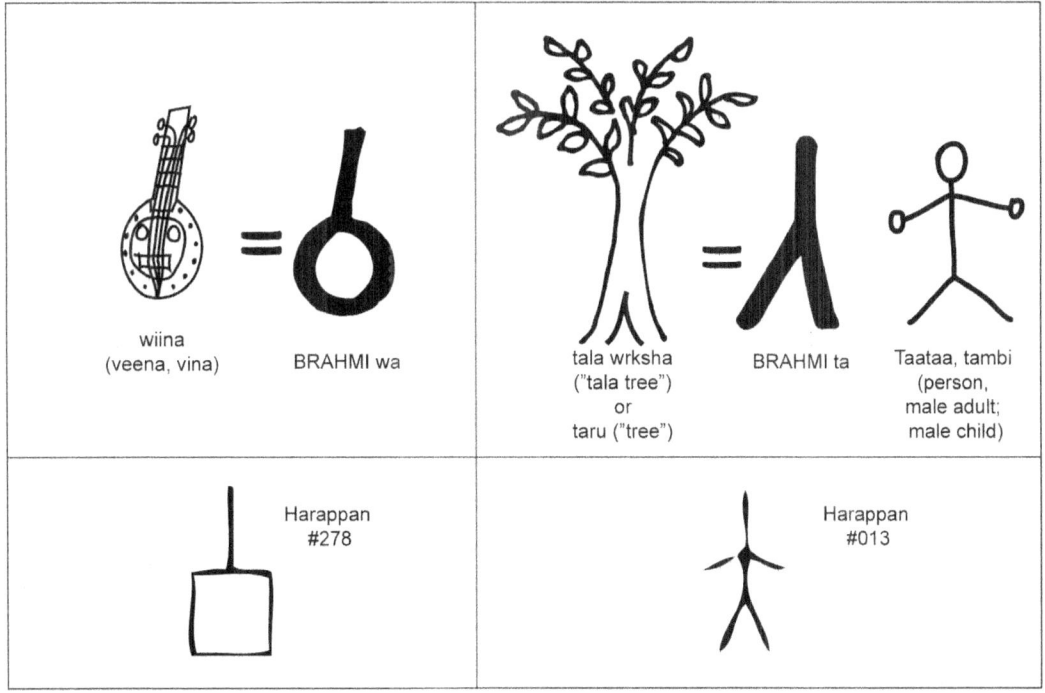

Chapter 2: Writing: Methods of Transcription and "Alphabets"

Although we might today consider an ideographic orthography "primitive", it in fact has one great advantage over nearly all other types of orthography in terms of communications between people speaking different languages: The same ideograph can be understood by someone speaking virtually any language. Thus, if we draw a picture (ideograph) of a tree, an English speaker may say "tree", a French speaker "arbre", a German speaker "Baum", a Mandarin speaker "mu' " and a Hindi speaker "ped..", yet all would understand the meaning of the ideograph.

This is of course exactly what happens in China today, where a multitude of languages share a single orthography and so are able to inter-communicate easily in writing, though the languages are mutually unintelligible! And of course, the Chinese are able to carry out the most technically sophisticated communications in their ideographic script, of supposed "primitive" origins!

A *syllabic* writing system is, as the name implies, one in which each glyph represents a *syllable*, e.g. [ka] or [ki] or [ku]. Such a writing system, a *syllabary*, is convenient for languages such as Japanese, which have a limited number of syllables, usually not more than about 50. It is less convenient for languages with large numbers of syllables or multiples and clusters of non-vowels, such as Hindi.

2.4 THE REBUS PRINCIPLE, ADDITIONAL STANDARD ORTHOGRAPHIC TERMS (*DETERMINATIVE, LOGOSYLLABIC, LOGOPHONETIC, ABJAD, ALPHABETIC, ABUGIDA, FEATURAL*) AND SOME NEW TERMS (*MAATRAIC, PHONOGRAPHIC*)

The earliest writers soon realized that to assign a separate picture (glyph, *ideogram*) to every word in their language made writing unmanageable. They soon learned a nice shorthand: To assign a symbol used for a word to other words that merely *sounded* like that word, with perhaps a marker of some sort for some distinction.

Thus, as a hypothetical example, to write English *treat* we could use the symbol we've already come up with for *tree*, which happens to be a picture of a tree, and add a mnemonic dot at the end to indicate the final *t* of *treat*. Or to write *God*, we could use some symbol we've already come up with for *got*, with perhaps a little halo marker for the deity.

This principle was developed universally in *all* orthographies that were originally ideographic, and is known as the **Rebus Principle**. The little distinguishing markers, such as the little halo to turn *got* into *God*, are called ***determinatives***. When we use determinatives that are indicators of the phonetic value of a glyph (e.g. "should rhyme with *bang*"), the determinatives are sometimes called ***phonetic complements***.

Let us now move further along with this Rebus principle and its associated determinatives. Now taking the *A* symbol for Semitic *'alef*, the head of an ox, we could assign this symbol to *all* words in our language which began with the same sound, [*aa*], with suitable mnemonics or determinatives. The determinatives could be symbols for particular semantic groups, e.g. gods (such as the halo cited in the previous paragraph) or animals or verbs indicating movement. Thus, for example, the later Sumerian and early Old Persian cuneiforms have specific symbols for "god" and "king". This is in fact the beginning of a phonetic transcription, and is the way the phonetic Semitic and Western (Roman, Greek) "alphabets" evolved from ideographic scripts. Sumerian ***cuneiform*** ("wedge-form", Latin *cuneus*, "wedge") writing, one of the earliest orthographies, also evolved from ideographs, as seen in **Fig. 2-2** above. These ideographs had to be simplified dramatically to allow for representation by the wedge-shaped styli used for writing. (This evolution, as hypothecated for the Indian scripts, is also shown in **Fig. 2-2**.)

As the ideographic scripts developed along Rebus principle lines, they quite evidently acquired a phonetic element. Many however remained a hodge-podge mixture of ideographic elements and some phonetic elements, these phonetic elements usually being syllabic. These scripts can be generally described as *logosyllabic* or, more accurately, ***logophonetic***. The most well-known *logophonetic* script of course is the later Egyptian. (Some linguists also use the rather inaccurate term ***morphosyllabic*** for most *logophonetic* scripts to note that each glyph represents a *morpheme* - a term defined later in this book - but we can ignore this terminology for now.) Perhaps a more accurate denotation for *logophonetic* would be ***ideo-phonographic***, i.e. indicating a mixture of *phonograms* (a glyph representing a single phone) and ideograms!

In introducing the term *ideo-phonographic* in the previous paragraph, we have also inadvertently introduced the more general term ***phonographic***. A *phonographic* script is one based on "***phonographs***" (also, "*phonograms*", the Webster English dictionary [SCr-45] defines both *phonograph* and *phonogram* approximately as synonyms). That is to say, it is a script in which each *glyph* ("letter", "symbol") represents a *separate phone,* and one strives to assign to each *phone* a separate *glyph*. (Unfortunately, in everyday English, a "phonograph" also signifies an instrument that plays old vinyl (music) records. No confusion is intended; it's just that the terms *phonographic* and *phonograph* are the most accurate way of describing the representation of each *phone* with a separate glyph! And, citing the Webster's English dictionary again, a *phonograph* is defined both as a glyph representing a phone and an instrument that plays vinyl records.)

The modern Western linguistics literature uses the term ***abjad*** to describe any orthography that is of the Semitic type. That is to say, a script in which each glyph stands for a non-vowel, and the vowels are then filled in either by the reader (as in the early Semitic scripts), or by diacritic marks (as in modern Arabic). It then distinguishes this *abjad* from an ***alphabet***, which it defines as a script which has separate glyphs for both vowels and non-vowels, examples being the Greek or Roman scripts.

The Western linguistics terminology then further denotes the Indian-type scripts, such as Dewanaagari, as ***abugidas***. (Apart from the Indian scripts and those derived therefrom, such as those of most South East Asian languages, the only major *abugida* is that for Amharic, a language of Ethiopia.) We may cite here a typical definition given for an *abugida*, one in the Daniels/Bright book [SCr-1]:

Chapter 2: Writing: Methods of Transcription and "Alphabets"

> *"....(a script)... in which each character (i.e. glyph) stands for a consonant accompanied by a particular vowel, usually /a/, and the other vowels (or no vowel) are indicated by consistent additions to the consonant symbols".*

...(2.1)

This sort of definition however betrays a *fundamental misunderstanding* of how the Indian scripts work.

For starters, each character (glyph) does *not* stand just for a consonant - there are characters (glyphs) for vowels as well. More importantly, the two fundamental features in the working of Indian-type scripts are the use of *maatraa*s (literally, "markers" or "indicators") for changes to a phone, be it a non-vowel (consonant) *or* vowel, and the use of *ligatures*, i.e. condensed joining-together of adjacent phones, usually but not always non-vowels. *The ligatures appear to be uniquely prominent only in Indian scripts*, and appear to be a carryover from the undeciphered Harappan (Indus Valley) script. This script clearly had ligatures (see depiction in the chapter on the Indian phonological classification in the first *NAVLIPI* volume), though it was also clearly not an *abugida* (it was most likely a *logophonetic* script).

A better way of visualizing the completely different Indian manner of thinking on scripts is as follows: Let us take the Roman letter *p*. To make the syllables [pa] or [pi] or [pu], we of course add another letter representing the vowel, i.e., *a, i* or *u*. The Indian manner of thinking in this respect would however have been to modify the original letter *p* itself in some way, with an indicator or *maatraa* representing the vowel. Thus, e.g., we could add a head-hyphen to the *p* to represent *i*, and a tail-hyphen to represent the *u*, thus obtaining *-p* and *p-* to represent [pi] and [pu] respectively, the hyphens being joined to and continuous with the *p* when written cursively. To represent a vowel alone, e.g. [u], one would still use a separate glyph.

In view of the above discussion, a better appellation for *abugidas,* i.e., Indian-type scripts, in this author's opinion, would be *maatraa-based*, or, to coin a new word, **maatraic** scripts.

Turning now to another type of script, the majority of Western linguistics literature distinguishes another type, most prominently represented by the Korean *Haangul* script [SCr-46 to SCr-52], as *featural*.

Chapter 2: Writing: Methods of Transcription and "Alphabets"

This type of script is the ultimate development in truly scientific orthography: For each characteristic or property of a phone, such as voicing or aspiration or artition (articulation position), is provided an *indicator*, in the form of a *sub-glyph*, i.e. part of the full glyph. Haangul also attempts to go even further, in trying to make the sub-glyph resemble the feature being described. Thus, the bilabial indicator is in the form of a sub-glyph that resembles the two lips, etc. Although this author would prefer a less ambiguous terminology such as **phono-indicative** (i.e. "indicating the characteristics or properties of the phone"), we will nevertheless stay in this book with the term *featural* when describing scripts of the Haangul type. It is noteworthy that the Japanese syllabary also qualifies as a *partially* featural script, as it has clear *indicators* (i.e. markers or *maatraa's*), e.g. for voicing, in both Hiragana and Katakana [SCr-55].

Some scripts do not fall neatly into any category, or may overlap several categories. We have already seen an example above: The Japanese script is a *syllabary* but also has *featural* characteristics. Among the most unique scripts that overlap several categories is that of the great Persian kingdoms of the middle of the 1st millennium B.C. (with prominent Emperors Darius, Xerxes, etc.) [LAi-39 to LAi-43]. Scholars in this kingdom borrowed a part of the Indian phonological classification but then adapted it to cuneiform. This created a curious cuneiform script in which some of the glyphs resembled those extant for other languages in the region, but had a highly scientific, phonetic classification within the cuneiform component.

2.5 MORE SPECIFIC CHARACTERISTICS OF SCRIPTS AND THE NEW TERMS *COMPLETENESS, VAIGYAANIC, EMPIRICITY, UNIPHONOGRAPHIC, UNIPHONEMOGRAPHIC, QUASI-PHONETIC* AND *PHONEMO-IDIOSYNCRATIC*

There are more specific characteristics and features of scripts not covered by the simple terms, such as *abjad* and *abugida*, given above. These are perhaps even more important for a modern, universal script. We list them below (along with brief definitions for them) and then look at them briefly in the ensuing paragraphs:

1. ***Completeness***: How completely the script is able to address all phones found in all of the world's languages.
2. ***Systematic and Scientific Organization***: How well the script is organized and presented, and how systematic and scientific this organization is.
3. ***Quasi-Phonetic or Phonetic***: Whether the script has a truly phonetic (i.e., phonological) nature or only a partial (i.e., *quasi-phonetic*) one. There are degrees of quasi-phoneticity, with some scripts as used for certain languages being more or less phonetic than others.
4. ***Empiricity***: Whether there is an ad-hoc, "adapt-as-you-go" nature to way the script represents a language, and whether there are certain empirical rules that must be learned along the way.
5. ***Uniphonographic*** characteristics: Whether one glyph represents one and only one phone, and vice versa.
6. ***Uniphonemographic*** characteristics: Whether one glyph represents one and only one phoneme in the language that the script addresses, and vice versa.
7. ***Phonemo-idiosyncratic***: Whether the script addresses phonemic idiosyncrasies found across the world's languages.

Completeness in an orthography, quite obviously, is the property which determines how *completely* it describes *not only the language or languages that are its immediate target, but more generally, all the world's languages*. In our definition of *completeness*, we expressly refer to *all* the world's languages, not just a subset thereof. The lay reader might immediately guess that very few, if any, of the world's extant orthographies are *complete*. As examples, the standard Roman alphabet is unable to describe all the phones in Arabic (e.g. the uvular *[k]*) or Hottentot (the various clicks) or even Spanish (the bilabial fricative), and the standard Dewanaagari alphabet is unable to describe the new phones found in Hindi which were borrowed from Persian (e.g. *[z]* or *[ʃ]*) or Arabic (e.g. the uvular *[k]*). On the other hand, the IPA's "alphabet" is reasonably complete or at least strives to be so. Thus, we can characterize scripts as being **complete** or **incomplete**.

Scientific and Systematic Phonological Organization and Presentation: This property describes whether an orthography is organized, presented and learned in a manner that is organized along scientific phonological principles. We readily know that our Roman "alphabet", i.e. [*a, b, c, d, e, f, g* ......] is definitely *not* systematically and scientifically organized. It is completely ad-hoc, unorganized and unscientific, nor is it taught in any way that gives us some scientific knowledge of phonology or organization.

Similarly, although the IPA orthography is frequently presented in a scientific way (for a specific language, it is a presentation in tables organized along proper, scientific phonological principles), its basis nevertheless remains the same, ad-hoc Roman "alphabet", and it is not organized along any scientific principles. Indeed, it may be said to be even more ad-hoc than its parent Roman "alphabet", since glyphs (letter symbols) have been added in an "as-you-go-along" fashion, as the IPA expanded from its narrow European base in the 19th century to cover more of the world's languages.

On the other hand, the Indian scripts are organized in a scientific and systematic way, with what is basically a 2-dimensional matrix representation with distinctions along voicing/devoicing, aspiration/non-aspiration, artition (articulation position), plosive/stop/fricative, etc., etc.

At the other extreme, the Korean Haangul is extremely systematically and scientifically organized and presented; in fact, it appears to be the most systematic and scientific script to date, although it lacks *completeness*.

If we attempt to call this property of scripts *scientific-systematic-organization/-presentation* or something of that nature, the terminology becomes too long. We thus find again that it is better to coin a new term for this property. We use **vaigyaanic**, a Hindi corruption of the Sanskrit *vaijnaanik* meaning "scientific". Scripts can then be termed either *vaigyaanic* or its opposite, ***avaigyaanic***.

There is a caveat in the *vaigyaanic-avaigyaanic* opposition. We use the term *vaigyaanic* only for those scripts that are completely so. Thus, if a script has its vowels very scientifically and systematically organized, but its non-vowels not so, then it is still *avaigyaanic*. There are then obviously degrees of this property, which we can call ***vaigyaanicity***, in that some scripts will be more *vaigyaanic* than others. Thus, the Japanese script has systematic and scientific organization and presentation in its vowels and in the separation of voiced from unvoiced non-vowels. However, the rest of the script is completely unorganized as it is presented. Thus, we would say that the Japanese script is *avaigyaanic*, although it is certainly less so than the Roman script as used for English.

Quasi-Phonetic and Phonetic character and degrees thereof: A script may be termed ***phonetic*** if some attempt, however small, is made to have a correlation between a glyph and a particular phone. Thus, the IPA's script is of course truly *phonetic*, but the Roman script as used for English is only very partially phonetic, i.e. it is ***quasi-phonetic***. There are of course, again, degrees of quasi-phoneticity. For example, the Roman script as applied to English or Dutch is certainly much less phonetic than when it is applied to Spanish. However, both the English and Spanish transcriptions are still quasi-phonetic.

Empiricity is a property that may perhaps be a little difficult for the layman to grasp. *Empiricity* implies that the rules of the transcription, especially as relating to the assignment of one glyph to represent one phone, are learned as one goes along, on a case-by-case basis. A rudimentary set of rules may be laid down at first, but this is only a very rough guide. One soon learns that there are more exceptions than the rules, and each exception must be learned *empirically*, as one goes along in the language, in a completely ad-hoc fashion.

The best example of such an *empirical* orthography is the Roman script as applied to modern English and Dutch. Thus, in modern English, one must learn that the digraph *gh* can be silent (*light*), be articulated as an [f] (*laugh*), be articulated as an unaspirated [g] (***ghost***), or as a partially aspirated [gh] (***ghoul***). These phones, [silent], [f], [g] and [gh] have little relation to each other. These rules are learned as we go along in the language, and in no other way. Similarly, in Dutch, one must learn that the digraph *ui* as in *huis* is not pronounced anything like [u+i], but rather as [au]. Citing English again, we need to learn that the diphthongs in the transcriptions *light, white, whyne* are all the same. In effect, then, we are committing to memory *three* separate representations, *igh, i* and *y* for the same diphthong. And on and on! We then later need to commit to memory that the symbol *y* represents many other sounds besides the above diphthong. And this is something we learn *empirically*, as we learn the language. Scripts can then be termed ***empirical*** or ***non-empirical***. For convenience, we may forego the term *non-empirical* in our descriptions of scripts. That is to say, we will assume all scripts are non-empirical. Only when we encounter an empirical script, such as the Roman script as used in English,

Chapter 2: Writing: Methods of Transcription and "Alphabets"

will we use the term *empirical* to describe it.

Uniphonography is a relatively easy principle to grasp, represented in the following rule:

> *One and only one glyph ("letter", "character")*
> *for each separate phone. And conversely, one*
> *and only one phone for each separate glyph.*
>
> **…(2.2)**

To revert to an example from modern English cited earlier, in a **uniphonographic** orthography we could, hypothetically, assign the digraph symbol *gh* to represent the phone [ʃ] *only*. It would then represent no other phones, and no other symbols would represent [ʃ].

All Indian scripts are *uniphonographic*, as are all scripts derived from them, such as Thai, Khmer, Burmese, etc. It is important to recognize that, for purposes of our definition, digraphs and multigraphs would still be considered as single glyphs when used to represent single phones.

Uniphonemography: In an analogous fashion to *uniphonography*, a **uniphonemographic** orthography would be one in which there would be a one-to-one correspondence between each glyph and each *phoneme*. Necessarily, such an orthography may be specific to a language or group of languages.

The original Sanskrit scripts, Braahmi and its predecessors, were *uniphonemographic*. Their later descendants, e.g. Dewanaagari, are only partially so. However, if Dewanaagari is applied in its strict, original connotation to Sanskrit, then it does end up being *uniphonemographic*.

We can now understand the above terminology by applying it to several modern scripts:

1) ***Japanese*** (both Hiragana and Katakana, but not the Kanji characters [SCr-55]): In our terminology, we would define this as an *incomplete, avaigyaanic, phonetic syllabary*. It is *non-empirical*, and it is also <u>not</u> *uniphonographic (because it is a syllabary)*, <u>not</u> *uniphonemographic* <u>nor</u> *phonemo-idioysyncratic*. However, we do not need to specify these latter terms in describing it. Actually, Japanese is <u>*partially*</u> *vaigyaanic*, since its vowels are organized and presented scientifically and systematically, and its non-vowels are separated according to

Chapter 2: Writing: Methods of Transcription and "Alphabets"

71

voicing. However, in the rest of its organization and presentation, it is definitely *avaigyaanic*. Thus, per our definition above, we return *avaigyaanic* to characterize Japanese.

2) **Roman script as used for English**: *Incomplete, avaigyaanic, quasi-phonetic, empirical.*

3) **Roman script as used for Spanish**: *Incomplete, avaigyaanic, quasi-phonetic* (though much less so than English). There is some *empiricity* with respect to different accents, but nothing even close to that of English. For example, the letter *s* may be pronounced as a palatal sibilant ([sh]) in the standard Madrid accent, an attribute that is learned by Madrid speakers, whereas it is pronounced as the standard dental sibilant ([s]) in South American Spanish.

4) **Dewanaagari script as used for Sanskrit; Thai script**: *Incomplete, vaigyaanic, phonetic, uniphonographic, uniphonemographic*. It is interesting to contrast the Dewanaagari script as used for Sanskrit with that as used for Hindi. The latter is *not uniphonographic*, since, e.g., the letters used for [ph] and [w] can also be pronounced as [f] and [v], respectively, at the speaker's discretion. However, the Hindi Dewanaagari *is uniphonemographic*, for the [ph]/[f] and [w]/[v] pair represent the same phonemes! Thus, here, we have a unique case of a *uniphonemographic* script that is *not uniphonographic*!

5) **Arabic script as applied to standard Arabic**: *Incomplete, avaigyaanic, phonetic, empirical*. This script is *uniphonemographic* only with respect to non-vowels, thus we cannot use this term for it in a general sense. It is also empirical with respect to its vowels only.

6) **Haangul**: *Incomplete, vaigyaanic, phonetic, uniphonographic, uniphonemographic*. Except for its lack of *completeness* and lack of certain other characteristics (*recognizability, ease of writing*) discussed elsewhere in this book, Haangul [SCr-46 to SCr-52] is a nearly perfect script!

7) **Pitman shorthand** [SCr-56 to SCr-57]: *Incomplete, vaigyaanic, phonetic, uniphonographic*. This script, when applied to a language such as Spanish (but not, e.g., French), is also *uniphonemographic*. It is incomplete because, in its original formulation, there were no glyphs for clicks, implosives and other rare phones, although adaptations since have accommodated these phones.

Chapter 2: Writing: Methods of Transcription and "Alphabets"

8) ***Turkish "alphabet" [LAs-19], Malay/Indonesian script [LAs-31], Swaahili "alphabet" [LAs-32] (all Roman-based)***: *Incomplete, avaigyaanic, phonetic, uniphonographic, uniphonemographic.*

9) ***Cherokee script***: The Cherokee script [SCr-62 to SCr-64] is a new construct from the 19th century. It is also *incomplete, avaigyaanic, phonetic, uniphonographic, uniphonemographic.*

10) ***"Alphabet" of the IPA*** [SCr-2 to SCr-4]: *Complete, avaigyaanic, phonetic, uniphonographic.* We say that the IPA's alphabet (referred throughout this book as "the IPA") is *avaigyaanic* because there was never any systematic or scientific organization in its origins in the Roman alphabet, although when presented in tabular form in the IPA Chart or for a particular language, it is presented in a scientific and systematic manner. Its "alphabetic" order and didactic representation are of the same unorganized, ad-hoc fashion as its parent Roman alphabet, with its later expansion from its original form being even more ad-hoc. The IPA is of course also not *uniphonemographic*, since it does not accommodate specific phonemes found in particular languages. However, we may note, the IPA is the only script we have discussed thus far that is truly *complete.*

After having sized up the various extant, modern scripts, we finally come to the script that is the subject of this book, **Navlipi**. As we will show later in this book when the script is presented, *Navlipi* qualifies as *complete, vaigyaanic, phonetic, uniphonographic* and *phonemo-idiosyncratic*. Like the IPA, it simply cannot qualify as *uniphonemographic* since it attempts to represent all the world's languages. However, it also uses the peculiar construct of *phonemic condensates*, a concept not found in any other world script. Again, like the IPA, it is *complete*. However, it is the sole script having the *phonemo-idiosyncratic* property. With regard to the *vaigyaanic* property of *Navlipi*, the reader may note that, like the IPA, it too is based on the ad-hoc Roman script. Thus, it should technically qualify as *avaigyaanic*. However, the presentation of *Navlipi*, in highly systematic and scientifically organized matrices, qualifies it as *vaigyaanic*. As emphasized ad nauseam in this book, the Roman script is used as *Navlipi's* base simply for purposes of recognizability and universality.

The various terms presented above are summarized, for convenience, in the **Tables** below.

Chapter 2: Writing: Methods of Transcription and "Alphabets"

Table 2-1 (*cont. overleaf*): Summary of *standard* orthographic terms used in the current state of the art as presented in discussions above.

TERM	DEFINITIONS	EXAMPLES AND COMMENTS
Abjad	Each glyph represents a single non-vowel. Vowels are either "filled in" by the reader or indicated by diacritics or other markers.	Modern Arabic and Hebrew scripts.
Abugida	Non-vowels and vowels are represented by single glyphs. The addition of a vowel to a non-vowel is further indicated by *maatra's*, i.e. markers or indicators of some sort.	All Indian-type or Indian-base scripts, including modern South-East Asian scripts.
Alphabet	Each glyph represents a single non-vowel or vowel. Said to be a further development from *abjads*.	The Greek alphabet. The Roman alphabet as originally used for Latin and used today for Spanish.
Featural	Each glyph has markers or indicators indicating the properties of the phone, such as voicing, phonochromaticity and artition (articulation position).	Haangul (Korean) is the prototypical example.
Ideographic, pictographic	Each glyph in the script represents a word, an object or an idea.	Modern Chinese script. Can be used with convenience for inter-communication between totally different languages, as in China today

(Table 2-1, cont.)		
TERM	**DEFINITIONS**	**EXAMPLES AND COMMENTS**
Logographic	Similar to ideographic, but narrowed to *words* only	
Logosyllabic, logophonetic	An ideographic script is further developed to the point where originally ideographic glyphs are used to represent phones having sounds similar to the original ideographs. This is frequently done with the use of *determinatives* and *phonetic complements*. The principle by which it is done is denoted as the *Rebus principle*. *Logosyllabic* and *logophonetic* apply respectively to syllables and phones.	
Morpho-graphic	Similar to ideographic, but narrowed to *morphemes* only	
Syllabic, syllabary	Each glyph in the script represents a syllable.	Modern Japanese script. Convenient for languages, such as Japanese, with limited number (< 50) syllables, but inconvenient for languages with > 50 syllables (such as Hindi).

Chapter 2: Writing: Methods of Transcription and "Alphabets"

75

Table 2-2 (*continued overleaf*): Summary of *new* orthographic terms as introduced and discussed above.

TERM	DEFINITIONS	EXAMPLES AND COMMENTS
Completeness	Property of a script whereby it is able to represent all phones in all the world's languages.	The IPA and *Navlipi* are the only scripts that appear to qualify.
Empirical	Property of a script whereby rules used for relating phones to glyphs are learned as one learns the language and are specific to the language. These empirical rules start as exceptions to nominal phonetic rules.	The Roman script as used for English and Dutch.
Phonemo-idiosyncratic	Property of a script whereby it is able to represent phonemic idiosyncrasies found across the world's languages.	*Navlipi* would appear to be the only script that would qualify.
Phonographic	Each glyph in the script represents a phone, i.e. it is a *phonograph* or *phonogram*	
Maatraic	Script of the Indian type, i.e., one that uses *maatraa's* (markers or indicators) for vowels and ligature (close joining together) of adjacent phones, where applicable.	All Indian and South-East Asian scripts (except the ancient Nomic Vietnamese and the modern Roman-based ones such as modern Vietnamese and Indonesian/Malay) are *maatraic* scripts.
Quasi-Phonetic vs. *Phonetic* character	Property of a script whereby its glyphs have a reasonably phonetic, i.e. uniphonographic, connotation.	Roman script as used originally for Latin and, to a large extent, as used today for Spanish.
Uniphonemographic	There is a one-to-one correspondence between glyphs and phonemes in the script	Most modern Indian-type scripts are uniphonemographic, including Hindi written in Dewanaagari.

(Table 2-2, cont.)		
Term	**Definitions**	**Examples and Comments**
Uniphonographic	There is a one-to-one correspondence between glyphs and phones in the script.	Many modern Indian-type scripts are uniphonographic. Hindi written in Dewanaagari is *not*.
Vaigyaanic	Property of a script whereby it is organized and presented in a systematic and scientific manner based on phonological principles.	

Chapter 2: Writing: Methods of Transcription and "Alphabets"

2.6 TOOLS AVAILABLE FOR THE MODERN ORTHOGRAPHER: TRANSFORMED LETTERS, DIACRITICS, MULTIGRAPHS, LINE POSITION, POST-OPS, PRE-OPS

Before starting out on the long journey of constructing a new script, one must take stock of the "tools of the trade" available to us, as it were. That is to say, we try to answer the question, "What tools are available to us as orthographers, for distinguishing different phones as well as relating similar phones?". We enumerate below just a few of the more common tools. The list below is representative and will give a good idea of what is available. It is however by no means exhaustive. The list is presented below and then discussed in the ensuing paragraphs:

"TOOLS OF THE TRADE" AVAILABLE TO ORTHOGRAPHERS

> - *Transformed glyphs or letters.*
> - *Diacritics.*
> - *Multigraphs.*
> - *Line position.*
> - *Post-ops* (post-positional operators).
> - *Pre-ops* (pre-positional operators).

....(2.3)

Transformed letters: The IPA has been expert at using transformed letters, which are basically just common letters (glyphs) of an existing script transformed in some way, e.g. by *inverting, rotating, turning left-to-right, expanding* or *contracting* a part of the letter, etc. The partial list in the **Table** below gives some transformed *vowels* used by the IPA:

Chapter 2: Writing: Methods of Transcription and "Alphabets"

Table 2-3: "Transformed letters", i.e., letters transformed from the original Roman letters, as used by the IPA. Only vowels are shown for simplicity. Reproduced with permission from the IPA Handbook [SCr-3]. (Copyright 2005, all rights reserved by the IPA).

ɐ	ɑ	ɒ	æ	a
i	ɪ	ɨ		
ǝ	ə	ɛ	ɜ	ɞ
ɟ	ɉ	j	ɺ	
ʉ	ʊ	ɯ	u	

As can be seen from a glance at the above list, transformed letters present problems when the nature of the transformation is not intuitive for the new phone it represents. Transformed letters can then be quite confusing and difficult to distinguish.

On the other hand, if the transformation is more intuitive, transformed letters can be very useful in a new script. The **Table** below of the common nasal phones in *Navlipi* shows an example of this more intuitive use.

Chapter 2: Writing: Methods of Transcription and "Alphabets"

Table 2-4: The common nasal phones in *Navlipi*, showing a more intuitive use of transformed letters. (Excerpted from the *Navlipi* SUMMARY TABLES in PART 1.)

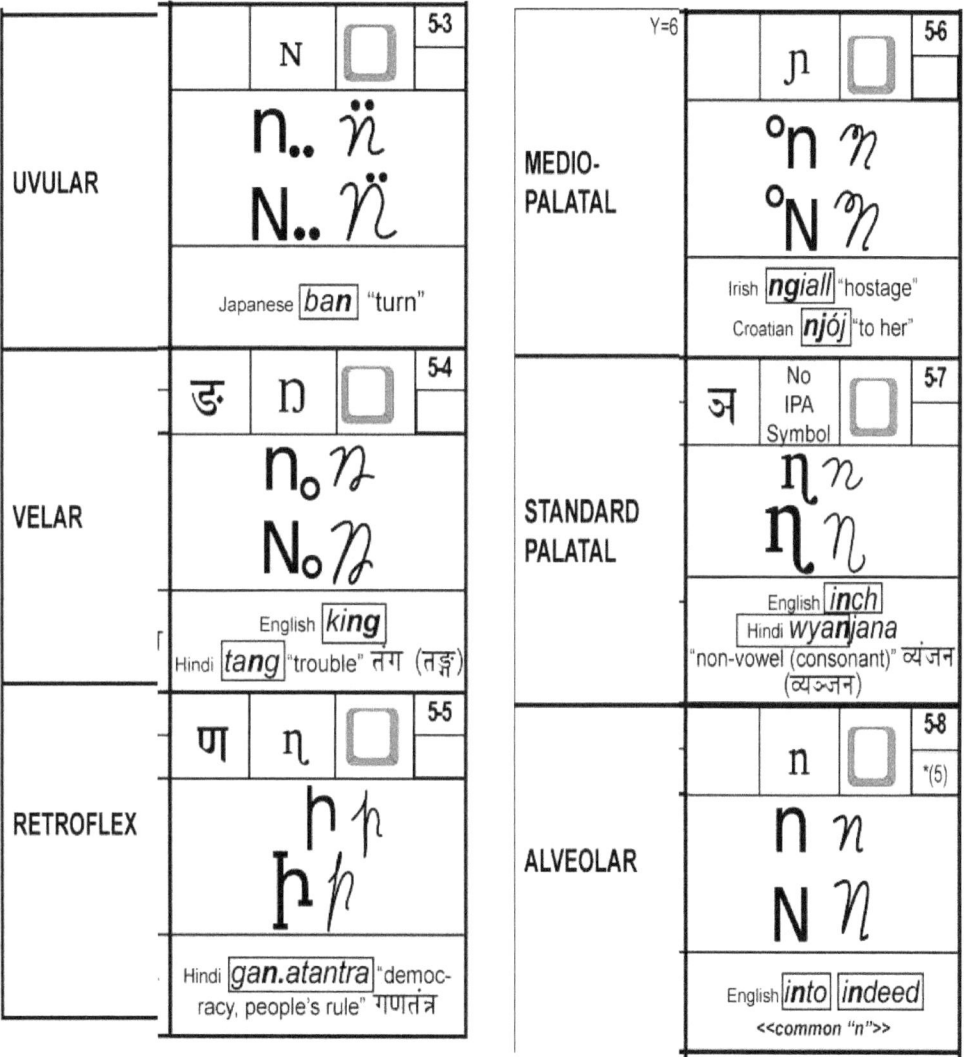

Chapter 2: Writing: Methods of Transcription and "Alphabets"

80

Diacritics: Diacritics have been another favorite with past orthographers. They are found in fair abundance in the IPA, and in absolute profusion in certain other new scripts such as the version of the Roman script used by Vietnamese. An example of the latter is shown in the **Figure** below.

As one can see by the Vietnamese example in the **Figure** below, diacritics are extremely cumbersome to transcribe in all three forms of importance: *cursive, print* and *keyboard*. They slow down cursive writing excruciatingly. And they can be confusing and cumbersome for non-native speakers who are learning a new language having many diacritics in its script. For this reason, *Navlipi* uses diacritics *as little as possible*.

> <u>**Fig. 2-3**</u> *(starting overleaf)*: An example of a script (Vietnamese) which uses diacritics in confusing profusion. The Vietnamese "alphabet" is shown first, followed by a typical short passage in the language. (*Vietnamese alphabet after ref. [Scr-126], reproduced with permission. Vietnamese passage from the transcription later in this book.*)

Chapter 2: Writing: Methods of Transcription and "Alphabets"

(Fig. 2-3, cont.)

Letter	Name	IPA
A a	a	aː
Ă ă	á	a
Â â	ớ	ə, ɜ
B b		ɓ, ʔb
C c	xê	k
D d	dê	northern pronunciation: z, southern pronunciation: j
Đ đ	đê	ɗ, ʔd
E e	e	ɛ
Ê ê	ê	e
(F) (f)	ép	
G g	rê	ɣ, ʒ (before i, ê, and e)
H h	hát	h
I i	i, i ngắn	i
(J) (j)	gi	
K k	ca	k
L l	en-lờ, lờ	l
M m	em-mờ, mờ	m
N n	en-nờ, nờ	n
O o	o	ɔ
Ô ô	ô	o
Ơ ơ	ơ	əː, ɜː
P p	pê	p
Q q	quy, cu	k
R r	e-rờ, rờ	southern pronunciation: ʐ, ɹ
S s	ét, ét-sì	s, southern pronunciation: ʂ
T t	tê	t
U u	u	u
Ư ư	ư	ɯ
V v	vê	v, southern pronunciation: j
(W) (w)	vê kép, vê đúp, đúp liu	
X x	ít, ít-xì	s
Y y	i, i dài, i-cờ-rét	i
(Z) (z)	giét	

Chapter 2: Writing: Methods of Transcription and "Alphabets"

(Fig. 2-3, cont.)

Một người đàn ông cao lớn đột nhiên tỉnh dậy và nhảy ra khỏi giường như thể anh ta vừa trải qua một giải mộ khủng khiếp. Anh nhìn ra bên ngoài của sổ. Thời tiết thật là đẹp. Mặt trời đang tỏa ánh nắng, vẫn là ánh nắng màu da cam của buổi sáng sớm mặc dù đến lúc này đã lên cao tận đường chân trời. Anh ngáp một cái, vươn vai rồi sau đó mở của sổ.

Multigraphs: Multigraphs are just multiple letters. Of multigraphs, **digraphs** are the most common. In English, for example, digraphs having the letter *h* are used to represent the very different single phones or affricates highlighted in the words *shoot*, *chat*, *this*, *think*. Multigraphs are definitely a very useful tool, and are used in *Navlipi*, primarily in the form of post-ops (see below).

Line position: Anyone using ruled paper may remark: "Why not use the *position* with respect to the writing line as a feature to distinguish different phones, and thereby limit the number of new letters one must arrive at in a new script?" For example, one could simply use the letter *a*, written at three different positions with respect to the writing line, to distinguish three different vowel phones (highlighted in bold in the example words provided): Normal, on line: *but*. Above line: *father*. Below line *fat*.

The answer to the above question is that it is simply not practical in the everyday world of today (2006), where ruled papers (or other ruled writing media) exist almost exclusively in primary schools only, for use by children. Printed texts, computer screens, etc., do not use lined media. Although it is certainly possible, detecting the position of a glyph (letter) with respect to an imagined writing line on an unruled piece of paper or a computer screen may be difficult and lead to misidentification. For this reason then, we must remove *line position* as a variable to be used in devising any new script.

Chapter 2: Writing: Methods of Transcription and "Alphabets"

Post-positional operators (post-ops): In the transcription [*kh*] for the unvoiced, aspirated, velar stop, the letter *h* is a post-op, operating on the *k* (the ***operand***) to transform it into an aspirated stop. The property of this post-op is thus *aspiration*. In French, the letter *n* is used as a post-op to indicate *nasalization* of a vowel, e.g. in *bon* ("good"). Post-ops are found abundantly in Dewanaagari, in the form of its "*maatraas*", which are essentially just post-ops.

Post-ops are extremely convenient in transcription, and greatly reduce the number of new letters needed in a new script. They also increase recognizability, distinctiveness, ease of transcription (keyboarding, cursive, print), and all the other properties we have identified (see **PREFACE**) as essential requirements for a universal orthography. Indeed, a chapter in the first *NAVLIPI* volume comes up, as an exercise, with a new script based entirely on post-ops. A limited number (about 13) post-ops are used in good measure in *Navlipi*.

Pre-positional operators (pre-ops): The opposite functionality of a post-op, where the operator is placed *before* the operand, yields pre-ops. There is no fundamental reason that post-ops should be preferred over pre-ops, since other features and properties remain virtually identical. Post-ops just happen to be more established out of habit, especially in the Roman script. Pre-ops are extremely rare in extant scripts (even Dewanaagari). An example is the digraph *gn* in languages such as French and Italian. Here, the *g* can be said to be a pre-op that operates on the *n* to palatalize it (e.g. in *co**gn**ac* or ***gn**occhi*). However, even this interpretation may not be strictly correct, since the alternative interpretation (that *gn* is simply a digraph for *[nj]*, the palatalized nasal) is also correct.

Chapter 2: Writing: Methods of Transcription and "Alphabets"

84

Summary of orthographic tools available. To summarize the discussion above then, we find that, of the full list of tools given earlier for *Navlipi*, it would be convenient to use the following:

SUMMARY OF **ORTHOGRAPHIC TOOLS**
AVAILABLE FOR CREATING A NEW SCRIPT
FROM AN ESTABLISHED, WIDELY RECOGNIZED SCRIPT SUCH AS THE ROMAN

The following would be very convenient to use, based on the discussion above:

- ***Transformed letters*** (judiciously transformed, with the IPA's experience in mind!).
- ***Multigraphs***.
- ***Post-ops*** (post-positional operators).

For the reasons enumerated above, however, it would *not* be convenient to use the following:

- ***Diacritics***.
- ***Line position***.
- ***Pre-ops***.

...(2.4)

Chapter 2: Writing: Methods of Transcription and "Alphabets"

2.7 EXERCISES

(1) Define, with examples, the terms *ideographic, logographic, syllabic, rebus principle, determinative, logosyllabic, logophonetic, abjad, alphabetic, abugida, featural, maatraic* and *phonographic*.

(2) Define, with examples, the terms *completeness, vaigyaanic, empiricity, uniphonographic, uniphonemographic, quasi-phonetic, phonemo-idiosyncratic* and *multigraph*.

(3) Discuss the tools available for modern orthographers in constructing a script from scratch. Define *post-op* and *pre-op*.

Chapter 2: Writing: Methods of Transcription and "Alphabets"

CHAPTER 3.
PHONOLOGICAL CLASSIFICATION AND SOME NEW PHONOLOGICAL TERMS

TABLE OF CONTENTS

3.1 NOTE ON IMPORTANCE OF THIS CHAPTER 88

3.2 THE TERM *PHONOLOGICAL VARIABLE* AND THE NEW TERMS *ARTITION*, *PHONOCHROMATICITY*, *PHONOCHROME*, *FORWARD FRICATIVE* 89

    3.2.1 THE *PHONOLOGICAL VARIABLE* AS APPLIED TO VOWELS, AND ITS DISCRETIZATION AND LIMITATION 89
    3.2.2 THE PHONOLOGICAL VARIABLE AS APPLIED TO NONVOWELS: A*RTITION* AND *PHONOCHROMATICITY* AND THE 15 ARTITIONS AND 35 PHONOCHROMES 92
    3.2.3 THE *FORWARD FRICATIVE* 96
    3.2.4 LINGUISTIC SIGNIFICANCE OF THE FORWARD FRICATIVE 97

3.3 THE TERMS *PHONEME*, *TONEME*, *CHRONEME* AND THE NEW TERM *GALATOPHONE* 99

    3.3.1 THE *PHONEME* AND THE *ALLOPHONE* 99
    3.3.2 THE *TONEME*, THE "*ALLOTONE*" AND THE *CHRONEME* 101
    3.3.3 THE *GALATOPHONE* 102

3.4 THE ALL-IMPORTANT *PHONEMIC CONDENSATE* 106

3.5 OTHER, MISCELLANEOUS PHONOLOGICAL TERMINOLOGY 110

3.6 EXERCISES 112

Chapter 4: The World's Major Language Families- A Primer

3.1 NOTE ON IMPORTANCE OF THIS CHAPTER

It should be noted at the outset that an understanding of many of the new terms introduced in this chapter - for example ***galatophone, forward fricative*** and, above all, **_PHONEMIC CONDENSATE_** - is extremely important for an appreciation of the later discussion in this book, and, indeed, of the first *NAVLIPI* volume.

Thus, once again as for Chapters 1 and 2, *both the layman and the experienced phoneticist are respectfully encouraged to read this chapter.*

Chapter 4: The World's Major Language Families- A Primer

3.2 THE TERM *PHONOLOGICAL VARIABLE* AND THE NEW TERMS *ARTITION, PHONOCHROMATICITY, PHONOCHROME, FORWARD FRICATIVE*

3.2.1 THE *PHONOLOGICAL VARIABLE* AS APPLIED TO VOWELS, AND ITS DISCRETIZATION AND LIMITATION

Variables in Vowel Phones: In our discussion in an earlier chapter, we have seen that *a vowel can be distinguished by the following characteristics*, which we can consider to be **independent variables**:

INDEPENDENT VARIABLES CHARACTERIZING VOWELS

VARIABLE	DESIGNATION	VALUES	NUMBER
Jaw position, vertical	x_1	*Close, close-mid, open-mid, open*	(Four (4) in all)
Jaw position, horizontal	x_2	*Forward, mid, retracted*	(Three (3) in all)
Lip position	x_3	*Stretched, rounded, flat*	(Three (3) in all)
Tongue position	x_4	*Forward, central, back*	(Three (3) in all)
Articulation position (usually of the tongue, but also of the lips, etc.)	x_5	Designated by the various possible contacts: We consider only *neutral, uvular, retroflex, dental, central, lateral, bilabial.*	(Seven (7) in all)
Duration of articulation	x_6	*long, short* and, in some languages, further distinctions	(Two (2) or three (3) in all)

…(3.1)

Use of each of these independent variables leads to a product, the **dependent variable**, which in this case is in fact the **phone** produced.

For example, we can describe the phone **[i]**, as in English *hit*, using the following in dependent variables (not including factors of *compensation* discussed in an earlier chapter):

- *jaw position, vertical = close-mid;*
- *jaw position, horizontal = mid;*
- *lip position = stretched;*
- *tongue position= forward;*
- *tongue contact = neutral;*
- *duration of articulation = short.*

.... (3.2)

In a mathematical analogy, the six (6) independent variables listed above can be considered as x_1, x_2, x_3, x_4, x_5 and x_6, and the dependent variable, the resulting phone, can be taken as y, which is a function of x_1, x_2, x_3, x_4, x_5 and x_6,. We then define the *independent variables* above as the **phonological variables**. The product of their use, the *dependent variable,* is then called the **phone**. That is to say:

> ➢ vowel phone = dependent variable = function of six (6) independent variables
> ➢ $y =$ *the vowel phone* $= f(x_1, x_2, x_3, x_4, x_5, x_6)$

.... (3.3)

We also use the methodology established in current linguistic practice, **square brackets**, to designate phones. Thus, the close-mid, rounded-lip, tongue-back, short vowel is written **[u]**, whilst the bilabial de-voiced plosive is written **[p]**.

Need for discretization and limitation of the vowel phonological variables: There are several important points to reiterate, as originally discussed in an earlier chapter, with regard to the phonological variables.

Firstly, the phonological variables are continuous variables. They *must* however be **discretized** for practical purposes, to keep out classification within manageable limits. For example, the lip position is a continuous variable, with many intermediate and continuously variable positions between the discretized *stretched, rounded* and *flat* that we have selected. Similarly, the jaw position can of course be continuously varied from fully open to fully shut, and one must needs discretize this for practical purposes. We could technically have an infinite (or at least a very large number) of intermediate positions between these, but we really cannot afford to.

Secondly, *even after discretization and limitation* along the above lines, we still have a very large number of independent variables. Thus, even after discretization, we need to *further limit* the variables. Using the lip example again, we must limit ourselves to just three. For example, we must omit "partly stretched", "partly rounded", etc.

To appreciate the large number of possible, articulatable vowels, i.e. *the total number of possible ways a vowel phone can be constructed*, we can take all the possible values for the six variables listed in the box above (e.g. four (4) values for "jaw position, vertical", variable x_1), as follows:

NUMBER OF POSSIBLE VOWELS
(based on the above six independent variables $x_1...x_6$):

4 X 3 X 3 X 3 X 7 X 2 (respectively for ($x_1, x_2, x_3, x_4, x_5, x_6$) = **1,512**

.... (3.4)

That is to say, *the vocal apparatus is truly capable of articulating 1,512 distinct vowel phones*! Quite obviously, all 1,512 possible vowels are not used even in all the world's languages combined!

Thus, a further limitation we must make in the application of the phonological variables is a practical one, i.e. to **limit them to the production of phones that are actually used in one of the world's languages**. This very practical limitation brings the number of vowel phones down from 1,512 or more to a more manageable figure.

As we now see in the next Section, these same principles apply to the non-vowel phones as well, of reduction of the total number of possible phones, can be applied.

3.2.2 THE PHONOLOGICAL VARIABLE AS APPLIED TO NONVOWELS: *ARTITION* AND *PHONOCHROMATICITY* AND THE 15 ARTITIONS AND 35 PHONOCHROMES

Variables in the Nonvowel Phones: In a fashion similar to the treatment of vowels above, and again from our first treatment of the subject in an earlier chapter, the *phonological variables* as applied to ***non-vowels*** are as below. (These also appear in the **Summary Tables** in **VOLUME 1**.) We note again that they and the classification they represent are based on the ancient Indian phonological classification, discussed in more detail in a chapter in the first *NAVLIPI* volume. It is noted however that we expand considerably on this original Indian classification.

All non-vowels can be defined precisely by just two *classes* of phonological variables:

11) *Articulation Position*, which we condense to ***ARTITION*** (as already noted in an earlier chapter) for convenience.
12) ***PHONOCHROMATICITY***, the "color" of the phone.

Both definitions will be apparent from the descriptions in the boxes overleaf:

ARTITIONS (ARTICULATION POSITIONS, POINTS OF ARTICULATION)

We identify a total of *15 artitions*. Starting from the back of the articulation apparatus (the throat) and progressing towards the front (exactly as in the ancient Indian classification), we have:

1. *Glottal*
2. *Pharyngeal*
3. *Uvular*
4. *Velar*
5. *Retroflex*
6. *Medio-Palatal*
7. *Palatal*
8. *Alveolar*
9. *Apico/Medio-Dental*
10. *Standard Dental*
11. *Pharyngealized Dental*
12. *Interdental*
13. *Infralabio-Supradental*
14. *Supralabio-Infradental*
15. *Bilabial*

...(3.5)

Chapter 4: The World's Major Language Families- A Primer

PHONOCHROMATICITY ("COLOR" OF THE PHONE):

We identify a total of **35 phonochromes**:
1. *Unvoiced/unaspirated*
2. *Unvoiced/aspirated*
3. *Voiced/unaspirated*
4. *Voiced/aspirated*
5. *Nasal*
6. *Fricative/unvoiced*
7. *Fricative/voiced*
8. *Flap/unaspirated*
9. *Flap/aspirated*
10. *Flap/nasal*
11. *Flap/fricatized*
12. *Trill/normal*
13. *Trill/fricatized*
14. *Click, ingressive, central, single, unvoiced*
15. *Click, ingressive, central, single, voiced*
16. *Click, ingressive, central, single, nasal*
17. *Click, ingressive, central, trill*
18. *Click, ingressive, lateral, single, unvoiced*
19. *Click, ingressive, lateral, single, voiced*
20. *Click, ingressive, lateral, single, nasal*
21. *Click, ingressive, lateral, trill*
22. *Click, egressive, central*
23. *Click, egressive, lateral*
24. *Ejective, unvoiced*
25. *Ejective, fricative*
26. *Implosive, unvoiced*
27. *Implosive, voiced*
28. *Semivowel, simple*
29. *Semivowel, pharyngeal*
30. *Semivowel, central*
31. *Semivowel, lateral, unaspirated*
32. *Semivowel, lateral, aspirated*
33. *Semivowel, lateral, fricatized*
34. *Semivowel, lateral, palatalized*
35. *Semivowel, lateral, pharyngealized*

…(3.6)

Chapter 4: The World's Major Language Families- A Primer

Once again taking a mathematical analogy, as for vowels, we can think of **phonochromaticity** and **artition** as our *independent variables*, respectively *x*, and *y*. As our *dependent* variable, we have the nonvowel phone, which we can tentatively designate as *NV*. Once again, as for vowels, we have:

NUMBER OF POSSIBLE <u>NON-VOWELS</u>

Non vowel phone (NV) = dependent variable = function of 35 x 15 independent variables.

*NV= The **nonvowel** phone =* **f** *(x, y)*
(*x = phonochromaticity, y= artition*)

35 phonochromaticities X 15 artitions = 525 *possible, articulatable* <u>nonvowels</u>!

...(3.7)

Discretization: Once again, as for vowels, it is clear that all these 525 possible nonvowel phones are not in use in the world's languages!

In addition, we note that some limitation has already been effected in the Tables above. For example, we do not have a listing for *"implosive, nasalized"*. And many of the intermediate articulation positions, such as *"palato-alveolar"*, are not listed.

And another important observation is worth noting: From a perusal of the ***Navlipi*** SUMMARY TABLES in **PART 1**, it is seen that there are many blank cells in the (27 X 15) nonvowel matrix. These are of course the nonvowel phones that are not found in use in *any* language of the world (to the best of published knowledge).

Chapter 4: The World's Major Language Families- A Primer

3.2.3 THE *FORWARD FRICATIVE*

Once we have an understanding of the phonological variable as applied to nonvowels, understanding of the term *forward fricative* is relatively straightforward.

FORWARD FRICATIVE

The **FORWARD FRICATIVE** of a particular phone is just the *fricative formed at the articulation position which is one position ahead of the articulation position of that phone*. It retains all the other properties (especially voicing) of the original phone.

...(3.8)

As one example, the forward fricative of **[p]**, the bilabial unvoiced plosive, is the fricative formed at the next position, the infralabio-supradental, i.e. **[f]**. Since [p] is *unvoiced, so is its forward fricative*, [f]. thus, [f] is said to be the forward fircative of [p], while [p] is said to be the *parent phone* of [f].

The **Table** below gives several other examples of forward fricatives, together with their parent phones. It is to be noted that this is by no means an exhaustive list. It is once again seen in the examples in this Table that an unvoiced phone always yields an unvoiced forward fricative, a voiced phone always yields a voiced forward fricative, etc.

Chapter 4: The World's Major Language Families- A Primer

97

Table 3-1: A few other *examples of forward fricatives* together with their parent phones. It is seen in the examples herein that an unvoiced phone always yields an unvoiced forward fricative, a voiced phone always yields a voiced forward fricative, etc. The list is by no means exhaustive.

PHONE	FORWARD FRICATIVE AND EXPLANATION IF APPROPRIATE
[b]	The forward fricative of **[b]** is [v]
[w]	The forward fricative of **[w]** (bilabial semivowel, as in English *wow*) is also [v]
[k]	The forward fricative of **[k]** is [sh] (the palatal unvoiced fricative, as in English *shoot*)
[g]	The forward fricative of **[g]** is [zh] (English *pleasure*)
alevolar-[t]	The forward fricative of **alevolar-[t]** is [s]
dental-[t]	The forward fricative of **dental-[t]** is ["th"] (as in English *thought*)
dental-[d]	The forward fricative of **dental-[d]** is ["thh"] (as in English *though*)

3.2.4 LINGUISTIC SIGNIFICANCE OF THE FORWARD FRICATIVE

The sharp reader, especially one who is multilingual, will immediately notice that many of the above parent-phone/forward-fricative relationships appear to have linguistic significance.

For example, an instantly recognizable one is the [p]/[f] pair, as seen in Latin *pater* vs. English *father* (a transition that forms part of Grimm's law). Someone familiar with German may then also recognize some words, such as *pferd* ("horse") which appear to capture the parent-phone-to-forward-fricative transition. As another example, the reader familiar with Indian as well as European languages will recognize the [k]/[sh] pair in such cognates as the Sanskrit nominal roots *vaak, vaach* and Latin nouns *vox, voctis* (all meaning "speech"). Indeed the parent-phone-to-forward-fricative transition again appears to be captured in the common element [*ksh*] found in so many Sanskrit words (e.g. in the verbal root *waksh*, "to wax (increase)"). (In Sanskrit, the parent-phone/forward-fricative pair is also captured in verbal conjugations as the "strong form" and "weak form" of verbal stems, but that is too much of a digression here.) As another example, the Indo-European parent phone [t] (dental, unaspirated, unvoiced plosive) becomes its forward fricative, [*th*] (interdental/supra-dental, unaspirated, unvoiced, fricative) in the transformation *Te* (Sanskrit "they") to English *they*.

As will be seen later in this book, the forward fricative *is* indeed of great significance in phonemic condensation, phonemic idiosyncrasies, and ***phonetic shifts within language families***.

Chapter 4: The World's Major Language Families- A Primer

3.3 THE TERMS *PHONEME, TONEME, CHRONEME* AND THE NEW TERM *GALATOPHONE*

3.3.1 THE *PHONEME* AND THE *ALLOPHONE*

Once we have understood the concept of the phonological variables, and the phones that they produce, the ***phoneme*** is relatively facile to understand. It can be defined thus:

PHONEME

➢ *The phoneme is a set of one or more phones that has a <u>linguistic</u> value.* The linguistic value inherently implies a "functional" or "practical" value.

➢ *The phoneme is recognized by the fact that its substitution in a word by another phoneme causes a change of meaning of the word.*

➢ *Phonemes are different and distinct in different languages, and sometimes in different dialects and "accents" as well*

...(3.9)

In the tradition established in current linguistics, phonemes are written between *forward slashes*. Thus, **[p]** indicates a *phone*, and /**p**/ indicates a *phoneme*.

The best way to understand phonemes is to take several illustrative examples. We first use the two Indo-European languages with the largest number of speakers, English and Hindi/Urdu.

In the English word pairs *seat-seed, though-dough,* and *clue-glue*, we can clearly see that the highlighted phones [t]-[d], ["th"]-[d] and [k]-[g] clearly *change the meaning of the word when they are interchanged*. They are thus, quite clearly and obviously, distinct phonemes.

When however we consider the *p* in English *spy* and *put* (in the British, American, Australian etc. pronunciation but not the Indian or Irish pronunciation!), the situation is a bit more complex. Here, the *p* in *spy* is unaspirated, whereas in *put* it is slightly aspirated. I.e., the phone is, respectively, [p] and [ph]. (If the reader is equivocal about the *p* in *put* being aspirated, he/she may hold a small, lighted match in front of his/her lips while articulating the word and will see that it goes out.) However, the **value** of these two phones in the English language is the *same*. Using an American, British or Australian accent, they are, in English, two different phones that represent *one phoneme*. We say that they are **allophones** of the same phoneme. /p/. (The exceptions to the Indian and Irish pronunciations are because Indians and Irish will generally pronounce the *p* in *put* without the aspiration.)

On the other hand, in Hindi, [p] and [ph] have *different values*, as seen in the words *pal* ("a short duration of time, an instant") and **phal** ("fruit"). That is to say:

> *in Hindi/Urdu, substitution of [p] by [ph] has changed the meaning of the word, whereas in English ("spy, put"), it has not. Thus, in Hindi/Urdu, [p] and [ph] represent different phonemes, whereas in English they do not.*

…(3.10)

Thus, [p] and [ph] are different phonemes in Hindi, designated /p/ and /ph/, whereas they represent the same phoneme in English (and Tamil, incidentally), designated just /p/. We also note that the Hindi word *bal*, "strength", indicates that [p] and [b] are also different, distinct phonemes in Hindi. They are also distinct in English, witness the **putt-butt** opposition. But, as we will see further below in this section, in some of the world's languages, such as Mandarin, [p] and [b] are not always distinct phonemes.

We can now turn, for another example, to another widely spoken Indo-European language, Spanish. In Spanish **Dios**, "God", the phone [d] is an alveolo-dental voiced plosive. However, in most South American Spanish *todos*, the *d* is a different phone, a voiced fricative, as in the English *though*. Nevertheless, in Spanish both these phones represent the same phoneme, whereas in English, as is obvious in the word pair **though-dough**, the equivalent phones are clearly different phonemes.

Another important feature is observable in the [p], [ph] examples from English and Hindi/Urdu above: In some cases, e.g. Hindi [p], [ph] and [b], *each phone represents a distinct phoneme*. However, in other cases, e.g. English [p]/[ph], the phoneme that we designate /p/ in English actually consists of two (allo)phones, [p] and [ph]. Phonemes may comprise more than two phones. In the English of the British Midlands, the *r* in the words *crude* and *try* can be pronounced using three different phones: An alveolar central tap, an alveolar central roll, and a retroflex central semivowel. All three are allophones of the same phoneme, designated /r/. Conversely, a phoneme can also consist of a *combination* of phones. This is seen in the German cognates of the English words *tide* and *ten*: *zeit, zehn*. Here the *z* is a combination of two phones, [t] and [s], i.e. [ts]. (Actually it is another combination showing the parent-phone/forward-fricative transition.) However, it represents a single phoneme, designated /z/ in German.

The relation of phonemes to *accents* within a language can be very confusing for a layman. To see how phonemes can differ within the different "accents" of the same language, let us look at some examples in English from across the globe.

The Australian pronunciation of the word *mate* uses the diphthong [aai], whereas the American pronunciation uses the diphthong [ei]. Does that mean that the diphthongs [aai] and [ei] are the same phoneme in a sort of global English? *NO!* We can see this if we look at the Australian pronunciation of the word *they*. Here, of course, the Australian uses the diphthong [ei], not [aai] (and the American does too!). If the Australian were to pronounce *they* with [aai], he may not be understood in Australia, let alone in America! We thus establish that [aai] and [ei] are indeed different phonemes (more rigorously, combinations of phonemes, since they are diphthongs). The Australian pronunciation of *mate* with a different phoneme than the American pronunciation is just a case of a different *accent*. We have the same situation in the American vs. British English pronunciations of the vowels in words like *can't* and *stop*. And for more extreme examples within the English-language world, we can cite the Yorkshire vs. the RP (Received Pronunciation, "Queen's English") pronunciation of *bus* and the Cockney pronunciation of *heel* which sounds more like *hill*.

3.3.2 THE *TONEME*, THE *"ALLOTONE"* AND THE *CHRONEME*

In a manner closely analogous to the relationship between a *phone* and a *phoneme*, a **tone** bears a relationship to something called a *toneme*. Thus, just as a phoneme has constituent phones (allophones) which are clearly different and distinct but have the same linguistic value, a toneme has constituent tones which are clearly distinct but have the same linguistic value: When substituted for each other, they do not change the meaning of a word.

Thus, e.g, the first tone of Cantonese (level, high) degenerates into a different tone (falling, high to low-mid) before pause, e.g. between words. Both these tones can be considered "*allotones*" of a single toneme. Similarly, the third tone of Mandarin (falling/rising, mid –> low –> mid) is normally heard just as a low tone (level, low) when not before pause. These two tones are then again just two allotones of the same toneme.

In an analogous manner, a *chroneme* has constituent phones which differ in the length of utterance. This is typically applied to vowels, which may have differences of length, typically two (short, long), and sometimes three (as in Mixteco, a language of the Oaxaca province of Mexico).

3.3.3 THE *GALATOPHONE*

We frequently arrive at a situation where **a phone that is strongly present in one language simply does not exist in another**. And this mostly occurs not with rare phones, but with very common ones. Examples abound, as seen in the **Table** below.

It must be noted that the situation exemplified in the **Table** below is *quite different from the Hindi vs. English, [p] vs. [ph] example* cited above. Here, both phones *do* exist in both languages; they are simply not distinguished phonemically in one (English).

Table 3-2: Examples of situations where a phone that is strongly present in one language but simply does not exist in another.

PHONE	DESCRIPTION/COMMENTS
[p]	The phone [p] does not exist in Arabic
[l] (alveolar central, or for that matter, *any* central)	The phone [l] (alveolar central, or for that matter, *any* central) does not exist in Japanese
[r] (alveolar lateral flap)	The lateral phones, e.g. [r] (alveolar lateral flap) do not exist in most southern Chinese languages
[k..] (uvular de-voiced unaspirated plosive)	The phone [k] (uvular de-voiced unaspirated plosive) does not exist natively in most languages excepting Arabic and certain other Semitic languages
aspirated plosives [ph], [bh], [kh], [gh]	The aspirated plosives, e.g. [ph], [bh], [kh], [gh], do not officially exist in Tamil, the "most Dravidian" of the world's languages. Only the corresponding unaspirated plosives exist
retroflex non-vowels	The retroflex non-vowels are absent in nearly all languages of the world except the Dravidian and the Indian sub-branch of the Indo-European family
fricatized lateral, *ll* and fricatized central *r^*	The fricatized lateral, *ll* of Welsh, and the fricatized central *r^* of Czech, exist in very few other languages.

Now frequently, when such a situation occurs, the native speaker of the language in question will *mistake one and only one particular phone from his/her own language for the missing phone. This is usually a close cognate in terms of artition*. To take the examples from the above Table again:

⇄ The Arabic speaker will always mistake [p] *only* for [b], which *does* exist in Arabic, but *never* for any other phone, e.g. the cognate bilabial [w] (or for that matter, [s] or [k] or [m] or [r]!). All three phones, [p], [b] and [w], are close cognates in terms of artition - they are all bilabials. Thus he/she may pronounce English *pay* as *bay* (as in "I will *bay* you some money") but never as *way*.

Chapter 4: The World's Major Language Families- A Primer

- The speakers of Chinese languages will mistake **[b]** for **[p]**, which *does* exist in their languages, but again, never for any other phone, such as **[w]**.
- The phone **[l]** (alveolar central, or for that matter, *any* central) does not exist in Japanese. Thus, the Japanese speaker may mistake **[l]** for **[r]**, a close cognate in terms of artition. He/she may then pronounce English *flow* as *frow*.
- The lateral phones, e.g. **[r]** (alveolar lateral flap) do not exist in most southern Chinese languages. Once again, southern Chinese speaker may mistake **[r]** for **[l]**, a close cognate in terms of artition Thus, the Cantonese speaker may pronounce English *fried* as *flied*.
- The phone **[k..]** (uvular de-voiced unaspirated plosive) exists natively in almost no language except Arabic and certain other Semitic languages. Thus, the English speaker will invariably pronounce Arabic *k..alb* ("heart", sometimes written *qalb*) as *kalb*, i.e. with a velar initial.
- The aspirated plosives, e.g. **[ph]**, **[bh]**, **[kh]**, **[gh]**, do not officially exist in Tamil, the "most Dravidian" of the world's languages. Only the corresponding unaspirated plosives exist. Thus, the Tamil speaker may pronounce Hindi *bhiik* ("begging") as *biik*.
- The retroflex nonvowels of the Indian languages will be pronounced as the corresponding alveolar nonvowels by native Europeans.
- The Welsh fricatized lateral, *ll*, is approximated by English speakers by prefixing *f*, as in *Floyd* for *Lloyd*. Similarly, the Czech fricatized central *r*^ is approximated by English speakers by *[-rch-]*.

With regard to the above discussion, one observation is elementary and self-evident, yet important, to remember. It is further supported by the above examples: That, almost always, ***only one, specific phone is mistaken***. Additionally, it is apparent that the phone that is mistaken ***is almost always of the same or very close artition to the phone that it is mistaken for***. Thus, for the Arabic speaker mistaking [p] for [b], both are bilabial plosives (one is un-voiced, the other is voiced). For the Japanese speaker mistaking the [l] for an [r], both phones are alveolar semi-vowels (one is a lateral and the other a central, the two being interchanged simply by changing the tongue breath egress position). And for the English speaker mistaking Arabic [k..] (uvular) for [k] (velar), the articulation positions are next to each other, and both are un-voiced, unaspirated plosives.

We coin a new word *for the phone that is mistaken*: ***GALATOPHONE.*** This is taken from colloquial Hindi/Urdu *galti* ("mistake", of Arabic borrowing), i.e. a ***"mistaken phone"***.

Chapter 4: The World's Major Language Families- A Primer

*Each **galatophone** must always be associated with a parent phone*. We then say that the galatophone ***"is a galatophone for the parent phone"***. Thus, e.g., we say that in Arabic, *"[p] is a galatophone for the parent phone [b]"*, and we say that in Japanese, *"[l] is a galatophone for the parent phone [r]"*, etc.

One other feature of galatophones is important: ***They almost always have the same phonemic value as the parent phone***. Thus, when an Arabic speaker mistakenly substitutes [p] for [b] in a word, it will not change the meaning of the word. Similarly, when a Japanese speaker substitutes [l] for [r] in a word, it will not change the meaning of the word. Thus, in a sense, galatophones are ***"nonexistent allophones"***. And frequently, these nonexistent allophones may actually be articulated! Thus, some Arabic speakers may in fact occasionally pronounce [b] as [p].

Some commonly encountered galatophones are listed in the Table below:

Table 3-3: Commonly encountered **galatophones**, together with their associated parent phones and the corresponding phonemic condensate.

LANGUAGE	GALATOPHONE	MISTAKEN FOR (PARENT PHONE)	PHONEMIC CONDENSATE
Japanese	[l]	[r]	central + lateral sounds
Arabic	[p]	[b]	voiced + unvoiced sounds
Cantonese	[b]	[p]	voiced + unvoiced sounds
Tamil	[ph], [bh], [th], [dh], [kh], [gh], [ph], [bh]	unaspirated phones **[p], [b], [t], [d], [g], [p], [b]**	aspirated + unaspirated sounds

Galatophones are important in the discussion of *phonemic condensates* (next Section), and, in general, in the treatment of the phonemic idiosyncrasies of different languages, which of course is what this book is all about.

Chapter 4: The World's Major Language Families- A Primer

3.4 THE ALL-IMPORTANT *PHONEMIC CONDENSATE*

A *phonemic condensate* can be defined as below:

> **PHONEMIC CONDENSATE**
>
> *An entity, normally a letter (glyph) or multigraph of the Navlipi script, that represents one or more phones that are part of (are allophones of) the same phoneme in one language, but represent different phonemes in another language. These phones are usually, but not always, closely related in terms of articulation position.*

...(3.11)

Once again, it is best to illustrate the definition with *examples*:

- ⇌ A *phonemic condensate that represents* (**aspirate + non-aspirate**). If, hypothetically, we use a *subscripted circle* to represent this, then, e.g., **[p]** would be used to designate the unaspirated phone (here the bilabial unvoiced plosive), **[ph]** would be used to designate its aspirated counterpart, and {p_o} would be used *to designate the unaspirated as well as aspirated phones.* Thus, *p* and *ph* would be used separately in Hindi, to represent the distinct phonemes that they are in Hindi. However, in writing English, we would use p_o to indicate that this may be either [p] or [ph], both being constituents of the same phoneme. *This would then be especially useful to the native Hindi speaker reading English.*

- ⇌ A *phonemic condensate that similarly represents* (**voiced and un-voiced**). Once again, if, hypothetically, we use a *subscripted double circle* to represent this, then, e.g., *p* would be used to designate the unvoiced phone, *b* would be used to designate its voiced counterpart, and b_{oo} would be used to designate *the voiced as well as de-voiced phones.* Thus, *p* and *b* would be used separately in Hindi, to represent the distinct phonemes that they are in Hindi. However, in writing Cantonese, we would use b_{oo} to indicate that this may be either **[p]** or **[b]**, both being the same phoneme. *This would be useful to the native English speaker* *reading Cantonese.*

⇄ A *phonemic condensate that represents **lateral as well as central** articulation, e.g. [l] as well as [r]*. Again hypothetically, if we use the subscripted number sign, #, to designate this, then, e.g., *l* and *r* would designate the alveolar lateral and central semivowels ([l], [r]), as used in English, and *r#* would be used to designate either lateral or central semivowel, and would be used in writing Japanese. *This would be then useful to the English speaker reading Japanese.*

It can be clearly seen from the above that phonemic condensates apply not only to phones that are genuinely present as part of a single phoneme in a language, such as the [p] and [ph] of English, **but also to galatophones**, e.g. the [p] and [b] example of Cantonese, or Arabic. In the former case, the [b] officially does not exist, but in everyday speech, one may frequently hear it. In the latter case, the [p] does not exist.

Further clarifying our definition of the phonemic condensate in light of the above then, we can say that it is, but one may frequently hear it in everyday speech:

> ### *PHONEMIC CONDENSATE AS USED IN TRANSCRIPTION*
>
> *A glyph, or symbol used to designate two or more allophones or galatophones of a phoneme in a particular language, for the benefit of the unfamiliar speaker of other languages.*

…(3.12)

We can now briefly look at *some* of the common *types* of phonemic condensates that may be found. These are listed in the **Table** below:

Chapter 4: The World's Major Language Families- A Primer

Table 3-4:   *Some* of the common *types* of *phonemic condensates*.

TYPE	EXAMPLE
Aspiration + Non-aspiration	[p] + [ph] (example also in text above)
Voicing + Un-voicing	[p] + [b] (example also in text above)
Plosive + Its Corresponding Fricative	[k] + [x]
Plosive + Its Corresponding Forward Fricative	[k] + [sh] or [p] + [f]
Plosive + Its Corresponding Semivowel	[b] + [w]
Semivowel + Its Corresponding Forward Fricative	[w] + [v]
Central + Corresponding Lateral Semivowel	[r] + [l]

So far, all of the above examples include phones with the *identical artition*, or, as in the case of the forward fricative, the *next position forward*. However, we also have situations where *phones of radically different articulation position or phonochromaticity* must form *one* phonemic condensate. Some examples are listed in the **Table** below:

Table 3-5: Some *examples* of situations where *phones of radically different artition or phonochromaticity* must form *one* phonemic condensate.

TYPE	EXAMPLE
Central + Corresponding Lateral Semivowel + Corresponding Nasal	**[r] + [l] + [n]**. This represents an extremely common phonetic shift or interchange found throughout the world's languages, from East Asia through West Europe and West Africa. Examples are Spanish/Portuguese *playa/praia*, Sanskrit *ruci-luci* ("light") and *roma-loma* ("hair"), Sanskrit-German *kalabha-knabe* ("young offspring, knave"), etc.
Uvular Fricative + Alveolar Flap or Trill	This, **[x..] + [rrr]**, is a combination of radically different phones, found in the French/German /r/ phoneme.

We may now further classify phonemic condensates as below:

Table 3-6: Classification of *phonemic condensates* into three (3) types.

TYPE	DESCRIPTION AND EXAMPLE
Simple	Having the *same articulation position*. Examples are the *aspirated/non-aspirated, voiced/un-voiced* and the **[r]-[l]** pairs cited above
Similar	Having *closely related articulation positions*, as in the *plosive + forward fricative* examples cited above
Unrelated	*Very different artitions*. As in the **[x..]/[rrr]** of the French/German /r/ phoneme cited above

3.5 OTHER, MISCELLANEOUS PHONOLOGICAL TERMINOLOGY

In closing this chapter, we mention some phonological terms that are common and may be encountered in this book and elsewhere. These are listed in the **Table** overleaf. The reader is also referred to the **Glossary** elsewhere in this book. We also note that there are a very few other terms, such as *continuant* and *liquid* which have been dealt with elsewhere in this book.

Chapter 4: The World's Major Language Families- A Primer

Table 3-7: Some additional, common phonological terms.

TERM	DEFINITION OR DESCRIPTION
Affricate	A combination phone that is composed of a stop followed by a fricative of the same artition. Example: [t] (phone) + [s] (fricative = [ts] (affricate).
Approximant	IPA term used to denote semivowels. The IPA, somewhat confusedly, further distinguishes just plain approximants, to which category the semivowels [r] and [j] would belong, and "lateral approximants", to which the semivowel [l] would belong! Then, to further confound the issue, it further categorizes the semivowel [w] as, sometimes, a *"velar* approximant" and sometimes a *"labio-velar* approximant"! It does not classify [w] as a "bilabial approximant" at all. In contrast, *Navlipi* prefers to stay with the term **semivowel**, which preserves the parent-vowel relationship of the semivowels and their facile derivation from these parent vowels.
Geminate	A twin or dual *non-vowel* phone, usually expressed by a dual letter, phonemically distinct from the corresponding single phone. Example: Hindi *pakaa* ("ripened"), *pakkaa* ("sure, certain, pucca").
Rhoticity	IPA term used to denote vocalic central phones, i.e. *vocalic –r*.
Sandhi (Sanskrit "union")	Term borrowed from Sanskrit grammarians denoting the *euphonic* ('*eu-phon*, "good sounding", =*su-bhan*) joining together of two adjacent phones, usually accompanied by a phonological reduction or change of some sort. Denoted sometimes by other terms, e.g. *liaison* in French (as in *a + il = a t'il*, done for euphony). This melding together of adjacent phones occurs naturally in most languages. Thus, in English, we have the following examples of Sandhi: *want + to = wanna; give (let) + me = gimme (lemme); got (did)+ you = gotcha (didja),* etc. etc.. Sanskrit Sandhi originated in similar, natural, common usage but then degenerated into rigid grammatical rules that *had* to be followed *every time, without fail!* This would be the equivalent of being told, in English, that *got + you* could *never* be pronounced as *got you*, but *always* had to be changed into *gotcha*! A few Sanskrit Sandhi rules are given elsewhere in this book.

Chapter 4: The World's Major Language Families- A Primer

3.6 EXERCISES

(1) Define the term *phonological variable* in the most general manner possible, with examples. Enumerate the independent phonological variables applicable to vowels and non-vowels, and, in this fashion, arrive at the total number of possible, distinct vowels and non-vowels capable of being articulated by the human speech apparatus.

(2) Define, citing examples, the terms *artition, phonochromaticity, discretization, phoneme, allophone, toneme, chroneme, galatophone, affricate, approximant, semivowel, geminate* and *rhoticity*.

(3) Define the term *forward fricative* and discuss its linguistic significance.

(4) Define, with several examples, the term *phonemic condensate*.

CHAPTER 4.
THE WORLD'S MAJOR LANGUAGE FAMILIES- A PRIMER

TABLE OF CONTENTS

4.1 OBJECTIVES OF THIS CHAPTER 116

4.2 SUMMARY OF WORLD LANGUAGE FAMILIES AND THE SEVEN PREDOMINANT LANGUAGE FAMILIES 117

4.3 LANGUAGE vs. DIALECT: A MORE EXACT DEFINITION 147

4.4 THE INDO-EUROPEAN (INDO-GERMANIC) FAMILY 150

    4.4.1 EXTENT AND NUMBER OF SPEAKERS 150
    4.4.2 INDIAN ("INDIC") BRANCH 152
    4.4.3 IRANIAN (PERSIAN) BRANCH 157
    4.4.4 GREEK BRANCH 158
    4.4.5 BALTO-SLAVIC BRANCH 159
    4.4.6 ARMENIAN BRANCH 160
    4.4.7 ALBANIAN BRANCH 161
    4.4.8 GERMANIC BRANCH 161
    4.4.9 ROMANCE (ALSO CALLED *ITALIC*) BRANCH 162
    4.4.10 KELTIC (*CELTIC*) BRANCH 162
    4.4.11 EXTINCT INDO-EUROPEAN LANGUAGES 163

4.5 THE SINO-TIBETAN FAMILY 164

    4.5.1 EXTENT AND NUMBER OF SPEAKERS 164
    4.5.2 THE CHINESE LANGUAGES 165
    4.5.3 THE TIBETO-BURMAN LANGUAGES 168

4.6 THE NIGER-CONGO FAMILY 169

Chapter 4: The World's Major Language Families- A Primer

4.7 THE AFRO-ASIATIC (FORMERLY CALLED HAMITO-SEMITIC) FAMILY 172

4.8 AUSTRONESIAN (FORMERLY MALAYO-POLYNESIAN) FAMILY 174

4.9 ALTAIC FAMILY AND JAPANESE 178

    4.9.1 URALIC, ALTAIC, "URAL-ALTAIC", "FINNO-UGRIC" AND JAPANESE 178
    4.9.2 EXTENT AND NUMBER OF SPEAKERS 179
    4.9.3 TURKIC BRANCH 179
    4.9.4 TUNGUSIC (SIBERIAN) AND MONGOLIC (MONGOLIAN) BRANCHES 179
    4.9.5 SCRIPTS OF THE ALTAIC FAMILY AND JAPANESE 180

4.10 DRAVIDIAN FAMILY 181

    4.10.1 DRAVIDIANS AND THEIR ORIGINS IN THE INDIAN AND WORLD CONTEXTS . 181
        4.10.1.1 Are Dravidians Native to India or Were They Migrants from the Iran/Iraq Region? *181*
        4.10.1.2 Dravidians, Aaryans (Aryans), Haplogroups and The Last Ice Age. *185*
        4.10.1.3 Tamil, Elamite and "Proto-Dravidian" *188*
        4.10.1.4 Recent DNA Studies and Archaeological Excavations Shedding Some Light on Dravidian Origins *192*
        4.10.1.5 The Likely Dravidian/Aaryan (Aryan) Tapestry in the Indian Geographical Context From About 10 000 BCE *193*
    4.10.2 EXTENT AND NUMBER OF SPEAKERS 201

4.11 AUSTRO-ASIATIC FAMILY 203

4.12 DAIC FAMILY 205

4.13 NILO-SAHARAN FAMILY 207

4.14 URALIC FAMILY 208

4.15 HMONG-MIEN (ALSO CALLED MIAO-YAO) FAMILY 209

4.16 KHOISAN (!XHOSAN) FAMILY (*THE "CLICK" LANGUAGES*) 210

4.17 ORIGINAL LANGUAGE FAMILIES OF NORTH AND CENTRAL AMERICA, THE CARIBBEAN AND EASTERNMOST SIBERIA 211

4.18 ORIGINAL LANGUAGE FAMILIES OF SOUTH AMERICA 216

4.19 OTHER LANGUAGE FAMILIES 218

4.20 EXTINCT, MORIBUND OR INACTIVE LANGUAGES *OF SIGNIFICANCE* OF THE ANCIENT WORLD 219

4.21 LIVING LANGUAGE ISOLATES 228

4.22 "SUPRA" OR "MACRO" LANGUAGE FAMILIES 232

4.23 LANGUAGES WITH AN "ENGLISH-LIKE" ("*ANGRAMAYA*", A NEW TERM) STRUCTURE (WITH BASE FROM ONE LANGUAGE FAMILY, ALL 'HIGHER' VOCABULARY FROM OTHER FAMILIES) 233

    4.23.1 THE STRUCTURE OF ENGLISH 233
    4.23.2 SOME OTHER "*ANGRAMAYA*" LANGUAGES BESIDES ENGLISH: *HINDI/URDU, INDONESIAN/MALAYSIAN LANGUAGES, KHMER, THAI, MYANMARI (BURMESE), SWAAHILI (SWAHILI), OTHERS* 236

4.24 BRIEF SYNOPSIS OF PHONETIC SHIFTS BETWEEN LANGUAGES IN FAMILIES 241

4.25 LANGUAGE, ETHNICITY, "RACE" AND COLOR 248

4.26 EXERCISES 258

4.1 OBJECTIVES OF THIS CHAPTER

Extant introductory books and articles on the *world's language families* and closely related subjects present limited information that frequently lacks detail [LN-6, SCr-1, LAs-1]. Alternatively, they have a presentation that may be confusing or overwhelming for the layman. In some cases, they do not cover all the subjects relevant to a good appreciation of the field. This is especially true of the introductory books used in linguistics courses in the English-language world. (See also **Section 1.9** in **Chapter 1**, discussing extant texts in introductory linguistics.) Some presentations, for example the graphical presentations found in some atlases [LAs-2] also have many inaccuracies, simplifications or outright errors.

On the other hand, the more specialized literature, focusing on very specific language groups [cf. LAi-30, IEu-17] is too specialized, too narrow, too difficult or too tedious for a casual perusal by the non-specialist or the inquisitive layman who may be eager to get a quick grounding in the subject. And mid-level literature, such as the *Ethnologue* presentations [LN-2], are also somewhat difficult for the layman to navigate through and comprehend.

In this context then, this chapter attempts to gives an overview of the field in a very simple, frequently *graphical*, format comprehensible to the layman. It also seeks to present the variegated subjects relevant to the field *"under one roof"*, as it were. At the same time, it seeks to present *far more detail* than found in the extant introductory literature. And it also presents material usually not discussed much for various reasons, such as the inter-relation of "race", migration and language.

The chapter also presents much <u>new</u> *material*. It also gives more exacting definitions in such subjects as *dialect vs. language* and phonetic transitions between languages. Finally, it also presents entirely new concepts, such as that of ***Angramaya*** languages.

The reasons for inclusion of this chapter in this book are self-evident: In order to have an appreciation of a script (*Navlipi*) purported to apply to all the world's languages, one must have at least a rudimentary knowledge of these languages, the families they belong to, and the variety inherent in them.

4.2 SUMMARY OF WORLD LANGUAGE FAMILIES AND THE SEVEN PREDOMINANT LANGUAGE FAMILIES

THE WORLD'S LANGUAGES: The world at the time of this writing, 2005, still possesses about *7,000 distinct languages*. The median number of speakers per language is thought to be only 6,000, showing that more than half the world's languages are extremely rare [LN-2, LAs-33].

The language family which is most well known, through fortunate or unfortunate happenstance, is of course the Indo-European (also called Indo-Germanic). This and a few other language families, have a very large number of *members* as well as a large number of *speakers*. Others, e.g. the Sino-Tibetan, have just a few major members, but nevertheless a very large number of speakers. And still others have only one member and are called *language isolates* [LAs-1, LAs-33 to LAs-39].

Although 7,000 may seem a large number, the world's languages are said to be dying at the rate of two a month at this writing (in 2005) [LAs-33, LN-79 to LN-82]. Many languages in a wide geographic range, from Komi and Mari (languages of the Finno-Ugric family) in northern Russia to Monchak in Mongolia to more than a hundred languages of Papua New Guinea, are expected, as of this writing, to be extinct by 2015 [LN-79 to LN-82].

A language embodies a culture and, more importantly, a particular way of thinking. Thus, some linguists feel that the loss of language diversity is akin to the loss of genetic diversity and the shrinking of the gene pool: Just as the latter is known to compromise genetic strength in such areas as the ability of a species to fight disease, the loss of language diversity and the shrinking of the language pool may lead to the lack of diverse approaches to tackling problems. It thus may perhaps, in the long run, lead to a lessened ability of humans to overcome sociological and technological problems of the future.

PREDOMINANT LANGUAGE FAMILIES AND METHODS OF ESTIMATION OF NUMBER OF SPEAKERS AND INHERENT ERRORS THEREIN: There are just a bit more than a handful of language families, just *seven* (*7*) to be exact, *each with more than 200 m speakers*, *which dominate the world's languages* [LN-2, LAs-1 to LAs-3]. We list these seven below, together with the number of speakers of each estimated, for the year *2005*, in a rough, "back of the envelope calculation" sort of way.

Chapter 4: The World's Major Language Families- A Primer

118

Table 4-1: The seven (7) largest language families in terms of number of speakers. The figures cited for the number of speakers are estimated figures for *2005* [LN-2, LAs-1 to LAs-3].

THE SEVEN LARGEST LANGUAGE FAMILIES IN TERMS OF ESTIMATED NUMBER OF SPEAKERS (AS OF 2005)
(Listed in order of decreasing number of speakers.)

INDO-EUROPEAN (ALSO CALLED *INDO-GERMANIC*)

With more than **3.0 billion** speakers. This includes, e.g., English and Hindi/Urdu. Among these, Hindi/Urdu is spoken or understood by an estimated 635 million people and English is spoken or understood by an estimated 500 million people across several continents. Geographically, Indo-European has the widest distribution of any world language family.

SINO-TIBETAN

Includes the Chinese languages, with more than **1.4 billion** speakers. Among these, standard Mandarin is spoken or understood by an estimated 750 million people.

NIGER-CONGO (A PART OF WHICH WAS FORMERLY DENOTED AS *BAANTU (BANTU)*)

Encompassing more than **585 million** people and including such prominent African languages as Yorub a, Swaahili and Zulu.

AFRO-ASIATIC (FORMERLY CALLED *HAMITO-SEMITIC*)

With more than **380 million** speakers. Its *Semitic* branch, includes Arabic which has nearly 300 million speakers across a wide geographic area.

(**Table 4-1, cont.**):

AUSTRONESIAN (FORMERLY CALLED *MALAYO-POLYNESIAN*)

Includes the languages of, e.g., Malaysia, Indonesia and the Philippines, and encompasses more than **370 million** people.

ALTAIC AND JAPANESE

With more than **345 million** people and including such languages as Turkish, Korean, Japanese and Mongolian. (Regarding the inclusion of Japanese, see discussion further below.)

DRAVIDIAN

With about **230 million** speakers, mainly in South India and Sri Lanka. This includes Tamil, the extinct ancient language Elamite and the nearly extinct, modern Brahui.

There are several reasons that the estimation of the number of speakers can only be *approximate*:

Firstly, due to the effects of globalization and concomitant multilingualism, and the dearth of *accurate, detailed* language censuses (as opposed to national censuses that simply ask a person what their native language is, whose results are not entirely accurate), it is difficult to arrive at truly accurate first (and second and subsequent) language data.

Secondly, the estimated figures that we cite necessarily include *double (and triple and more) counting*, one of the bugbears of language censuses. For example, the ethnic Panjaabi in Pakistan who speaks mostly Hindi (Urdu) in daily life and at home, but may occasionally lapse into Panjaabi with close family, would be counted among both Hindi/Urdu and Panjaabi speakers. (Officially, about 60% of Pakistanis list Panjaabi as their first language, although they may speak Hindi/Urdu most of the time [LAi-47].) Similarly, an ethnic Welsh person in Gwynnedd county in Wales who speaks mostly English in both business and at home but may occasionally lapse into Welsh with the closest family, or a Peruvian who speaks Quechua at home but counts Spanish as his first and best language, would both be included in the censuses of both applicable languages (Welsh/English and Quechua/Spanish respectively). In both cases, these persons are likely to list the language they know less well (Welsh and Quechua respectively) as their first language in censuses, for patriotic or other reasons. Thus, quite obviously with such examples in mind, simple addition of the total number of speakers *may yield a number exceeding the population of the regions in question*!

The estimates of the number of speakers cited below and elsewhere in this chapter also don't include those persons who can "get by" in a language, such as, for example, non-English-speaking scientists attending a scientific conference held in English.

Thirdly and finally, we note that the figures we cite are for the most recent population censuses for each country [LAs-3]. None are older than 2001. Even the most recent Internet postings available for country populations frequently rely on the most recent national censuses. For convenience, our language counts also *do not include countries with < 1 million population*, and we round off to the nearest million. A rough calculation shows that these approximations affect the final, overall figures very little. A detailed breakdown of the estimates for the number of speakers is provided under the discussions of the individual language families later in this chapter.

THE PRIMACY OF ENGLISH: Based on the figures cited above, English is only the *third* most widely spoken/understood language of the world, at about 500 million speakers quite behind Mandarin (est. 750 million) and Hindi/Urdu (est. 635 million). We can summarize this quickly as follows:

- *Mandarin*: Spoken/understood by 750 m (est., 2005)
- *Hindi/Urdu*: Spoken/understood by 635 m (est., 2005)
- *English*: Spoken/understood by 500 m (est., 2005)

However, as we all know, in spite of this mere third place, English is today rapidly taking over as the *lingua franca* in most of the world, although the recent work of Ostler contends that this may eventually change [SCr-1-b(ii)]. This is true even in places where it had no history or foothold, such as Mongolia and Indonesia. For example, in Mongolia, the government is itself taking the initiative in promoting English as the second language, to be taught from primary school onwards, and to replace Russian [LAs-27].

Indirectly, English is also causing the extinction of more and more languages. As an

Chapter 4: The World's Major Language Families- A Primer

121

example of the beginnings of such extinction in completely unexpected regions, and in a matter little noticed thus far, the children of India's affluent classes are rapidly starting to use English as their main language, with the language of their maternal or paternal ancestors sometimes not spoken or known by them at all. Similarly, and even more surprisingly, this has also started to happen among the affluent classes in Indonesia, a country with no known history of English colonial or other influence. With the continuation of this trend, it is conceivable that in another four or five generations, the Indian languages will be spoken only by the very poor, and available in written form only in archaic literature. This would then, in some ways, resemble what happened to Irish or Welsh vis-á-vis English. Indeed, this book, although written by an author of Indian ethnic origin, is written in English, for the simple practical purpose of reaching the widest and most influential audience. Needless to say, and notwithstanding the strong arguments put forth for diversity in language in the previous section above, that is the way of the world and not a subject that the present book concerns itself with. Nor is it an object of contention in this book.

The world's language families in tabular form are listed in **Table 4-2** below. It lists in summary form the above *seven* language families as well as *most* of the other major language families of the world along with some important language isolates or isolate groups. This **Table** s a summary list of *most* of the world's language families, listed in decreasing order of estimated number of speakers, *as of 2005* [LN-2, LAs-1 to LAs-3]. Prominent example languages in each are also listed. The estimated number of speakers for each is detailed (e.g. by country or ethnic group) later in this chapter. The method of estimation of number of speakers has been briefly described above.

The Table is grouped in three parts, comprising the languages with more than 50 million speakers, those with less than 50 million speakers and language isolates or groups of isolates. The precise breakdown of the sum figures for each language family by language, region or country are given later, under the brief discussions of the individual language families.

The **Figures** immediately following **Table 4-2** show the "language trees" for each of the seven predominant language families.

Table 4-2, PART A:
LANGUAGE FAMILIES WITH *MORE THAN* 50 MILLION ESTIMATED SPEAKERS, *AS OF 2005*

(Listed in order of decreasing number of estimated speakers; a question mark in the Estimated Number of Speakers column indicates that estimation is difficult and so it is best not to even hazard a guess.)

LANGUAGE FAMILY	PROMINENT EXAMPLE(S)	ESTIMATED NUMBER OF SPEAKERS (2005)
(1) *Indo-European (Indo-Germanic)*	Hindi/Urdu, English, Baanglaa (Bengali), Russian, French	> 3.0 billion
(2) *Sino-Tibetan*	Mandarin, Cantonese, Myanmari (Burmese), Tibetan	1.3 billion
(3) *Niger-Congo (including Baantu languages)*	Yoruba, Igbo, Swaahili, Zulu	585 million
(4) *Afro-Asiatic*	Arabic, Amharic, Hebrew	380 million
(5) *Austronesian (formerly Malayo-Polynesian)*	Bahasa (Bhaashaa) Malaysia (Malay), Bahasa Indonesia (Indonesian), Tagalog, Maori	370 million
(6) *Altaic+Japanese*	Turkish, Japanese, Korean	345 million
(7) *Dravidian*	Tamil, Kannadaa, Elamite	230 million
(8) *Austro-Asiatic*	Vietnamese, Khmer, Mundaa (Jhaarkhand, India), Khaasi (N.E. India)	115 million
(9) *Daic*	Thai, Lao	75 million

(Table 4-2, cont.)

Table 4-2, PART B: LANGUAGE FAMILIES WITH *LESS THAN* 50 MILLION ESTIMATED SPEAKERS, *AS OF 2005*

(Listed in order of decreasing number of estimated speakers; a question mark in the Estimated Number of Speakers column indicates that estimation is difficult and so it is best not to even hazard a guess.)

LANGUAGE FAMILY	PROMINENT EXAMPLE(S)	ESTIMATED NUMBER OF SPEAKERS (2005)
Nilo-Saharan	Maasaai (Kenya/Tanzania), Songay (Niger), Nubian (Egypt/Sudan), Kanuri (Nigeria), Fur (Darfur, Sudan)	*30 million*
Uralic	Finnish, Hungarian	*18 million*
Hmong-Mien	Western Hmong (Miao)	*7 million?*
Caucasian (Kavkaz): Kartvelian (South Caucasian)	Georgian	*< 6 million?*
Quechuua-Aymaran ("Quechuamaran")	Quechhua, Aymara (Peru, Bolivia)	*< 2 million?*
Caucasian (Kavkaz): North-Central Caucasian	Chechen (Chechnya)	*< 6 million?*
Caucasian (Kavkaz): Northwest Caucasian	Abkhaz (Abkhazia)	*< 1.5 million?*
Navajo (Athabaskian)	Navajo ("Navaho", Arizona, U.S.)	*< 1 million?*
Khoisan ("Click")	Nama (Namibia)	*< 1 million?*
Algonquian	"Algonkin" (U.S./Canada)	*?*
Arawakan (Taino)	Various languages of the Caribbean (extinct)	*?*
Australian Languages	Still disputed whether single family or multiple isolates	*?*
Caddoan	Caddoan (southern U.S.)	*?*
Carib	Various languages of the Caribbean (extinct)	*?*
Caucasian (Kavkaz): Northeast Caucasian	Avar (Dagestan)	*?*
Chibchan	Various languages of Central America	*?*

(Table 4-2(B), cont.):

LANGUAGE FAMILY	PROMINENT EXAMPLE(S)	ESTIMATED NUMBER OF SPEAKERS (2005)
Chukotko-Kamchatkan	Chukchi, other languages of the Kamchatka, Chukotka peninsula (eastern Russia)	? *(endangered)*
Eskimo-Aleut	Inuit (Canada, Greenland)	?
Iroquoian	Iroquois (U.S./Canada)	?
Je (Macro-Gé)	Various languages of southern Brazil	?
Maayan (Mayan)	Yucatec, Chol (southern Mexico, Guatemala)	?
Mixe-Zoque	Various languages of Central America	?
Muskogean	Muskogean (Florida, U.S.)	?
Oto-Manguean	Mixteco (near Oaxaca, Mexico)	?
Panoan-Ticuanan	Various languages of Peru, Bolivia	?
Siouan	Sioux (U.S./Canada Midwest)	?
Tucanoan	Various languages of northwestern S. America	?
Tupian	Guarani (Paraguay)	?
Uto-Aztec	Nahuatl ("Aztec", Mexico)	?
Yuman	Yuman (southwestern U.S., Mexico)	?

(Table 4-2, cont.)

Table 4-2, PART C:
EXAMPLES OF *SOME* LANGUAGE ISOLATES OR GROUPS OF ISOLATES *OF SIGNIFICANCE*
(*Listed in order of decreasing number of estimated speakers, or alphabetically if unknown*)

LANGUAGE ISOLATE OR ISOLATE GROUP	PROMINENT EXAMPLE(S)	ESTIMATED NUMBER OF SPEAKERS (2005)
Papuan languages	More than 1 000 unrelated languages of inland Papua-New Guinea	*< 8 million*
Ainu	Hokkaido, Japan	*nearly extinct*
Basque	Basque (Euskara) (France/Spain)	*est. < 3 million*
Burashaski	Burashaski (Paakistaan)	*endangered*
Etruscan	Etruscan (Italy)	*extinct*
Patagonian	Kawesqar (southern Chile)	*extinct by 2015?*
Sumerian	Sumerian	*extinct*

Chapter 4: The World's Major Language Families- A Primer

Fig. 4-1: Approximate geographic distribution of the nine largest language families (in terms of number of speakers *in 2005*).

Fig. 4-2 (*cont. overleaf*):

LANGUAGE FAMILY-TREE DIAGRAMS

FORMAT USED FOR THE LANGUAGE FAMILY-TREE DIAGRAMS PRESENTED IN THIS CHAPTER (STARTING OVERLEAF)

Points to note are:

(1) The **closeness** of the languages is represented on the x-axis and their **estimated age** (before the present time, BCE) on the y-axis.

(2) **Dotted** (as opposed to solid) boxes indicate multiple languages.

(3) **Circles** indicate languages of another family or group having significant influence on the language shown.

(4) For large language families, such as the Indo-European or Sino-Tibetan, a **"top-level"**, i.e. **"tree-trunk"** level diagram, without a y-axis, may be presented first.

Chapter 4: The World's Major Language Families- A Primer

(Fig. 4-2, cont.)

LANGUAGE FAMILY TREE PRESENTATION
Format and legend

FIRST ("TREE-TRUNK") LEVEL
(Branches only given, no time distinction, *NO Y-AXIS*)

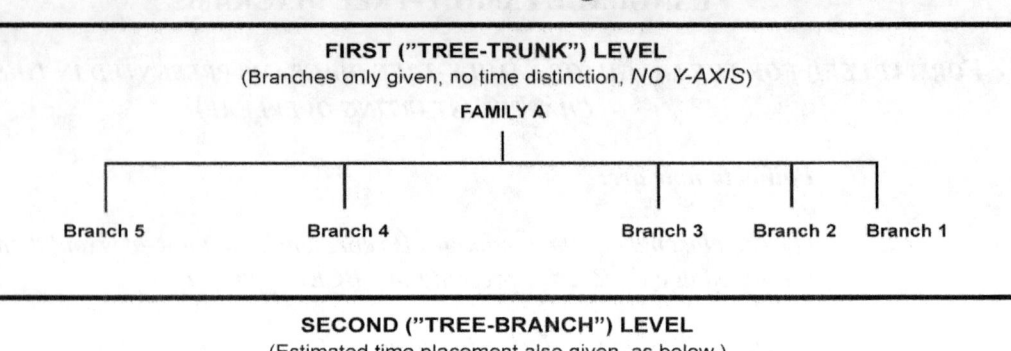

SECOND ("TREE-BRANCH") LEVEL
(Estimated time placement also given, as below.)

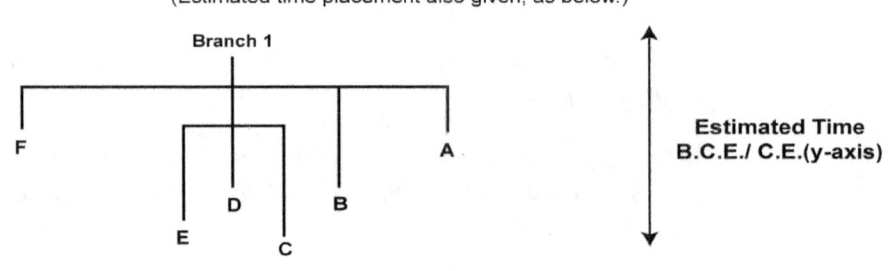

THIRD LEVEL

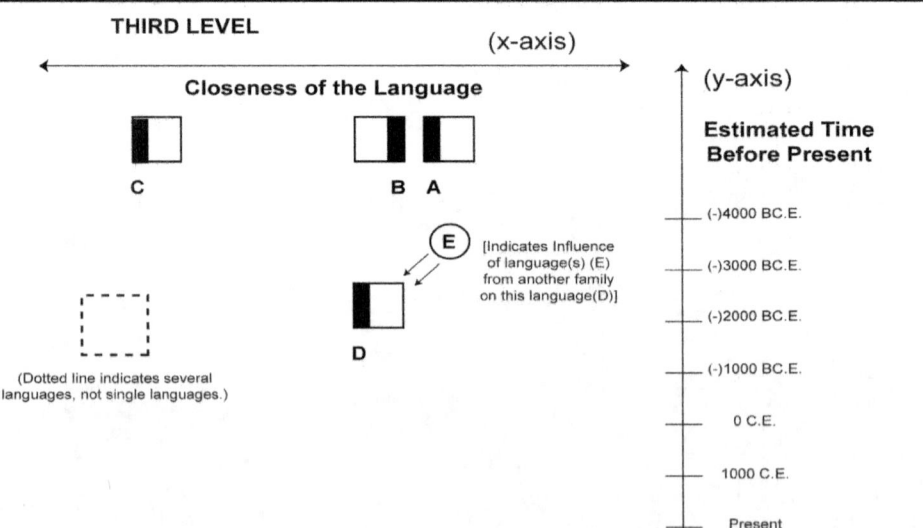

Chapter 4: The World's Major Language Families- A Primer

Fig. 4-3 *(starting overleaf, following pages)*:

LANGUAGE FAMILY-TREES OF THE SEVEN LARGEST LANGUAGE FAMILIES ONLY

In terms of estimated number of speakers, *2005.* Presented in order of decreasing number of speakers. See **Table 4-2, PART A**, above for list of these language families. Format used is described in the previous Figure. It is to be noted that *no temporal relationship is indicated by this diagram.*

Chapter 4: The World's Major Language Families- A Primer

(Fig. 4-3, cont.)

INDO-EUROPEAN, FIRST (TREE-TRUNK) LEVEL LF-2

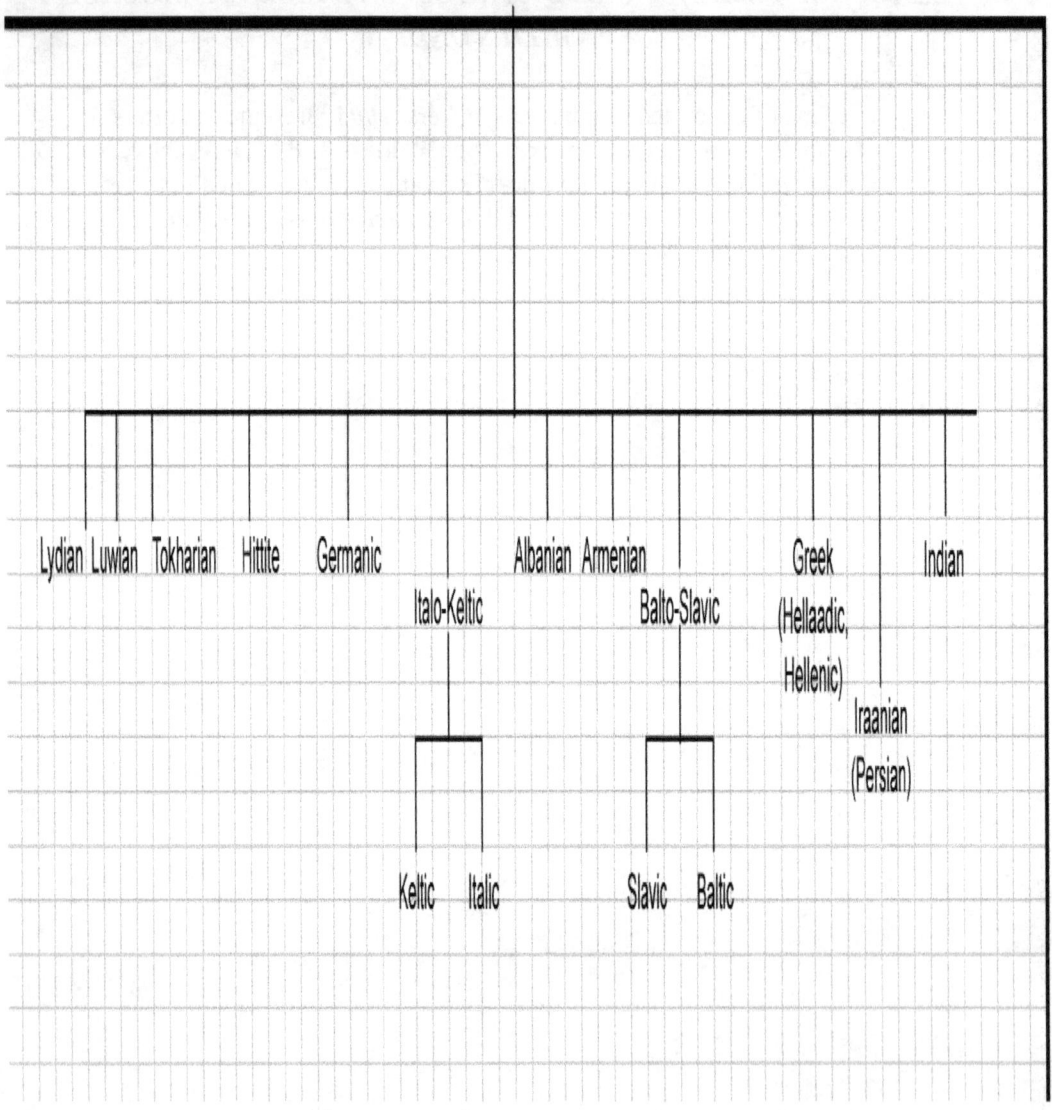

Chapter 4: The World's Major Language Families- A Primer

(Fig. 4-3, cont.): INDO-EUROPEAN, cont.: Indian ("Indic")

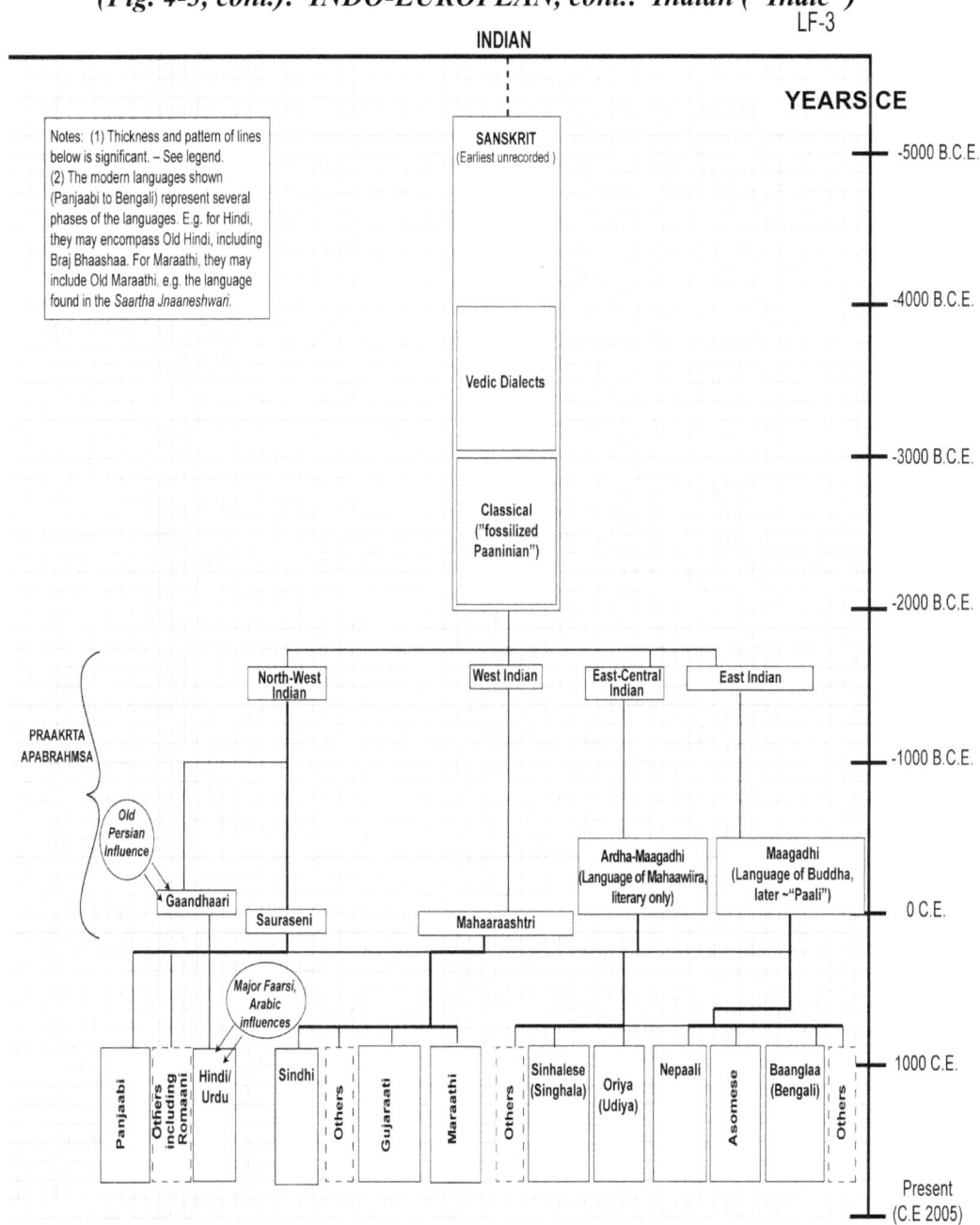

Chapter 4: The World's Major Language Families- A Primer

132

(Fig. 4-3, cont.): INDO-EUROPEAN, cont.: Iranian (Persian)
IRAANIAN (Persian)   LF-4

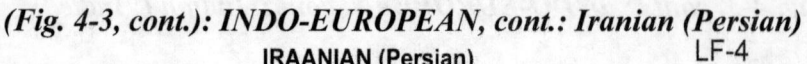

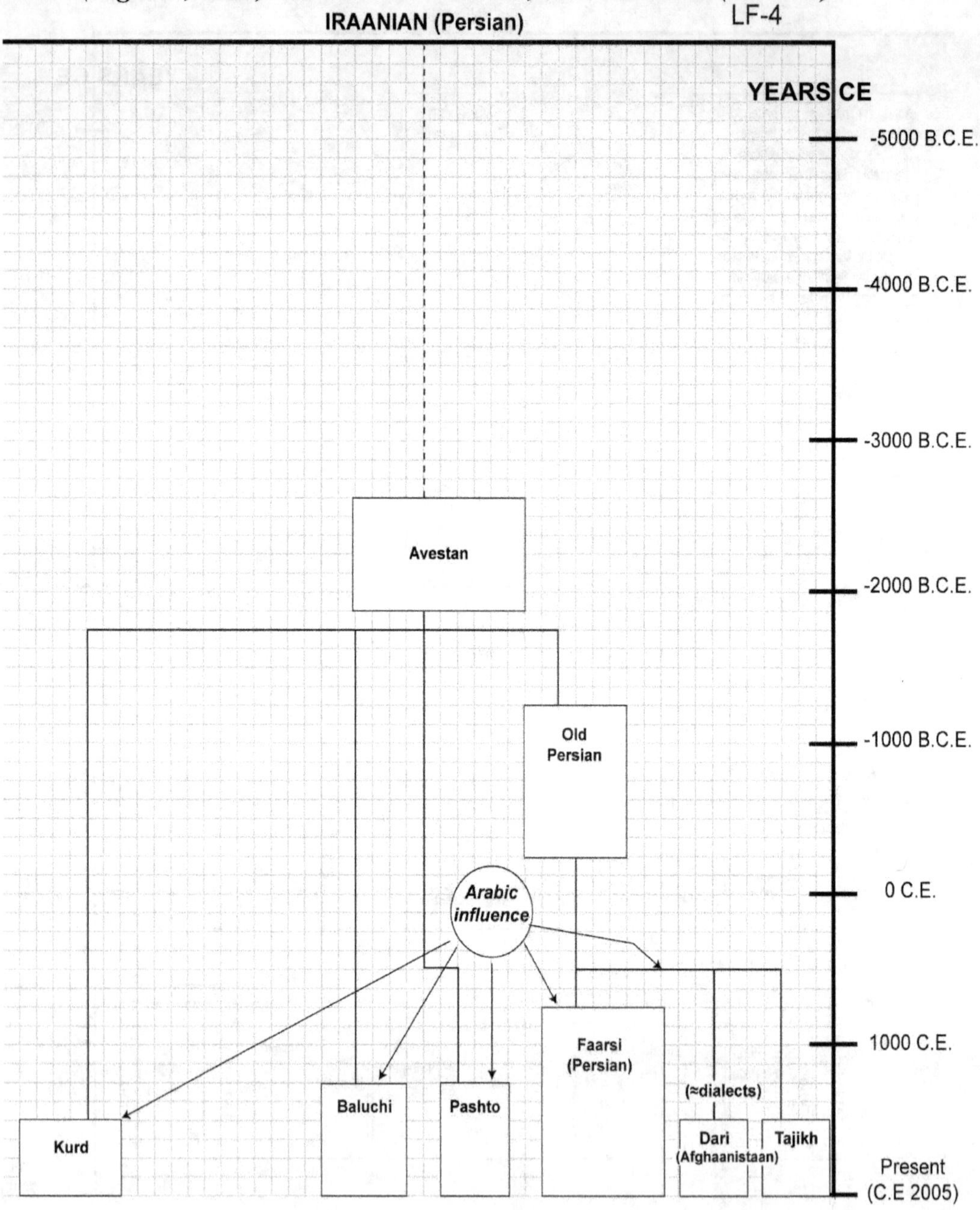

Chapter 4: The World's Major Language Families- A Primer

(Fig. 4-3, cont.): **INDO-EUROPEAN,** *cont.: Greek (Hellenic, Helladic)*

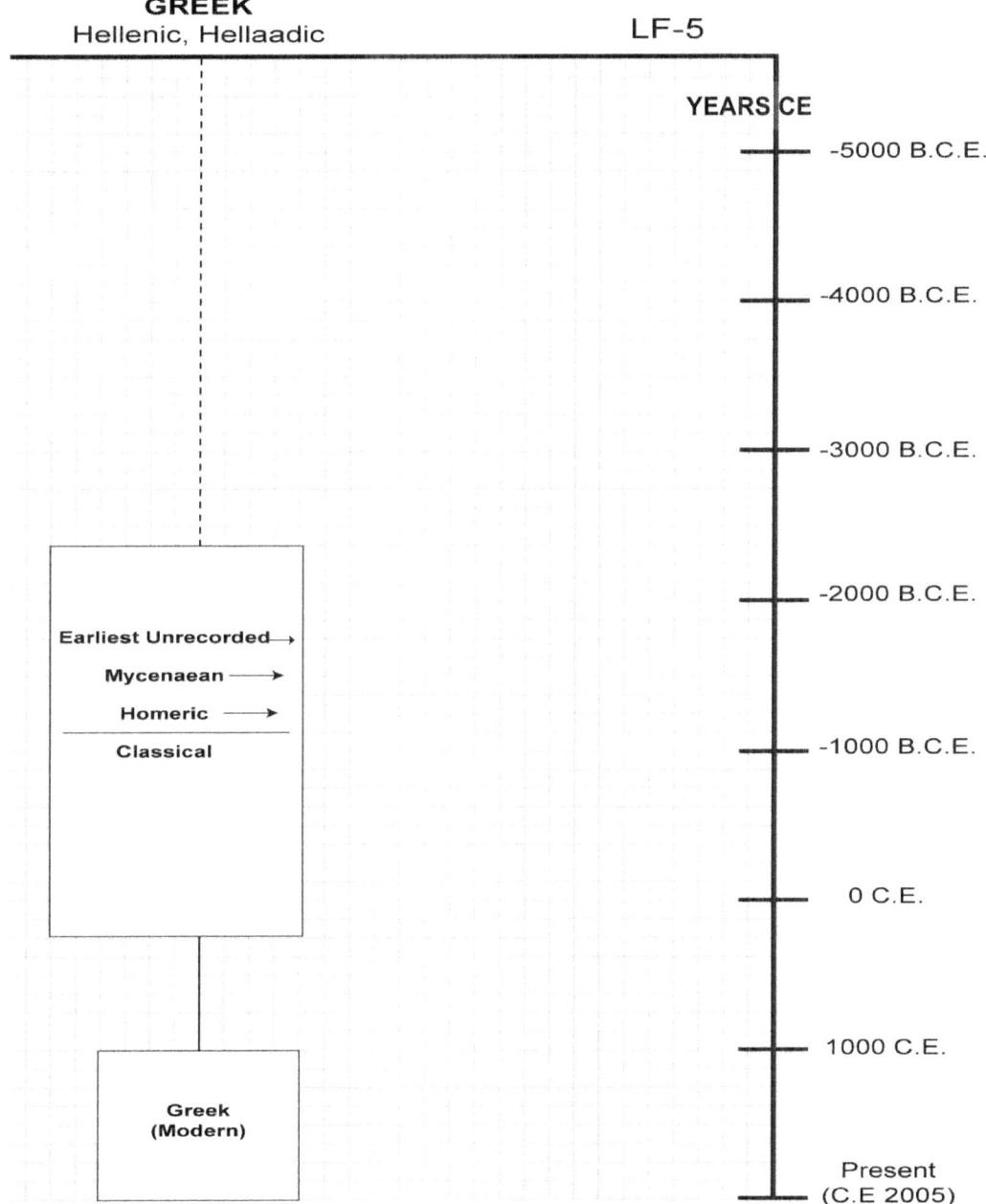

Chapter 4: The World's Major Language Families- A Primer

(Fig. 4-3, cont.): INDO-EUROPEAN, cont.: Balto-Slavic

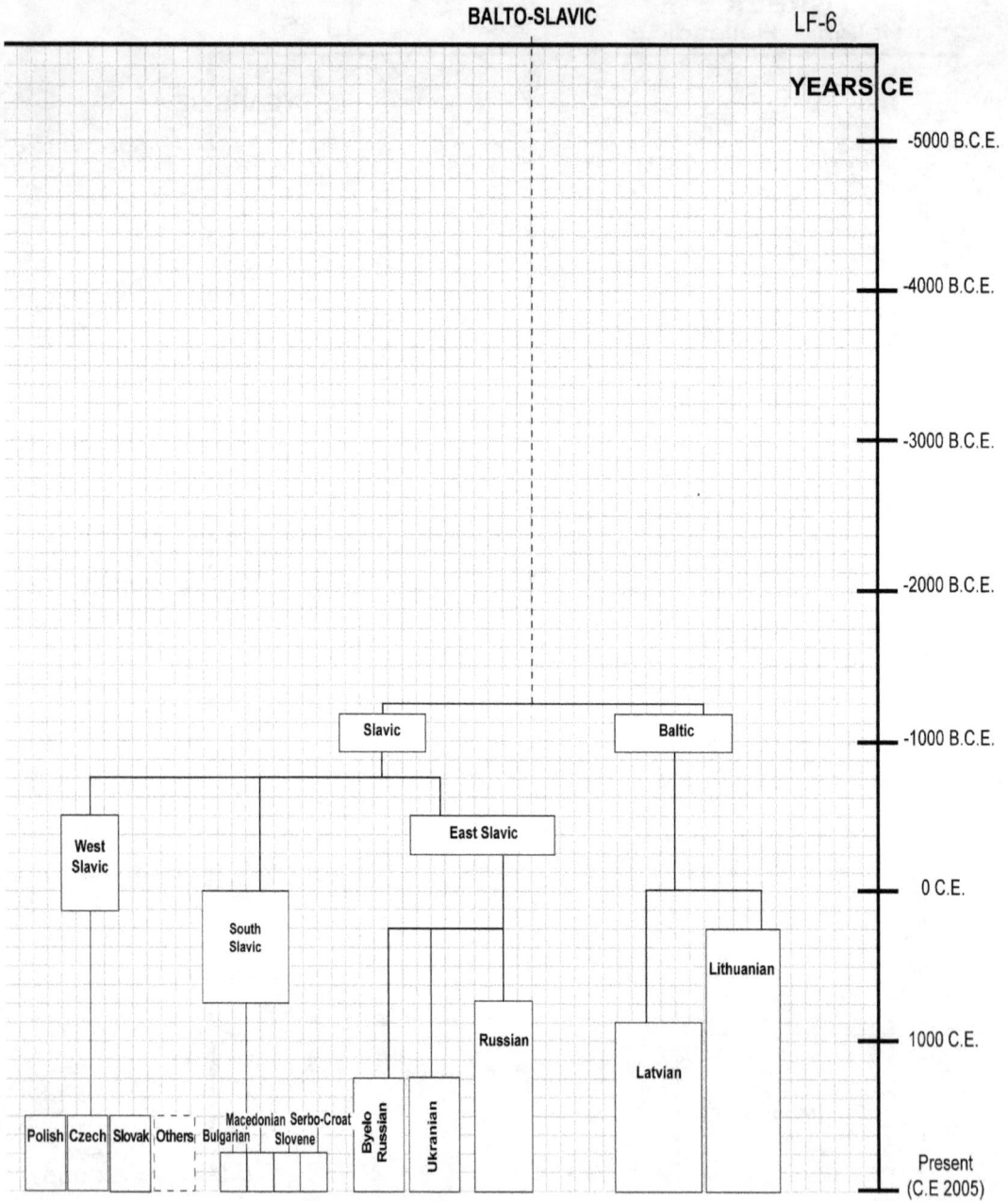

Chapter 4: The World's Major Language Families- A Primer

(Fig. 4-3, cont.): INDO-EUROPEAN, cont.: Keltic

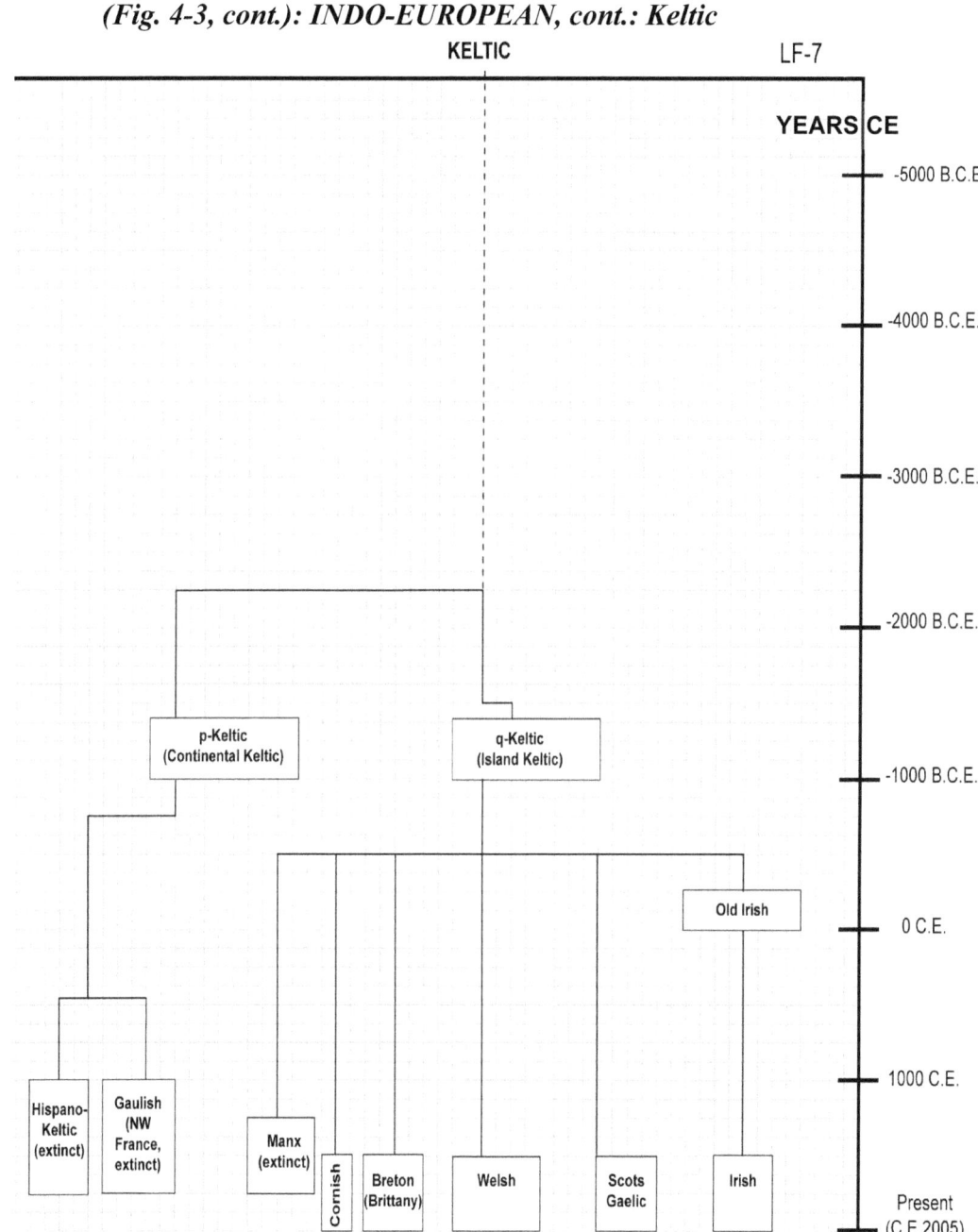

Chapter 4: The World's Major Language Families- A Primer

(Fig. 4-3, cont.): INDO-EUROPEAN, cont.: Italic (Romance)

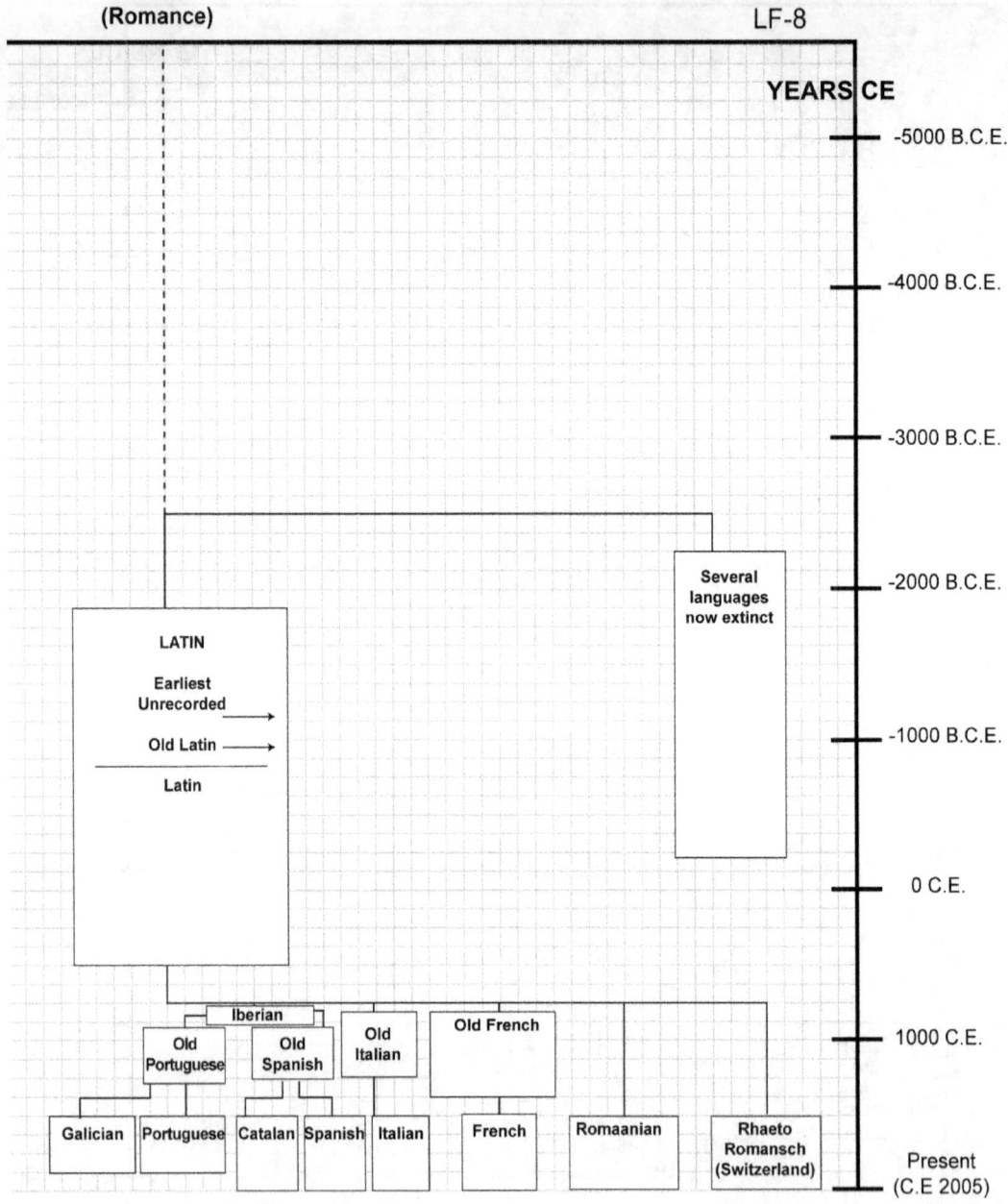

Chapter 4: The World's Major Language Families- A Primer

137

(Fig. 4-3, cont.): INDO-EUROPEAN, cont.: Germanic

GERMANIC   LF-9

YEARS CE

- −5000 B.C.E.
- −4000 B.C.E.
- −3000 B.C.E.
- −2000 B.C.E.
- −1000 B.C.E.
- 0 C.E.
- 1000 C.E.
- Present (C.E 2005)

East Germanic → Gothic (Extinct)

West Germanic → Old High German → German; Dutch
West Germanic → Anglo Saxon (Old English) → Middle English → English (← French, Latin, Classical Greek)

North Germanic → Danish, Norwegian, Swedish; Faroese; Icelandic

Chapter 4: The World's Major Language Families- A Primer

138

(Fig. 4-3, cont.): SINO-TIBETAN: Top Level

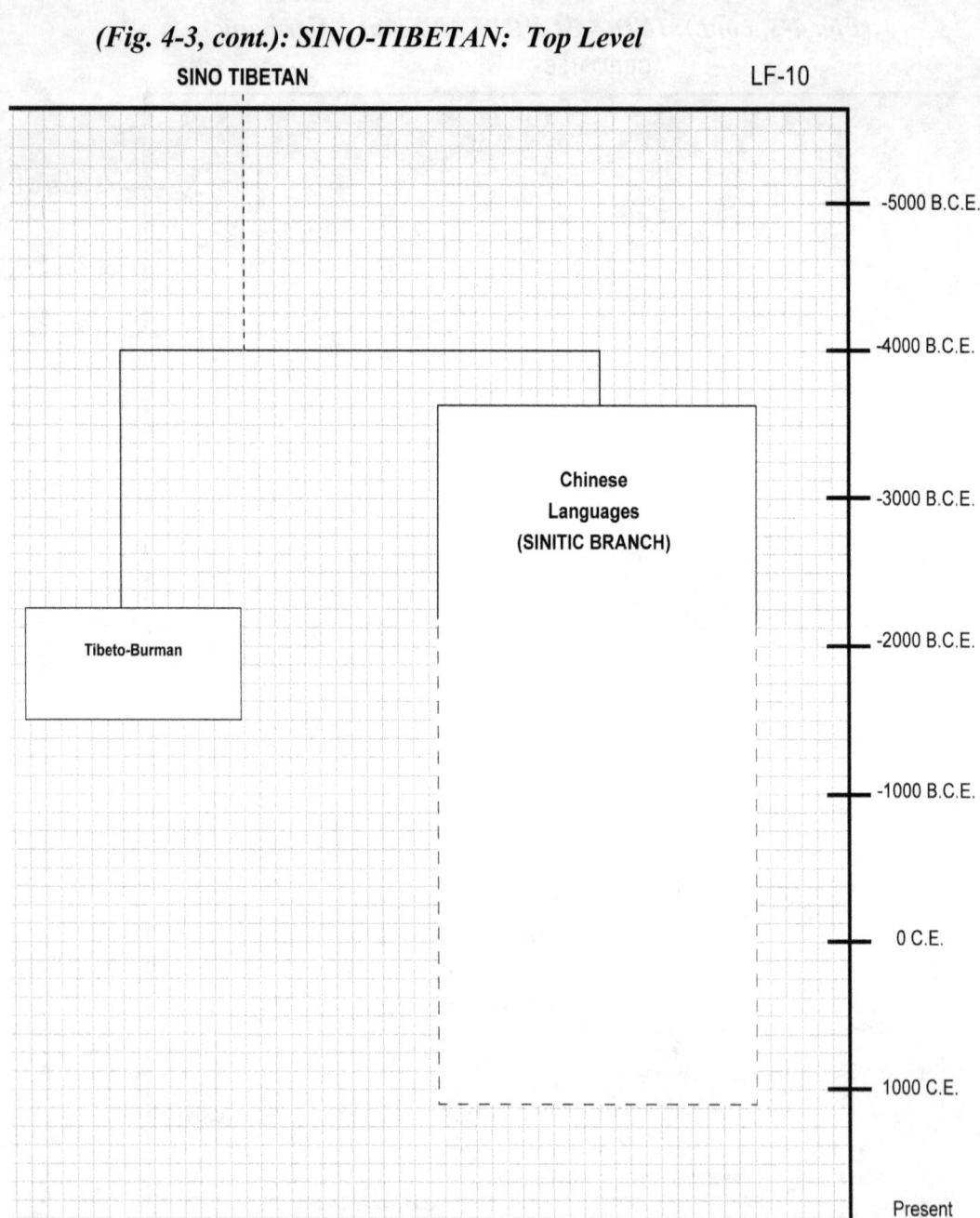

Chapter 4: The World's Major Language Families- A Primer

(Fig. 4-3, cont.): SINO-TIBETAN, cont.: Tibeto-Burman Branch

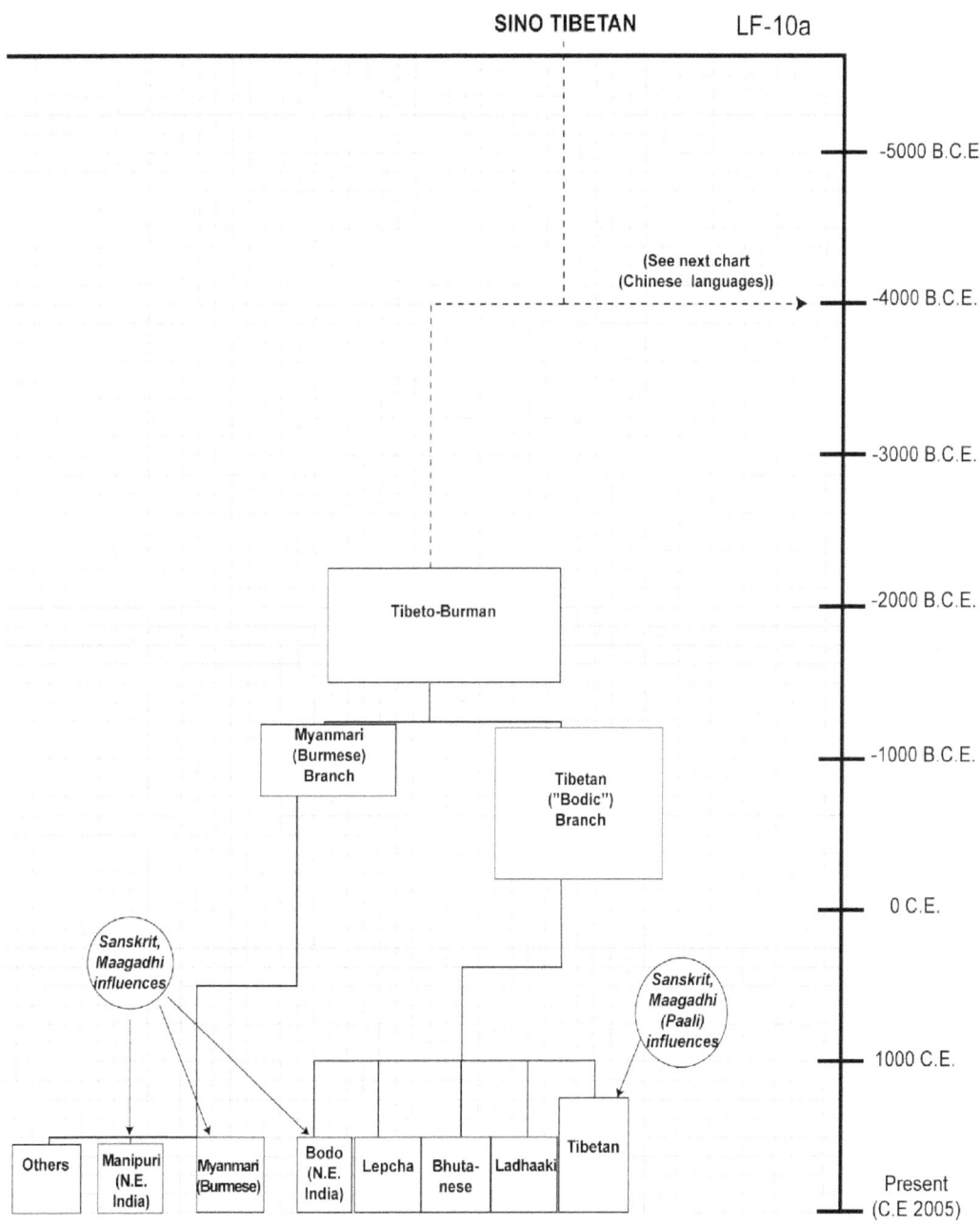

Chapter 4: The World's Major Language Families- A Primer

(Fig. 4-3, cont.): SINO-TIBETAN, cont.: Chinese (Sinitic) Branch

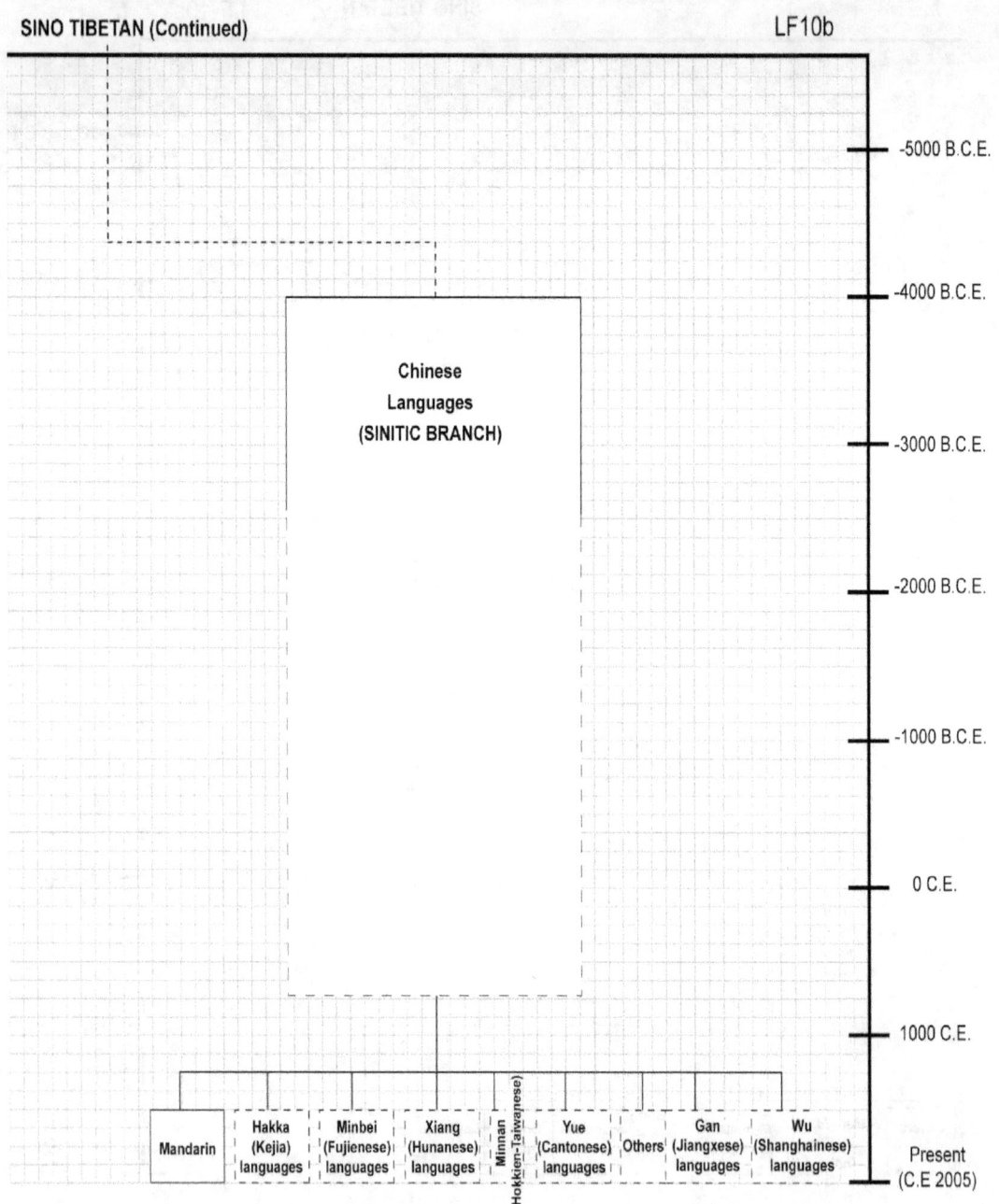

Chapter 4: The World's Major Language Families- A Primer

(Fig. 4-3, cont.): NIGER-CONGO (formerly "BANTU"):

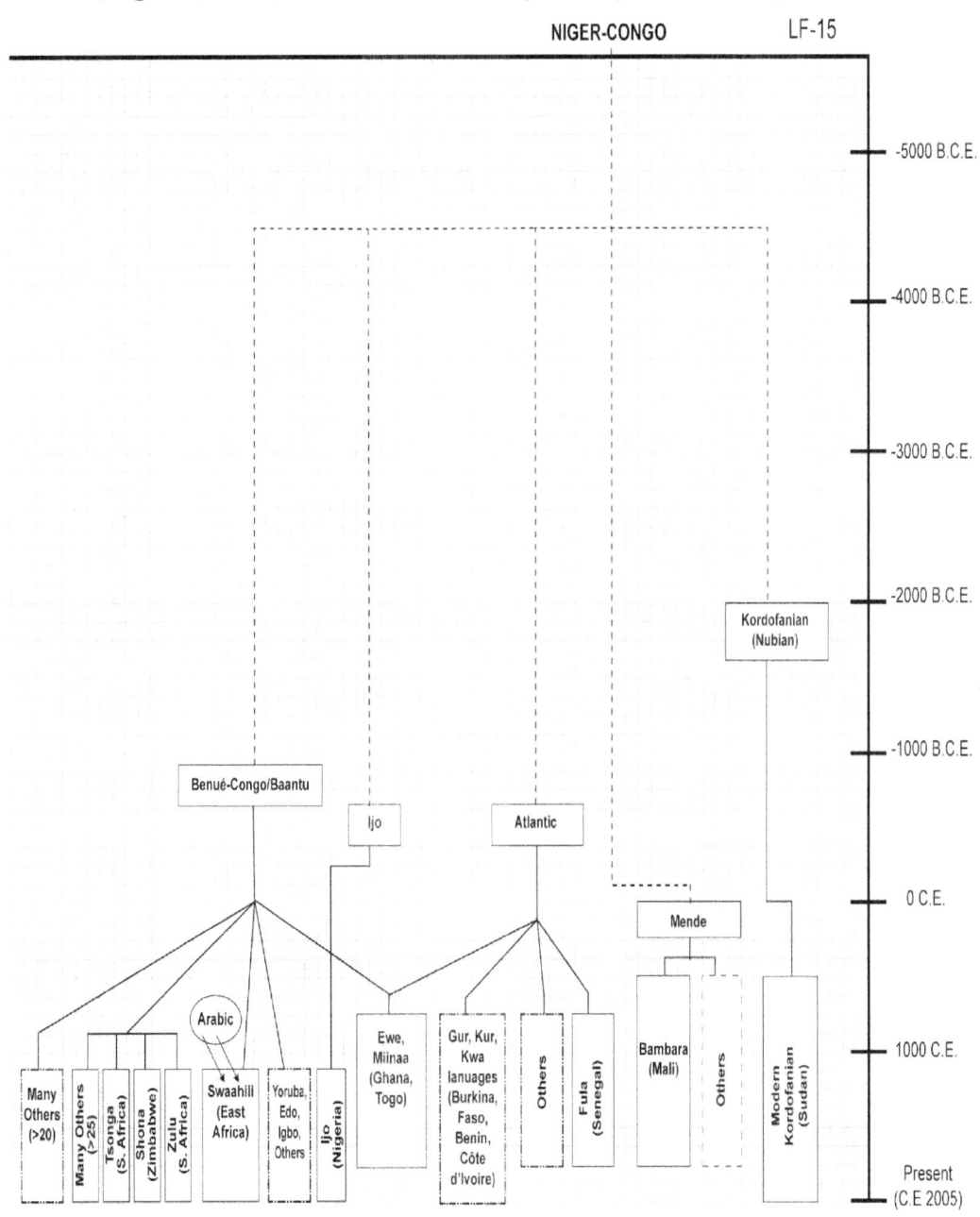

Chapter 4: The World's Major Language Families- A Primer

(Fig. 4-3, cont.): AFRO-ASIATIC (formerly HAMITO-SEMITIC)

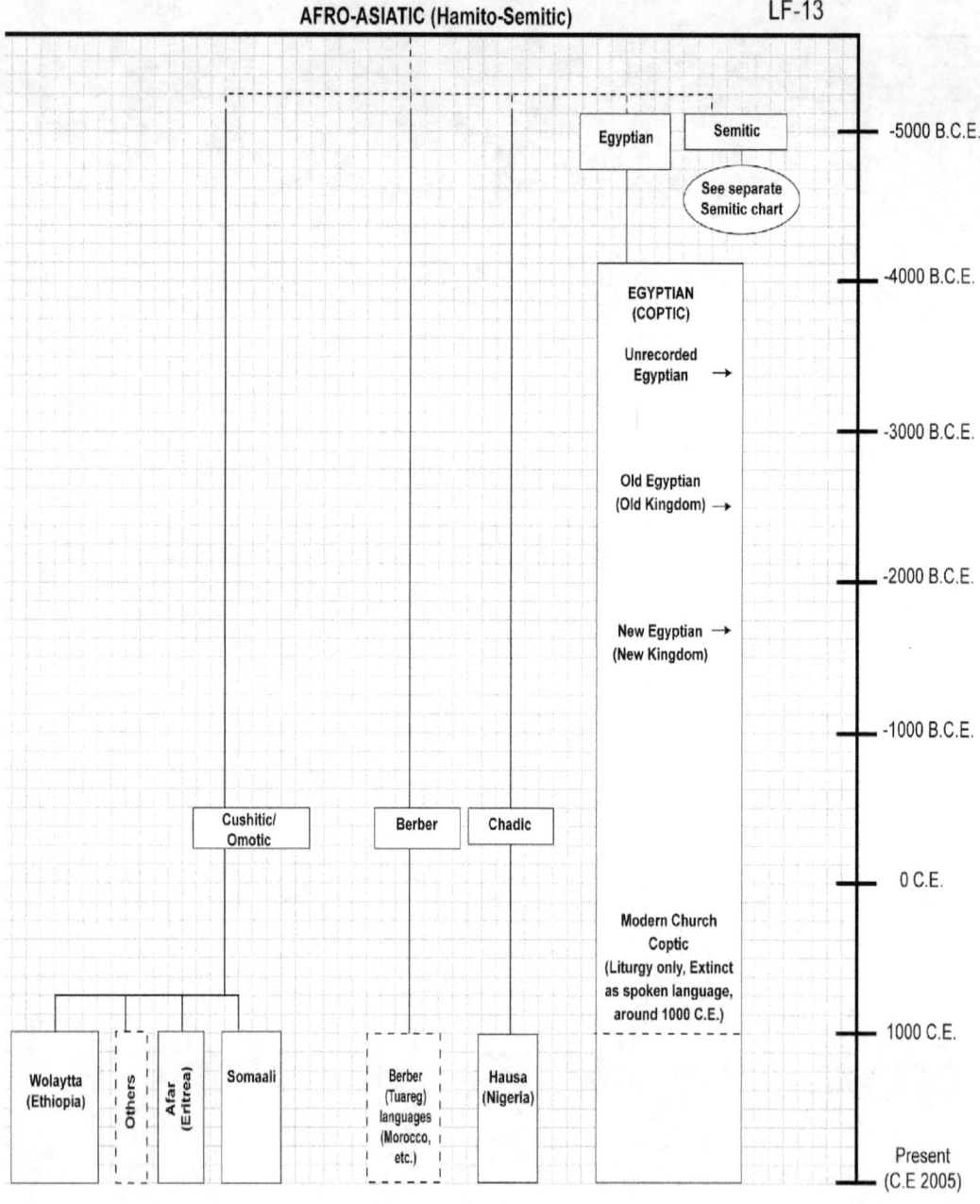

Chapter 4: The World's Major Language Families- A Primer

143

(Fig. 4-3, cont.): AFRO-ASIATIC (HAMITO-SEMITIC) cont.: Semitic Branch

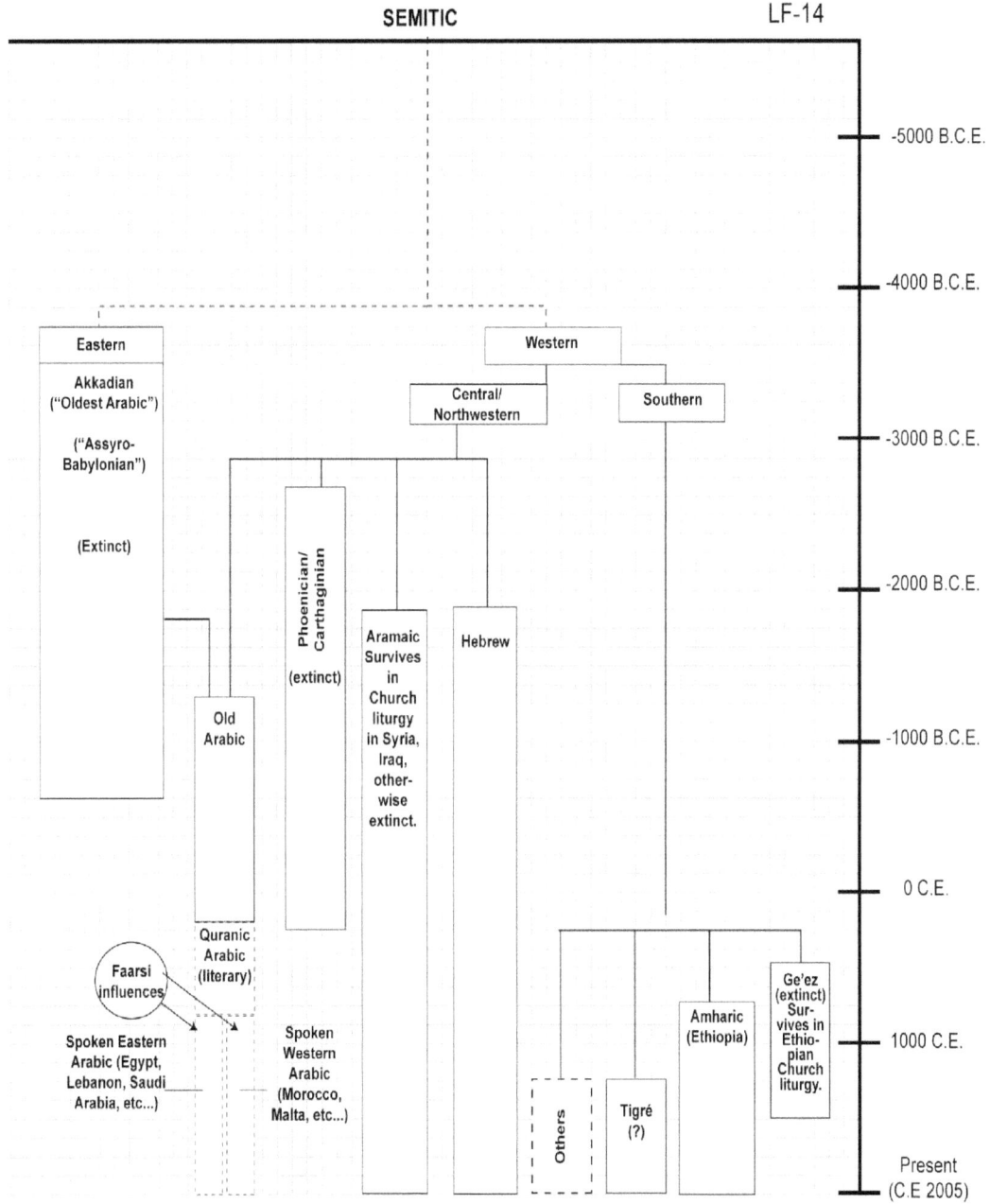

Chapter 4: The World's Major Language Families- A Primer

(Fig. 4-3, cont.): AUSTRONESIAN (formerly MALAYO-POLYNESIAN)

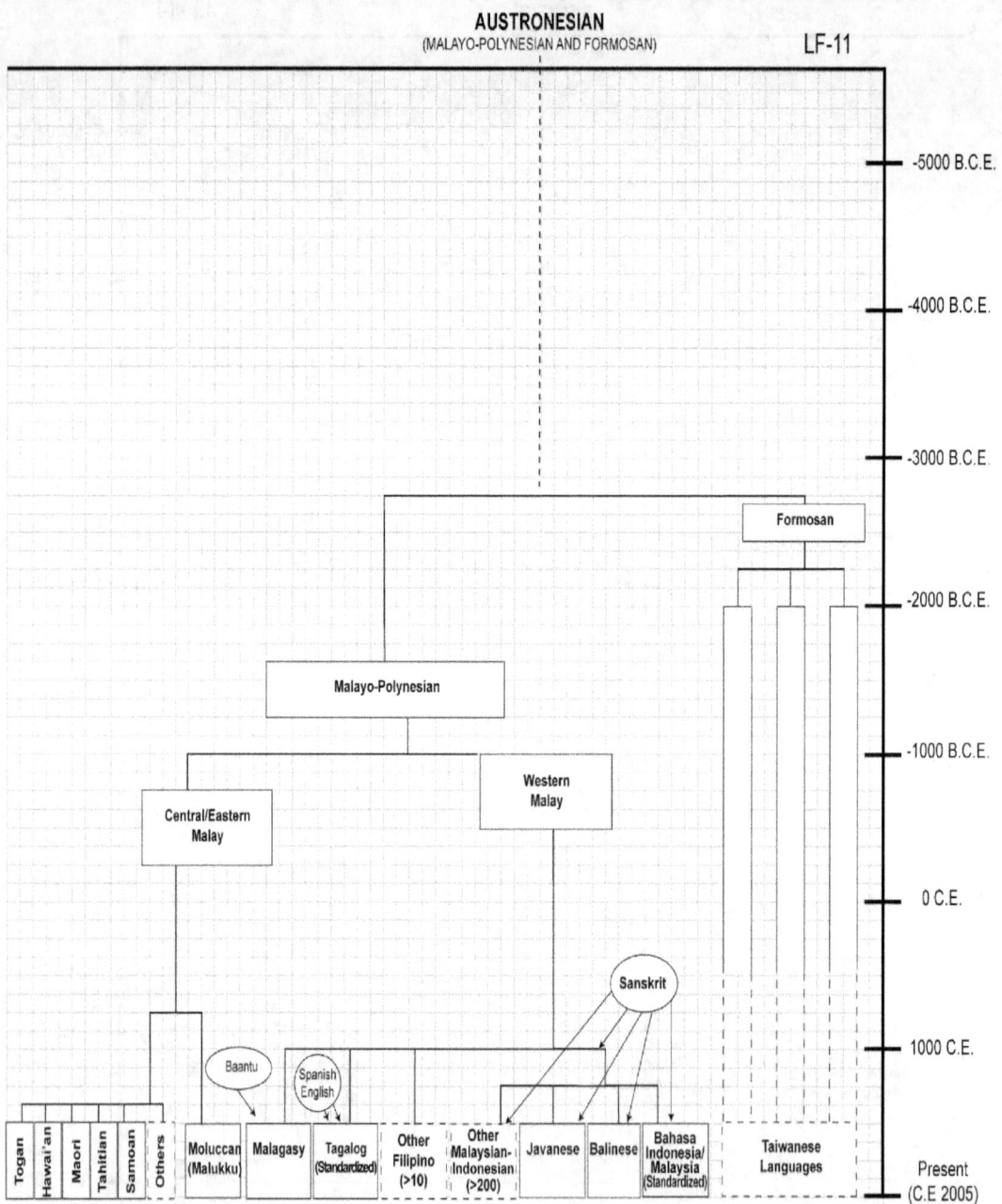

Chapter 4: The World's Major Language Families- A Primer

145

(Fig. 4-3, cont.): ALTAIC AND JAPANESE

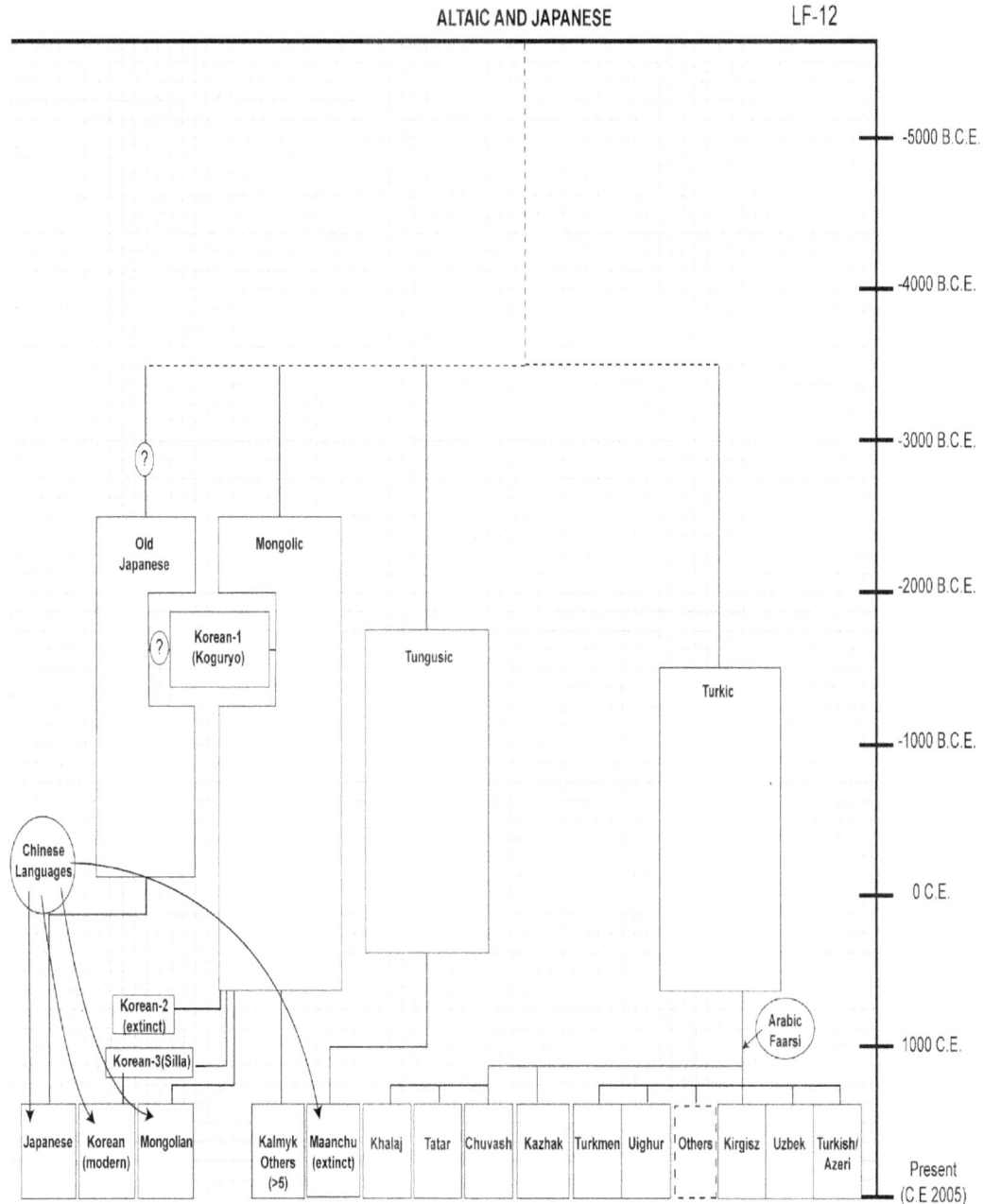

Chapter 4: The World's Major Language Families- A Primer

(Fig. 4-3, cont.): DRAVIDIAN (also called "ELAMO-DRAVIDIAN")

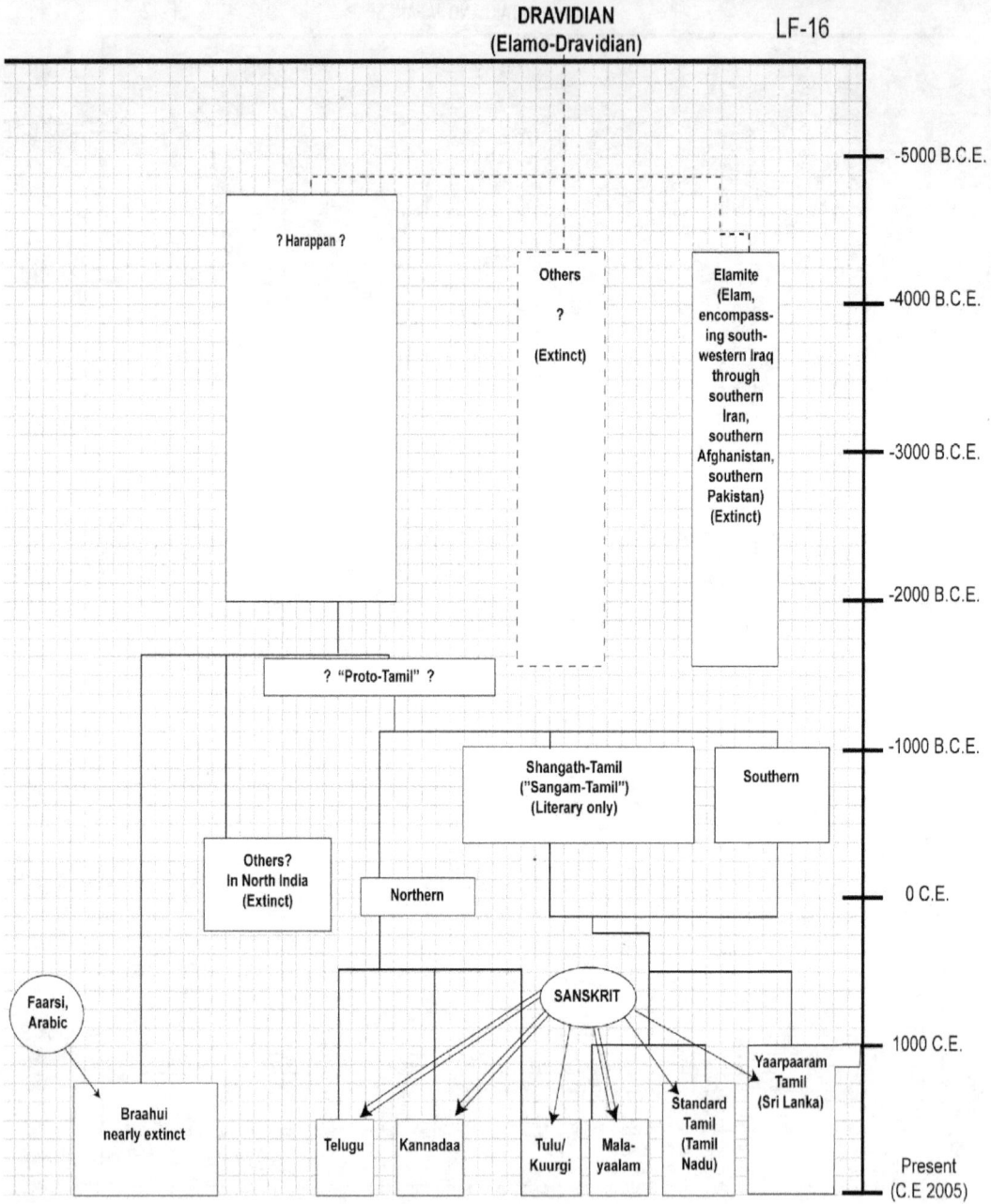

4.3 LANGUAGE vs. DIALECT: A MORE EXACT DEFINITION

Before presenting the language families, we need to briefly revisit an important question: What, in the broadest sense, distinguishes a *language* from a *dialect*?

Linguists use some specific tests too detailed for a primer such as this to determine this [LN-3 to LN-30, LN-34 to LN-41]. In spite of this, however, in many cases they still do not agree on whether a particular tongue is truly a language or just a dialect! Many linguists may then jokingly revert to an older, facetious definition of a language: *"A language is a dialect which has its own army and navy"* !

For our purposes in this chapter, however, we outline the following much more ordinary but nevertheless very comprehensive and broad rule:

> When two tongues are **both mutually unintelligible** (i.e. in *both directions*) *in a practical fashion* we can say with fair confidence that they are **distinct languages** as opposed to dialects.

...(4.1)

The key words in our rule above are *"both"* and *"in a practical fashion"*, as we now elaborate below.

Turning first to the word *"both"*, we give, as an example of its significance, the following examples: The most accented of Québécois French is, for practical purposes, unintelligible to a Parisian ("it sounds like Italian" a Parisian might say). *However, the situation is not true vice versa*, i.e. the Parisian's French is perfectly intelligible to a rural Québécois. Thus, we say that Québécois and Parisian French are dialects, not distinct languages; because the unintelligibility goes *only in one direction*.

Turning now to another example, the case is very similar for a speaker of the standard Hindi/Urdu, *Khari Boli* ("standing speech", i.e. standard pronunciation) from Delhi vis-à-vis a villager, from rural Haryaanaa (Haryana) province just outside Delhi. The

Chapter 4: The World's Major Language Families- A Primer

Haryaanvi's language has a few different words, but for the most part it is Hindi and he can understand someone from Delhi well, although the Delhiite may find it difficult to understand the Haryaanvi's speech. Haryaanvi and Delhi Hindi can thus still be considered dialects. Once again, the *unintelligibility goes only in one direction*.

And as a third example, all of us in the English-speaking world have occasionally run into a native of the nether regions of England whom we could not understand at all, but that person was of course speaking English and could understand London RP (Received Pronunciation)-English perfectly well! His is again just an English dialect, although perhaps some words are used differently and many words are pronounced differently.

Thus, the *Québécois French, Haryaanvi Hindi and nether-regions-English, of the three examples above, are all mere dialects*, not distinct languages: The unintelligibility goes only in one direction, not both ways.

When however we come to Portuguese vs. Spanish, to cite an example of what are considered distinct languages, not dialects, we encounter a distinctly different, but still a bit nebulous, situation: The Portuguese speaker never before exposed to Spanish may say he/she can follow *a good deal* of what a Spanish speaker is saying. On the other side, however, the Spanish speaker most likely cannot follow the Portuguese's speech at all. The key here then lies in the second set of words in our definition above, *"in a practical fashion"*. Although the Portuguese speaker can follow *some (a very small part)* of what the Spanish speaker is saying (much like a Hindi speaker can follow some Panjaabi or an Italian speaker can follow some Spanish or a Dutch speaker can follow some German), *for practical purposes* the Portuguese speaker cannot carry on a *full conversation* with the Spanish speaker. We thus have two distinct languages rather than dialects.

As a counter-example to Portuguese/Spanish, the Azeri speaker can follow Turkish well, and the Turkish speaker can follow Azeri equally well, so we say that Azeri (the language of Azerbaijan) is merely a dialect of Turkish (or perhaps we can say that Turkish is a dialect of Azeri!). Indeed, most Turks and Russians do not even consider Azeri a separate language, just calling it Turkish.

One of the key points to note with respect to the expression *"in a practical fashion"* is the following: If the person initially having trouble understanding the speech of the dialect expends some, even minimal, effort to listen very carefully, he/she will immediately start to comprehend the dialect: Thus, the standard-Hindi speaker will immediately notice that just a few words in the Haryaanvi's speech differ, e.g. *aggon, pachchhon* for standard-Hindi *aage, piichhe* ("ahead, behind"). Similarly, the Parisian will notice that the Québécois *quarent* ("forty") that he thought sounded so Italian is actually just the French pronounced with the original "rolled *r*", a straight [aa], and a diphthongized *"...ent"*, corresponding to original Northwestern French from about the 16th century, before the phonetic shift to the "uvular French *r*" occurred; most French immigrants to Quebec came from this region. And to go to our third example, with a little straining of the ear, the posh Londoner can easily understand the speech of the outlander Englishman. Thus, ***practically speaking,*** in each of the above three examples, the standard-pronunciation speaker can understand the dialect-speaker after just a few hours of good effort. These are then true dialects. That is however not the case with the Portuguese/Spanish example above: The Portuguese speaker will need many days of proper instruction before he/she can start to carry out a full conversation in Spanish (although it would certainly be much easier for him/her than, say, for a German). Thus, Portuguese and Spanish are distinct languages.

The reader will appreciate that, not withstanding our discussion above, as in all matters of human artifice such as language, there still remain decidedly grey areas. For example, in the year 2004, in an age when television and the Internet have spread standard pronunciations and transcriptions of a language far and wide, this author has in travels just 120 km north of aristocratic Vienna encountered German dialects which use markedly different words not resembling anything in modern German. They use, for instance, *ka-sii* for non-subjunctive "I am" as also "I was". This is perhaps a corruption (strictly speaking in linguistic parlance, metathesis) of a subjunctive form, *Ich sei*, or perhaps an archaic Gothic form. But this is still very different from the standard Viennese *Ich bin* or *Ich war*. When the natives in this region do not wish visiting Viennese to understand them, they can carry out entire conversations in their "dialect". And if written in Roman transcription, this "dialect" would not resemble German in any way! Were it not for communication with the larger German-speaking world via radio, newspapers, TV, the Internet, etc., the tongue of these outland Austrians would quickly evolve into a distinct language.

4.4 THE INDO-EUROPEAN (INDO-GERMANIC) FAMILY

4.4.1 EXTENT AND NUMBER OF SPEAKERS

The geographic extent of this family today is the widest among the world's language families [LAs-2, LN-2 to LN-11]. It ranges from North America and Europe to easternmost Siberia to Australia and New Zealand. Natively, this group is today concentrated in the non-southern regions of the Indian subcontinent (except for one exception, Sinhalese of Sri Lanka, which is in a southern region), in Europe, and in parts of the Near and Middle East (Iran and the Kurdish regions of Turkey, Iraq, Iran and Syria). However, through migration, the group has been spread to North and South America, Australia and South Africa. The limited Indian diaspora have preserved the languages of this family within their own communities in some parts of the world, e.g. East Africa, but in others, e.g. the Caribbean, Fiji, Seychelles, and the United Kingdom, they have mostly adopted the language of their country of residence.

We have given an estimate of more than 3.0 billion speakers for this family (as of **2005**), using the methods of estimation as defined earlier in this chapter. This estimate can be briefly broken down as in the following bullets (in decreasing numerical order, all figures for 2005). The figures are also conveniently summarized in the **Table** further below.

- ❖ ***Romance languages:*** Speakers of *Romance* languages in North, Central and South America and the Caribbean (including Quebec province in Canada) can be estimated at 548 m. Speakers of *Romance* languages in Europe can be estimated at 202 m. The total for *Romance* languages is thus **750 m**.

- ❖ ***Hindi/Urdu:*** We can similarly estimate *Hindi/Urdu* speakers as follows (figures based on 2001 census): (1) Pakistan, est. 2/3 of the population, though for many as a second language: 107 m. (2) First or major language in Indian states of Bihar, Chattisgarh, Delhi, Haryana, Himachal Pradesh, Jharkhand, Madhya Pradesh, Rajasthan, Uttaranchal (Uttarkhand), Uttar Pradesh: 458 m. (3) Second language in Indian states of Gujarat, Jammu & Kashmir, Maharashtra, Punjab, 1/3 of total population: 61 m. (4) Nepal, second language, 1/3 of total population: 9 m. Total Hindi/Urdu est. **635 m**.

- ❖ ***English:*** We can estimate *English* speakers as follows: US/Canada 335 m;

Chapter 4: The World's Major Language Families- A Primer

151

Australia/New Zealand 25 m; U.K/Ireland 65 m; S. Africa est. 10 m. Caribbean/other, 5 m. Indian subcontinent est. 50 m. Miscellaneous (e.g. Liberia) 10 m. Total English est. **500 m**.

❖ ***Other Indo-European languages, outside India:*** Speakers of *other Indo-European languages* not in the Indian subcontinent (such as Russian and Faarsi) can be estimated at **602 m**.

❖ ***Other Indo-European languages, within India:*** Speakers of other Indo-European languages in India can be estimated at 253 m. The remaining (non-Hindi/Urdu) speakers in Nepal can be estimated at 18 m and in Pakistan at 54 m. This yields a subtotal of other Indo-European languages in the Indian subcontinent of about **325 m**.

❖ ***Baanglaa (Bengali):*** Speakers of *Baanglaa (Bengali)* in Bangladesh can be estimated at 160 m and in West Bengal state in India at 80 m, for a total of **240 m**.

❖ ***TOTALS:*** The above totals add up to **3,052 m** for the estimated total number of speakers of Indo-European languages for the year 2005.

Table 4-3: Summary breakdown of *estimated* **number of speakers**, presented for the *Indo-European family* only. Estimated figures for *2005*. The figures do *not* include those speakers using a language from another family as a secondary language, e.g. a Basque speaking fluent Spanish at work. However, it *does* include speakers of dialects who use the standard language at least 50% of the time. The totals add up to 3,052 m. [LAs-2, LN-2 to LN-11].

LANGUAGE OR GROUP	ESTIMATED NUMBER (2005)
Hindi/Urdu	635 m
Other I-E languages [e.g. Russian, Faarsi, German, not in Indian subcontinent; includes, e.g., South African Dutch (Afrikaans)]	602 m
Romance, all regions *except* Europe (i.e. North, Central, South America, Caribbean)	548 m
English	500 m
Other I-E languages, Indian subcontinent	325 m
Baanglaa (Bengali)	240 m
Romance, Europe	202 m
TOTAL	3,052 m

4.4.2 INDIAN ("INDIC") BRANCH

The *Indian* sub-branch is given the curious name *"Indic"* in current Western linguistic jargon (perhaps because *Indian* may have originally had Native American connotations). It is also sometimes called *Indo-Aryan* in the modern Indian linguistics jargon. We prefer to stay with the term *Indian*. The Indian sub-branch is prevalent mainly in the *non*-Southern regions of India.

In approximate decreasing order of number of speakers, the *major* modern languages in this group are: *Hindi/Urdu, Baanglaa (Bengali), Maraathi, Panjaabi, Gujarati, Udiya (Oriya), Sindhi, Nepali, Assamese, Sinhalese, Kashmiri, Bhojpuri, Pahaadi* ("mountain language", also called *Kumaoni* or *Almori),* and several other modern Indian and South Asian languages. These languages also mostly correspond to modern provinces (states) of South Asia, e.g. Gujarati is spoken mainly in the state of Gujarat, Panjaabi in Punjab (both Indian and Pakistani Punjab), Marathi in Maharashtra, Sindhi in Sindh, etc. Of the modern Indo-European languages of India, it is felt by many scholars [LAi-45, LAi-46] that Maraathi is the closest in form and word construction to Sanskrit.

Readers will notice that in our language tree figures above, we have given the Sanskrit language much greater antiquity than is conventionally given in Western linguistic circles. The archaicness of Sanskrit as compared to all other Indo-European languages, and the reasons for assigning it such antiquity, are discussed in some detail in a chapter, on the Indian phonological system, in the first *NAVLIPI* volume. That chapter also gives, among other things, detailed comparative paradigms of verb conjugation and pronoun declension, which serve to illustrate the relative antiquity of Sanskrit as compared to all other Indo-European languages. We touch upon this subject only briefly here.

Very recent archaeological findings [HIi-1] appear to support a much greater antiquity for the Harappan ("Indus Valley", presumably Dravidian) civilization. They also appear to support some extraordinary features, e.g.: **(1)** Urbanization starting as early as 7000 BCE (Mehrgarh, Baluchistan [HIi-1]). **(2)** A much earlier provenance of Aaryans (Aryans) into India [HIi-11 to HIi-20]. **(3)** And a possible combined Aaryan/Dravidian character to the Harappan civilization, as evidenced by Harappan writing being found in places known in Indian tradition to be "Aaryan" such as Krishna's Dwaarakaa city in Gujarat; these have been radiocarbon dated to ca. 1900 BCE [HIi-10]. These factors in turn support a much greater antiquity for Sanskrit, more in line with what is evident from linguistic comparisons, e.g. of Sanskrit with the oldest of the other Indo-European languages such as Mycenaean Greek and Hittite, and with what Indians have contended all along. It is of course very different from the 1500 BCE date unfortunately parroted just about everywhere until very recently, a date based on a "back-of-the-envelope" calculation by F. Max Müller; this calculation which has no archeological, linguistic or any other evidentiary basis. The archaicness as well as the near parent-like nature of Sanskrit in the overall Indo-European context can be seen clearly in comparative paradigms of personal pronouns or verbs, available elsewhere. This was recognized early on by Western scholars such as Friedrich von Schlegel [IEu-13] and, to a lesser extent, William Jones [IEu-14], but has received "bad press", as it were, in more recent publications. However all these rather controversial matters are properly the subject for another book!

For reasons for not using the term "Indo-Iranian branch", see the discussion under the Iranian branch below.

Among the Indian languages, there are several sub-groupings, corresponding to the languages or groups of languages prevalent in India from about 700 BCE to about 500 CE, from which the modern languages are descended [LAi-9, LAi-50 to LAi-59]. These older languages were:

(1) *Maagadhi,* in the areas surrounding modern-day Bengal, Bihar and Nepal. The term *Maagadhi* has a broad temporal as well as geographical connotation. Temporally, it encompassed a period from about 700 BCE, through the time of Buddha and Mahaawiira (about 500 BCE), of Ashoka's inscriptions and of Vikramaaditya (ca. 100 BCE) to about 500 CE Geographically, it may have included various dialects in various regions. Buddha is said to have preached in Maagadhi. One form of Old Maagadhi has come down to us as *Paali,* the language of the Buddhist scriptures.

(2) *Ardha-Maagadhi* ("half-Maagadhi"), a literary construct of the Jain religious literature which nevertheless represents a co-mingling of Old Maagadhi and other languages a bit to the west of it. Whether it was actually a spoken language remains in question.

(3) *Mahaaraashtri*, in the areas surrounding modern-day Maharashtra, Gujarat and Sindh (present-day Pakistan).

(4) *Sauraseni*, in the areas surrounding modern-day Delhi, Haryaanaa, Punjab (Indian and Pakistani), Rajasthan, Madhya Pradesh.

(5) *Gaandhaari,* in the areas of Gandhaara (present-day Kandahar in Afghanistan) and present-day Baluchistan.

There is another intermediate "language" contemporary with the above which is frequently mentioned in Western discussions of Indian languages because it is mentioned by such eminent Indian linguists as Patanjali [LAi-8, LAi-9]. This is **Paisaachi**. In this author's opinion, this is an erroneous citation based again on a Western misunderstanding relating to the semantics of the word *Paisaachi* and its parent, *Pisaacha*. Pisaacha, which basically has the connotation "ghost" or "wild person", was a term, similar to *Raakshasa,* that was applied to any of a number of tribal peoples living in the hills or forested fringes of India. Paisaachi thus means the language of these people, a term which the mainstream Indo-European-speaking population used for languages they did not understand. It has the connotation of "gibberish" or "gobbledy-gook", what a human might, in J.R.R. Tolkien's stories, use for the language of hobbits or other nether-beings. It is thus not a term having any linguistic significance per se. It likely represented any of a number of Austro-Asiatic (Mundaa) or, less likely, Dravidian languages of India. It is thus not part of our list above.

According to Indian tradition, the above-mentioned languages were given the collective appellation **Praakrt**. The later phases of these languages were also sometimes given the collective appellation **Apabrahmsa** by strict Sanskrit grammarians. This is a derogatory appellation, roughly translated as "corruption", simply used to distinguish the existing speech of the common masses from the refined Sanskrit of the literature. It is thus a very lose term that does not denote any specific language. Sometimes, Apabrahmsa and Praakrt may be used synonymously. Once again, the connotation of *Apabrahmsa* seems to have been misunderstood by modern linguists.

The languages descended from Maagadhi, which we might give the appellation *"East Indian"*, include, for example, Baanglaa (Bengali), Nepaali and Assamese. The languages descended from Mahaaraashtri, which we might give the appellation *"West Indian"*, include, for example, Maraathi, Gujaraati and Sindhi. The languages descended from the components of Ardhamaagadhi, which we might give the appellation *"East-Central Indian"*, include, for example, Odiya (Oriya), Bhojpuri and Sinhalese. The languages descended from Sauraseni, which we might give the appellation *"North-West Indian"*, include, for example, Hindi/Urdu, Panjaabi and Maarwaari (which also has a blend of Mahaaraashtri).

Most of the modern Indian languages of Indo-European descent, such as Hindi/Urdu, Maraathi and Gujaraati, started taking form about 1100 - 1200 CE, i.e. rather recently. In the interim period that we have not discussed, about 500 CE to 1100 CE, there appears to have been a substantial mingling of the various Apabrahmsa.

It is worth noting that there are several modern tongues (we use "tongues" to avoid the word "languages") within the Indian family that are extremely difficult to classify as languages, as opposed to just dialects. This is even if we use the very specific rule we have tried to establish above. Falling in this category are, for instance: *Maarwaari*, a dialect (?) of Gujarati and a language of traders spoken in the border region of Gujarat and Rajasthan provinces in India, and spread eventually by these migrant Maarwaari

Chapter 4: The World's Major Language Families- A Primer

traders to regions as far away as Tamil Nadu; *Dogri*, a tongue spoken in the Jammu region of Jammu and Kashmir province, which resembles a cross between Panjaabi, Hindi and *Pahaadi*; and *Tulu* or *Kuurgi*, a dialect (?) of Kannadaa spoken in the Kuurg region of Karnataka province in South India.

It is also important to note that while the four major Dravidian languages of South India have a Dravidian base, a vast majority of their higher vocabulary in all except Tamil is derived from Sanskrit. This is much like English having a Germanic base but with the vast majority of its higher vocabulary derived from Latin and Greek. (A language of this sort is given a unique appellation, "*Angramaya*", later in this book.)

Romaani, the language of the Romaa, formerly called "Gypsies" (from a corruption of *Egyptian*), is currently spoken in various mutually intelligible dialects by about 7 million Romaa, mostly concentrated in the Balkans and southeastern Europe (Bulgaria, Romania, Hungary, Czech Republic, Slovakia). It has an interesting parentage. It was the language of a group of people in what is now the provinces of Raajasthaan (Rajasthan) in India and Sindh in Pakistan around 600-700 CE who were wandering musicians even at that time. These people fled *west* during the first Muslim invasion of India. Their language, descended from the medieval Sauraseni, today sounds like an archaic Hindi, appearing to provide somewhat of a bridge between Hindi and Sanskrit. This is exemplified in the following words: *triin* for "three" (Hindi *tiin*, Sanskrit *tri*); *chataar* for "four" (Hindi *chaar*, Sanskrit *chatur*); *maa ro!* for "don't cry" (Hindi *mat ro*, Sanskrit *maa roda*). Indeed, this author, for whom Hindi is a first language, is able to follow a movie made in Romaani fairly well, without any prior exposure to Romaani.

Script(s): Most interestingly, and perhaps most uniquely in a single branch (Indian) of a single language family (Indo-European), most languages in this group *have their own, distinct script.* In spite of this apparent variety of scripts, however, all these different scripts, i.e. all modern Indian scripts, including the scripts of the Dravidian languages of India, are descended from one common source, the **Braahmi** script of ancient India [LAi-60 to LAi-64]. (Braahmi is also the parent of the scripts used for the languages of South-East Asia such as Thai, Burmese and Khmer, and, before the post-independence Romanization, Indonesian [LAi-65 to LAi-73].) Braahmi and related subjects are dealt with in the chapter on the Indian phonological classification in the first *NAVLIPI* volume.

Hindi, Maraathi, Bhojpuri, Paahaadi and Nepaali, along with the ancient Sanskrit, are written in the *Naagari* ("urban", also called *Dewanaagari*, "refined urban") script. There is some minor variation in the script between the languages (a little bit more than the minor variations between Spanish and English), for example to accommodate a retroflex central in Maraathi, or flaps and non-Indian-origin phones such as [f] in Hindi, Maraathi and Sindhi. The other major languages, e.g. Baanglaa/Assamese, Odiyaa (Uriya), Gujaraati, Panjaabi (Punjabi) each have their own script. Kashmiiri (Kashmiri) is written in its own script (called *Shaarada* and now confined to use by (Hindu) Kashmiiri Pandits) as well as in Arabic script, whilst Sindhi is today written in Arabic script in Pakistan and Dewanaagari script in India. Hindi is denoted as Urdu when its higher vocabulary is derived from an Arabic or Persian base (even though the same words are also available from a Sanskrit base and may be used concomitantly). Urdu, written in Arabic script, is the official language of Pakistan today, but it is a language that is not native to any region in Pakistan. Rather, it is a creation (from a Hindi base) of the court of the erstwhile kingdom of Oudh (Awadh, Ayodhya), near modern day Lakhnau (Lucknow) in Uttar Pradesh, India. Panjaabi has a curious, religious division in its writing: It is written in *Gurmukhi* script by Sikhs in East (Indian) Punjab and the rest of India, in Arabic script by Muslims in West (Pakistani) Punjab (a version called *Shahmukhi* by some), and, rarely, in Dewanaagari script by Hindu Punjabis, such as those living today in Delhi. Romaani is written in Roman script.

4.4.3 IRANIAN (PERSIAN) BRANCH

Faarsi or modern Persian includes dialects such as Dari spoken in Afghanistan (including the Kabul region) and Tajikh (a more archaic Faarsi) spoken in Tajikistan.

Pushtu (also called Pashto, Pashtu, Pakhto, Pakhtuun), is the main language of the southern and eastern regions of Afghanistan (i.e., of the Pathaan or Pushtuun or Pakhtuun ethnic group). Curiously, the main language of Kabul city proper is Dari, a dialect of Faarsi, although most of its residents are Pushtuun.

Kurdish is spoken in the border areas of Syria, Turkey, Iran and Iraq, i.e. "Kurdistan".

All the modern Iranian languages have significant borrowings from Arabic. However, these borrowings are not sufficient so as to allow them to be classed as *Angramaya* languages (see section below on these languages).

In the Western linguistics literature, a further sub-class called *Indo-Iranian* is created, due to the similarities between Avestan (and its descendant Old Persian), and Sanskrit. In this author's humble view, these undoubted but somewhat superficial similarities neglect more important differences between Sanskrit and Avestan: The extreme grammatical hyperstructure of Sanskrit [LAi-2 to LAi-12], as compared to the more simplistic and incomplete grammatical structure of Avestan [IEu-23 to IEu-28], and the overwhelming presence of archaisms in Sanskrit found in no other Indo-European language (see the comparative paradigms presented in a chapter, on the Indian phonological classification, in the first *NAVLIPI* volume). It is true that there is striking closeness between Sanskrit and Avestan in some grammatical aspects. But it is also true, for example, that there is striking closeness between Sanskrit and Classical Greek [IEu-29 to IEu-33] in other grammatical aspects not shared with Avestan. (These are evident from the verbal paradigms also presented in the chapter in the first *NAVLIPI* volume referenced above, q.v.) Yet Western linguists do not create a sub-class, "Indo-Greek".

Thus, in this author's opinion, if one were to use a classification *Indo-Iranian*, one should also use another classification, *Indo-Greek*, which, in this author's view, has more relavence from a grammatical affinity point of view. Furthermore, the descendant languages of Sanskrit and Avestan have a wide difference, much more than that between the Baltic and Slavic languages, another widely used joint classification in the Western linguistic tradition (Balto-Slavic). For these and other reasons, this author declines to use this joint sub-class appellation, *Indo-Iranian*, preferring instead to use two distinct classes, **Indian** and **Iraanian** (Iranian) *while fully acknowledging their closeness*.

Script: Modern Iraanian languages are written in a modified Arabic script. Kurdish may also be written in the (Roman-based) Turkish script in the Kurdish regions of Turkey. Avestan was written in its own script. On another note, the script history of Persian is actually quite interesting: Persian tried to adapt whatever script was available, including cuneiform and Greek [LAi-39 to LAi-44] (see below under the section on ancient languages).

4.4.4 GREEK BRANCH

The distinctive Greek branch has only one language, in all its various dialects, from ancient times to the modern [LN-1, LN-2, IEu-29 to IEu-33]. Mycenaean Greek is the most archaic form [IEu-29 to IEu-33, SCr-39]. The later Homeric Greek is the language fossilized in Homer's famous epics [IEu-30]. Still later Classical Greek is what most people identify as Ancient Greek and is the Attic dialect of that time. Modern Greek is as different from Classical Greek as Italian is from Latin, although we may perhaps be misled by both having "Greek" in their names! The relation of ancient to modern Greek is described at some length elsewhere in this chapter, in the section on extinct, moribund and inactive languages.

Classical and Homeric Greek have striking similarities to Sanskrit in their grammatical structure, especially verbal conjugations [LAi-1 to LAi-12, IEu-29 to IEu-33]. To cite one example, both Sanskrit and Classical Greek use the same augment to construct the imperfect tense, the same type of reduplication to construct the perfect tense, and the same augment + reduplication to construct the pluperfect tense (7th aorist in Sanskrit). These similarities are shared in full force *with no other Indo-European languages, even Avestan*: For example, the reduplication is moribund and barely identifiable in Latin and Gothic (an older Germanic language), fleeting in Avestan, and non-existent in any other Indo-European language. The augment shows up only fleetingly in Avestan [LAi-2 to LAi-12, IEu-17 to IEu-21, IEu-23 to IEu-28, IEu-44 to IEu-49].

Script: Greek is of course written in the Greek script, which is substantially the same as the ancient Greek script (differences discussed in a later section in this chapter).

4.4.5 BALTO-SLAVIC BRANCH

This has two sub-branches, *Baltic* with modern members Latvian and Lithuanian, and *Slavic* [LAs-40, LAs-41, IEu-37, LN-1].

This branch's modern members include Russian, Polish, Bulgarian/Macedonian, Ukrainian, Czech, Slovak, Serbo-Croat and Slovenian. Bulgarian/Macedonian and Serbo-Croat are nearly mutually intelligible, whilst Ukrainian and Byelorussian are somewhat mutually intelligible with Russian. Very recently, post 2000, there have been attempts to divide Serbo-Croat into Serbian, Croatian and Bosnian variants, for political reasons, with new words being coined. The Slavic languages are further subdivided by most linguists into: *Eastern*: Russian, Ukrainian and Byelorussian. *Western*: Czech, Slovak, Polish. *Southern*: Bulgarian, Macedonian, Serbo-Croat, Slovene (Slovenian), all of which are nearly mutually intelligible.

Lithuanian and Latvian are unique and curious in superficially preserving some verb forms found elsewhere only in the most ancient Indo-European language (Sanskrit). We can cite two quick examples: The singular and plural (but not dual) present tense conjugation of one of the several Sanskrit verbs that mean "to be" (*as*), e.g. Sanskrit *asmi,* modern Lithuanian *esmi,* "I am"; and the formation of the inflected future tense by use of a *-sya-* affix (e.g. Sanskrit *daasyaami*, "I will give" vs. *dadaami*, "I give"). However, this resemblance is rather superficial, since neither Lithuanian nor Latvian has anywhere near the complexity or hyperstructure of grammar, nor the full complement of declensions and conjugations, nor the dual number, etc. etc., found in Sanskrit. Nor do they possess the myriad of moods, voices and tenses of the Sanskrit verb.

In addition, the Balto-Slavic group is said in the older Western classification to belong to the *shatem* bifurcation of Indo-European languages (vs. the *centum* group that Germanic, Romance, etc. belong to). However, this *shatem/centum* bifurcation, like many other early Western classifications, has now largely been discredited. The *shatem/centum* classification is far less important than much more significant classifications based on grammatical form. One of these, between Classical Greek and Classical Sanskrit, has been alluded to earlier in this chapter. If properly considered, they would, place, e.g., Classical Sanskrit (a *shatem* language) and Classical Greek (a *centum* language) very close. But that again is a subject for another book!

Script: Languages such as Russian, Ukrainian and Bulgarian are written in the Cyrillic script, a script based on the Greek. Polish, Czech and Slovenian are written in the Roman script. Serbo-Croat has a curious religious/ethnic divide: Christian Orthodox (mostly Serbian) speakers write in Cyrillic, whilst Catholic (mostly Croat) and Muslim (mostly Bosnian) speakers write the same language in Roman script!

4.4.6 ARMENIAN BRANCH

Although it has superficial resemblances to the Balto-Slavic group and to Greek, Armenian is generally given its own independent branch. It is considered a so-called *shatem* language in the older Western classification. Uniquely, the two dialectical variations, Eastern (Armenia) and Western (Turkey) Armenian, have differences in the written language as well.

Script: The language uses a script modeled on the Greek alphabet and said to be invented by one St. Mesrob in 407 CE [SCr-65]. The script attempts to have one letter for one phone, a total of 36. During Soviet times, the Cyrillic script was also in use. After the disbanding of the Soviet Union, there were some efforts at a Roman-based script.

4.4.7 ALBANIAN BRANCH

Again, this is generally given its own independent branch, although having superficial resemblances to the Balto-Slavic group and to Greek and Armenian. Standard, southern Albanian, called Tosk, is also the written language, whilst a northern (Kosovar) dialect, Gheg, was close to diverging into a separate language until modern times, when it has come closer to Tosk.

Script: Written today in Roman script.

4.4.8 GERMANIC BRANCH

Among surviving modern languages, the Germanic branch [IEu-17 to IEu-21, IEu-38 to IEu-43, LN-2] has the sub-branches *West Germanic* with major modern descendants English, Dutch, German, and *North Germanic*, with major descendants Swedish, Danish, Norwegian, Icelandic, Faroese, etc.. The *East Germanic* branch has no modern survivors (a major member, *Gothic*, is extinct) [IEu-17, IEu-19]. Within North Germanic, Norwegian and Swedish are very close, closer than Spanish and Portuguese; Swedes for example say that they can frequently follow Norwegian conversations. Within West Germanic, there are some *standardized* dialectical variations, e.g. Swiss German, which, for instance, uses *zwo* for *zwei* ("two").

As is well known, and as discussed at some length later in this chapter, English is unique among all these Germanic languages in having a Germanic base but a large majority of its higher vocabulary borrowed from Latin, Greek and French bases. These words have close cognates, e.g., in French. English is thus an *Angramaya* language, as discussed later in this chapter.

In a similar vein, German is unique among these languages in *two* ways: Firstly, it has the vast majority of its higher vocabulary derived from Germanic rather than Latin or Greek base words. Secondly, and more importantly, it is the *only* modern Indo-European language that preserves the old Indo-European *pre-verb/verb* (Sanskrit *upasarga/dhaatu (anga)*) structure in full force. This is discussed in more detail in the section later in this chapter on Vedic vs. Classical Sanskrit.

Script: All Germanic languages are today written in the Roman script.

4.4.9 ROMANCE (ALSO CALLED *ITALIC*) BRANCH

In approximate decreasing order of number of speakers, the *major* modern languages in this group [LAs-42, LAs-43, LN-2] are: Spanish, Portuguese, French, Italian, Romanian, Rhaeto-Roman ("Rhaeto-Romansch", an Italian-like language of Switzerland that is closer to Latin than modern Italian). All are descended from late Latin.

Catalan, from the region of Barcelona in Spain, and Galician, from the northwestern regions of the Iberian peninsula, are considered separate languages, rather than dialects, respectively, of Spanish and Portuguese. In this author's humble opinion, they lie in a very grey area in this respect. Catalan may be unintelligible to a Madrid native; but then so are many Italian dialects to a Rome native! Although separate literatures have been cultivated, many Spanish and Portuguese authorities claim that their recognition as languages may possibly also have a political element (perhaps the need to suppress nationalistic urges by prematurely recognizing regional "languages"!).

It is also noteworthy that, unlike the Indian and Germanic sub-branches, there are no higher medieval or pre-medieval groupings in the Romance languages. E.g. French and Italian are not descended from a "French-Italian" parent, but rather from older versions of the same languages, i.e., Old French and Old Italian.

The Italic branch also had another sub-branch along with Latin, surviving through the later Roman era, as our language tree figure above shows. All the languages in this self-branch are extinct today.

Script: All these languages are today written in the Roman script.

4.4.10 KELTIC (*CELTIC*) BRANCH

The *major* modern descendants are Irish (also called Gaelic in more common parlance), Welsh and Scots Gaelic [LAs-44 to LAs-47, LN-2]. The Keltic languages are nearly extinct today for all practical purposes, i.e. in terms of daily usage. They are spoken today, along with English, in outlying areas of Britain and Ireland, by older speakers. One of the Keltic languages, Manx (of the Isle of Man), is truly extinct. None are in active use, e.g. in everyday commerce, today; they have been superseded by English.

There are periodic revival attempts for Irish and Welsh, and Welsh is taught as a compulsory language in schools in Gwynnedd County and other regions of Wales.

Other, minor descendants include Breton (of Brittany in northwestern France), also not in active use today.

The Keltic group is widely believed to have been the first Indo-European linguistic "wave" to occupy Europe, its speakers supposedly conquering and imparting their language to native Europeans. Thus, among modern European languages, the Keltic group shows the largest "distance" from the parent.

Some linguists further subdivide Keltic into two groups, *Island* Celtic (also called *q-Celtic*, including, e.g., Irish, Scots Gaelic, Welsh, Breton and Cornish) and *Continental-*Celtic (also called *p-Celtic*, including, e.g., Gaulish of Northwestern France and a remnant called Hispano-Celtic in Spain).

Script: Written today in the Roman script.

4.4.11 EXTINCT INDO-EUROPEAN LANGUAGES

These are covered in a separate section below, q.v..

4.5 THE SINO-TIBETAN FAMILY

4.5.1 EXTENT AND NUMBER OF SPEAKERS

Sino-Tibetan languages [LN-1, LN-2, LAs-48] do not extend beyond China, Tibet, Myanmar (Burma) and Southeast Asia, except as part of the Chinese, Tibetan or other diaspora. Within Southeast Asia, they extend into the border areas of Laos and Thailand.

This family is further divided into *Sinitic* (i.e., Chinese) languages and *Tibeto-Burman* languages.

Much of the modern linguistics literature further divides Tibeto-Burman into a number of sub-branches. However, in this author's humble opinion, the total scholarship in this field is very sparse and very little of it is by native speakers of these languages. And in what little scholarship there is, there are major conflicts, e.g. with some researchers claiming that "Sinitic" languages are merely a sub-branch of Tibeto-Burman, and using appellations such as "Sino-Bodic" [LAs-1, LAs-48, LN-1].

Consequently, this author feels that the "jury is still out", as it were, with respect to further divisions within the Tibeto-Burman branch. We will thus not treat of sub-branches of the Tibeto-Burman languages

The number of speakers of Sino-Tibetan languages can roughly be broken down as follows (all figures estimations for the year *2005*): China **1,216 m**, Myanmar **44 m**, Taiwan **21 m**, Hong Kong **7 m**, Tibet **3 m**, Regions of India (Ladhak, Sikkim etc.) **7 m**, Diaspora (including Singapore) **7 m**. This yields an approximate total of *1,305 m*.

The number of people who can speak or understand Mandarin is estimated to be about **750 million** [LAs-49]. A more detailed discussion on this subject is presented below.

The languages of the Himalayan regions of India (Ladhak, Sikkim) and of Bhutan and the Tibet-abutting regions of Nepal *not* in general intelligible with the Tibetan of Tibet. For example, Ladhaaki and Tibetan are, according to our definition, given earlier in this chapter, distinct languages.

Many linguists believe that Sino-Tibetan speakers have geographically taken over regions in southern China thought to have once been populated by speakers of *Austronesian, Tai,*

Austro-Asiatic, and other language families, which are thought to have originated in southern China [LN-83, GDn-17 to GDn-19].

4.5.2 THE CHINESE LANGUAGES

It is very important for the layman to recognize that the many Chinese *languages* (listed below) *are **distinct languages**,* using the broadest definition that we have established above of two languages being distinct, viz. mutual unintelligibility (see Section on language vs. dialect above). This may go quite counter to the not uncommonly held wisdom in the lay world, of a single language called "Chinese". It may, unfortunately, also go against the official position of the Chinese government and the appellation given by its bodies to the various Chinese languages, as "dialects"! Many contend [LAs-48 to LAs-50] that this serves more of a political than a linguistic purpose, keeping diverse China more united. The Chinese languages today are at least as distinct as Italian is from French, and in some cases more so. Admittedly, however, most are not as distinct as French is from German.

In addition, in certain parts of China, especially the southern regions, dialectical variations sometimes increase from village to village, with the result that, across say a dozen villages, one encounters a truly distinct language rather than dialect. One recent article in the popular press [LAs-49] noted that:

> "The Han speak as many as 1500 dialects, with the bulk of those concentrated in the southern half of the country..... Many of the Han dialects are almost entirely mutually incomprehensible, ***more distinct than languages from disparate regions of Europe***.....The degree of difference among dialects is much higher than the degree of difference among European languages. In Europe they call them languages, but in China, we share a culture, so *the central government* would like to consider that one language is shared by many different peoples..."

...(4.2)

While some of these statements in the above, like the one hinting at 1500 distinct dialects, may not be entirely accurate linguistically, the gist of the article is clear. Through all these variations however, the *written unity of the languages is maintained* due to the ideographic nature of the script [SCr-25 to SCr-31].

Chapter 4: The World's Major Language Families- A Primer

All Chinese languages are thought to be derived from a common origin - the earliest, written record of Chinese is in the so-called "bone-inscription" ("turtle-shell") documents of about the 2nd millennium BCE) [SCr- 25 to SCr-31].

The Chinese languages can be further sub-categorized broadly into the sub-families given in the several paragraphs below. Except for Mandarin, these are generally identified by the geographical region of China where they are most prominent.

Mandarin is centered approximately in the vicinity of the Beijing area, with several geographically determined dialects. The official accent, equivalent to the "Queen's English" or "Received Pronunciation" in England, is known as *Putonghua*, whilst the corresponding official written language is known as *Baihua*.

In order to estimate the number of speakers of Mandarin, it is necessary to estimate the number who speak it as a second language. However, such an estimation is difficult in those regions of China where it cannot be considered a first language. For example, it is established (both officially and unofficially) that Mandarin is not the first ("native") language in the provinces of Anhui, Hubei, Hunan, part of Jiangsu, Guangdong, Guangxi, Yunnan, Guizhou, Fujian, Gansu, Guangxi, Zhejiang, Inner Mongolia and in the Shanghai metropolitan region, as also Tibet. However, official Chinese government or other census data do not give information on the second language fluency of the population in these (or any other) regions. The official Chinese government position, apparently for reasons of harmony, national unity related political considerations, is that most of the population in such provinces and regions is familiar with spoken Mandarin (*Putonghua*). This position is however not fully credible. For example, a traveler to even highly developed areas of Guangdong or Fujian province will find it impossible to communicate with the majority of the population when speaking standard Mandarin.

Nevertheless, a rough estimation of Mandarin speakers can be made by meticulously poring through official and unofficial data available from public sources, primarily on the Internet. Such analysis was carried out for this chapter in 2006. On this basis, Mandarin is estimated to be spoken or understood by approximately **750 m** people, making it *the most widely spoken single language in the world*, far exceeding English.

Minbei (Fujienese), (also called **Northern Min** or just **Min**) is found in Fujien province (near Guangdong) and also eastern Guangdong.

Hakka (Kejia) is found in Southeastern China, in parts of Fujien, Guangdong and Jiangxi provinces. There are several other Chinese languages broadly classed under **Others** in the language tree presented earlier in this chapter.

Yue (Cantonese) is spoken in the vicinity of Guangdong ("Canton") and Guangxi Zhuang provinces (near Hong Kong), and of course in Hong Kong proper. In terms of number of speakers, this is the largest of the Chinese languages after Mandarin. Interestingly, much of the older Chinese diaspora, e.g. in the Chinatowns of San Francisco and New York, speak Yue or Hakka, but the newer diasporas try to speak Mandarin, if they speak any Chinese languages at all.

Gan (Jiangxese) is centered in Jiangxi and parts of Hubei province.

Xiang (Hunanese) is spoken primarily in Hunan province.

Wu (Shanghainese, Zhejiangese) is centered around Shanghai and the provinces of Zhejiang, southern Jiangsu and southern Anhui. It is as close to Mandarin as Spanish is to Portuguese, and is also somewhat close to Jiangxese (Gan).

Minnan (Hokkien-Taiwanese) (also called ***Southern Min***) is found in Taiwan and in the Chinese mainland directly across from Taiwan.

Script of the Chinese Languages: Uniquely, all Chinese languages share *one, single, script* which is primarily ideographic, although having some logo-phonetic elements [SCr-25 to SCr-31]. This single script is derived from the ancient Chinese ideographic scripts, with first records, the so-called "turtle-shell inscriptions" or "bone inscriptions", dating from about 1000 BCE (Western dating, although the Academia Sinica accords an older date) [SCr-25, SCr-26]. Many characters are unchanged from that time.

This common script gives the Chinese languages an uncommon and unique identity not seen in any other language families. It would be the same as if, in a common European *written* language, there would be a picture of a tree. The German would read it as *Baum*, the French person as *arbre* and the English person as *tree*, but all would understand it to mean the same object, a tree.

4.5.3 THE TIBETO-BURMAN LANGUAGES

Tibetan Languages: Although of Sino-Tibetan origins, modern Tibetan, especially the literary language, is somewhat like English (see discussion further below), in having a large part of its higher vocabulary taken from a language of different origin, in this case Sanskrit. It is an *Angramaya* language.

Within this branch, we must also include the tongues spoken in the Himalayan regions Bhutan, Sikkim and Ladhak, many of which are related to Tibetan. Other Tibetan languages include ***Bodo*** of Northeast India, which has a Tibetan base but much borrowing from neighboring Indo-European languages [LAs-48].

Script of the Tibetan languages: Tibetan has its own script, derived from the ancient Indian Braahmi script.

Myanmari (Burmese) and Related Languages: Modern Myanmari (Burmese) has some borrowings from a Sanskrit base for its higher vocabulary, i.e. it is also an *Angramaya* language (see discussion below). Manipuri is a language of the state of Manipur in India which is related to Myanmari, but has significant input from Sanskrit for its higher vocabulary (i.e., it is another *Angramaya* language).

Script of Myanmari/Burmese: Burmese is written in its own script, which, like other South-East Asian scripts (Thai, Khmer and the old Indonesian script now replaced by a Roman-based script), is based on the ancient Indian Braahmi script.

Sub-classifications: Tibeto-Burman languages are given many sub-classifications, such as Burmese-Lolo, Nung, Qiang and Karen. However, scholarship by native speakers of the languages is especially lacking for these languages, and, in this author's opinion, much more thorough work needs to be done before settling on the classifications currently given in modern linguistics texts.

Chapter 4: The World's Major Language Families- A Primer

4.6 THE NIGER-CONGO FAMILY

Extent and Number of Speakers: These languages are most closely identified with Africa [LAs-9 to LAs-15, LN-2]. They were originally given the broad appellation ***Baantu*** (Bantu) in the older Western linguistic literature. Baantu is now considered a subset of Niger-Congo. Most linguists today enumerate 177 branches of the Niger-Congo family. The geographical extent of the Niger-Congo family today is West Africa, East Africa and Southern Africa. They include the major West African languages such as ***Yoruba*** and ***Igbo***, major languages of Nigeria, ***Zulu***, one of the major languages of South Africa, and, in an oblique way, ***Swaahili***, the lingua franca of East Africa. Baantu speakers migrated quite recently from their West African home, to the regions such as southern and eastern Africa where Baantu languages are found today. By some assertions, this occurred as recently as 1000 CE

The breakdown of the number of speakers is roughly as follows (in decreasing order, all figures estimates for 2005): Nigeria (est. 113 m), D.R. Congo (Kinshasa, 63 m), Tanzania (41 m), Kenya (38 m), Uganda (31 m), Ghana (24 m), Mozambique (22 m), Côte d'Ivoire and Cameroon (19 m each), Angola (18 m), Burkina Faso and Niger (15 m each), Malawi and Zimbabwe (14 m each), Senegal (13 m), Mali and Zambia (12 m each), Chad, Rwanda and Benin (9 m each), Guinea and Burundi (8 m), Somalia and Togo (6 m each), Sierra Leone (5 m), Central African Republic (4 m), Congo (Brazzaville, 3 m), Namibia, Lesotho, Guinea-Bissau, Gambia, and Gabon (1 m each). **Total 584 m**.

Branches of the Niger-Congo family include ***Kordofanian (Nubian)***, with very few speakers; ***Mende***; ***Ijo***; ***Atlantic***; and ***Benué-Congo***, with the largest number of speakers. There appears to be some cross-fertilization between the Benué-Congo and Atlantic branches, as shown in our language tree depiction earlier in this chapter. This is either due to borrowing owing to geographical proximity, or due to a possible common parent, or both.

As noted above, until more recently, the entire Niger-Congo family was given the name ***Baantu (Bantu)***. The Baantu languages are however now recognized by most linguists as merely *a sub-branch of one of the branches of this family (specifically, the Benué-Congo/Baantu branch)*, although with a very large number of speakers. They further assign as many as 500 "languages" to the sub-branch.

However, this author notes the caveat that most of these studies are by non-native speakers residing primarily in England and the U.S; there is still very little linguistics scholarship within Africa (barring South Africa). Many of these so-called Baantu "languages" are considered dialects by native speakers [LAs-9 to LAs-17]. This is analogous to scholars in these same institutions [LN-73, LN-74] listing "Rajasthani" (whatever that is - ask any Indian to identify this "language"!) as a separate language from Hindi and claiming that India has "hundreds of languages"! Thus, we reiterate that there must be some healthy skepticism in these pronouncements of hundreds of Baantu languages by non-natives of the region.

Nevertheless, there is general agreement on one point: That the Baantu languages spread through migration from a small area in West Africa, roughly corresponding to modern-day Nigeria and neighboring countries, starting around 500 BCE.

Interestingly, the Benué-Congo languages are unique in that they have both tonal and non-tonal members [LAs-12, LAs-14, LAs-15]. The tonal character of some of the languages may be original, or it may have been acquired from languages which these languages eventually supplanted. If the former is the case, then many of these languages subsequently lost their tonal character. The fact that the tonal languages are concentrated in the West African region, the presumed homeland of these languages, supports the view that all languages of this sub-branch were originally tonal. The analogy, in an opposite sense, would be Vietnamese, an Austro-Asiatic language which was originally *not* tonal but which acquired tonal characteristics from the influence of neighboring Sino-Tibetan languages.

To cite a few examples of important languages of the *Baantu* sub-branch, **Yoruba** is a major, tonal language of Nigeria (along with Hausa of the Afro-Asiatic family). Languages such as **Igbo**, and **Fulfulde**, also of the West African region, are close cognates. **Zulu** is one of the major languages of South Africa. **Miinaa** and **Ewe** are two languages of the Togo-Benin-Ghana region which have very interesting and complex tonal structures (one of the *Navlipi* language transcriptions presented in this book is in Miinaa). **Swaahili** is structurally another *Angramaya* (English-type) language (as discussed later in this chapter): Its base words are of Baantu origin whilst the higher vocabulary is mostly of Arabic origin, with some recent borrowings even from English.

There are of course many other Niger-Congo languages of significance which we have not listed here due to space reasons.

Scripts of the Niger-Congo Languages: All the above languages are written in Roman script or slight modifications thereof, but many have had a history of also being written in the Arabic script or adaptations thereof, and many other have had unique scripts invented specifically for them, such as the Vai script; these scripts are discussed in a chapter in the first *NAVLIPI* volume. Swaahili adopted the Roman script in the late 19th and early 20th centuries, being written in Arabic script before then. Prior to the advent of Europeans in West Africa, there is some history of Yoruba having been written in the Arabic script.

4.7 THE AFRO-ASIATIC (FORMERLY CALLED HAMITO-SEMITIC) FAMILY

Extent and Number of Speakers: This family's original geographical sway is primarily North Africa and the Middle East. It has the fourth-largest number of speakers in the world, after Indo-European, Sino-Tibetan and Niger-Congo. Its largest single member is of course Arabic. It was originally given the appellation *Hamito-Semitic* [LAs-11, LAs-13, LAs-51 to LAs-55, LN-1, LN-2]

The breakdown of speakers is roughly as follows (in decreasing order, all figures for 2005): *Arabic* has approximately **295 m** speakers [LAs-53 to LAs-55], comprising those in Egypt (76 m), Algeria (32 m), Morocco (31 m), Iraq (30 m), Saudi Arabia (25 m), Yemen (23 m), Syria (20 m), Sudan (18 m), Tunisia (10 m), Libya (6 m), Jordan (6 m), UAE (4 m), Lebanon (4 m), Palestine (4 m), Kuwait (3 m), Oman (3 m). There are several countries with under one million people which are not in our count, for example Qatar and Bahrain. *Other Afro-Asiatic* speakers number **87 m**, including those of *Amharic* (Ethiopia, 62 m), *Hausa* (Nigeria and environs, 15 m), *Hebrew* (Israel, 7 m) and *Berber* languages (Algeria, Libya and Morocco, 3 m). The **total** for Afro-Asiatic is thus **382 m**.

Semitic Branch: This comprises *Arabic, Amharic* (an Ethiopian language spoken in the Addis-Ababa region), and *Hebrew* as well as several extinct or moribund languages, such as Aramaic, the language thought to be spoken by Jesus Christ and now used only in the Syrian and Iraqi church liturgy.

Hebrew is unique among present-day languages in that it is one of the few examples of a language *brought back from virtual extinction to vibrant, everyday use*: It was extinct as an everyday language since well before Roman times (it is said that the Jews of the Roman era actually spoke Aramaic in everyday use) until the establishment of the state of Israel. Today, however, it is very much the vibrant, everyday language of Israel.

Arabic also has an interesting history, in that it was originally confined to the Arabian peninsula until about 600 CE. It spread rapidly during the Mohammedan conquest and took over (i.e., replaced) languages spoken by the peoples of North Africa and the Middle East which were mostly also of the same family. Since then, it has started to segment, with, e.g., Moroccan Arabic no longer being mutually intelligible with Egyptian Arabic, although the latter is still mutually intelligible with Lebanese, Saudi, etc. Arabic. Until very recently, "taught Arabic" differed markedly from "street Arabic", but modern language courses have changed this.

Chadic Branch: ***Hausa***, spoken in the northern Nigeria region. It serves as a non-English, non-French lingua franca for much of Nigeria and neighboring West African nations [LAs-10, LAs-15].

Berber Branch: ***Berber*** is spoken by former nomads of northwestern Africa, e.g. the Tuaregs. Most of these peoples are bilingual, speaking North African Arabic as well.

Cushitic Branch: This is spoken today in parts of Ethiopia, Somalia and northern Kenya. The most well-known of Cushitic languages is ***Orominga***, spoken in some parts of Kenya and southern Ethiopia.

Egyptian Branch: A modern version of ancient ***Egyptian*** survives only in the Coptic Church liturgy.

Scripts of the Afro-Asiatic Languages: Arabic is of course written in the Arabic script. Hebrew is written in its own script. The Arabic and Hebrew scripts are extremely similar, and even the names of the letters (in Arabic *'alif, beth, gimmel, daleth* etc.) are nearly identical. Both are written right to left and descended from a North Semitic alphabet of around 1500 BCE, which itself was an amalgam of cuneiform, hieroglyphic and syllabic systems of varying parentage. This North Semitic alphabet was adopted by the Akkadians (ancient Arabs) and popularized by the seafaring Phoenicians. The original Semitic consonant-only scripts have been adapted in Arabic and Hebrew for vowels through the use of diacritics (dots, dashes) and other glyphs. Amharic is written in its own script, said by Ethiopians to pre-date the Semitic scripts [SCr-70]. Hausa mainly and the Berber languages are written in the Arabic script. With the advent of Christian missionaries in the early 20th century, Hausa and the Cushitic languages have started to be written in the Roman script. Orominga, a prominent Cushitic language, was formerly written in the Amharic script. Egyptian was of course written in *Hieroglyphic* script, originally purely ideographic. Its subsequent versions included *Demotic* and several cursive versions found in many papyri. In the early Christian era, it was also written in an adaptation of the Greek script.

4.8 AUSTRONESIAN (FORMERLY MALAYO-POLYNESIAN) FAMILY

Extent and Number of Speakers: This family was originally called ***Malayo-Polynesian*** or just ***Malay***. After the discovery of a number of very varied languages of this family on the island of Taiwan (formerly Formosa) [LAs-56, GDn-18, GDn-19], a bifurcation was made between Malayo-Polynesian and ***Formosan***, both then being inserted under the umbrella of a group denoted as ***Austronesian*** [LN-1, LN-2, LAs-1, LAs-58]. Unfortunately, the appellation *Austronesian* creates some confusion for the *layman,* since it can easily be confused with *Austro-Asiatic*, and, further, with *Australian, Melanesian, Micronesian* and other similar terms. On the other hand, *Malayo-Polynesian* has a clear geographical connotation simple for the layman to understand. Nevertheless, since the linguistics literature now uniformly uses *Austronesian*, we shall stay with this.

Geographically, this group extends from southern Thailand through the Malaysian and Indonesian archipelagos to the Philippines, Hawai'i [LAs-57] and New Zealand in the East and Madagascar in the West [LAs-58].

The original homeland of the Austronesian languages is thought by many linguists to have been southern China [LAs-56, LAs-58, GDn-18, GDn-19, LN-83]. The Austronesian language family is then thought to have spread from southern China, first to Taiwan, and thence to Malaysia, Indonesia, Polynesia, etc.. However, this hypothesis, like so much scholarship in the field of linguistics, is based on entirely circumstantial and speculative evidence, coupled with unfamiliarity with the region in question, once again due to non-native scholarship. For example, much of the evidence cited for the hypothesis is the presumed absence of archaeological artifacts (such as pottery) within Indonesia or Malaysia which is said to point to the absence of a population earlier than the seafaring Malay peoples [LN-83, GDn-19].

However, much of this lack of archaeological evidence may simply be due to a combination of such factors as the lack of money, and in many cases, permission, for archaeological digs in these countries. Additionally, the pre-Malay inhabitants of the region may simply have not been inclined much towards producing archaeological artifacts such as pottery! This may in turn have been due, in part, to their transient lifestyle (spending much of their lives seaborne) and the abundance of substitutes for pottery, such as gourds, palm nut shells, etc. which would not be found in archaeological digs due to their biodegradable nature. The very large ethnic variety in the "aboriginal" population of Taiwan ostensibly speaking Austronesian languages (the Saisiyat, Thao, Tsou, Rukai, Paiwan, Yami, Puyuma, Amis, Bunun, Kavalan and Atayan ethnic groups) also suggests that this hypothesis may be simplistic. [LAs-56, GDn-18, GDn-19]. There are thus many, including this author, who hold opposing views.

This author feels that another hypothesis on the origins of the speakers of the Austronesian languages must be considered: That they are a remnant of some of the most recent littoral-hopping waves of migrants from Africa who developed a special expertise in seafaring as compared to their contemporaries, around 20,000 to 10,000 BCE [GDn-17, GDn-19]. This may account for the fact that Austronesian languages are found today *exclusively in littoral or archipelago areas, along the major west-to-east seafaring route from the horn of Africa*, a wide arc from Madagascar through New Zealand. This may also, possibly, explain the lack of any remnant Austronesian languages in geographically isolated inland regions in Southeast Asia or southern China, such as inland mountains, which is somewhat at odds with the hypothesis that later Sino-Tibetan speakers flushed out earlier Austronesian speakers from all these regions: In India, where similar multiple linguistic migrations occurred, the more original inhabitants invariably remained in more isolated mountains or forested regions; today, these peoples are denoted by the government as "scheduled castes/scheduled tribes," inhabit isolated forested and mountainous areas, and invariably speak Austro-Asiatic or Andaman languages.

The approximate breakdown of the number of speakers is as follows (in decreasing order, all figures estimates for 2005): Indonesia (232 m), Philippines (89 m), Malaysia (27m), Madagascar (19 m), Miscellaneous Polynesia, (including remnant Maaori in New Zealand and Hawaai'ian languages, 5 m), Timor (1 m). **Total 373 m.**

Major languages: The *major* languages of this family, in decreasing order of speakers, are: **Bahasa (Bhaasha) Indonesia and Bahasa Malaysia** (also called *Malay*), which are nearly identical differing rather like British and American English [LAs-31] ; *regional Malay languages* of the Indonesian and Malaysian Archipelagos (such as Balinese, Javanese, etc.); *Tagalog* and other Filipino languages; *Malagasy*. (Madagascar); *Hawaa'ian*; *Maaori* (New Zealand); varied *Formosan* (Taiwanese) languages; *Other* regional languages of the Polynesian region (e.g. *Tahitian* which is similar to Hawaai'ian [LAs-57]).

Bahasa (Bhaashaa) Indonesia and Bahasa Malaysia (Malay), and Other Languages of the Indonesian and Malaysian Archipelagos: Bahasa (Bhaashaa) Indonesia and Bahasa Malaysia (also called Malay), are nearly identical as noted above [LAs-31]. We may thus consider them as a single language. This language is another one with an *Angramaya* (English-like) structure (see later in this chapter), in that the base language is definitely of Austronesian origin, but nearly all the higher vocabulary is of Sanskrit (i.e. Indo-European) origin, emanating from cultural colonization by South Indians starting from before the Christian era. Bahasa Indonesia and Bahasa Malaysia differ mainly in certain elements of the higher vocabulary such as technical terms, which were coined by the respective governments. The resulting differences are said to be slightly more than those between British and American English [LAs-31]. As any person of Indian heritage on a visit to Indonesia will tell you, he/she is able to instantly recognize many of the common words in everyday use from their Sanskrit origin, starting from Bahasa (*Bhaasha*, "language, speech") to proper names (Meghaawati Sukarnoputri, a recent Indonesian president comes to mind). Indeed the original name of the country of Indonesia was to be *Nushaantara* (*Nusha*, "islands" + Sanskrit *antara* "distance, separation"). Indonesian authorities officially recognize more than 2,000 words of Sanskrit origin among the basic, everyday vocabulary of the average, uneducated Indonesian [LAs-31]

In addition to the standardized Bahasa, there are many other languages within the geographical extent of Indonesia and Malaysia. The Indonesian archipelago alone is said to have **241** distinct *languages*, distinct from Bahasa Indonesia [LAs-31]. These include, e.g., major languages such as **Balinese** and **Javanese**.

It is important for the layman to understand that these Indonesian languages are really *distinct languages*, mutually unintelligible with Bahasa Indonesia. Some of these have a very large number of speakers. For example, Javanese, a distinct language on the island of Java, has more than 100 million speakers. As examples of other Indonesian and Malaysian languages with distinct names, we can cite **Taba** (also called **Moluccan** or **Makian**) and **Tukang Besi** (also known as **Sulawesi**). Languages such as *Balinese* (from the Indonesian island of Bali) have a further unique and interesting structure in that they have three usage "levels", depending upon whether one is addressing family or persons of lower social status (lowest level), everyday commercial uses (middle level), or highly honored members of societies such as Hindu priests (highest level). Bahasa Indonesia is used as a lingua franca by Indonesians from diverse islands.

Tagalog is the major language of the Philippines. This has substantial borrowings from Spanish, and a few recent ones from English. In contrast to other languages we have discussed, however, its structure is *not* English-like, not Angramaya,. **Malagasy** is the language of Madagascar. It has some Baantu and Arabic borrowings, to be expected due to geographical proximity to Africa and the Arabian peninsula. *Hawaai'ian*, the language of the Hawaiian islands, is today practically extinct as a spoken, everyday language. *Maaori* is the language of the original peoples of New Zealand, again today practically extinct as a spoken, everyday language. There are many other *Polynesian* languages such as *Tahitian*. *Formosan languages* are of more archaic structure than any of the other Austronesian languages. They also display much more variation between themselves than the other Austronesian languages. They are now nearly extinct, having been superseded by Mandarin and Minnan (Hokkien-Taiwanese) languages on Taiwan.

Script of the Austronesian Languages: Like many languages of Southeast Asia (such as Thai, Khmer and Burmese), Bahasa Indonesia was originally written in an Indian script derived from southern Paali script (and thus ultimately from Braahmi). Inscriptions in old temples in Indonesia are still found in this script. At independence, Indonesia and Malaysia officially adopted the Roman scripts they use today. Malagasy and Maori and Tagalog are written in the Roman script. Taiwanese is written in the Chinese (ideographic) script.

Chapter 4: The World's Major Language Families- A Primer

4.9 ALTAIC FAMILY AND JAPANESE

4.9.1 URALIC, ALTAIC, "URAL-ALTAIC", "FINNO-UGRIC" AND JAPANESE

In the earlier Western linguistics literature, up to about 1945 CE, the now distinctly recognized ***Uralic*** and ***Altaic*** language families were considered one family, called ***Ural-Altaic*** [LAs-23 to LAs-25]. This family included, as important members, ***Maagyaar*** (Magyar, Hungarian), ***Finnish***, ***Turkish***, ***Mongolian*** and ***Korean***.

Later studies, primarily by Hungarian-language and English-language authors broke up this family into *Uralic* and *Altaic* components [LN-2, LAs-1, LAs-21, LAs-22, LAs-26]. Some other authors have made the controversial contention that this was based less on academic scholarship and more on the fact that many Europeans of the time wanted a distinction between the European and Asian branches [LN-2, LAs-1, LAs-21, LAs-22, LAs-26]. We shall not touch this controversy, but do note that there has been little scholarship in this area from native Korean [LAs-29, LAs-30], Japanese and Turkish [LAs-19] speakers. We nevertheless follow the now well-established distinction of ***Uralic*** and ***Altaic*** as separate language families, since that is what is used in most literature on the subject. A sub-branch called ***Finno-Ugric*** is designated within the Uralic family for the Finnish, Estonian (considered a dialect of Finnish by some), Maagyaar (Magyar, Hungarian) and related languages. It nevertheless remains true that distant languages, such as Korean and Finnish, *do show clear affinities* [LN-2, LAs-1, LAs-20, LAs-22].

In addition to the above controversy, there remains even today a perhaps more important prevailing academic controversy. This is on the precise placement of ***Japanese***. Many authors working in this field [LAs-29, LAs-30, LAs-59 to LAs-61, LN-83] include Japanese in the Altaic family, as a very distant relation of Korean. This has much to do with a linguistic interpretation of Korean history (or a historical interpretation of Korean linguistics, depending upon one's viewpoint) held by such authors as Diamond [LN-83]: These authors contend that Korea had three distinct language groups, the southeastern-most one of which migrated to Japan, whilst the dominant among the other two eventually extinguished the other languages from the Korean peninsula. In the present author's view, however, this view pays more attention to historical events as opposed to linguistic analysis, which indicates affinities between modern Korean and Japanese which could just as easily be ascribed to borrowing. Other authors, including many prominent Japanese-origin authors [LAs-59, LAs-60, GDn-22, GDn-23, GDn-37], are more inclined to assign Japanese *its own, distinct language family*. I.e. they consider Japanese a *language isolate*. For the purposes of this book, nevertheless, Japanese is included within the overall *Altaic* family.

4.9.2 EXTENT AND NUMBER OF SPEAKERS

Barring Indo-European, the Altaic family has the broadest geographic extent of any family, from western Turkey through Mongolia to Korea and perhaps (see note on controversy in previous paragraph) Japan.

The approximate breakdown of the number of speakers is as follows (in decreasing order, all figures estimates for 2005): Japanese 128 m, Turkish 75 m, Korean 48 m (South) and 24 m (North), Uzbek 28 m, Kazhak 15 m, Azeri Turkish 9 m, Kyrgysz, Uyghur est. 6 m, Turkmen 5 m each, Mongol 3 m. **Total 346 m**.

4.9.3 TURKIC BRANCH

Among major languages are ***Turkish/Azeri, Uzbek, Kirghiz, Kazak, Uyghur (Uighur), Tatar*** [LAs-20]. Many languages of the Turkic group are in fact mutually intelligible dialects. For instance, Turkish and Azeri are mutually intelligible. (Azeri is basically Turkish with regional words and dialectical variations; and as noted elsewhere in this book, most Turks do not consider Azeri a separate language at all, but just call it Turkish!)

4.9.4 TUNGUSIC (SIBERIAN) AND MONGOLIC (MONGOLIAN) BRANCHES

Within the *Tungusic* branch is only one major language, *Maanchu*, once the language of the Manchu dynasty of China and the Manchurian region, which for all practical purposes is extinct (it has been supplanted by Mandarin) [LAs-28]. Several other Tungusic languages are expected to be extinct by 2015.

The major languages within the *Mongolic* branch are *Mongolian* and *Korean*, which are extremely close. Mongolian speakers will remark how easy it is for them to learn Korean because many words in the two languages are mutually intelligible and the grammatical structure is so close [LAs-27]. Nevertheless, it is noted that the current linguistics scholarship does not put Korean squarely in the Mongolic branch, but rather gives it a separate, undefined placement. Based on extensive conversations with native Korean and Mongolian speakers, this author begs to differ.

4.9.5 SCRIPTS OF THE ALTAIC FAMILY AND JAPANESE

All *Turkic* branch languages of the Altaic family were originally written in scripts derived from the Arabic script. For example, Turkish was written in a variant of Arabic called the "Kufic" script. Turkish adopted a Roman-based script under the directive of Kemal Attatürk after the demise of the Ottoman Empire. (It is said that Attatürk even contributed substantially to this script, working with the linguist Ismet Inönü. Along with the change of script, many words of Arabic and Faarsi origin were replaced by Turkish-origin words [LAs-19]. The script is uniquely adapted to Turkic languages, and has the added feature of one-phone-one-letter (no digraphs etc. are used). The Turkic languages falling under the old Soviet Union adopted the Cyrillic script, but their governments are as of this writing (2005) talking of changing back to Arabic or further to Roman-based scripts (with the Turkish script as a base). Uighur is still written in an Arabic-based script in many parts of China's Xinxiang province.

Old Mongolian was originally written in Phagspa, a script based ultimately on Braahmi [SCr-53, SCr-54]. In more recent times, among other Altaic languages, Mongolian was, due to Soviet influence, written in the Cyrillic script in recent times. However, very recently (2004), the Mongolian government talked of converting to a Roman-based script [LAs-27]. Korean is written in its own script, called *Haangul* [SCr-46 to SCr-53]. This was adopted under the directive of a 16th century king. It is one of the most scientific if not *the* most scientific script devised anywhere. It shows some influence from Buddhist literature, and thus, ultimately, the Braahmi script. It is discussed in much more detail elsewhere in this book.

The Japanese script is well known. It is a syllabary, a form highly convenient for Japanese because Japanese has just over 40 syllables [SCr-55]. It has versions, *Hiragana* and *Katakana*, for words of native or foreign origin, and *Kanji* characters, adapted from Chinese characters, thus giving it a small ideographic flavor.

4.10 DRAVIDIAN FAMILY

4.10.1 DRAVIDIANS AND THEIR ORIGINS IN THE INDIAN AND WORLD CONTEXTS

4.10.1.1 Are Dravidians Native to India or Were They Migrants from the Iran/Iraq Region?

Among major language families, especially those identified with ancient civilizations, the **Dravidian** family remains perhaps the *most mysterious in terms of origins and affinities*.

Recent (from about 1980 to 2005) studies have nevertheless shed much more light on this subject. These include, e.g.:

(1) The seminal *linguistic* studies of McAlpin on Elamite [LAi-24] and studies on related subjects by others [LAi-25 to LAi-38].
(2) Recent *DNA* studies, such as those of Barnabas and coworkers, Bamshad and coworkers, and others [GDn-25 to GDn-36, GDn-67 to GDn-70].
(3) Very recent *archaeological* digs, such as the ones carried out by the Archaeological Survey of India at Dholavira in Gujaraat, Sanauli in Uttar Pradesh, Adichchannallur in Tamil Nadu and Bhirrana in Haryana and by Pakistani scientists at Mehrgarh in Pakistan [HIi-1 to HIi-9].
(4) And earlier *archaeological* digs by the Meadow group of Harvard University [HIi-5]).

As a result of these studies, the view is now gaining ground that ***Dravidians might, possibly, be native to present-day India/Pakistan*** and have spread west *to* Iran and Iraq, rather than being migrants *from* the Middle East, as originally hypothesized by many [HIi-1 to HIi-9, GDn-25 to GDn-36, GDn-67 to GDn-70].

A generally accepted belief is that the language(s) of the Indus Valley (Harappan) civilization was (were) Dravidian [LAi-13 to LAi-23, HIi-21, HIi-22]. However, it is also true that ***there is as yet no hard linguistic, archaeological or any other type of evidence to support or negate this belief***. Nevertheless, for reasons that will be apparent from the discussion in the sequel, this remains a plausible belief, and we will give it high credibility in our subsequent discussions.

Chapter 4: The World's Major Language Families- A Primer

Within India itself, it is a widely held belief - one would even clarify it as a "collective people's memory", which are known to be sometimes quite credible - that the Dravidians are somehow integrally associated with India. This is in sharp contrast to views expressed in literature meant primarily for a Western audience, whether authored by Indians or non-Indians.

Thus, according to this view, the origins of *the Dravidians may actually be placed in India proper*, from the beginnings of farming communities in Neolithic times. This view is supported by excavations at **Mehrgarh** in present-day Pakistan [HIi-1], which have revealed *semi-urban* developments dating to earlier than 7000 BCE, as a prelude to the great Harappan-era cities. These semi-urban developments were advanced, even having, for instance, established dental practices, with evidence of the first dental drilling of a live patient to access a root canal [HIi-1]! This appears to show a clearly *Indian*, as opposed to Middle Eastern, origin for the Harappan-era (presumably though not certainly, Dravidian) civilizations.

Indeed, today, Dravidian-speaking peoples seem to be such an integral part of the of Indian heartland (i.e. central and southern India) that it is difficult to imagine that their origins may have been outside the Indian subcontinent. This is especially so given the fact that the Dravidian languages are today found nowhere else in the world. On the other hand, many examples exist in the world to show that the speakers of a language or group of languages may be supplanted from their original homes - the Austro-Asiatic, Austronesian and Indo-European families, and even, presumably, Japanese, are just a few such examples of this. There is also, of course, clear evidence that Dravidian languages stretched to present-day eastern Iraq in ancient times, certainly to the Elamite regimes [LAi-24 to LAi-28], but with affinities with the Hurrian and other ancient Middle Eastern languages also possibly indicated [LAi-28, LAi-29].

It is also reasonable to presume, based on linguistic, DNA and other evidence (see below), that *the most likely geographical extent of Dravidian peoples in ancient times was approximately from modern-day Iraq and western Iran through the Deccan and coastal regions of South India* (see also maps in **Figs. 4-4**).

Thus, before we discuss Dravidian origins further, it is worthwhile to reconstruct the background tapestry of the flow of peoples in the context of which they must be presented. That is to say, the background of prior peoples and linguistic groups within the region relevant to Dravidians. We now do this in brief.

Chapter 4: The World's Major Language Families- A Primer

183

Our reconstruction must necessarily start with the migration of hominids from Africa as it pertains to the Indian and Middle Eastern context. Much of the more recent developments relating to this migration are based on ***DNA studies***. In this respect, a caveat on their limitations is thus worth mentioning at the outset: The accuracy of the *"molecular clock"*, assumptions in the concept of ***genetic drift***, and the accuracy of genetic dating in general, have all been questioned by eminent authorities in recent articles in the genetics literature [GDn-38, GDn-39]. And in some cases, e.g. the placement of the first ex-Africa migration about 70,000 years ago, they contradict archaeological evidence. We nevertheless proceed on the assumption that *modern DNA dating and evolutionary biology techniques have some, reasonable accuracy*.

Neglecting for the moment the much earlier migrations of *Homo erectus*, it is generally agreed that some of the first migrations of *Homo sapiens* from the horn of Africa were around 70,000 BCE, from a population thought to number as little as 2,000 (though again that is also very contentious!— cf. refs. [GDn-1, 8, GDn-17, GDn-19, GDn-23]). Very recently, in 2003, the discovery of a "thoroughly modern" human skeleton in Tianyuan Cave near Beijing, dated to about 40,000 BCE, has challenged even this theory [GDn-20] as have other recent studies [GDn-21, GDn-10].

Such migrations would have brought modern humans through the Middle East and into northern India as far as the Deccan, no doubt intermingling with or displacing prior *Homo* species. Much of this migration may have been littoral initially [GDn-17], subsequently progressing inland only slowly. In recent (1996 et seq.) work, Barnabas, Bamshad and coworkers, and others, genetically documented the route of the M haplogroup from Africa to India and showed that their study supported the "southern", littoral route of migration [GDn-25 to GDn-30]. They showed that, subsequently, there was much *in situ*, i.e. *indigenous*, genetic differentiation.

The *first* linguistically significant littoral-hopping migrations [GDn-17] from the west into India might be considered to be those of what are known, for want of a better appellation, as the "*Negrito*" peoples. The descendants of this migration today are presumed to remain only in the Andaman/Nicobar Islands, and in isolated pockets in the Indian mainland, such as the Kaadar and Pulaiyan people of Parambikkulam and adjoining areas near the Annamalai hills in Tamil Nadu [HIi-22]. Little anecdotes of anthropological and/or archaeological evidence buttress the view of such littoral-hoping "Negrito" (again, for want of a better word) migrations from Africa, across India, to the Indonesian archipelago. For example, the womenfolk of the above-mentioned Kaadar people use a unique type and shape of comb with a very unique, intricate, serpentine design. The identical comb, with *absolutely identical design*, is also found among the Semangs of Malaysia, another short-statured "Negrito" people. This is very unlikely to be mere coincidence. "Negrito" skeletons of men of very short stature have been unearthed at various places in the Indian heartland, e.g. at Vaadnagar near Baroda (Vadodara) [HIi-23, HIi-24] Etc. etc. In terms of language, it is reasonable to presume that these early peoples' language(s) belonged to a separate family or families. The language isolates surviving in the Andaman and Nicobar Islands of India, and apparently unrelated to any known languages, may be the descendants of these.

The *next* (second and beyond) migrations into India are easier to postulate with some credibility, since they have apparently left stronger linguistic evidence: A second migration of Austro-Asiatic peoples, progenitors of the Mundaa peoples. Mundaa languages survive all over India even today (2005), though they are concentrated in certain provinces, such as Jhaarkhand and, to a lesser extent, Chhatisgarh. Then, a third, continuous migration of Mongolian peoples (from the East, probably across Tibet and what is today Arunaachal Pradesh). Elements of Sino-Tibetan languages are incorporated into the languages of the hill peoples of India and Nepal such as Almori, Paahaadi and Nepaali. As any traveler to these regions will have noted, in a superficial, "racial" sense, there is an increased prominence of the epicanthic fold as one progresses onto the higher elevations in the Himaalayan foothills, or east through Bengal to Arunaachal Pradesh, etc. However, recent (ca. 2000 et seq.) Y-chromosome studies appear to indicate a very recent overlay of Tibeto-Burman-speaking populations on earlier Austro-Asiatic-speaking populations in the Indian subcontinent [GDn-26, GDn-27, GDn-67].

The Dravidian migration into India, *if there was one*, might then be placed concurrently with these, second and third, migrations. On the other hand, *if the Dravidian peoples were native North or Central Indian descendants of the Neolithic peoples who first took to farming on the Indian subcontinent, then there would have been no migration*. The latter view is supported by excavations of semi-urban developments in Mehrgarh in present-day Pakistan dated to ca 7000 BCE, cited earlier in this chapter, which appear to be precursors to Harappan cities [HIi-1]. Also as noted above, a recent (2006) mtDNA study by the Barnabas group [GDn-26] supports *in situ* genetic differentiation within India of groups carrying the M haplogroup that arrived from Africa 70,000 to 30,000 years ago.

To the above picture of the linguistic groups of India thus far, we must add the caveat that there may have been other language families or isolates that were supplanted by the Austro-Asiatic, Sino-Tibetan, Dravidian and other groups, which today show no traces.

4.10.1.2 Dravidians, Aaryans (Aryans), Haplogroups and The Last Ice Age

Now following the initial migrations out of Africa, estimated at around 30 000 to 20 000 BCE, there was a major event elsewhere in the world, which ultimately had a profound effect in the Indian and Eurasian context. This was the last *Ice Age*. This may not have significantly affected peoples in warmer climates such as Africa or the Middle East or North, Central and Southern India, but it did apparently serve to "tie up" human populations in the temperate region, until it ended, around 8 000 to 6 000 BCE.

In the Indian and Dravidian context, the people of most relevance that were "tied up" in this fashion by the last Ice Age were those corresponding to the ***R1a haplogroup***, the so-called "***Aaryan (Aryan) haplogroup***", in regions near the Caspian, Black and Aral Seas [GDn-29 to GDn-36, GDn-40, GDn-67 to GDn-69]. (To clarify once again, *haplogroups* are groupings of the most common *haplotypes* in the Y (male) chromosome, thus passed down among males only. *Haplotypes* in turn are a type of mutation within the Y chromosome called a *Single Nucleotide Polymorphism*, SNP or "Snip" for short.)

The R1a haplogroup has received much interest. Scholars working in the field, such as the groups of Semino, Passarino and Wells have declared a *Ukrainian* origin for this haplogroup [GDn-44]. The reasons given for the Ukrainian assignment are based on three separate types of study: (1) Principal component analysis. (2) Frequency distribution. (3) Microsatellite variation. According to this reasoning, "the greater the microsatellite diversity of a haplotype at a particular geographical location, the closer that location is to that haplotype's likely geographical point of origin. In the case of R1a, the highest level of microsatellite diversity is found in Ukraine" [GDn-40 (a)]. Therefore, Ukraine is presumed to be the geographical origin of this haplogroup.

Respectfully, however, this reasoning is seriously faulty, in that it ignores the fluid, migratory nature of human populations. It assumes that the present population composition of a particular geographic area (the Ukraine in this case) has strong relation to its past composition. As an example, if an entire village or group of villages got up and moved 500 km east of its original location, e.g. due to extreme conditions such as flood or drought or flight from an invader, the above reasoning would be invalid. Perhaps then, the terms "geographical location" in the quote above would be more accurately replaced by "concentration of population". This would remove the tie-up with geographical location but retain it with a particular ethnic stream. The reasoning may then have more validity.

Chapter 4: The World's Major Language Families- A Primer

More recent genetic studies relating to the R1a haplogroup have indicated a possible Indian subcontinent origin for this group [GDn-34 to GDn-36]. In the context of this controversy, then, this author believes that other evidence, such as archaeological, and, more particularly, linguistic, should perhaps be given equal weight to genetic analyses.

The linguistic evidence, primarily the far greater archaicness of the Sanskrit language when compared to all other ancient Indo-European languages (see analyses and paradigms presented elsewhere in this chapter and in a chapter in the first *NAVLIPI* volume) indicates a temporal closeness of the parent R1a haplogroup to the Sanskrit language. In turn, due to the slowness of ancient travel and migration, this would indicate a geographical closeness of the location that Sanskrit first found itself in, i.e. (modern-day) eastern Afghanistan and western Pakistan.

This linguistic evidence must be taken together with such other factors, as the apparent **westward** *migration of Iranian offshoots of the Indo-European group from India*, which is supported not only by theological arguments (presented elsewhere in this chapter and in a chapter in the first *NAVLIPI* volume), but also by the following facts: Although modern-day Iranians speak an Indo-European language (Faarsi), *their gene pool has very little of the R1a haplogroup but a great contribution from haplogroups identified with Semitic and other Middle Eastern and Mediterranean populations* [GDn-40 to GDn-42]. In contradistinction, populations from eastern and northern Afghanistan through Pakistan, Kashmir and down into central India, as well as Brahmin populations of the deep Indian South, have a very strong presence of the R1a haplogroup [GDn-34 to GDn-36].

(As noted elsewhere in this chapter as well, genetic analyses of Indian populations are unfortunately complicated by divisions of *caste*, which originally reflected racial and ethnic divisions, and the subsequent, resultant endogamy practiced over millennia. This has been strongly corroborated by a recent genetic studies by Bamshad et al. and others [GDn-29, GDn-32, GDn-34 to GDn-36, GDn-67 to GDn-70]. Thus, in some respect, when one is analyzing different castes in India, one is effectively analyzing the remnants of entirely different racial or ethnic groups or even nationalities, although diluted over the millennia by intermingling.)

Also in contradistinction to the Iranians, the Tajiks (Tadzhiks), placed today in northern Afghanistan, Tajikistan, Kyrgyszstan and Turkmenistan, *are noted in many genetic studies to have among the highest incidence of R1a haplogroup presence, nearly 64%, surpassed only by the Ishkashimi and Kashmiri Pandits at 68% or more* [GDn-40 (a)]!

Finally, there is also the evidence, though limited, that the tree line during the LGM (last glacial maximum, i.e. the height of the last Ice Age), lay just south of cold, icy desert, was somewhere in the middle of modern-day Ukraine, but veered off sharply south at more eastern latitudes, going eventually through the middle of modern-day Turkmenistan and Tajikistan [GDn-71].

This would imply that the populations originally migrating eastward from Africa and the Middle East would have been "stuck", to wait out the Ice Age, exactly within modern-day Turkmenistan and Tajikistan. Thus, the likelihood that substantial human populations were isolated in the regions north of Afghanistan must be taken into serious consideration.

In view of the arguments presented above, it is this author's considered opinion that the "migration" of the R1a haplogroup, i.e. the Aaryan "migration", would more likely have occurred from what is today Uzbekistan and Turkmenistan and perhaps parts of northern Afghanistan and through the Kubha (Kabul) valley. This author also feels that, under the circumstances then, a more accurate term for this "migration" is *slow co-mingling. There is no archaeological (or other) evidence whatsoever of any Aaryan "invasion" or other sort of rapid migration* as such, although there is genetic evidence of strong superimposition of a presumably non-indigenous haplogroup (the R1a) onto the Indian population [GDn-34 to GDn-36]. In this context, it is noted that Tajikistan and Turkmenistan are today very much a desert or very arid region. However, around 7 000 to 5 000 BCE the approximate date of our discussion, they would have been a temperate desert bordering a lush grassland, the border bifurcating the territory [GDn-71]; this would have been very much like the northern Sahara in Africa, which also started drying up around 5 500 BCE [GDn-71].

The relative placement of the Dravidians and Aaryans in the Indian context is depicted in maps presented in **Figs. 4-4** *et seq.,* further below, at the end of the discussion in this section.

At a much, much later time than the Aaryan migrations (or "co-minglings", as this author prefers), there were migrations into India, all from the west: Greek, Hun, Persian, Arab, Central Asian, etc. etc. Although the linguistic influence of these groups on Dravidian languages is small, it is nevertheless present: For example, some common Tamil words today are of Arabic and Faarsi origin.

4.10.1.3 Tamil, Elamite and "Proto-Dravidian"

We have now set up, above, a basic, background tapestry of the Indian heartland in the context of the early peoples settled therein, above. One of our first stopping points subsequently must be the very important work of McAlpin [LAi-24] and others [LAi-25 to LAi-37] in attempting to relate *Elamite* and other Dravidian languages.

Elamite was the language of Elam, a kingdom or republic that was prominent in the region of western and southern Iran and easternmost Iraq in the late 4th and early 3rd millennium BCE. (Elam still means "homeland" in Tamil and was used by the Tamil Tigers, the LTTE, as a name for their desired Tamil nation in Sri Lanka.) One of its achievements was the development of a unique script, given the appellation "Proto-Elamite", which has been successfully deciphered [LAi-25, LAi-26, SCr-21] It is noted that there are several variations of Elamite that one must deal with: Old Elamite, Middle Elamite, Achaemenid Elamite (from the royal Achaemenid inscriptions and other tablets from Persepolis), etc. [LAi-24 to LAi-27]. The Elamite we refer to and discuss in this book encompasses *all* these variants.

We have briefly alluded to McAlpin's work in Chapter 1 of this book. Therein, we have noted some of McAlpin's somewhat glaring errors, for example the use of many Tamil words of obvious Sanskrit (i.e. Indo-European) borrowing, e.g., *kutiira* ("hut, settlement"), *shawa* ("corpse") and *channa* ("beauty").

Nevertheless, McAlpin's conclusion that Elamite and Tamil are both Dravidian and are related appears to be *eminently correct*, and his contribution is thus seminal. This is especially evident to a Tamil speaker such as this author, or to several scholars, native speakers of Tamil, consulted for the present book, who reviewed McAlpin's work in detail. The very large number of definitively Dravidian cognates amongst the most common words (personal pronouns, numerals, etc.) which are known to change least in languages [LN-84], e.g., *Nii*, "you", *ulh*, "home, inside", *naal.*, "day", *paara*, "look (at)", are irrefutable. More so to a native Tamil speaker, or someone familiar with the language (such as this author). They simply cannot be ascribed to mere coincidence.

Presented in the **Table** below are just some of these cognates. In considering these, it must be borne in mind that we are comparing a modern language (Tamil) with a language more than four thousand years removed from it (Elamite). This would be the equivalent of comparing English words with Sanskrit words. Thus, the cognacy is all the more striking.

In this author's opinion, just this limited list of cognates irrefutably establishes the cognacy of Tamil and Elamite, and thus places Elamite firmly in the Dravidian family. It also however shows that there is some significant distance between Tamil and Elamite, as is to be expected over a span of four thousand years or more.

What is most striking to this author about Elamite is that it has rather poor grammatical form and structure and is more like a periphrastic language. In that sense, its contrast to Tamil, with its high (superficially) inflectional character and structure, is quite striking.

This would appear to indicate that, if Elamite and Tamil had a common parent, Elamite was already significantly degenerated ("metathesized" in modern linguistic jargon) from this parent language. This may have been due, perhaps, to the influence of other Middle Eastern linguistic groups it had come into contact with. In contrast, proto-Tamil would have escaped this outside influence until it encountered Sanskrit, sometime, according to this author's contention, around 3100 – 3500 BCE This then would yield *a much greater age for a parent language, a "**Proto-Dravidian**", possibly well into the 5th or 6th millennium BCE* (Regarding the dating of Sanskrit to 3500 BCE as compared to Max Muller's "back-of-the-envelope" calculation of 1500 BCE which subsequently stuck, as a sort of unquestioned gospel, in all subsequent Western and many Indian publications, see the extensive discussion in a separate section in in a chapter in the first *NAVLIPI* volume, on the Indian phonological classification).

With respect to the discussion on Elamite above, some evidence has also been presented lending credence to the possible affinity of Dravidian languages with *other* languages of the Middle East besides Elamite. These include **Hurrian, Susian, Kassite**, all now extinct. Thus, e.g., Hurrian is an agglutinative language that appears to have little Dravidian component, but on closer analysis, it reveals many words of obvious Dravidian provenance [LAi-28]. Whether these are merely borrowings from Elamite or native to Hurrian may be left for scholars in this field to decide [LAi-27, LAi-28]. Caldwell, Haimendorf [HIi-23, HIi-26] and others have done extensive linguistic comparisons of Tamil with Susian and Elamite before proposing affinities. Geographically, the Hurrian and Elamite lands in the Middle East correspond to modern-day eastern Iraq and western Iran, with some stretch into present-day Baluchistan.

Chapter 4: The World's Major Language Families- A Primer

Table 4-4 (*cont. overleaf*): Selected cognates of ancient Elamite and modern Tamil, from the seminal work of McAlpin [LAi-24]. *In considering these cognates, it must be borne in mind that we are comparing a modern language (Tamil) with a language more than four thousand years removed from it (Elamite). Thus, the cognacy is all the more striking.*

[Note that the transcriptions into Roman script are rough, to avoid diacritics and under-marks required to render Dravidian languages into Roman script. Thus, e.g., [**t.**] and [**r.**] can both represent the retroflex and alveolar flaps as well as a host of other phones, whilst [**l.**] represents a retroflex lateral.) In this author's opinion, just this limited list irrefutably establishes the cognacy of Tamil and Elamite, and thus places Elamite firmly in the Dravidian family.]

(The especially strong or important resemblances are double-asterisked.)

(MODERN) TAMIL	(ANCIENT) ELAMITE	WORD MEANING
**chinna	tsinna, chinna	small; young (person)
**naal. naalaki	naa, naan	day; today
**nii	nii	you (singular)
**ondru, undru, colloq. onna, unna	unra	one; each; one (thing)
**paara	paara	look (at), look, watch over
**pori	paari	to pluck, pull
**ul, ulla	ulhi, ulh	inside; interior; room; house; dwelling
aanpu	Haan	kindness; love, friendship
aarii (inf. aari-girada)	shaarra, shaarri	to collect, gather, investigate
at.i, ad.i	hat.a	to hit, beat, strike, destroy; (but note Indo-European co-incidental cognate *hat (*to hit)!)
chiiru, shiiru chiirudai, shiirudai	shiil(in)	wealth, abundance, prosperity, beauty rich, fancy clothes
er.i	eri	burn, blaze, bake; baked brick
id.u	iddu	to distribute, give (flour, etc.)

(Table 4-4, cont.)		
(MODERN) TAMIL	(ANCIENT) ELAMITE	WORD MEANING
irai, iraiwan	irshai	great person, great, large
it.aayan	hit., hit.u	herdsmen; herds
karu	kari(ri)	young of animal, kid
katt(il)	kat	cot, bed; bed-place
muut.u	muuhtu, muuti	female animal
pat.ai, par.ai (remains in Malayaalam only, defunct in Tamil)	pera	to speak, say; to read
pohal, pokal	puk(ta)	refuge; help
taar..	tsaar.a, saara	to go down, bend; below, under
tall.u	tallu	to push down, thrust; to write (cuneiform)
tir.ai	tserum, serum, ser	tax, tribute
tonru, tond.u	tonpa, tumpa	to appear, be visible
tul.ai (verb, inf. ~irada)	tullin	a hole; to make a hole, bore, cut, breach
tuvai; tukai	tuhai	to pound, crush; to wash clothes (pounding them on a wash stone)
ud.ai ottai	ud.u, hud.u	to break, break into pieces, make holes a hole, gap
uppat., uppar. uppar.avar	uppat.	bricklaying, brickwork (caste of) construction workers

It is also worth noting that there are also some superficial examples of name similarities which may or may not indicate a western migration of Dravidians from India. Some examples of these are: The affinities of the names *Dramila* (found in Mycenaean descriptions whence supposedly *Tamil*) with *Draavida*; the Lycians of Anatolia calling themselves Tamils (*Trimmlai*); or the name for "town, city" being *ur* in both modern Tamil and Sumerian. There are many such examples which can be cited. And finally, there is much anthropological and related evidence as well, to indicate a common "Dravidian" element in civilizations as varied as the Harappan, Sumerian and Minoan:

Matriarchal lineage; prominence of the mother-goddess culture; strikingly "Dravidian" place names; a very specific type of bullfighting as a quasi-religious or quasi-ritualistic sport, practiced even today in regions as far apart as Tamil Nadu in India, Crete and Iberia. Etc. etc. etc..

Krishnamurthi [LAi-30] has produced a rather thorough and detailed comparative grammar of the Dravidian languages. Unfortunately, because of its very technical and specialized presentation, it is difficult for even the well-informed linguist to peruse, and can be directed only to an audience heavily specialized in the Dravidian languages. It also gives little insight into the origins of Dravidian languages or their relation to non-Indian languages such as Elamite (though it of course does not seek to).

4.10.1.4 Recent DNA Studies and Archaeological Excavations Shedding Some Light on Dravidian Origins

Another element in completing our background tapestry for Dravidian languages is important **DNA work**, primarily by the Barnabas' group, originally at the National Chemical Laboratory, Pune, India, and several other workers [GDn-25 to GDn-36, GDn-67 to GDn-70]. To cite some of their very first work, Barnabas and coworkers carried out an analysis of mitochondrial DNA variation (mtDNA) of 100 working class or farmer individuals belonging to 14 language groups in North, South and Central regions of India, using the same set of six restriction enzymes used in the study of other world ethnic groups. They found 29 mtDNA types and constructed maximum parsimony trees. They found that 12 of the 29 gene types of South Indians were the same as those found in "Caucasians" in the Zagros region of Iran and Iraq (coincidentally, exactly corresponding to the location of the Elamite kingdom). The South Indians shared only four gene types with East and Southeast Asians. *Most surprisingly, they found that North Indians and South Indians shared only two mitochondrial gene types with each other*, indicating a huge North/South Indian, "Aaryan/Dravidian," divide. The use of farmer or working class subjects as in the Barnabas study, minimized the otherwise pernicious and unpredictable effect of caste in the Indian context, lending further credence to it. Her analysis indicated that South Indians and inhabitants of the Zagros region of Iran and Iraq had a strong genetic affinity. In the context of this study, statements such as made by Diamond and Bellwood in their well-cited 2003 article in *Science* [LN-83] viz. "...South Indians today are phenotypically and genetically so unlike peoples of the Fertile Crescent.", display, in this author's humble opinion, a surprising ignorance of others' DNA studies.

The above work was corroborated by further studies by the Barnabas and other groups [GDn-25 to GDn-36]. A prominent such recent (2006) study was a high-resolution mtDNA study of a larger sampling of the Indian population with implications for the Paleolithic settlement of the Indian subcontinent [GDn-26]. This study included sequencing of the non-transcribed HVSI region to derive maximum maternal lineages. The target sample comprised *non-tribal* Indians. (Any analysis of Indian populations is fraught with complications due to caste, which originally reflected racial and ethnic divisions; hence the exclusion of tribal ("Scheduled Caste/Tribe" in Indian government jargon) individuals is important.) A key finding of this study was that there was significant *in situ* genetic differentiation of the Indian population from great antiquity. This would also lend credence to great antiquity of the Dravidian peoples within India proper.

The very recent *excavations* by the Archaeological Survey of India at Dholavira in Gujarat, Sanauli in Tehsil Barot, Taluka Bhagpat in Uttar Pradesh, Adichchannallur in Tamil Nadu and Bhirrana in Haryaanaa [HIi-2 to HIi-9] have revealed two features of potential note in a Dravidian context. Firstly, they have shown that the (possibly Dravidian) Harappan civilization extended throughout India, as far East as the eastern Gangetic Plain, to the southwest to all parts of Gujarat, and, possibly (pending identification of Adichchannallur as definitively Harappan or pre-Harappan), *as far south as Tamil Nadu*. Secondly, the burial customs and gold diadems at Adichchannallur have a striking resemblance to those found not only in the Middle East but as far west as Mycenae; these resemblances cannot simply be ascribed to coincidence. They again appear to indicate a Middle Eastern connection to the southern Indian (Dravidian) peoples, whether through westward migration from India or eastward migration from the Middle East.

4.10.1.5 The Likely Dravidian/Aaryan (Aryan) Tapestry in the Indian Geographical Context From About 10 000 BCE

Now that we have laid our background tapestry, giving some orientation to the Dravidians in the Indian and world context, we can attempt to discuss the origins of the Dravidian language family in more detail.

The picture we have painted above can be summarized in a rough *map* of a possible *placement of the Dravidian* (including Elamite) *peoples* with respect to other peoples, starting from about 10 000 BCE through around the 5th and 4th millennia BCE, in the Indian context. This is presented in **Figs. 4-4a-c.**

Chapter 4: The World's Major Language Families- A Primer

194

Figs. 4-4a-c (*starting overleaf*):

ROUGH MAPS OF A POSSIBLE PLACEMENT OF THE DRAVIDIAN (INCLUDING ELAMITE) PEOPLES WITH RESPECT TO OTHER PEOPLES AROUND THE 10TH TO 4TH MILLENNIA BCE, IN THE INDIAN CONTEXT

The placement of the Aaryan (Aryan) peoples in the maps is based on genetic evidence from the R1a, "Aaryan" (Aryan) haplogroup, for just after the end of the last Ice Age. Very recent studies, which appear to ascribe a purely Indian subcontinent origin to R1a, appear to cast some doubt on this placement ([GDn-34 to GDn-36], see text for discussion). The earliest map shown presumes that the Dravidian and Aaryan peoples had some contact with each other and knew of each other, but had not yet mingled, and is drawn in consideration of the presumed distribution of vegetation in the millennia after the Last Glacial Maximum, LGM [GDn-71]. This would be more in line with the opinions held in India (as opposed to in the West) relating to the lack of archaeological or related evidence for an "Aaryan invasion" into India as also the most recent excavations [HIi-2 to HIi-9, GDn-25 to GDn-36, GDn-67-GDn-70]. The maps still accommodate the radical difference between the Indo-European and Dravidian language families and the clear, later clash of cultures recorded in the later, Hindu literature as well as in sharp North/South Indian divide in DNA distributions still prevalent today (2003-2008) [GDn-67 to GDn-70]. These original ethnic divisions in good probability led to the eventual caste divisions. It is also presumed that the Sino-Tibetan groups had not yet made significant inroads into the Indian heartland, which is also corroborated by recent Y-chromosome studies [GDn-32]. Along with the Sino-Tibetan groups, the Austronesian groups, which also were thought to have not as yet impinged on the area of interest, are also not shown, for clarity.

(*Figure starts overleaf.*)

(Figs. 4.4, cont.): (a)

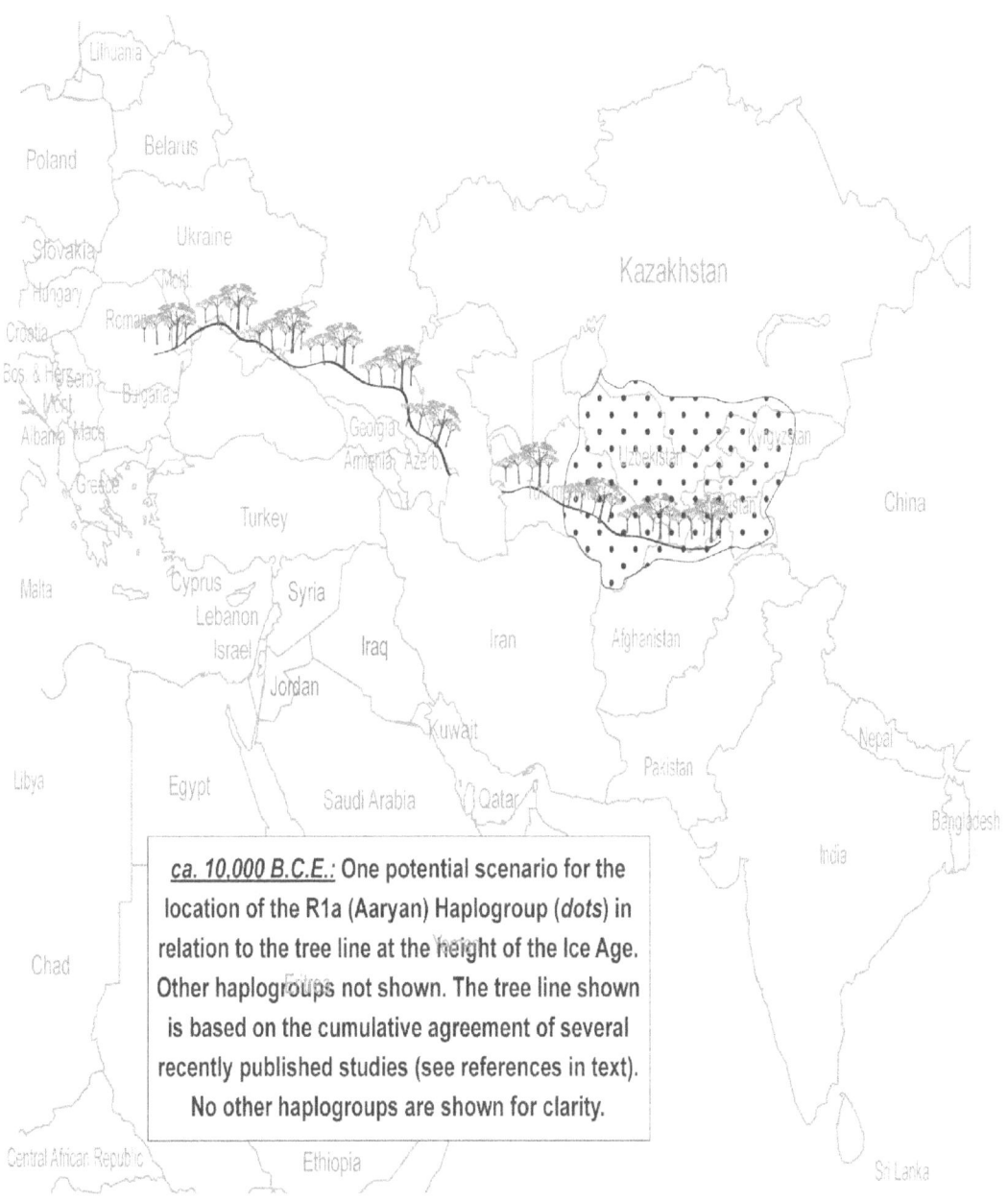

ca. 10,000 B.C.E.: One potential scenario for the location of the R1a (Aaryan) Haplogroup (*dots*) in relation to the tree line at the height of the Ice Age. Other haplogroups not shown. The tree line shown is based on the cumulative agreement of several recently published studies (see references in text). No other haplogroups are shown for clarity.

Chapter 4: The World's Major Language Families - A Primer

(Figs. 4.4, cont.): (b)

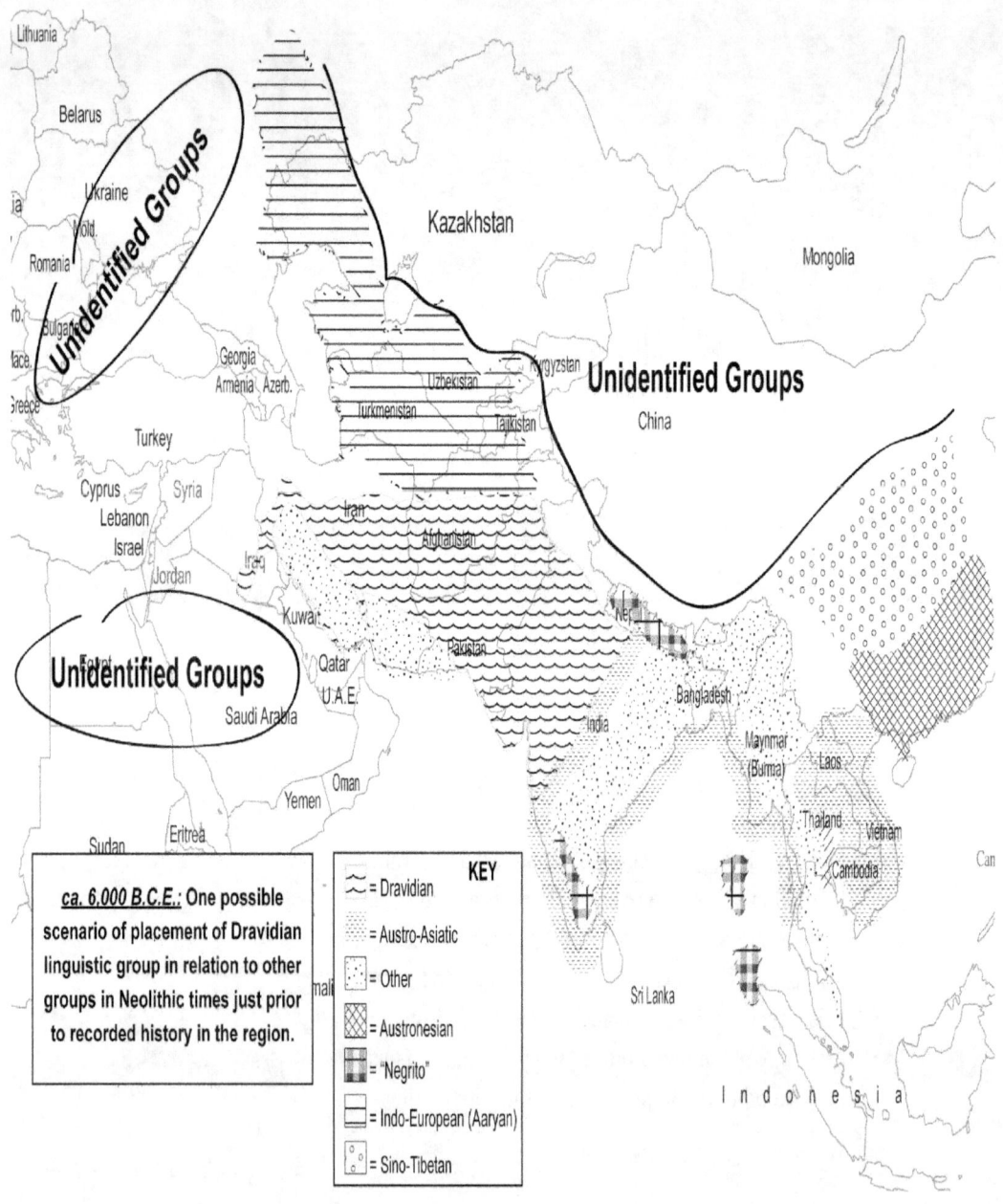

ca. 6,000 B.C.E.: One possible scenario of placement of Dravidian linguistic group in relation to other groups in Neolithic times just prior to recorded history in the region.

KEY
≈ = Dravidian
= Austro-Asiatic
= Other
= Austronesian
= "Negrito"
= Indo-European (Aaryan)
= Sino-Tibetan

Chapter 4: The World's Major Language Families- A Primer

(Figs. 4.4, cont.): (c)

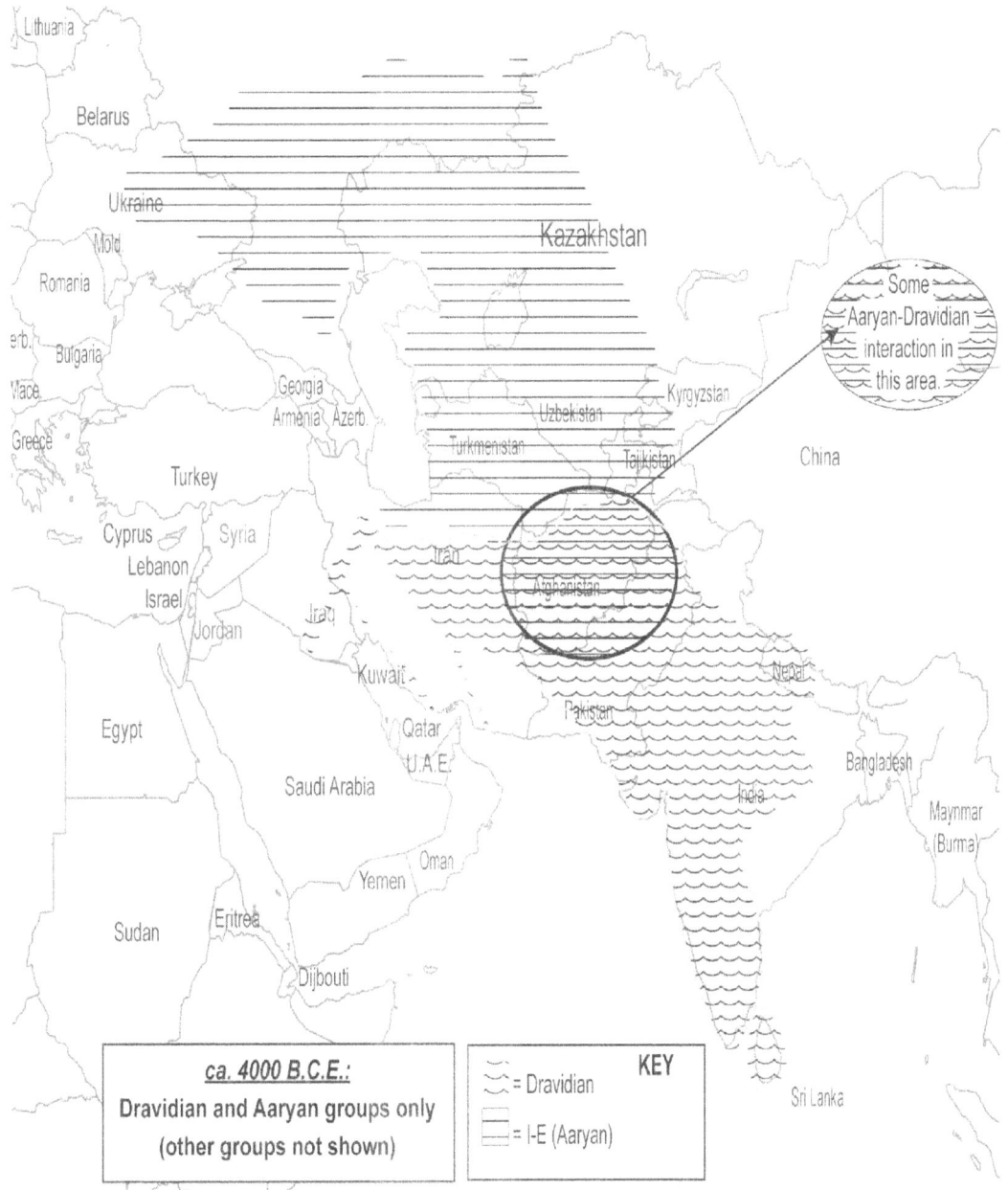

Chapter 4: The World's Major Language Families- A Primer

The placement of the Aaryan (Aryan) peoples in our above maps is based on genetic evidence from the ***R1a**, "**Aaryan" haplogroup*** for just after the end of the last Ice Age. However, very recent studies, which appear to ascribe a *purely Indian subcontinent origin to R1a*, appear to cast some doubt on this placement [GDn-34 to GDn-36]. The map presumes that the Dravidian and Aaryan peoples had some contact with each other and knew of each other, but had not yet mingled. It would also account for the citation of peoples such as the merchant *Pani* (plural *Panaya:*) as distinct from the *Daasa* in the *RgWeda (Rig Veda)*.

As a final point on the subject of Aaryan-Dravidian co-mingling, or otherwise, we need to note that this has recently (2006-2008) become a very controversial topic in India. There are those in India, primarily on the religious right, who contend that there was never any Aaryan-Dravidian divide. Unfortunately, many of them gloss over the reality that the Aaryan (Indo-European) and Dravidian language families radically differ from each other, with no hint of cognacy. Furthermore, they gloss over the fact that Indian society still shows radical fissures, in the form of *castes*. These appear to be the remnants, 5000 years later, of some sort of very serious ethnic and/or racial clash, which may have included pre-Dravidian peoples such as the Mundaa and Negritos. These divisions, originally along ethnic and color lines, persisted even after the original color distinctions vanished; the word for caste in Sanskrit is *warna (varna)*, which means "color". We can perhaps pardon the ancient perpetrators of this societal division by noting that there were no university sociology departments or psychologists to counsel these ancient peoples or interpret for them! But caste does show how such ethnic and sociological problems can be perpetuated, for thousands of years, if not dealt with early on and nipped in the bud. Anti-Aaryan (also translated as anti-Hindu and anti-Brahmin) antipathy persists in southern India even today – interview any politician from one of the Dravidian political parties in Tamil Nadu! Indeed, E. Ramasami Naicker, founder of the Dravida Kazhagam, the successful Dravidian movement, fled to atheism to escape the clutches of Hinduism.

There was definitely an Aaryan/Dravidian divide in ancient India, and at some point in time, Aaryans and Dravidians were geographically separate; the effects of this divide are strongly present even today in South India. This author however subscribes to the view that Aaryans and Dravidians were separate but proximate. At the end of the Ice Age, perhaps 6000 BCE (see maps in **Figs. 4-4** above), Aaryans, who had been geographically isolated, and evolved separately, for perhaps 10 000 years in, possibly, the area just north of present-day Afghanistan, started to move out. They first headed south to present-day northern India, and *only later*, as the climate warmed in Europe, to the northwest to Europe. This would explain the relative antiquity of Sanskrit as compared to all the other ancient Indo-European languages (see treatment of this subject elsewhere in this book).

It is also apparent that a small sub-branch of the Aaryan people then went *west*, to Iran, after an apparent theological feud with the main Aaryan group; witness the fact that Avestan (the parent of Old Persian) is the only Indo-European language in which *daiwa* means "demon" rather than "god" (sort of like modern Greek being the only Indo-European language where *nai* means "yes")! And the Aaryan *Asuras* (demons) have become Iranian *Ahuras* (gods).

Also, in the context of Aaryan/Dravidian co-mingling, it is worth noting the work of the Greek-Russian scholar Viktor Sarianidi. His painstaking, 30-year work at the *Bactria-Margiana Archaeological Complex (BMAC)* in Turkmenistan unearthed evidence, in a very small part of this vast complex, of Vedic-type rituals, including oblations offered with *ghrtam* (ghee) and Soma juice (juice of a narcotic plant), all dated from about 2000 B.C. Dr. Sarianidi, perhaps under the influence of Max Müller's dates (see elsewhere in this book for a discussion of F. Max Müller's horrendously erroneous "back-of-the-envelope" dating of Indian events), immediately jumped to the conclusion that this was evidence of Aaryans transiting through this area *before* arriving in India! Now the ancient peoples at BMAC were shown to be great traders (situated as they were at a crossroads of trade routes), with artifacts from far and wide, e.g. Sumerian cuneiform seals found next to Harappan seals. Thus, a more logical explanation for the BMAC findings could just as well be Aaryans visiting from India and performing a ceremonial oblation for some occasion (perhaps a business dinner?!), one of many travelers visiting the BMAC peoples. This is especially probable in view of the fact that this evidence of oblations was found in only one small part of the vast complex, with the rest of the complex indicating a totally different culture. It is also in line with the influence of Indians from the east on the Mittani and Kassites, discussed elsewhere in this book. However, this equally plausible explanation of the evidence was unfortunately entirely neglected by Dr. Sarianidi!

Earlier in this section, we have posited the hypothesis that "Proto-Dravidian" may have had extreme antiquity, possibly well into the 5th or even 8th millennium B.C.E (cf. the excavations at Mehrgarh, dating from around 7100 BCE). This is based on the structure of Elamite in relation to that of Tamil as well as other factors.

What the maps in **Figs. 4-4** then tell us together with this presumed extreme antiquity for a "Proto-Dravidian" is that there may have been a geographical continuity, and linguistic dominance, of Dravidian-language peoples from eastern Iraq through most of India, including the deep south of India, around this time. We can then conjecture that a common *parent* of ancient-day Elamite, Susian, Hurrian and modern-day Tamil may have been spoken even earlier, perhaps *as early as 7,000 BCE*

As noted earlier, all the data presented in the discussion above of course do not necessarily imply a Middle Eastern origin for the Dravidian peoples of India. They could easily as well imply a ***westward*** migration of Dravidians *from* the Indian heartland *to* these Middle Eastern regions. This is a less conventional view, nevertheless supported by recent (1996 – 2008) DNA and archaeological studies [GDn-25 to GDn-36, HIi-1 to HIi-9], as discussed at some length above.

On this basis, the Dravidian-speaking peoples may then be considered as one of the first human converts from a hunter-gatherer lifestyle to a farming lifestyle, one of the world's first farmers. That is to say, they may be considered among the world's first civilizers, contemporaneous with or perhaps (in this author's opinion and as hinted at by recent archaeological studies [HIi-1 to HIi-9]) even earlier than their Sumerian counterparts. This earlier antiquity would accord well with the sudden appearance of a fully developed writing around the middle of the 3rd millennium BCE in the Harappan civilization, with little if any evidence of any earlier stages of development [HIi-1]. It would also accord with very recent archaeological findings of Harappan writing from the middle of the 4th millennium BCE, pre-dating the earliest Sumerian writing [HIi-5, HIi-6].

In view of the extensive discussion above, the present author then subscribes to the following view:

> ***The Dravidian peoples may, possibly, be native to northern, northwestern and central India and the region around modern-day Baluchistan, and southern Afghanistan. They may have migrated <u>westward</u> to western Iran, Iraq (Mesopotamia) and perhaps Anatolia, thereby giving rise to such languages as Elamite***.

...(4.3)

Detailed discussion of this subject is best left to another book, but it is definitely relevant to mention it here, since it is relevant to the origin of the Dravidian languages of India.

4.10.2 EXTENT AND NUMBER OF SPEAKERS

The list of Dravidian languages surviving today is short. The major languages can be listed as follows, along with their geographical extent:

- ❖ *Tamil* (mainly in Tamil Nadu province in India, northern and coastal areas of Sri Lanka);
- ❖ *Kannada* (mainly in Karnataka province in India);
- ❖ *Malayalam* (mainly in Kerala province in India);
- ❖ *Telaguu* (Telugu) (mainly in Andhra Pradesh province in India);
- ❖ *Tulu* (also called *Kuurgi* or *Kodagu*, mainly in western Karnaatakaa province in India);
- ❖ *Brahui* (mainly in Baluchistan province in Pakistan but originally extending up to Helmand province in Afghanistan, nearly extinct). (Even as of 1908, the date of publication of Denys Bray's grammar of the Brahui language [LAi-38], the Brahui were said to number only 300,000. Since this is less than 1 m, Brahui does not figure in our census below.)

The approximate breakdown of the number of speakers is as follows (in decreasing order, all figures estimates for 2005):

- *Telaguu* 76 m;
- *Tamil* 63 m (Tamil Nadu) + 5 m (Sri Lanka);
- *Kannada* 53 m;
- *Malayaalam* 32 m;
- *Tulu* etc. 2 m;
- *Miscellaneous*, including diaspora, 2 m;
- **Total 233 m**.

Tamil and Malayalam are close, closer than Spanish and Portuguese, indicating a very recent divergence. Sri Lankan Tamil, called *Yaarpaal.am Tamil*, is an archaic Tamil; it however also has more influences from Sanskrit and other regional languages, such as Malayalam, than Indian Tamil. It bears the same approximate *temporal* relation to mainland Tamil as Québécois French bears to European French, but the difference in the language in the case of Tamil is greater. Tulu is considered by some to be a dialect of Kannada, but Tulu speakers think otherwise, and the two are not mutually intelligible.

All the five major Indian Dravidian languages derive much of their higher vocabulary from Sanskrit. Tamil does this the least, and is thus said to be the "most Dravidian" of the Dravidian languages. Thus, languages such as Telaguu (Telugu), Malayaalam and Kannadaa can be considered to be *Angramaya* languages, as defined later in this chapter, while Tamil should probably not be considered an *Angramaya* language.

Much has been made about **Brahui**, a modern Dravidian language of Baluchistaan. Even as of 1908, its speakers numbered less than 300,000, as noted above [LAi-38]; it is believed now to be well on its way to extinction. Now it is possible that Brahui is truly a survivor among Dravidian languages once widely prevalent in northern India. Its location in remote, mountainous regions of Baluchistaan, away from the major Afghan-Indian thoroughfare through the Khyber Pass, would support this view. However, this language could also easily be a medieval or earlier transplant from southern India, given the extensive seafaring of peoples of the Tamil Nadu region from about 1000 BCE through 1300 CE [HIi-22]. It could also be a remnant of South Indian cultural colonization dating from the early 1st millennium BCE, recorded in fleeting reference in old Tamil works such as those of the poet Maamuulanaar and the Sri Lankan Buddhist chronicle called the Mahaavamsa, both said to date from the 1st millennium B.C. [HIi-22, HIi-24]. F. Haimendorf [HIi-26] also proposed that Brahui was brought to Baluchistan by Tamil traders, but his voice was drowned out by later authors.

Thus, in brief summary, Brahui may still be an original Dravidian language of the region, but there is no strong evidence either way- i.e., either proving or disproving this. In this respect, the collective memory of the Brahui people, as recorded in the introductory passages in Bray's grammar dating from 1908 [LAi-38], is of no help! It states that the Brahui originated in Aleppo (in Syria)! This may be based on a story of the arrival of Braaho, or Ibrahim, from Aleppo, who ostensibly converted them to Islam in recent memory. Bray however notes that the Brahui did *look* very "different" from the neighboring Pathaan (Pushtuun, Pushtu) as well as Baluchi and Persian peoples. It is also noteworthy that, even as of 1908, the Brahui language of everyday usage was so laden with Baluchi and Faarsi borrowings as to nearly drown out the underlying Dravidian base [LAi-38].

4.11 AUSTRO-ASIATIC FAMILY

Extent and Number of Speakers: Geographically, these extend from eastern India through Vietnam [LN-1 to LN-4, LAs-62]. They include *Vietnamese* and *Khmer* (Cambodian).

The approximate breakdown of the number of speakers is as follows (in decreasing order, all figures estimates for 2005): Vietnam 88 m, Cambodia 15 m, India est. 10 m, Other 2 m. **Total 115 m**.

Like the Malay (Austronesian), Tai and Sino-Tibetan languages, these are also thought by modern linguists to have originated in southern China.

Interestingly, these languages have developed a variegated tonal character, possibly due to proximal influence from other language families: Some, e.g. *Vietnamese*, have strong tonal character (possibly due to the influence of Sino-Tibetan languages), whilst others, such as the Mundaa languages of India, have practically no tonal character. The number of speakers is similar to the Tai languages, in the tens of millions.

Modern linguistics texts [LN-1 to LN-4, LAs-62] bifurcate this family into two branches, *Munda* (*Mundaa*) and *Mon-Khmer*.
bhg3
Mundaa languages of India: These still survive amongst the Aadivaasi (aborigines) of the hill areas of India in provinces like Jhaarkhand (indeed, the Chief Minister of that state at the date of this writing, in 2006, had the surname Munda). Major languages include *Santhali* and *Mundaa* (also called Mundaari). *Khaasi*, a language of northeastern India, combines Mundaa and Sino-Tibetan elements.

Khmer (Cambodian): This is another *Angramaya (*English-like, see **Section 4.23** below) language, having an Austro-Asiatic base, but with nearly all the higher vocabulary, and even many everyday words, of Sanskrit origin. Examples of everyday words of Sanskrit origin in Khmer are *Aakkaa* for "sky" (Sanskrit, Hindi *Aakaash(a:)*); *Srii* for "woman" (Sanskrit, Hindi, etc., *Strii*). Proper names are immediately recognizable by persons of Indian heritage as of Sanskrit origin, for example, the late King *Norodom Sihanouk* (Sanskrit *Narottam Sinha*, "Finest among men, Lion"). Everyday Khmer vocabulary also has common or cognate words with neighboring languages such as Thai, but it is unclear to someone like this author, who is not fluent in these languages and their history, whether this is just due to proximal borrowing or genuinely common origins. Examples of such common words are Khmer *Reap* and Thai *Raap*, both meaning "kill".

Vietnamese: Vietnamese has very little Sanskrit-based superstructure, in contrast to Khmer. It is a strongly tonal language, possibly due to proximal influence from Sino-Tibetan (Chinese) languages. At one time, Western linguistic scholarship did not recognize Vietnamese as an Austro-Asiatic language, but rather placed it in the Sino-Tibetan family! This error has now been corrected.

Script of the Austro-Asiatic Languages : The Indian Mundaa languages are written in the script of the local mainstream language (Dewanaagari in Jharkhand, Telaguu in the border regions neighboring Aandhraa Pradesh). Khmer like many other Southeast Asian and Malay languages, was originally and still is written in an Indian-based script derived from South Indian Paali (and thus eventually from Braahmi). Vietnamese was written in a script called *Nom* which was derived from the Chinese script and is of ideographic origin [SCr-66, LAi-68]. This script was replaced by French colonialists with a Roman-based script laden with diacritics to represent the tones, and thus somewhat difficult to write (a sampling of this script was cited in an earlier chapter).

4.12 DAIC FAMILY

Extent and Number of Speakers: The geographic extent of this family is Thailand, Laos and parts of southern China and Vietnam [LN-1 to LN-4]. Its dominant languages are ***Thai*** and ***Lao***, which is close to Thai.

The approximate breakdown of the number of speakers is as follows (in decreasing order, all figures estimates for 2005): Thai 63 m, Lao 6 m, Other 6 m. **Total 75 m**.

There has been a significant change in nomenclature in the linguistics literature within the last two decades with respect to this family. Originally, the family was denoted as Tai, or sometimes even Thai. Today, ***Daic*** is used for the family. ***Tai*** is a branch within this family, the other branches being ***Kadai*** and ***Kam-Sui***, with very few speakers in southern China and some parts of Vietnam. *Thai,* the major language of Thailand, is a language within the Tai branch. *Lao* is the other major language in this branch.

The original homeland of the Daic languages is, like the Austronesian languages, thought by many modern linguists to have been Southern China. However, once again this, like so much in the current scholarship in the field of linguistics, is based on rather circumstantial and speculative evidence, and there are many in the current scholarship itself who hold opposing views [LAs-4]. Some authors, including this one, consider the Daic languages to be related to the Austro-Asiatic languages. This relation goes beyond common words between, say, Khmer and Thai, that many travelers to the region (including this author) will identify and which may be ascribed to simple cross-borrowing.

Thai and Lao constitute the major languages in this family. Like many other languages cited above, Thai also has an *Angramaya* (English-like) structure (see discussion further below): Proper names and much of the higher vocabulary are of Sanskrit (i.e. Indo-European) origin. For example, the name of the most recently reigning king, Bumibol Adulyadej, will at once be recognized by persons of Indian heritage as *Bhuumi-bala Atulya-tej(a:)* (Sanskrit "Having the strength of the Earth, of immeasurable brilliance"). Everyday Thai vocabulary also has common or cognate words with neighboring languages such as Khmer, as noted above.

Script of the Tai Languages: Like many other languages of Southeast Asia (such as Khmer, Burmese and Bahasa Indonesia/Malaysia), Thai is written in an Indian-origin script derived from southern Paali script (and thus ultimately from Braahmi). The official

Thai government line, as shown in an elaborate exhibit in the Thai National Museum in Bangkok, is that the script was brought from Amarawati, on the south-eastern coast of India (near modern-day Chennai and Kanchipuram).

4.13 NILO-SAHARAN FAMILY

Extent and number of speakers: These form a sort of buffer between the Afro-Asiatic and the Niger-Congo language groups in Africa, are not spoken in a geographically contiguous area, and have a very small number of speakers [LAs-10, LAs-16, LAs-17, LN-1 to LN-4]. A major member of note is ***Masaai***, the language of the Masaai ethnic group of Kenya/Tanzania. The approximate breakdown of the number of speakers is as follows (in decreasing order, all figures estimates for 2005): Sudan 10 m, Tanzania/Kenya 10 m, Somalia 3 m, Chad and Mali 2 m, Other est 5 m. **Total est. 30 m**. Interestingly, Masaai was the subject of a recent attempt, funded by major multinational software companies, of coining entirely new technical, scientific and computer-related words, to enable the language to adapt to modern times [LAs-17]. This author feels that such attempts are needed in many other languages of the world, most with far more speakers than Masaai!

Scripts of the Nilo-Saharan Family: These now primarily use the Roman script, which was introduced by Christian missionaries to the region.

4.14 URALIC FAMILY

Extent and Number of Speakers: The *Uralic* family is thought to have once extended through a good part of Siberia and the easternmost part of Eastern Europe [LAs-24 to LAs-26]. Today, its extent is in the area around Finland and Estonia, in Hungary and in scattered pockets in eastern Russia and Siberia. The generally accepted division is into the ***Samoyedic*** and ***Finno-Ugric*** sub-branches. Among the former sub-branch are many Siberian languages close to extinction. The major languages in the latter sub-branch are ***Magyar (Hungarian), Finnish, Estonian,*** and ***Saami.***

The approximate breakdown of the number of speakers is as follows (in decreasing order, all figures estimates for 2005): Hungary 10 m, Finland 5 m, Siberia 2 m, Estonia 1 m. **Total 18 m.**

Finnish and Estonian are close, and Finnish and Maagyaar (Hungarian) are as close as Italian and Portuguese.

Scripts of the Uralic Languages: All major *Uralic* languages (Maagyaar, Finnish, etc.) are written in Roman-based scripts.

Chapter 4: The World's Major Language Families- A Primer

4.15 HMONG-MIEN (ALSO CALLED MIAO-YAO) FAMILY

This is a small language group (in terms of number of speakers) [LAs-1, LN-1 to LN-4]. Its speakers number **less than 10 million**. Its major language is ***Hmong***, also called *Hmong Njua* ("Hmong of the West"), a language of Laos.

As an interesting aside, outside of Laos and neighboring countries, the only place that has a significant number of speakers of Hmong is of all places, the state of Minnesota in the U.S. Midwest. The speakers there are refugee immigrant descendants of anti-Communist fighters from Laos who have settled there. Their U.S.-born descendants of course speak English as their first language.

Script: That used today for Hmong is Roman-based, although Hmong has a rich history of attempts at creating new scripts for it [SCr-67].

4.16 KHOISAN (!XHOSAN) FAMILY (*THE "CLICK" LANGUAGES*)

Extent and Number of Speakers: The languages of South and Southwest Africa known in the 19th century Western linguistics literature as "Bushman" languages, and more recently as "Hottentot" languages, are now given the appellation ***Khoisan*** languages [LAs-7, LAs-8, PHo-21 to PHo-27]. The most prominent of these is ***Nama*** (also called *Hottentot*), spoken in Southern Africa, Botswana and prominently in Namibia. These languages are unique among the world's languages in employing *clicks* as major phonemes. The total number of speakers is estimated by some at less than one million.

Scripts of the Khoisan Family: Because of their use of clicks and other unique features, these languages have been very difficult to render in Roman-based scripts. Anyone trying to follow Roman transcriptions of them, with all their exclamation marks and pseudo-Greek/pseudo-math symbols used to represent the various clicks, will attest to this! Lacking native scripts, they must nevertheless necessarily be rendered in Roman-based scripts. The most widely accepted original Roman orthographies were those of Bleek, Schulz and Lepsius [SCr-68 to SCr-71] using pseudo-math symbols for clicks, including such oddities in orthography as a "not-equals" sign. The later, official South African government orthography dispensed with these, using simpler but nevertheless still highly confounding letters such as *C, Qc, Q, X*.

4.17 ORIGINAL LANGUAGE FAMILIES OF NORTH AND CENTRAL AMERICA, THE CARIBBEAN AND EASTERNMOST SIBERIA

Extent: We must obviously commence by noting the qualifying word "Original" in the section title above. Obviously, today, European languages of the Indo-European family, mainly English and Spanish, and to a lesser extent Portuguese, Russian and French, have totally supplanted the original languages of these regions. It also goes without saying that many of these languages, e.g. Cherokee of the North Carolina region of the U.S., survive in textbooks only. Their speakers have long abandoned them for the ubiquitous English (in Canada and the U.S.) or Spanish (in Mexico and Central America). The original speakers of some of the languages, especially in the Caribbean region, are extinct. Others' numbers have been decimated. As an example, the estimated original Native American population of the U.S. of about seven million is today reduced to about 500,000. Surviving speakers of the original languages of the Americas are mainly in South America (covered in the next Section) and to a lesser extent Mexico and Guatemala. In Peru, Bolivia and parts of Ecuador, we have speakers of Aymara, Quechua and other 'Peruvian' languages numbering in the millions. In Mexico, in the region of Oaxaca, one still finds speakers of Mixteco who know little Spanish.

Due to the dearth of linguistic scholarship in these languages in general as compared to, say, Indo-European languages, and the dearth in particular of scholarship by native speakers of the languages who would truly have an understanding of them, there is still an incomplete knowledge of them (see, e.g. Refs [LAs-63 to LAs-77]). Many controversies and disputes still exist in relation to these languages.

The most widely held scholarship posits about *17* distinct language families, not including isolates and unclassified languages. We list them here alphabetically:

1) *Algonquian-Ritwan*: Of the U.S. Northeast, Canadian Southeast and U.S. and Canadian Great Lakes region. It includes Blackfoot and Ojibway.

2) *Arawakan (*sometimes called *Taino*): The predominant family in the Caribbean islands prior to the extinction of the natives of this region by Europeans. It is believed by some historians to have arrived in the Caribbean in a migration from South America around 400 B.C..

Chapter 4: The World's Major Language Families- A Primer

3) **Caddoan**: Of the U.S. southern Midwest.

4) **Carib**: Of the southern Caribbean islands and of course the origin of the name *Caribbean*. There is overlap into South America (Venezuela, northern Brazil). Also suffering extinction similar to Arawakian.

5) **Chibchan**: Of southern Mexico and Central America. Once again, the distinction from Mayan is disputed.

6) **Eskimo-Aleut**: Including such regions as the easternmost regions of Siberia, Greenland, and the Canadian extreme northeast. The most prominent member of this family is of course *Inuit*, which, in various dialects, is still spoken in broad regions of Canada and Greenland.

7) **Iroquoian**: Of the U.S. Northeast and Canadian Southeast. Includes *Iroquois*, the language of the most prominent Native American ethnic group of the U.S. northeast.

8) **Mayan**: Of southern Mexico and Guatemala. Some linguists claim a connection with the Oto-Manguean and Mixe-Zoque families. *Chol* of this family is the most direct survivor of the language of the Mayan inscriptions.

9) **Miwok-Costanoan, Chumashan, Keresan** and **Yuman** are other language families of the western U.S. *Zuni* is a language isolate of New Mexico still having thousands of speakers.

10) **Mixe-Zoque**: Of southern Mexico and Central America. Once again, the distinction from Mayan is disputed. The language of one of the oldest civilizations of central America, the *Olmec*, is thought to have been of this family.

11) **Muskogean**: Of the U.S. Southeast, except Florida.

12) **Na-Dene:** In this family, the *Athabaskian* sub-family is the dominant component. Its most prominent member is *Navajo*. The Navajo population of the U.S. states of Arizona and New Mexico is the largest

single surviving ethnic group among Native Americans in the U.S. today, numbering several hundred thousand.

13) **Oto-Manguean**: Of southern Mexico and Central America. There are still many native speakers of languages of this family such as **Mixteco**, e.g. in the hills surrounding the southern Mexican provincial capital of Oaxaca, where many of the "Indians" do not speak Spanish at all. The distinction from Mayan is disputed.

14) **Siouan**: Its most prominent member is of course **Sioux**, of the Dakotas. It was prevalent in the U.S. and Canadian Midwest.

15) **Uto-Aztec**: Its most prominent member is **Nahuatl** ("Aztec"), the predominant language of Mexico during the Aztec empire. The Shoshone and Comanche languages of the U.S. are of the same family.

16) **Wakashan**, of the Northwest U.S. and Southwest Canada, includes Nootka, a language studied at some length by Edward Sapir, a well known linguist of the last century.

17) **Yuman**: Of southern (U.S.) and Baja (Mexico) California parts of Arizona.

18) **Unclassified, Undocumented or Isolates**: At least 30 known languages fall in this category. They include such well-known ones as **Seminole** (of the U.S. state of Florida).

Number of Speakers: As noted above, the total number of ethnic Native Americans in the U.S. and Canada is today less than 500,000, from an original population estimated at about seven million. Of these few speak their ancestral languages. The situation is better in Mexico and Central America, where many "Indians" speak both Spanish and their ancestral tongues, and some, e.g. in the isolated hilly regions surrounding Oaxaca in Mexico alluded to above, speak only their ancestral tongues and no Spanish. The total number of such bilingual and monolingual speakers in Mexico and Central America can be estimated at about three million.

Chapter 4: The World's Major Language Families- A Primer

Origins of Large Variation and of Large Number of Isolates: There has been much debate in academic circles about the (comparatively) large number of language families in North and Central America and the (comparatively) small number of language families in South America. This appears to defy another tenet of current (2005) linguistic scholarship, namely that temperate climates (such as the northern U.S. and Canada) breed relatively small numbers of language families with large numbers of speakers, whereas tropical and sub-tropical climates (such as Mexico, northern South America or Papua New Guinea) breed large numbers of language families [LN-1 to LN-4, LAs-1]. In the opinion of this author, one of the reasons that this tenet does not hold in the Americas is that, unfortunately like many other tenets of current linguistic scholarship, it is based on very limited observation, confined to a limited region (in this case, temperate Eurasia and tropical Polynesia), and may thus be inherently flawed.

There may however be other reasons for the large numbers of language families and isolates in the Americas. One of these may have to do with the history of sea-based migration to the North and Central American mainland from both the Atlantic and the Pacific side, coupled with the relatively sparse populations of these regions. We are all aware that many ancient peoples had highly developed naval, shipbuilding and navigation skills. This includes peoples ranging from the ancient Egyptians, Phoenicians, Indians and Chinese, to the comparatively more recent Greeks, Romans, Arabs and Scandinavians. Now there is absolutely no reason to assume that these peoples did not have the capability to journey to the Americas. This then gives rise to the possibility that these peoples landed in the Americas long before Columbus, whether by design (some brash, adventurous sea captain wanting to find out what lay at the edge of the ocean!) or by sad happenstance (lost in a storm and subsequently shipwrecked in better weather). There is some, scattered evidence for potential landings of such peoples on the American mainland. However, the only fairly well documented arrival is that of the Scandinavian Leif Erikson from Greenland to Newfoundland.

To put it in a more prosaic way, then, *"every Tom, Dick and Harry from the Old World who could get together a ship and a team of crewmates probably landed in the New World, long before Columbus"*! Thus, one argument is that, due to the very low population density of the Americas to begin with, the linguistic effect of scattered groups of shipwrecked wayfarers would have been sufficiently large so as to give rise to new languages at the extreme, or large numbers of borrowed words at a minimum. These languages or borrowings would be created by necessity upon the mingling of the wayfarers with American natives. They would be easily isolated from other languages due to the extremely low population density, and would leave little trace of their initial origins. Many of these would then have so few speakers as to become isolates due to the vastness of the Americas.

Script: Mayan languages had highly developed scripts [SCr-32 to SCr-38]. Today, a few languages of these regions still do not use a script, i.e. they are not written. Many languages, e.g. Cherokee and Navajo in the U.S., use transcriptions that are based on variations of the Roman script specially created for them [SCr-62 to SCr-64]. On the other hand, the Mayan languages had a highly developed ideographic script that has been deciphered. Recent findings appear to indicate that what is apparently the oldest civilization of North and Central America, that of the Olmecs, also had an ideographic script.

Chapter 4: The World's Major Language Families- A Primer

4.18 ORIGINAL LANGUAGE FAMILIES OF SOUTH AMERICA

Extent and Number of Speakers: The general statements made in the previous Section with respect to the North and Central American language families apply almost without exception to the language families of South America as well [LAs-73 to LAs-77]. As with the North/Central American group, there is still much that is unsettled. Additionally, some languages of some remote regions of the Andes and the Amazon remain unstudied and unclassified to this day. The Peruvian languages [LAs-77] appear to be the most studied of this group.

The generally agreed-upon state of understanding in current linguistic circles is that there are approximately ***nine (9)*** distinct language families, as below, plus many isolates or unclassified languages. These are roughly as follows:

1) ***Andean: Quechua-Aymaran*** (also called ***Quechuamaran***): The most prominent members (and most well studied by Western linguists) are ***Quechua*** and ***Aymara***. Some linguists consider Quechua a sub-family rather than a single language (for example, Cuzco Qeuchua of Peru and Bolivian Quechua are considered separate lanaguages) , and many others dispute the relation between Quechua and Aymara languages. Aymara languages are prominent in Bolivia.

2) ***Andean***: ***Panoan-Ticuanan***: Some linguists [LAs-77] feel this family is cognate with *Quechhua-Aymaran*.

3) ***Andean: Unclassified***: Several languages in the remote Andean regions have as yet to be classified.

4) ***Arawakian***: This Central American/Caribbean family leaves traces in northwestern South America (Colombia, Bolivia).

5) ***Carib***: Of Venezuela and neighboring regions (northern Brazil, Guyana, Suriname (former Dutch Guyana). Overlapping with the southern Caribbean islands.

6) ***Chibchan***: Of northwestern South America, overlapping with Central America.

7) ***Je*** (also called ***Macro-Gé***) Of the Brazilian southern coast and bordering hinterland, geographically the largest single Brazilian language family.

8) ***Miscellaneous Unclassified Languages and Language Isolates***: In spite of massive deforestation in the Amazon region, several languages indigenous to this region remain unclassified. Some may be isolates. Many languages of the southern portion of South America still remain undocumented and/or unclassified since, in many cases, the speakers have become extinct. Indeed, very recent language extinctions in this region have been documented in the popular press [LN-80 to LN-82].

9) ***Tucanoan***: Of northwestern South America.

10) ***Tupian***: Of northeastern and southern Brazil, and neighboring countries, including Paraguay. Its most important member is ***Guarani***, an official language of Paraguay.

Script: Original Scripts of most South American languages, if they existed, do not survive.

4.19 OTHER LANGUAGE FAMILIES

For reasons of space, we have not included detailed descriptions of other language families, such as the *Caucasian* family (which includes *Georgian* and, according to some scholars [LAs-1], *Basque*), the *Chukotko-Kamchatkan* family in the region of the Chukotka and Kamchatka peninsulae of Russia and the *Australian* family(ies). These are however covered in our summary Table presented above. Except for those of the Caucasian family, all the other languages are either seriously endangered or extinct. Most if not all of these are *expected to be extinct by 2050*. It is also noted that the Caucasus region includes, even today (2005), a very large number of distinct language isolates or families with just two or three members; these are again covered elsewhere in this book.

4.20 EXTINCT, MORIBUND OR INACTIVE LANGUAGES *OF SIGNIFICANCE* OF THE ANCIENT WORLD

WHAT WE MEAN BY LANGUAGES "OF SIGNIFICANCE": The first word in the title of this Section above, "*OF SIGNIFICANCE*", is inserted for a very important reason: One simply cannot cite *every* extinct or inactive language for which the world has a record, not least in a book that deals with a different subject, such as this. We thus cover only those extinct languages that have had or continue to have *a significant impact* on the world today.

Languages such as Classical Greek and Latin continue to have a very significant impact in Europe and America even today. Similarly, Sanskrit continues to have a significant impact in India today. Also, in families such as the Indo-European, the ancient languages are very useful in understanding interrelationships among their modern descendants. These are thus languages *of significance*.

On the other hand, languages such as **Etruscan**, and the many known (e.g. **Sumerian**) and unknown languages of the Middle East that existed before the advent of Semitic languages, have little impact today. Nevertheless, they retain important historical significance for the development of languages in the respective regions, or for the study of currently extinct but important ancient languages, such as Latin; for example, Etruscan may have had some significant impact on Latin, primarily in borrowed words and forms. Thus, we cover these languages as well, although in less detail than, say, Cl. Greek/Latin.

We can enumerate the *major* ancient languages of significance briefly as follows:

HITTITE, LYDIAN AND LUWIAN (INDO-EUROPEAN FAMILY): Spoken in Anatolia during the 2nd millenium B.C., according to current understanding. They are much degenerated from the parent Indo-European language. Extinct, no modern descendants. Luwian is thought by some to be the language of Troy. Some presume the Trojan language was an ancient Latin, given credence by the legend of Aeneas fleeing from Troy through Carthage to Italy to found Rome, although the majority view in this respect, and the view thought to have been held by the ancient Romans themselves, is that Latin speakers came to Italy from the North [IEu-44].

Chapter 4: The World's Major Language Families- A Primer

VEDIC AND CLASSICAL ("PAANINIAN") SANSKRIT (INDO-EUROPEAN FAMILY): Classical Sanskrit is the language as "finalized", "formalized" (critics would say "petrified"!) by the great grammarian and linguist Paanini and entirely unchanged since this "finalization". (Paanini was born around the 8th century BCE, though that again is the subject of a great dispute, in Sindh province, modern-day Pakistan, near Attock. He worked mainly in Gandhaara, modern Kandahar, Afghanistan). Paaninian Sanskrit is substantially the same as the language discussed by his 64 predecessor grammarians, which he cites as references in his work. Vedic Sanskrit is the older language of the *RgWeda (RgVeda, Rig Veda)*, the oldest written document in any Indo-European language (regarding the Hittite inscriptions at Boghaz-Koy, see further below).

Among the intriguing mysteries regarding the possible form of Sanskrit before Paanini formalized it (*Samskrtam,* "refined", "cultured") is the precise nature of the formalism. For example, the 2nd person singular pronoun in the nominative case is *twam*, i.e. *tuu-am* in Sanskrit. Since this pronoun appears as *tuu (tu)* or a close variant in virtually *all* ancient *and* modern Indo-European languages, from Latin to French to Spanish to Maraathi to Hindi/Urdu, it is a matter of conjecture if the *-am* suffix was simply added to formalize the word ("*bindam lagantam Samskrtam bhawantam"*!). Yet the *twam* does survive as *tum* in Hindi, *tumi* in Maraathi and Baanglaa, etc. etc. So which is it?! This is a difficult question to answer.

Paaninian Sanskrit also formalized **Sandhi**, i.e. the euphonic joining together of words (sort of equivalent to the *liason* of French). This made Sandhi *compulsory* and made the resulting language artificial: To cite a modern example from American English, compulsory Sandhi would be if one *always* had to write and pronounce *did you* or *want to* as *didja* and *wanna*. Thus, one is at pains to know what spoken Sanskrit, *without* compulsory Sandhi, was like. More importantly, this also tells us that, by the time that the *RgWeda* was first formalized, there appears to already have been an established literary tradition, and the form of the *spoken* language is already lost; this author's hypothecation of the form of an original, *spoken* Sanskrit, e.g. the existence of everyday words such as the nouns *udra* and *wadra* ("water") and the verb *wiir* ("to be manly, to wage war"), lost in the later language, appears elsewhere in these *NAVLIPI* volumes.

One of the several major differences between Classical and Vedic Sanskrit is that the Vedic retains the original Indo-European *separated pre-verb/verb-stem (upasarga/anga)* construction of verbs in full force, partially preserving the "natural, spoken" character of the language. In contrast, Classical Sanskrit, likes, for strict grammatical reasons, to combine the pre-verb and verb in conjugation, giving the language an even more artificial, literary character than Vedic Sanskrit. This pre-verb/verb separation is found today in full force, among modern Indo-European languages, *only* in modern German: For example, in the modern German, *Ich teile Ihnen mit* or *Er geht sofort ab* ("I will communicate (it) to you", "he goes out immediately") the verbs (*teilen, gehen*) are separated from their pre-verbs (*mit, ab*) by other parts of the sentence. Vedic Sanskrit also preserves some Indo-European archaisms not found in Classical Sanskrit, e.g. Vedic *dama: (damas)* (cf. Latin *domus*) vs. Classical *grham* for "house". Once again, this is a subject for another book. Vedic Sanskrit also sometimes has a more "conversational" character.

MYCEANAEAN, HOMERIC AND CLASSICAL GREEK AND THEIR RELATION TO MODERN GREEK [IEu-29 to IEu-33] *(ALL INDO-EUROPEAN FAMILY)*: Modern Greek is the only modern member of the Greek branch. Mycenean Greek is the oldest recorded Greek.

Homeric Greek (the language of the folk poems compiled by Homer) is an older form of Classical Greek, and is closer in grammatical form to Sanskrit than virtually any other Indo-European language. The Western Classics literature frequently assigns Homeric Greek a historical place, as if it were an intermediate stage between the oldest Greek and Classical Greek. While Homeric Greek has some archaisms (such as *tosoio* in place of Classical Greek *tou* for masculine 3rd person genitive (i.e. "his"), closer to the Sanskrit *tasia*), it is important to remember that **Homeric Greek** was simply one of a number of dialects of the older Greek. Specifically, it was a mixture of **Old Ionic** (whence the Attic-Ionic dialect which comes to us as standard Classical Greek) and **Aeolic**.

The modern Greek speaker would *not*, for the most part, be able to understand ancient Greek because, in addition to morphological and other changes as described in the next paragraph, so much of the vocabulary and sound changes (both phonological and as represented orthographically) are so vastly different in modern Greek after centuries of change. It is, in fact, comparable to how a modern French, Spanish, or Italian speaker would have to understand Latin (i.e., not very well, but would be able to glean meaning from cognates here and there). We just tend to assume that ancient and modern Greek would be more closely related simply because they are both called "Greek"! Among modern Greek dialects, the language of Cyprus is closest to Classical Greek.

With regard to a more technical description of the phonological and morphological changes from Classical to modern Greek, Modern Greek exhibits aspects of both linguistic continuity and change in relation to its ancient predecessor. While a variety of dialects of ancient Greek existed prior to the Hellenistic period, the post-classical standard became **Koine**, or 'common' Greek (a mixture of Attic and Ionic dialects), which later evolved into medieval, then modern Greek.

Individual phonological differences are too many to list here. However, significant shifts from ancient to modern Greek include the loss of a pitch accent in favor of a stress accent (paralleled in the Vedic to Classical Sanskrit transition), the regularization of vowel length, and a fricatization of aspirated phones *(ph, th, kh* to *f, th*, and *x,* respectively*)*.

Modern Greek, like its ancient counterpart, remains substantially an inflected language, with endings supplying most of the grammatical markers. Where ancient Greek utilized five cases (nominative, accusative, genitive, vocative, and dative), the dative has disappeared in modern Greek, and its functions have been subsumed into the genitive case. The dual number, already moribund in classical Greek, has been entirely lost in the modern language. The definite article (*ho, he, to*) remains largely the same in form and use, but the indefinite article in modern Greek is expressed by forms of the number 'one' (*enas, mia, ena*).

The verbal system of modern Greek exhibits marked changes from the ancient system, both in morphology and syntactical constructions. The structure of verb person remains the same for the modern language, with first, second, and third person forms in the singular and plural (aside from the dual, which, as in the case of nouns, has also disappeared). With respect to mood, the subjunctive and optative, distinct forms in ancient Greek, are replaced by periphrastic constructions; the imperative mood, however, retains inflectional endings. While ancient Greek distinguished between active, middle, and passive voice, in modern Greek the middle and passive have collapsed into one category, the 'medio-passive', in opposition to active voice. Verbal tense and aspect are also marked by shifts: the aoristic aspect does not occur in modern Greek, leaving only perfective and imperfective aspects. An inflected future tense appears in ancient but not modern Greek; it has been replaced by the future tense particle '*tha*', followed by a finite verb form of perfective or imperfective aspect. The variety of participial forms and constructions of ancient Greek becomes simplified in modern Greek, with only the imperfective participial form remaining.

OLD AND CLASSICAL LATIN [IEu-44 to IEu-49] *(**INDO-EUROPEAN FAMILY**)*: This branch is also designated ***Italic***, with a further distinction of ***p-Italic***, which was spoken in the south and central regions of Italy (Umbria, Campagna) and ***q-Italic***, whence Latin, the parent of the ***Romance*** languages, is descended [LN-1 to LN-4, LAs-1]. The lack of linguistically relatable archaeological evidence makes the origins of the arrival of Latin into Italy somewhat nebulous. One view is that speakers came down from the North, and this is supported by the fact that the *p*-Keltic branch of the Keltic language family has some affinity to **p-Italic**. (The *p-, q-* appellations come from the *pinte* vs. ***q**uinque (= **hw**inhwe)* distinction). The northern immigration is also supported by the fact that the original Latins who came into Italy from the north around 1500 BCE [IEu-44] cremated their dead, a practice that continued up to the cremation of Julius Caesar and the Roman institution of the vestal virgins, who looked after the sacred fire which was also the source of the cremation fire. (The original Indo-Europeans are widely believed to have cremated their dead, a practice surviving only in India today.) Another view is that the language was brought from Troy, in modern-day western Turkey, via Carthage, by Aeneas, according to the legend in the *Aeneid*. This would make the Trojan language (possibly Luwian) "proto-Italic". This view appears to have less credence.

OLD BALTO-SLAVIC (INDO-EUROPEAN FAMILY): This has two branches, **Baltic** with modern descendants Latvian and Lithuanian, and **Old Slavonic** (also called **Old Church Slavonic**), with modern descendants as noted in the previous section.

OLD GERMANIC LANGUAGES [IEu-17 to IEu-21] ***(INDO-EUROPEAN FAMILY)***: As noted above, among surviving modern languages, this has two sub-branches **West Germanic** and **North Germanic**. The oldest language in this group, **Gothic** (also called **East Germanic**), with oldest records dating from the 4th century CE, has no modern descendants, Old Prussian having died out in the Middle Ages. It is widely believed that the Germanic tribes first extensively populated the Baltic littoral area, being pushed west by the "Baltic" and Slavic tribes who were further east. They migrated thence into the Scandinavian peninsula, probably around 1000 BCE, conquering and assimilating with the native non-Indo-European Scandinavians and giving them an Indo-European language. The sudden and universal changeover in Denmark from burial to cremation of the dead around 1000 BCE (extensively documented, e.g., in the exhibits in the National Museum in Copenhagen), along with other archaeological evidence of large migrations from the Baltic regions at around 1000 BCE, are thought to support this view. (As noted above, the original Indo-Europeans are widely believed to have cremated their dead, a practice surviving only in India today.) The Germanic tribes also migrated from the Baltic area to the other parts of Europe which we today identify so clearly as "Germanic", including Germany, once again conquering and assimilating with pre-Germanic and pre-Indo-European groups.

OLD KELTIC LANGUAGES [LAs-44 to LAs-47] ***(INDO-EUROPEAN FAMILY)***: This branch is sometimes further sub-classed into ***p-Keltic*** and ***q-Keltic***, similar to the *p-* and *q*-Italic sub-classification above. Although the oldest documented language in this group is *Old Irish (Old Gaelic)* from about 800 CE, it is widely believed that the Kelts were the first Indo-European group to populate the regions of Western Europe. This was originally populated by a myriad of other non-Indo-European linguistic groups (with limited survivors such as Basque, Etruscan), through conquest, assimilation or other means. Some linguists also ascribe a common Italic-Keltic parent [IEu-7, IEu-10, IEu-12, LAi-2, HIi-14, HIi-48]. (Recent genetic findings have placed the origins of the vast bulk of the West Europeans, including inhabitants of the British Isles, in peoples isolated in northern Iberia during the last Ice Age, the so-called *R1b haplogroup* [GDn-40 (b)].)

AVESTAN AND OLD PERSIAN [IEu-23 to IEu-28, LAi-2, HIi-14, HIi-48] *(INDO-EUROPEAN FAMILY)*: Avestan is the language of the *Avesta,* the main scripture of the Zoroastrian religion (whose modern followers still include about 5% of the Iraanian population and, adhering to more orthodox and older traditions, the Paarsis of India. The latter are on the verge of extinction through assimilation, numbering less than 90,000 today. Old Persian is the language of the cuneiform inscriptions and epistles of the Persian Achaemenid kings and Darius (*Daaryawausha*) [LAi-39 to LAi-44]. (See next chapter for a discussion of the Old Persian cuneiform script). Old Persian can be considered a descendant of Avestan. Avestan is very close to Sanskrit in some grammatical aspects, but in others it has marked differences.

TOKHAARIAN (INDO-EUROPEAN FAMILY): From the region of western China bordering Tajikistaan, Kyrgyzstaan and Kazhakstaan. Extinct today.

ANCIENT LANGUAGES OF THE AFRO-ASIATIC FAMILY [LAs-11, LAs-13, LAs-51]: *Egyptian* (also called *Coptic*) [LAs-52, SCr-23]. The language of ancient Egypt. This language survives in the liturgy of the Coptic (Egyptian Orthodox) Church. *Akkadian* ("*Old Arabic*", also called *Assyro-Babylonian*). The oldest *known* Semitic language. Its record starts approximately with the conquest, by the Akkadian king Sargon, of the Sumerians of Iraq (Mesopotamia) dated by Western historians to around 2300 B.C. The languages known as *Babylonian* and *Assyrian* are considered dialects of Akkadian. *Aramaic* is something of a cross between Hebrew and Arabic (closer to the former), and survives in the liturgy of the Assyrian and Syrian churches (northwestern Iraq, eastern Syria). *Phoenician*; this language is of note because the alphabet used to represent it is the immediate antecedent of the Greek alphabet, and thence the Roman alphabet in which this book is written. Phoenecian was also spoken in Carthage in North Africa.

SUMERIAN (ISOLATE?), the language of one of the world's first civilizations (Sumer) in what is now southern Iraq and centered on the city of Ur, is also one of the oldest for which written documentation still exists [SCr-21, SCr-22]. Its cuneiform (wedge-form) writing, dating from about 2700 BCE, was only deciphered in the 19th century, following the decipherment of the trilingual Behistun inscriptions, containing Old Persian written in cuneiform. Thus, Sumerian is one of the ancient languages which have had the good fortune of being fully deciphered and understood.

Sumerian is a language *isolate*, but obviously an extremely important one. It is an *agglutinative* language, much like modern Malay or Hungarian. That is to say, declensional change for nouns, and conjugational change for verbs, are effected by agglomerations of uninflected words into compounds: e.g. *gal* ("man") and *lu* ("great") are compounded to get *lugal* ("king"); with the addition of the abstraction indicator *nam*, one gets *namlugal* ("kinship"). Plurals are formed exactly as in Malay, by repetition of terms (e.g. "house-house" means "houses"). There is evidence however that Sumerian may have been an inflectional language at an earlier time [SCr-22], degenerating into its later agglutinative character through influences from other linguistic groups. Some scholars have hinted at a relationship of the older Sumerian with Dravidian languages [HIi-22, HIi-26] which goes beyond superficial similarities which may be attributed to simple borrowing, such as the word and suffix *ur* for "city", still used in Tamil today.

The original geographical extent of Sumerian is a matter of conjecture. For instance, archaeologists recently unearthed a war zone in what is today Syria, with advanced weaponry similar to that used by Sumerians, dated to about 3500 BCE [HIh-8]. Did these people speak a language related to Sumerian?

ETRUSCAN [LAs-38, GDn-56] *(ISOLATE)* is another language having important influence in the ancient world, though arguably much less than Sumerian. It is also a language isolate. It was spoken in all of northern Italy before the advent of Latin. It was written in Roman script, contemporaneously with Latin. Recent DNA studies appear to indicate a Middle Eastern origin for the Etruscans [GDn-55, GDn-56].

THE ANCIENT (DRAVIDIAN?) HARAPPAN LANGUAGE OF INDIA: This of course survives in the (very limited number of) Indus Valley (Harappan) inscriptions, most famously the commercial cylinder seals used in that civilization and unearthed from sites as far-ranging as Gujarat, the Indus Valley and eastern Uttar Pradesh.

Unfortunately, the writing, and thus the language, is still undeciphered to this day. We thus still have no clue as to what language family it may belong to.

Chapter 4: The World's Major Language Families- A Primer

There are many wild and not-so-wild theories as to what the language may be: These include: **(1)** Sanskrit (propounded by the Vishwa Hindu Parishad in India). **(2)** An ancestor of Tamil, *the most common and perhaps the most logical theory*, making it a Dravidian language. (See the substantive discussion under the Dravidian Languages section above.) **(3)** A member of the Semitic family related to Akkadian, which this author personally finds incredible (!). **(4)** A cognate of Sumerian itself, this last theory based on the obviously close commercial links between Sumer and the Indus Valley.

Judging from the number of distinct glyphs (symbols or letters) found thus far in the Indus Valley script, just about 200, it was probably a combination ideographic and phonetic script, possibly logophonetic. It is however possible that this limited number of about 200 glyphs may simply represent the *commercial/trade portion* of the Harappan language. If so, one may have to propose different hypotheses for this script from the current ones.

In the context of the discussion here, this book does not wish to dignify, beyond this mention in passing, authors such as Farmer and Witzel, the latter at Harvard, who have made the incredible declaration that the Harappan civilization was illiterate [LAi-74] and that the Harappan writings are mystical, religious symbols. Firstly, it is difficult to envision how the engineering constructions and other achievements of the Harappan civilization could have been arrived at without the benefit of writing, just as it is difficult to envision how the Egyptian pyramids could have been constructed without the benefit of writing. A very scholarly recent analysis of the Harappan script by eminent computer scientists and the pre-eminent Indian Harappan scholar (Iravathan Mahadevan) has demonstrated beyond any doubt a linguistic structure to the Indus script [LAi-82]. (This author feels the study was unnecessary and leant unnecessary credence to the fanatic, fringe-group, naysayers such as the Farmer-Witzel cabal, simply by the fact that it was done, but that is another story.) Mahadevan has discussed this further in an eloquent if unnecessarily subdued and low-key review [LAi-15] and critique of Farmer-Witzel.

This author personally feels that the "scholarship" of authors like Farmer and Witzel is driven by virulent anti-Indian hatred. In this respect he quotes a possibly relevant anecdote: Zubin Mehta, the erstwhile conductor of the New York Philharmonic, once noted, "My good friend Henry Kissinger (former U.S. Secretary of State under Presidents Nixon and Ford) told me he always *hated* India – he could not explain why, but he always did...". (Kissinger had never even visited India at that time.) Although he could be wrong, this author feels that the virulent anti-India hatred of authors like Witzel may be founded on the same background as that of Kissinger: It possibly relates to the unfortunate symbolism associating India with Aaryans (Aryans), Sanskrit, swastikas and the like, in the propagation of which Indians had absolutely no part. In this world scenario then, everything associated with Hitler and Aaryans (Aryans), and, by extension, with India, generates a natural, knee-jerk hatred; it is related to the fact that everything *opposed* to India and Hitler, such as the British of several generations ago, is loved. Witzel has even gone so far as to get involved in local American politics, in the modification of the India sections of history books selected by local American school boards. In this respect, this author suggests that Witzel et al. should stick to study of their own civilizations – there is plenty still to study in Western civilizations – and *lay off India*! Also relevant in this context, Witzel's substantial ignorance of the Sanskrit language; this was exposed and apparent in severe mistranslations, as pointed out by eminent Indian Sanskrit scholars; it has been discussed elsewhere in the *NAVLIPI* volumes.

ANCIENT WRITTEN CHINESE (SINO-TIBETAN FAMILY): We need to qualify our subtitle with the word *written* because, being an ideographic language, we have only approximations of what the spoken language of ancient times actually sounded like. Archaic Written Chinese [SCr-25 to SCr-28], dating from about 300 BCE (although the first written inscriptions, on bronze artifacts and bones of the Shang dynasty date from about 1600 BCE), has been tentatively reconstructed, mostly by non-Chinese scholars (at least to the year 2005). Unlike the modern Chinese languages, it *did* have some inflectional character superimposed upon its monosyllabic base. It also apparently possessed phonemic opposition between voiced and unvoiced phones (e.g. [p]/[b]) which has disappeared today.

Chapter 4: The World's Major Language Families- A Primer

4.21 LIVING LANGUAGE ISOLATES

GENERAL NOTE ON LANGUAGE ISOLATES AND WHAT THEY TELL US ABOUT THE EVOLUTION OF LANGUAGE: Language *isolates* are of course single languages which appear to have no connection to any other languages or language families.

Well known examples from the ancient world are **Sumerian** and **Etruscan**, which we have already discussed above. Well known examples from the modern world are **Basque** in Europe, several **Caucasian** languages of the Caucasus Steppe region that do not belong to any family from that region [LAs-34, LAs-35], several **languages native to North America**, **Burashaski,** a language of northern Pakistan, the **Andaman/Nicobar Islands** languages, and a very large number (> 1,000) of languages of **Papua-New Guinea** [LAs-36]. There are other language isolates not in our list as well, such as some languages of Chattisgarh and Jhaarkhand states of India.

In our modern world today, we are used to the dominance of just a few language families. It is therefore difficult for us to envision today that the presence of a large number of language families, and a large number of language isolates, *may at one time have been the norm rather than the exception.*

Indeed, the fortuitous concurrence of two historical events probably led at one time to the development of a very large number of language families and isolates even in places, such as the Eurasian landmass, where there are relatively few today. These two events were:

> (1) The last *Ice Age*, which lasted tens of thousands of years and ended just about 8,000 to 6,000 BCE.
> (2) The evolutionary advancement of *Homo sapiens* to the level where language could develop to an advanced level, *apparently fortuitously coinciding with the Ice Age*, i.e. probably happening just about in the middle of this Ice Age.

Before we delve into these two events further, we need to briefly digress and touch upon a theory widely propounded in the current linguistic scholarship with regard to language isolates [LN-1 to LN-4, SCr-1, LAs-1, LAs-34 to LAs-39]: *That temperate climates (such as Europe and Central Asia) breed relatively small numbers of language families with large numbers of speakers, whereas tropical climates (such as Polynesia) breed large numbers of language families* [LAs-36, LAs-37]. The prototypical example cited in

Chapter 4: The World's Major Language Families- A Primer

229

support of this is the contrast between Eurasia (with perhaps a dozen dominant language families today in a vast geographical region) and Papua-New Guinea (with over a thousand language isolates on a mid-sized island).

In this author's humble opinion, however, not only is this theory based on *limited geographical observation*, but it also may be in error in the sense of "confusing the symptom with the disease". For example, if we broaden our geographical observation sphere to, say, the Americas or the Horn-of-Africa-Middle-East-India axis, we find that even in warm or sub-tropical regions such as the Middle East and the Horn of Africa, the number of surviving language isolates or families is small, whereas in cold or temperate regions such as North America, they are large.

In this author's considered opinion, the presence of language isolates may quite simply be *due to the presence of isolated populations* and nothing more! However, it is the *reasons for isolation of the populations* that can be very varied.

For example, in regions such as Papua-New Guinea the population had a comparatively sedentary, relaxed, peaceful and contented lifestyle, where they had *little occasion or reason* to interact with even neighboring linguistic groups. In contrast, the peoples of Eurasia had a more, shall we say, aggressive, lifestyle which made them constantly on the move in search of food, land and conquests. They thus constantly interacted with other linguistic groups. Similarly, the peoples of the Middle East or North India, busy in constant interaction with each other in the course of building civilizations, would quite obviously develop few language isolates. In occasions where tropical peoples *did* have occasion to venture out in search of food, conquest or other such things, for example the Austronesian or the Baantu peoples, their language family *did* dominate, and the number of language families was small and number of isolates minuscule. Thus, the Austronesian and Baantu languages are stark, concrete evidence today that refutes the above theory.

In this context then, the first event cited above, i.e. the last *Ice Age*, may have created a dichotomy of linguistic conditions. In the regions bordering the more than 1 km thick ice sheets, in Europe, northern Asia and North America, populations would have been isolated by climate. If they developed language, it would be in isolation. We have some genetic evidence of such isolation of populations, in the three Eurasian **haplogroups**, the **R2a, I** and **R1a**, corresponding respectively to the regions of northern Iberia, the Balkans and the Uzbekistan-Turkmenistan-Caspian-Sea region. (*Haplogroups* once again are groupings of the most common *haplotypes* in the Y (male) chromosome, thus passed down among males only.) More recent (2000 et seq.) genetic studies [GDn-2 to GDn-10,

GDn-41 to GDn-49, LAs-48] have supported the hypothesis that, in the colder climates, much movement of populations occurred as the Ice Age started to end.

One such study is that of Stephen Oppenheimer, a medical geneticist at the University of Oxford, England. Oppenheimer published [GDn-48] an extensive DNA study showing that the original populations of the British Isles (including Ireland) likely arrived from the region of Spain about 10,000 years ago, right after the last Ice Age concluded and as the ice sheets enveloping most of Europe up to southern France slowly receded northward. He posits that they spoke a language or languages related to modern Basque. Although the Anglo-Saxons imposed their language on the English and the Celts imposed theirs on the Irish, the actual gene pool contributed by these numerically inferior invaders appears to have been no more than 5%. [GDn-48, GDn-49].

The second event cited above, the first development of language coinciding with the 10,000 or 20,000 years of isolation caused by the Ice Age, is a conjecture of this author. It is however a conjecture that may have considerable credibility.

LANGUAGE ISOLATES OF OCEANIA: These are concentrated in the region of the interior of ***Papua-New Guinea***, which according to many linguistic studies has over 60 language families and nearly 1 000 languages [LAs-36]. In this still densely forested region, languages within tens of kilometers proximity are totally unrelated. Interestingly, the languages of the coastal region of Papua-New Guinea *do* belong to a single language family, the Austronesian, giving support to the hypothesis of littoral "island-hopping" migration of Austronesian peoples into Polynesia, either from the Indian subcontinent or from the Chinese mainland. The several ***Australian*** aboriginal languages are also an isolate, and Western linguists are divided on whether they constitute a single language family [LAs-37].

LANGUAGE ISOLATES OF EUROPE: The most prominent ancient language isolate of Europe is of course ***Etruscan***, dealt with in a separate section in this chapter. ***Basque*** is the only prominent modern language isolate. It is spoken in the Pyrenees mountain region on the French-Spanish border.

LANGUAGE ISOLATES OF THE AMERICAS: The Americas have so many language isolates, that they have been covered separately above, in the sections on North, Central and South American languages, *q.v.*. Interestingly, many of these isolates are continuing to become extinct even as of this writing. For example, the language designated ***Kawesqar,*** of the Patagonian regions of southern Chile, was documented to have only six, elderly speakers left in 2004 [LN-81]. *Zuni* is a language isolate found among Native Americans in the U.S. state of New Mexico which still has many thousands of speakers.

OTHER LANGUAGE ISOLATES: The language known as ***Burushaski*** is an isolate found in northern Pakistan. The language family designated ***Kamchatkan*** by linguists is found among non-Russian-ethnicity peoples in the Kamchatkan and Chukotko peninsulas of the Russian Far East. Interestingly, this family does not appear to have any relation to any languages of the Americas, even though the earliest humans are thought to have migrated into the Americas from a land bridge connecting eastern Siberia to Alaska.

Chapter 4: The World's Major Language Families- A Primer

4.22 "SUPRA" OR "MACRO" LANGUAGE FAMILIES

In the late 20th and early 21st centuries, there was much work on so-called "supra" or "super" or "macro" language families, which are purported to deal with parent language families spanning radically different groups such as the Indo-European and the Altaic. Among these is the *Nostratic* language family [LAs-78, LAs-79].

This author feels that scholarship in this new field is too sparse and weak to be able to come to any definite conclusions in this respect. Superficial similarities across language families, and their relation to children's phonology and the first phonemic differentiations of children, are apparent to any multilingual person: For example, *ni* ("you" in Mandarin), *ni* ("you" in Tamil), the radical root *ta*/*tad* (3rd person) in Sanskrit and by extension, all Indo-European languages, *thaa* (3rd person in Mandarin), etc. all have a dental artition, indicating a possible *parent dental phoneme for all 2nd and 3rd persons* ("*not-self*", see discussion in an earlier chapter). Similarly, one might conjecture that the Indo-European negation, dental *na* and the Semitic negation, dental-central *la,* are one and the same through the common *r-l-n* relationship. However, without further evidence, these could very well be coincidental resemblances.

Thus, this author feels that the subject of "supra" or "macro" language families is too much in its infancy, as of this writing (2005), to be treated of in this chapter.

It is also noted that the possible structure of a ***parent human language*** is discussed at some length in an earlier chapter of this book. For reasons explained therein, this is dubbed *"**anti-Nostratic**"*!

4.23 LANGUAGES WITH AN "ENGLISH-LIKE" ("*ANGRAMAYA*", A NEW TERM) STRUCTURE (WITH BASE FROM ONE LANGUAGE FAMILY, ALL 'HIGHER' VOCABULARY FROM OTHER FAMILIES)

4.23.1 THE STRUCTURE OF ENGLISH

As noted in passing in several places earlier in this book, many languages have a structure like that of English, where *a base language of a particular origin has superimposed upon it a higher vocabulary taken from an entirely different origin*.

Thus, for example, English has a native Germanic base, from its Anglo-Saxon roots before 1066 CE, before which the language somewhat resembled the German of today. Upon this is superimposed a higher vocabulary taken first from French, the earliest of Norman provenance, post-1066, but later brought through cultural and commercial contact as well. Later, Latin and Greek were also used for borrowing, as the English language developed and needed a higher vocabulary.

In the case of English, the superstructure of higher words happens to be taken from the same main language family (Indo-European). However, in most of the other examples listed in the Table below, the borrowed language is actually of a radically different provenance, i.e. from a very different language family.

Chapter 4: The World's Major Language Families- A Primer

We shall coin a new word for such English-like languages: ***ANGRAMAYA*** (literally, "English-like" in Sanskrit):

ANGRAMAYA:

A LANGUAGE TYPE WHEREIN THE BASE LANGUAGE, OF A PARTICULAR ORIGIN, HAS SUPERIMPOSED UPON IT A HIGHER VOCABULARY TAKEN FROM AN ENTIRELY DIFFERENT ORIGIN.

Some *examples* are **English** (base Germanic, higher vocabulary French, Latin, Greek), **Malay/Indonesian** (Bahasa Indonesia/Malaysia, base Austronesian, higher vocabulary Paali and Sanskrit), **Khmer** (base Austro-Asiatic, higher vocabulary Paali and Sanskrit). In the case of English, the languages from which the higher vocabulary is derived still happen to be of the same family (Indo-European). However, for Indonesian and Khmer, the higher vocabulary languages derive from an entirely different language family.

...(4.4)

If one has some doubts that such a structure, in which a higher vocabulary from a particular origin is superimposed on a base vocabulary of a different origin, is unique at all, one need only compare modern German and modern English. Now both of these are supposedly of "Germanic" origin. In German, nearly all the higher vocabulary is of truly *Germanic* rather than Latin (i.e. *Romance*) or Greek origin, and nouns are usually derived from variations of pre-verb/verb pairs.

For example, let us look at the words in the Table below, used in a financial context and found in a typical financial document. The German words in this Table are all clearly of Germanic origin, with lots of free use of pre-verb/verb (*upasarga/anga*) construction. Yet every single one of their English equivalents is clearly of Latin, Greek or French origin! A reader familiar with French will immediately be able to pick out the corresponding French equivalents, some of which (e.g. *instruction, documents*) may be identical to the English.

Chapter 4: The World's Major Language Families- A Primer

Table 4-5: Comparison of English and German words drawn from an everyday *financial* document, showing the *angramaya* nature of English.

*It is seen that although German and English are both supposedly of "Germanic" origin, in German, nearly all the words are of truly Germanic origin, whereas in English they are, as is quite evident, all ultimately of Latin, Greek or borrowed French provenance! This illustrates the **ANGRAMAYA** character of English.*

GERMAN	ENGLISH
Anweisung	*instruction*
Überweisung	*deposit*
Vereinbarung	*agreement*
Bestimmungen	*provisions*
Bedingungen	*terms*
Unterlagen	*documents*
anträgen	*apply*
tätigen	*transact*

Chapter 4: The World's Major Language Families- A Primer

4.23.2 SOME OTHER *"ANGRAMAYA"* LANGUAGES BESIDES ENGLISH: *HINDI/URDU, INDONESIAN/MALAYSIAN LANGUAGES, KHMER, THAI, MYANMARI (BURMESE), SWAAHILI (SWAHILI), OTHERS*

The short Table below lists languages that show this type of *Angramaya* structure. The last column in the Table, "Stability/Comments" is of relevance in *special cases*, as described below.

Table 4-6 (*cont. overleaf*): Some of the many languages displaying an "English-like" (*Angramaya*) structure, as described in text.

LANGUAGE	ORIGIN	ORIGIN OF SUPERIMPOSED HIGHER VOCABULARY	COMMENTS
English	Germanic sub-branch of Indo-European	Old and Middle French (*Romance* sub-branch of Indo-European) Latin (*Indo-European*) Classical Greek (*Indo-European*)	
Tibetan	Sino-Tibetan	Sanskrit, via North India (*Indo-European*)	
Myanmari (Burmese)	Sino-Tibetan	Sanskrit, via North India (*Indo-European*)	
Malay (Bahasa Indonesia/- Bahasa Malaysia)	Malayo-Polynesian	Sanskrit, via South India (*Indo-European*)	
Regional/- Local Languages of Indonesia (Balinese, Javanese, other)	Malayo-Polynesian	Sanskrit, via South India (*Indo-European*)	

(Table 4-6, cont.)			
LANGUAGE	ORIGIN	ORIGIN OF SUPERIMPOSED HIGHER VOCABULARY	COMMENTS
Khmer (**Cambodian**)	*Austro-Asiatic*	Sanskrit, via South India (*Indo-European*)	
Thai	*Tai*	Sanskrit, via South India (*Indo-European*)	
Hindi/Urdu	*Indo-European*	Arabic (*Semitic*) Faarsi (*Indo-European*) Turkish (*Altaic*)	Some feel this is a "meta-stable language" that has not found its footing yet!
Swaahili	*Bantu*	Arabic, via coastal traders (*Semitic*)	
Telaguu, Malayaalam, Kannada	**Dravidian**	Sanskrit (*Indo-European*)	
Korean	*Altaic*	Chinese (*Sino-Tibetan*)	Like Japanese, Korean falls into this category only with respect to the *written* language. Here, the borrowings are ideograms from literary Chinese. The spoken language is entirely different, and does *not* fall into this category.
Japanese	*Altaic? Isolate?*	Chinese (*Sino-Tibetan*)	Like Korean, Japanese falls into this category only with respect to the *written* language. Here, the borrowings are ideograms from literary Chinese. The spoken language is entirely different, and does *not* fall into this category.

Even among *Angramaya* languages themselves, there are some special cases.

For example, a somewhat special case is **Korean**, in which the borrowings for the higher vocabulary were in the form of *ideograms* from a *literary* language (Chinese), from a time when Korean was still written in Chinese ideographic script (pre-Haangul). Being ideograms, their pronunciation depends entirely on the language used to articulate them!

A much more special, one would say even extreme, case, is **Hindi/Urdu**. Hindi, a language which has undergone extreme stress due to invasions, and Urdu, a "language" of somewhat artificial origin, are of course in fact the same base language, but with different origins for their higher vocabularies. One may remark that these languages have still not found their footing for higher literary and commercial use today. They are in danger of either being "bastardized" by heavy English borrowings, or becoming entirely extinct.

Hindi/Urdu in fact has a very special and *extreme* place among *Angramaya* languages: Even some very basic, everyday words, such as the ones listed below, are foreign (Arabic or Faarsi or Turkish) borrowings, having displaced the original Sanskrit-based words:

Table 4-7: Table illustrating the *extreme ANGRAMAYA* nature of Hindi/Urdu, with even basic, everyday words being of foreign (mostly Arabic, Faarsi and Turkish, but some English as well) origin. The most likely, original Sanskrit-based words displaced by these borrowings are given in *italicized* square brackets, where applicable. The *"round-trippers"* among these words (see discussion below) are marked with a double asterisk. At the end of each entry, the language of origin is given in standard square brackets. *This short list is just exemplary and is an excerpt from a list of several hundred such words which has been compiled by the author and is available to the inquisitive reader.*

- *akhbaar* ("newspaper") *[patrikaa]* (See also *khabar* below.) [Arabic]
- *baad* ("after", with object; "afterwards") *[anantar, nantar* (cf. Maraathi)*]*. [Arabic]
- *baarish* ("rain") *[warshaa]*** [Faarsi]
- *baksaa* ("box") *[no common original word]*. [English]
- *botal* ("bottle") *[no common original word]*. [English]
- *dard* ("pain") *[vedanaa]* [Faarsi]
- *darwaazaa* ("door") *[dwaar]*** [Faarsi]
- *dikkat* ("trouble") *[kasht.]* [Arabic]
- *dil* ("heart", also figuratively) *[hrd]* [Faarsi]
- *diiwaanaa* ("crazy; intoxicated") *[muudh.a]* [Faarsi]
- *dost* ("friend") *[mitra]* [Faarsi]
- *duniyaa* ("world") *[jag]* [Arabic]
- *kalam* ("pen") *[likhantra (from likh-yantra)]* [Arabic]
- *khabar* ("news") *[samaachaar]*(see also a*khbaar* above). [Arabic]
- *khush* ("happy, contented") *[prasanna/-aanandit]* [Faarsi]
- *khuun* ("blood") *[rakta, lahu]* [Faarsi]
- *kitaab* ("book") *[pustak,* cf. Maraathi*]* [Arabic]
- *kursii* ("chair") *[aasana]*. [Arabic]
- *makaan* ("house, building"). *[ghar, griha]* [Arabic]
- *manzil* ("house, building, floor"). *[star]* [Arabic]
- *mulaakaat* ("meeting") *[milan; mishran]*. [Arabic]
- *mushkil* ("difficult") *[kathin]*. [Arabic]
- *sabzii/sabjii* ("vegetable", Faarsi "green") *[bhaaji]* [Faarsi]
- *saphed* ("white") *[shweta]*** [Faarsi]
- *sharm* ("shyness, bashfulness") *[lajjaa,* cf. Maraathi *laaz]* [Faarsi]
- *taariikh* ("date") *[dinaank]* [Arabic]

Chapter 4: The World's Major Language Families- A Primer

It is also to be noted that some words in the above Table, marked with double asterisks, are unique in an additional manner, in that they have made a *"round trip"*! For example, Sanskrit *shweta*, "white", to Faarsi *saphed*, borrowed back into Hindi/Urdu, cognate with English *white*, Anglo-Saxon *hwaeta*. Similarly Sanskrit *warshaa*, "rain" to Faarsi *baariish*, borrowed back into Hindi/Urdu; and again, Sanskrit *dwaar*, "door", to Faarsi *darwaazaa*, borrowed back into Hindi/Urdu.

This unique position of Hindi/Urdu is in contradistinction to, say, English, where most common, everyday words still remain "Germanic". For example, for some of words in the above Hindi/Urdu list, some corresponding English words are all still "Germanic", in comparison with what might have been their Latin-origin equivalents from Norman French if English had been an extreme *Angramaya* language:

- English: *book, blood, friend, world,* and *white*.
- Cf. German: *Buch, Blut, Freund, Welt, weiss*.

One might cite "could-have-been" Norman-French-origin English equivalents of the above English words, if English had been an extreme *Angramaya* language:

- *livre, sang, ami, monde, blanc.*

Chapter 4: The World's Major Language Families- A Primer

241

4.24 BRIEF SYNOPSIS OF PHONETIC SHIFTS BETWEEN LANGUAGES IN FAMILIES

In discussing this subject here, we will eventually develop certain *rules*, some of which are well known to linguists [PHo-1 to PHo-20], and others which we formulate for the first time here.

Now any layman will have observed certain obvious relationships between *phones* in related languages. These occur in words that are considered as *cognate* in the related languages.

Some immediate examples that come to mind among European languages are:

- ❖ The [*l*] and [*r*] relation between Spanish and Portuguese. Thus, e.g., Spanish *playa* ("beach"), *borsa* ("stock exchange") and *obligar* ("to compel"), become Portuguese *praia, borsa, obrigar* (though the latter changes meaning somewhat when used as a past participle, *obrigado*, "thank you"). Here the Spanish [*l*], an alveolar lateral semivowel, is correlated to the Portuguese [*r*], which is an alveolar central tap or trill.

- ❖ The [*d*]/["*th*"] and [*ts*]/[*t*] relations between German and English (in British pronunciation), as in German *der, dass* vs. English *the, that*. Here German [*d*], an alveolar voiced aspirated stop, is correlated to the English ["*th*"], which in British pronunciation is an interdental unvoiced fricative. And in the German *zehn, zwei* vs. the English *ten, two*, an English alveolar unvoiced stop [*t*] is correlated to a compound phone, [*ts*], corresponding to the same stop [t] plus its forward fricative.

- ❖ The [*p*] of the Romance languages and Latin appears to correlate to the [*f*] of the Germanic languages. Thus, e.g., Latin, Spanish *pater, padre*, "father" become English, German *father, vater*, Latin *pisces* correlates with German, English *fisch, fish*, etc. In general the [*p*] of the older Indo-European languages becomes [*f*] in the Germanic languages, e.g. Sanskrit *plu*, "to flow", *pr* "to fill" vs. English/German *flow/fluessen, fill/füllen*, etc. Here, the reader may immediately recognize that there was probably an intermediate stage, represented by the plosive [p] plus its forward fricative, [f], i.e. [*pf*]. This latter is of course still found in many German words, e.g. *Pflock* ("plug"), *Pflug* ("plough"), which appear to be on their way to becoming **Flock** and **Flug**. Thus, we have the likely transition *[p]* → *[pf]* → *[f]*.

Examples among Indian languages are:

- ❖ The **[w]** to **[b]** and **[a]** to **[o]** relations between certain Hindi and Baanglaa (Bengali) words. Thus, e.g., Hindi and Sanskrit *wimaan* ("airplane"), *warshaa* ("rain"), *wimal* ("without blemish"), become Baanglaa *bimaan, borsho, bimol*. And Hindi *jal* ("water") becomes Baanglaa *jol*.

The few examples cited above are meant to be illustrative. They illustrate the cardinal rule of phonetic shifts, well established in current linguistics practice:

If a phonetic shift occurs between diverging languages within a language family, the shift is always identical.

That is to say, a certain phone, e.g. **[p]** of Latin, will always be shifted to a certain other phone, e.g. **[f]** of German or English, as in *pater* to *vater* or *father*. (This rule does *not* apply to directly borrowed words, e.g. English *paternalistic*.)

...(4.5)

Two qualifiers are applied to the above rule:

- It occurs only *when the related words are of similar descent, i.e. are "cognate"*.
- It occurs when *the phonic environment of the phone that is shifted is of a specific type*.

The key qualifiers above are important. What they essentially mean is that the phonetic shifts do not *always* occur. They only occur in certain **cognate** groups of words.

Let us illustrate these qualifiers with one of our examples above, Spanish [*l*] always becomes Portuguese [*r*], in functionally related words of similar descent and when the environment of the phone is similar. *Playa/praia* ("beach"), *bolsa/borsa* ("bourse/stock market"), *obligar/obrigar* ("thank, oblige") are all descended from Latin parents that became the vernacular Spanish and Portuguese words with time. These words are of course *cognates*. And also, reflecting our second qualifier, the immediate phonic environment of the phone shifted in these words is similar: a preceding or following non-vowel. However, illustrating the applicability of the second qualifier, we have the examples, Spanish *linea* ("line"), *cual*, ("which") vs. Portuguese *linha*, *qual*. Here, even though the words *are* cognates, both descended from Latin, the phonic environment of the [*l*] is different: It does not have a preceding or following non-vowel. And so it *doesn't* become an [*r*] in Portuguese. To see a third instance of application of our first qualifier, we see that the shift does *not* occur when the words are *not* descended from the common parent, i.e. are *not* cognate, but rather, have been borrowed for technical uses after the daughter languages already evolved. This is seen in the Spanish and Portuguese *aorta* ("aorta"), a Latin borrowing for a medical term in which the [*r*] *is* followed by a non-vowel but a phonetic shift still doesn't occur. That is to say, we do not have Spanish *aolta* vs. Portuguese *aorta*.

Applying the qualifiers similarly to Hindi/Sanskrit vs. Baanglaa, we see, that certain words with initial [*b*] in Hindi and Sanskrit remain unchanged in Baanglaa, e.g. Hindi, Sanskrit *bol* ("speak"), *bal* ("strength") unchanged in Baanglaa *bol*, *bol*. The rule here thus seems to be "initial [*w*] of Sanskrit always becomes initial [*b*] of Baanglaa, but initial [*b*] of Sanskrit remains [*b*] in Baanglaa."

Now that we have our basic, cardinal rule of phonetic shifts and its two associated qualifiers, we can cite **a few additional, illustrative examples of typical phonetic shifts**. The reader may thus become more comfortable with them:

- For some Latin-based words in French/Spanish and English, [*l*] becomes Italian [*j*]. E.g. English, French *closed, clos*, "closed" from Latin *closum* or *clotum*, becoming Italian *chiuso*. English, French *flame* ("flame") from Latin *flama* becoming Italian *fiamma,* French, Spanish *blanc, blanca* becoming Italian *bianca*, etc. etc.
- Original Latin suffixes *-tio*, *-tionis* becoming English [*-shan*], French, Spanish [*-sion*] and German, Italian [*-tsion*], as in the words *information* or *nation* as pronounced in each of these languages.

- Some Arabic words with initial [s] becoming initial [sh] in Hebrew, e.g. Arabic *salaam aaleikum*, Hebrew *shaalom aleixem*, "peace be with you".
- In some languages, one finds both elements of a phonetic shift present, as if the shift were still in transition. Thus, in Sanskrit, we have the following examples:
  - Verb *ruch* "to shine, to be resplendent", noun *ruchi* "light, brightness" vs. verb *loch* "to shine; to see/view", *lochana* "illuminating" (in the latter, an original *luch* has taken a *guna* to yield *loch,* cognates Latin *luce* etc.). In these examples, the [l] and [r] are both present in Sanskrit, as if still in transition between each other.
  - *Loma:* "(long) hair", vs. *romasha* "hairy, shaggy". Here again, both [l] and [r] exist together, giving the same word a slightly different meaning.
  - Noun *Vaach* "speech, word, voice, sound" but in many declensionional forms of this noun, the [ch] (palatal stop) becomes [k] or [g] (velar stops), e.g. *vaakya* "that which is spoken, a sentence", *vaagbhis* (instrumental plural case) etc. Thus, here we have living evidence of the palatal <—> velar phonetic shift through the forward fricative, i.e. [k] <—> [ksh] <—> [sh] <—> [ch]

In view of the above, we may now formulate some clearly applicable *rules for phonetic shifts*. Most of these are presented for the first time here, although corollaries for some may be found in the linguistics literature. We state that, *whenever a phonetic shift of a phone occurs:*

> **RULE 1:** *The most likely shift is to a PHONE HAVING THE SAME ARTITION (articulation position) as the original phone.*
>
> **RULE 2:** *The next most likely shift is to a phone IN AN ADJACENT ARTITION; and among these, the most frequent shift is that of a PLOSIVE OR SEMIVOWEL TO ITS FORWARD FRICATIVE.*
>
> **RULE 3:** *Shifts sometimes involve simple ELISION of an entire phone.* These are uncommon.
>
> **RULE 4:** *Shifts may also involve ADDITION of a phone.*
>
> **RULE 5:** *The shift **least likely to occur** is to a phone clearly having no relation to the original phone.* Nevertheless, ***these shifts do occur.***

...(4.6)

We can now cite just a few illustrative examples for each of the above rules:

Illustrative Examples for Rule 1:

- The [*l*] and [*r*] relation between Spanish and Portuguese. Thus, e.g., Spanish *playa* ("beach"), *borsa* ("stock exchange") and *obligar* ("to compel"), become Portuguese *praia, borsa, obrigar* (though the latter changes meaning somewhat when used as a past participle, *obrigado*, "thank you"). Here the Spanish [*l*], an alveolar lateral semivowel, is correlated to the Portuguese [*r*], which is an alveolar central tap or trill. The [r]-[l] shift of course extends to [n] as well. The [r]-[l]-n phones are freely interchangeable through a slight change in the place of egress of the breath (central vs. lateral vs. nasal).

Chapter 4: The World's Major Language Families- A Primer

- The [w] to [b] relation between certain Hindi and Baanglaa (Bengali) words. Thus, e.g., Hindi and Sanskrit *wimaan* ("airplane"), *warshaa* ("rain"), *wimal* ("without blemish"), become Baanglaa **bimaan, borsho, bimol**.

- Many Sanskrit to Hindi and Maraathi transitions, e.g. Sanskrit *bhan*, "sound, speak", Maraathi *mhan*, "tell, say, mention"; Sanskrit *bhaginii*, "honored woman, sister", Hindi, Maraathi *bahin, behen*, Gujaraati *ben*.

The alveolar tap *r* becoming the trilled "rolled r" and reverting interchangeably to the tap in many world languages, such that the tap and the trill are interchangeable and allophones of the same phoneme.

Illustrative Examples for Rule 2:

- In the German *zehn, zwei* vs. the English *ten, two*, an English alveolar devoiced stop [*t*] is correlated to a compound phone (affricate), [*ts*], corresponding to the same stop [t] plus its forward fricative.

- The [*p*] of the Romance languages and Latin appears to correlate to the [*f*] of the Germanic languages. Thus, e.g., Latin, Spanish *pater, padre*, "father" become English, German *father*, *vater*, Latin *pisces* correlates with German, English *fisch, fish*, etc. In general the [*p*] of the older Indo-European languages becomes [*f*] in the Germanic languages, e.g. Sanskrit *plu*, "to flow", *pr* "to fill" vs. English/German *flow/fluessen, fill/füllen*, etc.. Here, the reader may immediately recognize that there was probably an intermediate stage, represented by the plosive [p] plus its forward fricative, [f], i.e. [pf]. This latter is of course still found in many German words, e.g. *Pflock* ("plug"), *Pflug* ("plough"), which appear to be on their way to *Flock* and *Flug*.

- There is strong evidence that the original Sanskrit third person plural indicative active ending *-nti* became the *-nsi* of Classical Greek through the intermediate *-ntsi*, since this ending is still evident in Hittite. The transformation is thus clearly through the *forward fricative*, i.e. [t] ---> [ts] ---> [s], as in other cases, e.g. the Germanic [p] ---> [pf] ---> [f].

Illustrative Example for Rule 3:

- Latin *negro* becomes Italian *nero*, with elision of the [g]. Similarly, many Italian words having their origins in Latin and still spelled with a *g* elide the [g] in pronounciation, e.g. *medaglio, intaglia* etc. In English, we elide the [gh] in pronunciation of words such as *light* even though the spelling still retains the letters. Etc. etc

Illustrative Example for Rule 4:

- The Old English (Anglo-Saxon) to modern English shifts of many vowels illustrate this shift: The pure vowels have been turned to diphthongs as a result: E.g. A-S *liht, niht*, English *light, night* (today's diphthongized pronunciation). Also cf: Gothic *mus, hus*, English *mouse, house*, A-S *nu*, English *now* etc. etc.

Illustrative Examples for Rule 5:

- The presumed original central tap or trill [r] of Latin and medieval French becoming the uvular fricative *r* of modern Parisian French.

- The [k] of many original Keltic words becoming [p] in Welsh only. The most well known example of this is *mae**k***, "son" becoming *mae**p***. Thus, Old Gaelic *MacRichard* ("son of Richard") becomes *MapRichard* and ultimately *Pritchard* in Welsh.

- Tamil *[w]* and *[g]* are sometimes interchangeable, although these two phones are completely unrelated.

It is to be noted that many of the above rules become apparent *in combination* when one language borrows words from another. E.g. English *printer* becomes Japanese *purinta*, English *bottle, box* become Hindi/Urdu *botal, baksaa*, etc.

4.25 LANGUAGE, ETHNICITY, "RACE" AND COLOR

One of the basic tenets of linguistics that is self-evident and apparent, from the everyday world, even to the monolingual layman with no knowledge of linguistics, is that there is, **today**, *little relation between language on the one hand and ethnicity, "race" or color on the other*. That is to say, we can formulate a crude but emphatic rule:

$$Language \neq Ethnicity \neq \text{``Race''} \neq Color$$

(*where in this case, the not-equivalent-to sign, $\neq$, implies "not related to"*)

...(4.7)

This tenet is, for instance, readily apparent in the many populations of African origin who now speak, say, Spanish, Portuguese or English, or the populations of Mexican Aztec origin (or mixtures thereof) who now speak Spanish, as their native, first and sometimes, only language.

The same layman may, however, readily conclude that, in historical times, *prior* to the recent era of massive migrations of the last 600 years or so of world populations, there *was some* relation between language and ethnicity, "race" or color.

What we would like to do in the brief discussion in this Section is to thoroughly *debunk this myth as well*. Let us start by taking some illustrative examples:

EXAMPLE 1: *THE TURKISH POPULATIONS OF ANATOLIA TODAY*: Turkish is a language of the Turkic sub-group of the Altaic family, a family that originated most probably in a region corresponding to western Mongolia today. It is important to note that it was brought to Anatolia by the invasion of *just 40,000* Seljuk Turks, who conquered a population estimated at about five to seven *million* [HIh-6]. Prior to this invasion, this "native" population spoke varied other languages: dialects of Greek in the western region, dialects of Faarsi (Persian) in the eastern region, and dialects of Arabic, Aramaic and other Semitic languages in the southern region, with Greek by far the major component.

Chapter 4: The World's Major Language Families- A Primer

However, within 150 years of the Seljuk invasion, *all Anatolians were speaking only Turkish*. What is more, even the predecessor languages were actually the result of conquest of and eventual dominance by Greek, Persian, Arab and other later arrivals, of yet earlier peoples, who spoke other languages, e.g. Elamite, Hurrian, Hittite, other Indo-European languages and other Semitic languages. Yet again, these in turn were, probably the result of invasion and conquest by the Elamites, Hurrians, etc. of yet other predecessor language families and language isolates! And so on and so forth. Thus, today, Turks superficially "look like" Greeks in western Anatolia, and Arabs and Iraanians in southeastern Anatolia. None of them however "look like" the Turkic-speaking Uighurs of what is today western China, and the gradual gradation of facial features, with the epicanthic fold increasingly evident, is readily visible as one goes from Turkey, through Azerbaijan, Kazakhstan, Turkmenistan, Kyrgyszstan, and Uzbekistan, to the Uighur region of China and eventually to Mongolia.

Our above analysis relating to the Turkish speaking peoples finds support among many genetic studies, including more recently those of Arnaiz-Villena et al. and Cinnoglu et al. [GDn-41, GDn-42]. Quoting from the former:

> "Turks (Anatolians) do not significantly differ from other Mediterraneans, indicating that while the Asian Turks carried out an invasion with cultural significance (language), *it is not genetically detectable.*"

…(4.8)

Thus, the adage "Turks are basically Greeks who speak Turkish", used by some to try to engender friendly relations between these two sometimes embittered peoples, does indeed have a lot of credence. Ethnically, the modern Anatolian is a mixture of Greek, Persian and other Indo-Europeans, Akkadians and other Semites, Elamites, Hurrians and other Dravidians, and, quite probably, a little Sumerian thrown in as well! A true embodiment of the ancient Middle East! Yet he/she speaks a "Mongolian", Altaic language. And all this happened fairly recently, around the 12th century CE

EXAMPLE 2: THE HUNGARIAN (MAGYAR, MAAGYAAR) POPULATIONS OF TODAY: As noted above, the Hungarian (Magyar) language is a member of the Finno-Ugric sub-branch of the Uralic branch of the Ural-Altaic family. The latter's members include Finnish, Korean and Mongolian. Genetic studies very similar to those cited for Turkish above appear to indicate that less than 10% of the genetic inheritance of modern-day

Chapter 4: The World's Major Language Families- A Primer

Hungarians is from the conquering Maagyaar tribes. It may be conjectured that the original Maagyaar had an epicanthic fold, nearly invisible today among ethnic Hungarians.

EXAMPLE 3: THE EGYPTIAN POPULATIONS OF TODAY: As a result of invasion and conquest around the 8th century CE, Arabic, a language of the Semitic sub-group of the Afro-Asiatic family, supplanted Egyptian, a language of the Egyptian sub-group of the same family. Egyptian itself however has a comparatively long residence time in Egypt, having of course endured there from pre-historic (i.e. pre-written-historical-record) times. Yet it is quite likely that Egyptian itself is an amalgamation of a prehistoric Afro-Asiatic base language with archaic Nubian, some other Nilo-Saharan language, or language isolates.

EXAMPLE 4: THE HINDI/URDU-SPEAKING POPULATIONS OF CENTRAL INDIA TODAY: An ethnicity vs. language analysis in India is, unfortunately, uniquely skewed by the caste system. (As noted elsewhere, this caste system is a remnant of the world's first attempt at "race"/ethnicity and color-based segregation of society, which was further given a religious sanction. Needless to say, an attempt that has left a permanent and horrible scar on that society, 5,000 years later, even when the original color and ethnic distinctions have been gone for thousands of years.) Thus, such an analysis must be confined to particular castes. We look for example at the modern Indian provinces of Madhya Pradesh, Chhattisgarh and Uttar Pradesh. If we then examine the middle castes (Vaishya, Kshatriya) only, these reflect successive overlayers of the following linguistic groups: Austro-Asiatic, Sino-Tibetan, Dravidian and Indo-European, with varying contributions from each group, depending on region and caste. Today, all these people speak an Indo-European language, Hindi/Urdu.

EXAMPLE 5: INDO-EUROPEAN SPEAKING POPULATIONS OF EUROPE TODAY: As one example of our perhaps distorted misconceptions on numbers of language families and isolates, the layman today, especially one schooled in the Western tradition, thinks of Europe as a homogeneous mass of people, nearly all of whom speak a language of the Indo-European family. Racial identifications of course immediately follow. Completely missed in this scenario is the likelihood that, prior to the advent of dominant linguistic groups such as the Indo-European and the Finno-Ugric into Europe, **there were most likely tens of language families and tens of isolates in Europe**. Some of these survived in regions where they managed to protect themselves by geographical isolation, e.g. the French-Spanish Pyrenees (*Basque*) or the Caucasian Steppe (*Caucasian languages*). Others, e.g. *Etruscan*, survived, if only temporarily, through political, economic or

Chapter 4: The World's Major Language Families- A Primer

military strength. The racial argument now completely counter to the homogeneous-race argument above, again follows logically: That Europeans today are actually a mish-mash of dozens of ethnicities (or "races", with the term used loosely, in the lay sense - biologists of course tell us today that the term "race" is genetically meaningless and nonsensical).

From the superficial teaching of historical linguistics in the primary and secondary educational systems today [LN-1 to LN-30, LAs-1, LN-85 to LN-87], and fed further by the extreme racist theories propounded by Europeans in the late 19th and early/mid 20th centuries, a layman might then readily arrive at the following rather racist picture of Europe from a linguistic perspective: An empty or nearly empty land, much like the New World once was, until, suddenly, Aaryan (Aryan) hordes sweep in from somewhere in Central Asia, where they had been curiously confined for thousands of years. They populate the land and give it its dominant Indo-European languages. Subsequently, successive waves of migration from branches of the same Indo-European family - in chronological order Keltic, Greek, Romance (Italic), Balto-Slavic, and Germanic - give Europe its present linguistic structure. Other language families, e.g. the Uralic, then take root in later Mongol migrations. Language families represented by Basque, Etruscan and the myriad languages of the Caucasus are quaint curiosities that we need not consider seriously! *We all know of course that this may in fact be a horribly incorrect scenario, in fact it is probably nonsense!*

Firstly, the land was not empty or humans, but, based on the archaeological record [LAs-4, LAs-5], fairly well populated. The people inhabiting it were "white" in their superficial appearance, but spoke non-Indo-European languages. We have surviving evidence for this in languages such as Etruscan, Basque and the multitude of Caucasian languages and isolates, the very languages that Western European linguists of the 19th century preferred to ignore. It is not unreasonable therefore to presume that there were tens, perhaps even more, language families and isolates in Europe prior to the Indo-European migration.

We also know, again from the archaeological record, that in some parts of Europe, the Indo-European migration was very recent, for example in Scandinavia. The Danish National Museum in Copenhagen records evidence of well-preserved burials from about 3 000 B.C. where the bodies show very light blond hair and other Nordic features. But in the same museum, there is also evidence presented of a massive migration from the region of the Baltic states (present-day Lithuania/Latvia, a known regrouping area for Indo-Europeans at that time), around 1 000 BCE This was the only major migration into Scandinavia, and there is therefore a strong presumption that it was the only migration of

Indo-European speakers into Scandinavia. Following this migration, burials are immediately replaced by *cremations*, a characteristically Indo-European method of disposing of the dead, practiced as recently as the cremation of Julius Caesar but surviving only in India today. (The migration of cremating Latins into northern Italy around 1 200 BCE [IEu-44] parallels this Scandinavian migration.) Thus, it is plausible to conclude from this that the "Nordic-looking" Scandinavians were actually non-Indo-European, and acquired their Indo-European language very recently, about 1 000 BCE, from an overlaying but probably numerically inferior migration of Indo-Europeans, whatever they looked like, from the region of the Baltic states. To use some crude, superficial racial phraseology, it is possible that the overlaying Indo-Europeans were less blond and darker than the native Scandinavians at that time. This would immediately trash the racist European theories of the 19th century, some of which tried to establish a Scandinavian origin for Aaryans (Aryans) due to an obsession of Europeans, at least at that time, with skin, hair and eye color. More importantly, it would appear to indicate a large number of "native" European languages which, except for a few like Etruscan and Basque, have been lost forever.

These conclusions from Denmark have their exact analogues in recent (2006-7) genetic studies of British populations, which have concluded that the *Germanic migrations of the 5th-6th centuries CE yielded only about a 5% contribution to British genes*, with the major Irish and British genetic component being the Iberian R1b haplogroup [GDn-40 (b), GDn-48, GDn-49]. In a similar vein, most central Europeans, *including Germans,* have a predominant genetic underpinning of groups such as the Balkan M haplogroup, *with only a superficial, ca 5% to 10%, overlayer of the Aaryan R1a haplogroup.* Indeed, it would appear that modern (early 21st century) DNA studies would have thoroughly debunked Hitler's racial superiority theories and might have shown that Germans were less Aaryan (Aryan) than most East Europeans, Baltics and Indians! Many recent (2000 onwards) genetic studies have provided overwhelming support to our above scenario [GDn-40, GDn-42 to GDn-49].

WAS THERE EVER ANY RELATION BETWEEN LANGUAGE AND ETHNICITY? The examples and arguments cited above appear to lean towards a counter-hypothesis, that there was **never** any relation between language on the one hand and race/ethnicity on the other. This also is an extreme hypothesis. In fact, it is the other extreme of the arguments presented in the previous paragraphs. It may *not* have been true at a certain time in human history. Let us briefly examine this hypothesis.

In an earlier discussion in this chapter, we have referred to a dichotomy in the isolation of human populations in the northern hemisphere during the last Ice Age, ca. 16,000 to ca. 6,000 BCE: In the colder regions, just south of the ice sheets, some populations may have become isolated for prolonged periods. Evidence for this appears in the R2a, I and R1a haplogroups discussed earlier. This population isolation necessarily implies linguistic isolation. In the warmer regions, e.g. the Middle East and northern India, extensive human interaction would minimize isolation.

We also noted in the discussion above *our thesis* that, exclusively in the colder, northern regions, *this trapping of human populations in certain narrow regions during the last Ice Age may have fortuitously coincided with the period of human evolution when language was developed from near scratch*.

These narrow regions probably numbered many more than just the three represented by the above three haplogroups. Thus, one would then have expected that the geographical isolation coincided with an ethnic isolation as well and was reflected in unique language families that were first developed at this time. Obviously then, these language families would have had no relation to each other. They would be an ethnic marker of sorts. But this would apply only for the colder regions just south of the ice cap (including in northern China). In the warmer Middle East, or Africa or India or Central America or southern China, free-flowing human populations might have prevented such isolated linguistic development.

Furthermore, if we were able to study the languages that evolved at this time *in the colder regions only*, we would be able to clearly and transparently see, in their structure, the development of language from first principles. Additionally, such development may not have followed the same pathway in each of these pockets of isolation. We would then have been clearly able to see what we presume are mono-syllabic sounds uttered by primordial humans gradually developed into verbs, nouns, pronouns, etc. perhaps in a distinct way for each language.

Further discussion of this subject requires an understanding of the hypothetical primitive phonemes of the first languages, of baby and child speech, and other subjects. These are discussed in another chapter, and so we must unfortunately recess until then.

"RACE", ETHNICITY AND LANGUAGE: From even the prematurely terminated discussion above, we can now arrive at the possible contention that, at this very remote period in *Homo sapiens'* past during the last Ice Age and only in the colder regions just south of the ice sheets where human populations may have been temporarily isolated, there *was*

indeed a correlation between ethnicity and language. Again, this occurred only among these populations isolated by the Ice Age, but not those in the warmer regions of Africa, the Middle East, India, southern China, Central America, etc. We can however see how quickly this correlation may have dissolved: As the Ice Age started to end and these isolated human populations started to move again, ethnic admixture with other human populations would thus have immediately re-started, and any ethnic distinctions would have quickly vanished. Thus, the arguments on ethnic ("racial") purity are truly nonsense!

To reiterate the argument with respect to Europe then, we have tried to demonstrate in the previous sections that a likely linguistic scenario in Europe was the following: Prior to the advent of dominant linguistic groups such as the Indo-European and the Finno-Ugric, there were most likely tens of language families and tens of isolates in Europe. Some of these survived in regions where they managed to protect themselves by geographical isolation or political strength, e.g. Basque, Etruscan and the numerous Caucasian languages. The racial argument then follows logically: That Europeans today are actually a mish-mash of dozens of "races", with the term used loosely in the lay, non-scientific, sense, and, here, in the sense of "sub-races." The only commonality is that they all have a very fair skin color.

Today, biologists, geneticists and anthropologists are generally in agreement that "race" as a concept is nonsensical and meaningless. Richard Lewontin was one of the first to note, as early as the 1970's [GDn-50], that nearly all human genetic variation can be found within a *single* "race". That is to say, if one focused on genes alone rather than superficial facial features and skin color, the difference between a European, an African and a Chinese individual would not be much greater than the difference between two Europeans, two Africans, two Chinese, etc.. Modern genetic methods have confirmed Dr. Lewontin's statements: It is indeed true that genetic variation within two individuals within a "race" is equal to or greater than that between individuals of two different "races". More recently (2007), Craig Venter, CEO of a firm that was one of the first to sequence the human genome, has noted that "race" is a social concept, not a scientific one [GDn-51].

Yet very recently, there has been much revisionist banter on this subject, in both academic papers, as well as articles in the popular press. This seeks to revive the concept of "race". For example, Armand Leroi, an evolutionary biologist at Imperial College, University of London, contended in a popular article in March 2005 [GDn-52] that while individual genetic features such as skin color or hair texture may vary more within a "race" than between one, when taken together, "certain skin colors tend to go with certain kinds of eyes, noses, skulls, bodies", to quote Dr. Leroi directly. It is the present author's humble opinion that this biologist's view is again skewed by blinding Eurocentrism.

The notion that certain skin colors may go with certain noses, skulls and bodies may partially apply, but only if one were to confine our observations to very limited regions of the world, e.g. certain parts of Europe and Africa only, such as would have been the narrow purview of Dr. Leroi's world view. They are completely confounded when applied to larger parts of the world, and especially regions of the world which were multi-racial and multi-ethnic since prehistoric times, such as India, the Middle East and Northeast Africa. For example, in many South Indian Brahmin (presumed more "Aaryan" than other groups) groups, we frequently find long, "Roman" noses not found in North India; ultra-thin lips; lightly wavy, non-Mongol-type hair; blue eyes; tall, thin build; and obviously "Caucasian" features. But these are all juxtaposed with jet-black skin of a hue comparable to that of an ethnic West African. This would then completely confound Dr Leroi's analysis of certain skin colors "going with" certain other "racial" features.

Indeed, if we had the luxury to be able to momentarily carry out a virtual, "thought" experiment, where we could paint over a person's color to get a universal dark brown, we would realize how nebulous "racial" or "ethnic" stereotyping is: To take one example, we would find, once they were all colored an identical brown and their hair was made of the same texture, that tall, big Scandinavians with flat heads ("brachycephaly" in 19th century racial jargon), flat noses and large lips - a common type found in Scandinavia even today - did not look too different from many West Africans! And if we were to further extend this virtual experiment by juxtaposing people from Somalia and northern Ethiopia ("blacks" of African origin according to our stereotyping) with this Swedish and West African group, we would see that these latter peoples contrasted radically with both the Swedes and the West Africans, in looking much more "Caucasian" to use a crude racial stereotype. . Indeed, one already sees how color alone can mislead in the following example: Many Indians who develop advanced leucoderma over their entire bodies, such that they become "white", are then immediately mistaken for Europeans, even by other Indians. As another example, in regions which were at the juncture of very recent migrations such as Poland or the Ukraine, we would find that if we colored everyone the same dark brown, the "facial types" then vary radically even in closely related people, sometimes even in the same family: Brachycephaly and dolicocephaly (long-headedness), epicanthic folds and no epicanthic folds, flat noses and long, "Roman" noses, thick and thin lips, jet-black hair with straight, "Mongol" texture and fair, wavy hair, etc., etc.. Yet if we were to carry out a DNA analysis of these people, we would find that their family relation, and hence "ethnic" closeness, is well substantiated by the DNA analysis, indicating that the superficial external "racial" features were probably meaningless.

In a lighter vein, we might conjecture, with respect to skin color as a stereotyping identifier, that it is possible that in the next 100 years, a skin dyeing technique may be put on the market by pharmaceutical companies. This might do for skin color what has already been done for hair color: the capability of choosing one's skin color of the week! It might then lead to a "democratization" of race in everyday life, and eliminate racial stereotyping which unfortunately still affects our lives everyday!

GENETIC DATING AND EVOLUTIONARY BIOLOGY TECHNIQUES AS APPLIED TO LINGUISTICS: We mention here in passing certain other developments in linguistics of the very recent past (since 2002). These are mentioned because this author feels they need to be strongly refuted: They are, in this author's opinion, a seriously wrong track of investigation by persons who unfortunately have little qualification in linguistics and almost no mastery over the languages they so freely pronounce on and make sweeping generalizations about. These pronouncements are then given serious consideration due to the academic or other pedigrees of the authors. Among others, these developments relate to the attempt *to apply evolutionary biology techniques to linguistics*.

As just one example of such studies (the only one we will consider here for space reasons and because this is not the main subject that this book deals with), we cite a recent article by Gray and Atkinson [LN-77], entitled "Language-tree divergence times support the Anatolian theory of Indo-European origin". In this article, these authors, who are, respectively, *a psychologist and a biologist*, couple computer-based evolutionary biology techniques (used, e.g., to backdate, by number-crunching, masses of SNP data from DNA analysis) with a very crude and deficient database of basic words in a number of Indo-European languages, to arrive at the conclusion of an Anatolian origin for Indo-Europeans. This study completely ignores linguistic relationships relating to grammatical structure, etymology and semantics among ancient as well as modern Indo-European languages, not to mention archaeological evidence. It does not help that there are many other glaring errors in this article which detract from its credibility, such as using "Afghaani" (a nonexistent language) for Pushto, "Waziristani" (a nonexistent language) for the language of Waziristaan (where the languages are actually Pushto and Dari, a Faarsi dialect), and a very egregious error in a "language-tree"; all of these errors were surprisingly not picked up by the editors. The authors appear to have little knowledge of any other language except English and not even a primer-level knowledge of a single ancient Indo-European language (such as Classical Greek or Latin). One may remark that before one can write with such sweeping conclusions about such serious matters as the origin of Indo-European languages, one must have, at a very minimum, at least a thorough understanding of the languages one is so freely pronouncing on.

More fundamentally, using an analysis technique borrowed from evolutionary biology, without a deep and underlying knowledge of the languages that form the object of the study (which the authors do not appear to have), is fraught with danger: Languages have complex, very subjective and "human" relationships and elements. And simple mathematical analysis of "cognates", with no consideration of what those cognates are, and their subjective relationship, e.g., whether they have a parent-child or just a sibling relationship, their degree of similarity, morphological and semantic, etc., will lead to glaringly wrong conclusions, not unlike those from the now discredited glottochronology.

As early as the mid-20th century, the dangers of applying mathematical (and hence, evolutionary biology) techniques to relationships among different languages had been clearly set forth [LN-78].

FLUX IN THE FIELD OF DNA-BASED PREDICTION OF HUMAN ORIGINS (AS OF 2005):
Finally, that we must take all our discussions above with a strong caveat: That this field, as of this writing (2003-2007), is in a state of great flux. Many recent finds, e.g. the discovery of hominid fossils in inconvenient places such as South Africa and other, unrelated DNA-based studies, the Flores islands of Indonesia, have turned extant theories on their head [GDn-57 to GDn-62]. We learn from recent studies that "convergent evolution" occurs not only in frogs [GDn-53, GDn-54], but also in humans, where lactose-tolerance apparently evolved independently in Africa and Europe within the last 6000 years [GDn-63, GDn-64].

And "re-discovery" of older work, such as the seminal work of the Soviet scientist Dmitri Belyaev [GDn-65], shows us that "niceness" and "nastiness" in entire ethnic groups may after all be inherited among humans as well (as we long suspected but never dared say!), just as we know with fair certainty that it is in, say, dogs or rats, where it has been purposely inbred by humans!

Chapter 4: The World's Major Language Families- A Primer

4.26 EXERCISES

(1) Contrast *language* with *dialect* giving examples from at least two languages.

(2) Enumerate the seven predominant language families of the world in decreasing order of number of speakers, citing at least two example languages from each family.

(3) Enumerate the major extant branches of the Indo-European language family. Enumerate at least three ancient, extinct languages from this family and discuss any significance or importance they may still retain today. Discuss major influences from outside this family, on at least three currently spoken languages from this family.

(4) Enumerate the major branches of the Chinese language sub-family and cite at least one language from each.

(5) Enumerate the major branches of the Niger-Congo language family and cite at least one language from each.

(6) Enumerate the major branches of the Afro-Asiatic language family and cite at least one language from each. How does the Semitic sub-branch of this family relate to the parent? What are the major currently spoken languages of the Semitic sub-branch and what if any is their mutual affinity?

(7) Enumerate the major branches of the Austronesian language family and cite at least one language from each.

(8) Enumerate the major branches of the Uralic language family and cite at least one language from each. What is the current (2009) scholarship with regard to the relation of Japanese to Korean and the Altaic family in general?

(9) Enumerate the major branches of the Dravidian language family and cite at least one language from each. In light of the most recent (to 2009) DNA and archaeological, what is the likely geographical origin of a putative parent Dravidian language? How might this relate to the Harappan (Indus Valley) civilization and Aaryans (Aryans) and their language?

(10) Enumerate the major branches of the Austro-Asiatic language family and cite at least one language from each.

(11) Enumerate the major branches of the Daic language family and cite at least one language from each.

(12) Enumerate the major branches of the Nilo-Saharan language family and cite at least one language from each.

(13) Enumerate the major branches of the Uralic language family and cite at least one language from each.

(14) Enumerate the major branches of the Hmong-Mien language family and cite at least one language from each.

(15) Enumerate the major branches of the "click" language family of Africa and cite at least one language from each.

(16) Enumerate the major branches of the original language families of North and Central American, the Caribbean and easternmost Siberia and cite at least one language from each.

(17) Enumerate the major branches of the original language families of South America and cite at least one language from each.

(18) Enumerate several examples of moribund ancient languages *of significance*. Discuss their significance.

(19) Enumerate several language isolates that are currently spoken and discuss their extent.

(20) Define the term *angramaya*. How are English, Hindi and Khmer *angramaya* languages?

(21) Clarify with examples. How does Hindi differ from the other *angramaya* languages?

(22) Discuss at least three phonetic shifts between languages in families, giving

Chapter 4: The World's Major Language Families- A Primer

260

several example words for each.

(23) Discuss language in relation to ethnicity and "race".

CHAPTER 5.
GRAMMAR AND GRAMMATICAL TERMS, THE *FORM* OF LANGUAGE, ORDER IN LANGUAGE, AND POSSIBLE STRUCTURE OF A SINGLE, PARENT HUMAN LANGUAGE, THE *"ANTI-NOSTRATIC"*

TABLE OF CONTENTS

5.1 SYNOPSIS OF GRAMMATICAL TERMS FOUND EXTENSIVELY IN THE LINGUISTICS LITERATURE AND THEIR UNDERLYING BASES 263

    5.1.1 PREMISE OF THIS CHAPTER AND WHAT IS COVERED AND NOT COVERED IN THIS CHAPTER.. 263
    5.1.2 THE VERB AS FUNDAMENT OF LANGUAGE 264
    5.1.3 ATTRIBUTES OF THE VERB: NUMBERS, GENDERS, TENSES, MOODS, VOICES AND OTHERS.. 264
    5.1.4 SUMMARY OF VERB ATTRIBUTES (PROPERTIES) AND FORMS 271
    5.1.5 ATTRIBUTES OF THE SUBSTANTIVE: NUMBERS, GENDERS, CASES AND OTHER ATTRIBUTES.. 272

5.2 THE *FORM* OF LANGUAGE: TYPOLOGY, MORPHEMES AND MORPHOLOGY 273

    5.2.1 TYPOLOGY 273
    5.2.2. DESCRIPTION OF THE VARIOUS TYPOLOGIES 275
    5.2.3 DIFFERENCES IN INFLECTION IN AGGLUTINATIVE VS. NON-AGGLUTINATIVE LANGUAGES: SYNTHETIC LANGUAGES 280
    5.2.4 POLYSYNTHETIC LANGUAGES 281
    5.2.5 OTHER CLASSIFICATION METHODS FOR TYPOLOGY 286
    5.2.6 COMBINATIONS OF TYPOLOGIES 286

Chapter 5: Grammar and Grammatical Terms, The Form of Language, Order in Language, and Possible Structure of a Single, Parent Human Language, the "Anti-Nostratic"

5.3 TRANSFORMATION BETWEEN TYPOLOGIES 287

    5.3.1 SOME EVIDENT PRINCIPLES REGARDING TRANSFORMATION BETWEEN TYPOLOGIES 287
    5.3.2 CAVEAT REGARDING TYPOLOGICAL CLASSIFICATION 288

5.4 FORM AND ORDER IN LANGUAGE 290

5.5 FAINT HINTS OF THE ORIGINS OF LANGUAGE: 297

    5.5.1 INFANT PHONEMES AND WHAT THEY MAY TELL US OF THE STRUCTURE OF EARLY HUMAN LANGUAGE; THE CONCEPT OF *SELF* AND *NOT-SELF*, TERMS BORROWED FROM IMMUNOLOGY 297
    5.5.2 OTHER FEATURES OF HYPOTHETICAL EARLY HUMAN LANGUAGES 303
    5.5.3 POSSIBLE FORM OF EARLY HUMAN PROTO-LANGUAGES 305
    5.5.4 CONCOMITANT MONOSYLLABIC AND HIGHLY INFLECTIONAL CHARACTER: IS IT POSSIBLE? 308

5.6 EXERCISES 310

Chapter 5: Grammar and Grammatical Terms, The Form of Language, Order in Language, and Possible Structure of a Single, Parent Human Language, the "Anti-Nostratic"

5.1 SYNOPSIS OF GRAMMATICAL TERMS FOUND EXTENSIVELY IN THE LINGUISTICS LITERATURE AND THEIR UNDERLYING BASES

5.1.1 PREMISE OF THIS CHAPTER AND WHAT IS COVERED AND NOT COVERED IN THIS CHAPTER

This chapter starts on the premise that much of the modern linguistics and phonology literature uses grammar and grammatical terms innately and extensively, assuming knowledge of these on the part of the reader that may not be there. For example, one may find terms such as *instrumental* or *locative* (case), *pluperfect* (tense) or *periphrastic* (form). The experienced linguist may be surprised to hear how many otherwise highly educated persons do not know what those terms mean. In fact, a quick street poll of passers-by in England or America will reveal that a majority of persons does not even know what terms such as *passive voice* mean! Thus, it becomes imperative to educate a layman in these before proceeding further in any discussion of languages.

As with other chapters in this book, however, this chapter also discusses or develops many more fundamental or new concepts, such as the somewhat counter-intuitive concept that ***the VERB is more fundamental to language than the NOUN (substantive).***

In the previous Section, we discussed grammatical terms that might be unfamiliar to the layman. There are however also grammatical terms that may be quite familiar to the layman. We have all encountered elementary grammatical terms in secondary school. In the English language, such terms may include, for instance, *(in)definite article*, *demonstrative pronoun, interrogative pronoun, subjunctive mood*. It is not the purpose of this chapter to discuss such elementary grammatical terms, which *are* assumed to be understood by the layman and for which reference texts are available.

Rather, what we seek to present in this chapter is somewhat more complex terms, such as *middle voice, causative form,* and *instrumental case.* These are not found in standard, reference grammar texts, but are nevertheless encountered extensively in the linguistics literature. From a quick conversation with recent secondary school graduates, even in countries with fairly high educational standards such as the United Kingdom or Japan, one will find that these terms *are,* indeed, unfamiliar to a vast majority of these graduates. However, without at least rough knowledge of such terms, one cannot really discuss language intelligently! Hence, the reason for commencing this chapter with a discussion of these terms.

5.1.2 THE VERB AS FUNDAMENT OF LANGUAGE

In the most archaic languages that have somehow been "fossilized" or otherwise survived without too much change from what one might conjecture are their putative Neolithic origins, one frequently finds, somewhat *counter-intuitively,* that **the VERB, rather than the noun (substantive), appears to take primary position as a linguistic element**.

The prototypical example of such a "fossilized" language is Sanskrit. The primacy of the verb was in fact recognized by the ancient Indian etymologists [LAi-11, LAi-12, LAi-3], and is in fact one of the fundamental theses in one of the world's first works on etymology, Yaaska's *Nirukta* [LAi-12]. In this and other Sanskrit etymological works, nearly **every noun is derived from a verbal root**. To this day, when one learns Sanskrit, one is shown **how nearly every noun in the language can be derived from a verbal root, and never vice versa**! This appears to apply even to so-called "denominative" verbs. (For those unfamiliar with this term, a modern English example of a denominative verb is "to bicycle" or "to bike", derived from the noun "bicycle" or "bike".)

This concept, i.e. *giving primacy to the verb over the noun*, may initially appear **counter-intuitive** to us. In our minds, we would expect names for objects (nouns) to be more "fundamental" than verbs to a hypothetical "caveman" first learning language! One would expect that the caveman first started assigning names to objects, and the first languages then developed from this. Nevertheless, from an analysis of "fossilized" languages as referenced above, *including ancient Sumerian and Chinese* [SCr-22, SCr-25, SCr-26], the verb *does* indeed turn out to have primacy over the noun! This concept is thus *taken as a thesis in our book*.

5.1.3 ATTRIBUTES OF THE VERB: NUMBERS, GENDERS, TENSES, MOODS, VOICES AND OTHERS

We are familiar, from secondary school grammar, with terms such as *transitive* and *intransitive* verbs (verbs which carry (*transitive*) or do not carry (*intransitive*) over to a complement, such as a direct object) and *reflexive* verbs (verbs which reflect back on to

Chapter 5: Grammar and Grammatical Terms, The Form of Language, Order in Language, and Possible Structure of a Single, Parent Human Language, the "Anti-Nostratic"

the subject, e.g. French *s'assoir* ("to seat oneself")). We are all also familiar with such verb forms as the *infinitive* ("to eat"), *past participle* ("eaten" or "having eaten"), *present participle* ("eating", as in "I am eating now"), *gerund* ("eating", noun, as in "eating is good"). In languages such as Hindi, English, French and German, we are also familiar with *auxiliary (helping) verbs* ("am", "have", "will", as in "I am eating", "I have eaten", "I will eat", etc. etc.). In the absence of inflectional affixes, these are used to arrive at tenses, conditions, moods, etc. in verbs. Verbs are actually however considerably more complex than just this, as the terms defined below show.

INFLECTION VS. AUXILIARY (PERIPHRASTIC) FORM: Once again, in Hindi, English, French or German, we are used to employing auxiliary verbs in expressing different tenses, moods, etc., as described in the previous paragraph. We also use separate words to indicate person, number etc. (e.g. "I eat", the "I" being separate from the verb "eat"). Auxiliary forms are also known as *periphrastic*.

In many languages, however, instead of using such auxiliary words, one employs an *inflection* of the verbs. That is to say, the verbs have *inflectional affixes* to indicate the person, number etc.. These are usually suffixes, i.e. endings, rather than prefixes or infixes. The survivors of such endings can be seen in such modern words as Italian *habiamo*, "we have", where the *-mo* ending is an inflection that indicates "we", or Spanish *somos*, "we are", where again the *-mos* ending (inflection) indicates "we".

Languages which use inflections are called *inflective* or *inflectional* languages. Classical Greek is a highly inflected language. Latin is somewhat less inflected. Sanskrit is said to be the most inflected language known in the world. Italian and Spanish have some remnants of inflection. Modern Hindi, Mandarin and English have very little inflection. (Turkish is highly inflected, but uses a different category of inflection than Classical Greek or Sanskrit, called *agglutination*. This is discussed in more detail later in this chapter.)

PERSON, NUMBER, GENDER, CONJUGATION, ANIMATION: Most readers will be familiar with the terms *first person* (e.g. "I", "we"), *second person* (e.g. "you"), and *third person* (e.g. "He", "she", "it", "they"). (In Sanskrit grammar, what one calls the *third person* in European languages is actually called the *first person*, but that is not of immediate relevance here.)

Most readers will also be familiar with the *singular* (one person, as in "I" or "he") and *plural* (several persons, as in "we" or "they") *numbers*. To this, however, we must add

Chapter 5: Grammar and Grammatical Terms, The Form of Language, Order in Language, and Possible Structure of a Single, Parent Human Language, the "Anti-Nostratic"

the *dual number*, representing two persons (as in "we two" or "those two"). This number is today found in a few languages: Examples are ancient languages, such as Sanskrit (where it appears in full force), and Classical Greek and Sumerian (in both of which it is somewhat moribund) and in modern Arabic (where it also appears in full force).

One can quite obviously have three *genders: masculine, feminine* and *neuter.* Very few languages (prominently, English, all the Chinese languages and Tamil) do not assign a gender to nouns.

In many native North American languages, such as Navajo, one also gives verbs an attribute of *inanimate* or *animate*. That is to say, just as one distinguishes the gender, person or number of the subject of the verb, one also distinguishes whether it is animate, such as a person, or inanimate, such as a rock.

When one writes out all the numbers and persons of a verb in a particular tense, one is said to *conjugate* the verb (e.g. *"I eat, you eat, he/she/-it eats, we eat, you eat, they eat"* would be the conjugation of the verb "to eat" in the present tense, indicative mood in English). Those readers familiar with French or Spanish would be familiar with *conjugation classes*. For example, French has three "regular" conjugations, with verbal infinitives ending in *-er, -ir* and *-re*. Other languages, such as Latin and Classical Greek, have more than three conjugation classes. Sanskrit has ten conjugation classes.

It is also important to note that in many languages, e.g. Hindi and Tamil, and partially in Russian, conjugation of verbs is different for masculine, feminine and neuter cases. Thus, in addition to number, in these languages we introduce another parameter, *gender*. Here then, one would not have an identical form of the verb for "he/she/it eats" (as we do in English, the form being "*eats*"), but rather, different forms for "he" vs. "she" vs. "it". For example, Hindi *Main jaataa huun* ("I go", masculine) vs. *Main jaatii huun* ("I go", feminine), where the form of the verbal stem is different (masculine *jaataa*, feminine *jaatii*).

In languages such as Navajo, "conjugation" of verbs (if it can be called that in such highly complex, "polysynthetic" languages) is different, not just for masculine and feminine, but also for inanimate vs. animate cases.

Now that we have recapitulated some of the basic properties of verbs, we can identify more specifically their important *characteristics* or *attributes*. We identify *eight (8) major* attributes of verbs. These are given in **Table 5-1** below. These attributes are by no means exhaustive, and there are several other characteristics that may be added for more obscure languages. However, for our purposes in this book, they suffice.

Table 5-1: Major *ATTRIBUTES* of **verbs**. These attributes are by no means exhaustive, and there are several other characteristics that may be added for more obscure languages. However, for our purposes in this book, they suffice.

> *1. Person.*
> *2. Number.*
> *3. Gender.*
> *4. Tense.*
> *5. Voice.*
> *6. Mood.*
> *7. Animation.*
> *8. Additional, unclassifiable attributes and forms.*

Person, number and *gender* have been discussed above. The other characteristics are now discussed.

TENSE: All the modern European languages carry a similar description for their tenses, modified from Latin grammar for each particular language. Thus, in English, we have the following common tenses:

Chapter 5: Grammar and Grammatical Terms, The Form of Language, Order in Language, and Possible Structure of a Single, Parent Human Language, the "Anti-Nostratic"

Table 5-2: Common (but by no means all) *tenses* used in English, illustrated with the verb "to eat". The complexity of tenses in English is clearly seen, in spite of it being a highly periphrastic (non-inflected) language.

- *Present* ("I eat")
- *Present continuous ("present progressive",* "I am eating")
- *Past ("imperfect")* ("I ate")
- *Past (imperfect) continuous ("past progressive")* ("I was eating")
- *Future* ("I will eat")
- *Future continuous ("future progressive")* ("I will be eating")
- *Perfect, present* ("I have eaten")
- *Perfect continuous* ("I have been eating")
- *Perfect ("past perfect",* "I had eaten")
- *Perfect continuous* ("I had been eating")
- *Future perfect* ("I will have eaten")
- *Future perfect continuous* ("I will have been eating")

Tenses of verbs can however be considerably more complex than those in the Table above.

For example, in Latin and Greek, we have the **pluperfect** tense (Latin *plus quam perfectum*, "more than perfect"), which is somewhat but not entirely similar to the English *perfect ("past perfect")* tense. The connotation of *"perfect"* is of an action already completed at some very definite time in the past (as in "I had eaten") as opposed to an action completed at an unspecified time (as in "I ate"). The Latin and Greek *pluperfect* denotes an action completed in the past, but at a *remoter* time than the English *past perfect*. In Sanskrit and Classical Greek, we also have a tense denoted as **aorist**, which indicates an action in the *past* that is totally *indefinite* (i.e. it may or may not have been completed in the past, and if so, either at a specified or at an unspecified time!). In fact, Sanskrit and Classical Greek have many aorists, denoting slightly different shades of time.

Chapter 5: Grammar and Grammatical Terms, The Form of Language, Order in Language, and Possible Structure of a Single, Parent Human Language, the "Anti-Nostratic"

VOICE: Nearly all languages of the world display two *voices* for their verbs: *Active*, as in "I eat", and *passive*, as in "I am eaten". In addition more structured languages such as Classical Greek and Sanskrit also display a voice intermediate between these, called the **middle voice** (*aatmanepada*, "word for oneself", in Sanskrit). This voice is best illustrated by an example from Classical Greek: *agoratso* (△ ≟λ△☐☐, "buy"), active voice - "buy", middle voice - "buy for oneself", to be contrasted with the passive voice, "be bought".

MOOD ("MODE"): The "regular" mood of a verb is denoted as the *indicative*, e.g. in "I eat". The other common moods that the reader may be familiar with include the *subjunctive* (e.g. in "It is necessary that I eat this", French *je fait* "I do", indicative vs. *que je fasse* "that I do", subjunctive) and the *imperative* (e.g. "Eat this!" (Command)).

Once again, however, verbs can have many other moods. For example, again turning to Classical Greek and Sanskrit, one has moods such as the **optative** indicating necessity or requirement of the action, "I *must* or *ought to* eat", which are of course expressed in English using the auxiliary words *must* and *ought*. In English, we also frequently encounter the **conditional**: For example, *indicative* "I eat", *conditional* "I can (could) eat". In Sanskrit, one finds other, peculiar mood forms, such as the **desiderative**, indicating a desire for the action of the verb ("I wish to eat") and **intensive**, indicating an intensification of the action or state of being represented by the word ("I eat very intensely (or quickly)"). All of these forms in Sanskrit have their own *inflectional endings* that are incorporated right into the verb stems during conjugation! Some languages, such as Tamil, also express **negation** in a peculiar way also by *inflecting* it right into the verb, giving rise to a *negative* mood (e.g., *naan pesharain*, "I am speaking", vs. *naan peshamaatai*, "I shall (very strongly) not speak", with *pesha* being the verbal stem for "to speak"). (In contrast, Sanskrit and Classical Greek use an auxiliary word for negation, denoted in their grammars as the "prohibitive particle", *maa* in Sanskrit and *me* in Cl. Greek- thus *maa kuruu*, "don't do" in Sanskrit; even though they are highly inflectional languages, they do not inflect negation.)

Incidentally, the reader will quickly notice from the above discussion that a language like English (or Hindi/Urdu), while not having the complex or highly structured inflections of Classical Greek or Sanskrit, is nevertheless able to express nearly *all* the fine distinctions of mood, voice and tense that the Greek or Sanskrit does, albeit with the help of auxiliary words!

UNCLASSIFIABLE VERB ATTRIBUTES (NEITHER TENSE NOR MOOD NOR VOICE): There are several attributes of verbs which are difficult to class as either tense, mood or voice, although many grammatical texts appear to place them into one of these classes. We will treat only one such attribute here, the *causative*.

The *causative* form a verb is best explained by example: *indicative* "I do", *causative* "I cause to do" or "I cause to have done".

Among modern languages, the causative appears to be most developed in Hindi/Urdu: Almost every verb can have a causative form, which frequently may have a slightly different meaning from a pure causative, as illustrated by the examples in the Table below:

> **Table 5-3:** Examples of *causative* voice in Hindi/Urdu, Sanskrit and some other Indo-European languages, and the occasional changes of meaning that are generated in going from the normal to the causative voice.

- *Karnaa*, "to do" vs. causative *karvaanaa*, "to make (someone etc.) do";
- But *padhnaa* "to read", causative *padhaanaa*, "to teach" (i.e., "to cause to read", a change of meaning).
- Such changes of meaning are more common in causatives of some of the older languages, e.g. Sanskrit *sthaa* "to stand", causative *sthaapa* (as in *sthaapaya*) "to stop" (i.e. "to cause to stand", whence the English/German etc. cognates).
- Once again, in many languages that use causatives, e.g. the Sanskrit and Hindi examples above, the causative form is effected by a distinctive change to the verb stem, i.e. an inflection, rather than the use of auxiliary words (such as the English words "to cause to....")

5.1.4 SUMMARY OF VERB ATTRIBUTES (PROPERTIES) AND FORMS

The above discussion on the properties and forms of verbs is summarized in the Table below.

Table 5-4: Verb *ATTRIBUTES* (properties), in summary. Under each property, only the most commonly occurring or most significant values are given. Thus, the list is by no means exhaustive. For definitions and explanation, see discussion above.

	ATTRIBUTE	**VALUES (AND DESCRIPTION, IF APPROPRIATE)**
1	Person	1st, 2nd, 3rd
2	Number	Singular, dual, plural
3	Gender	Masculine, feminine, neuter
4	Tense	E.g., *present, present continuous (present progressive), past, imperfect, past continuous (past progressive), future, future continuous (future progressive), perfect, perfect continuous, future perfect, future perfect continuous, pluperfect, aorist.*
5	Mood	E.g., *indicative, imperative, subjunctive, optative, conditional, desiderative, intensive, negative.*
6	Voice	E.g., *active, passive, middle.*
7	Animation	*Inanimate, animate.*
8	Other	*Causative.*

5.1.5 ATTRIBUTES OF THE SUBSTANTIVE: NUMBERS, GENDERS, CASES AND OTHER ATTRIBUTES

The word *substantive* is a more general, and more grammatically correct, term than the more crude *noun*, for what we know from primary school as a "name, place or thing". It encompasses all *nominal* forms, e.g. nouns, pronouns, etc.

Where the verbs in languages possess numbers and genders, substantives possess the same numbers and genders.

And, analogous to the conjugation of verbs, substantives are *declined*. Such *declension* of the substantives gives all their possible *cases*. The reader may be familiar with the *nominative* and the *accusative* cases of substantives, denoting respectively the *subject* and the *direct object* in a sentence. There are many other cases. Sanskrit has eight cases, Turkish nine, and Finnish as many as 15. Inflectional languages decline their substantives using inflection.

The most commonly used cases are best illustrated in a Table, as below.

Table 5-5: Commonly found *cases* used in the declension of **substantives** (nouns, pronouns). The word, "you" is used as an example for illustration.

CASE	SIGNIFICANCE
Nominative	Subject, e.g. "*you*"
Accusative	Direct object, "He hit *you*"
Instrumental	Instrument or agent, e.g. "*with* you"
Dative	Indirect object, e.g. "*to* you"
Ablative	From or out of, e.g. "*from* you"
Genitive or Possessive	Possession, e.g. "*yours, your*"
Locative	Indicating location, e.g. "*in* you"
Vocative	Calling, e.g. "*Hey you!*"

Chapter 5: Grammar and Grammatical Terms, The Form of Language, Order in Language, and Possible Structure of a Single, Parent Human Language, the "Anti-Nostratic"

5.2 THE *FORM* OF LANGUAGE: TYPOLOGY, MORPHEMES AND MORPHOLOGY

5.2.1 TYPOLOGY

We have been introduced briefly above to the concept that languages can be differentiated according to their *form* - e.g. whether their verbs are conjugated mostly in an inflectional vs. auxiliary-word manner. Modern linguists refer to this as *typology*.

A language can be *typed* according to its inflectional or auxiliary-word characteristics, or some other characteristic. This is called *morphological* typology. It can also be typed according to some other property, such as the preferred order of subject, object and verb in its sentences. This would be called *syntactical* typology.

Before discussing typology further, we need to introduce a very important concept, that of the *morpheme*. According to the Webster dictionary [SCr-45], a morpheme is:

> "*any word or part of a word, (such) as an affix or combining form, that conveys meaning, cannot be further divided into smaller elements conveying meaning, and usually occurs in various contexts with relatively stable meaning.*"

...(5.1)

Again, the concept of the morpheme is best illustrated with examples. In English, the words *search, find, the* are all morphemes. In the sentence *I searched for a sailor with happiness*, the *-ed* in *searched*, the *-or* in *sailor* and the *-ness* in *happiness* are also morphemes. *Search, find* and *the* are called *free morphemes* because they can appear independently and still convey linguistic meaning. On the other hand, *-ed -or* and *-ness* are called *bound morphemes*, since, quite obviously, they cannot stand alone. When used alone, they and convey no meaning. For everyday purposes, we may even think of a morpheme in any language as an entity somewhere in between a syllable and a word.

A morpheme can have slightly different forms, affected by the manner of use of the root word. For example, the English verb *learn* is converted to its past participle in three ways, yielding *learnt, learned* and *learned* (with the second pronounced *learnd* and the last pronounced *learn-id*, as in "a learn-ed person"). In this example, all three morphemes, *-t, -d* and *-ed*, achieve the same result, and are in fact the same morpheme.

Thus, in an analogy with phonemes vs. allophones, the components of this morpheme are called *allomorphs*.

Modern linguists classify languages according to the character of their morphemes, i.e. according to *morphological typology* [LN-88 to LN-94]. We first list here the many, varied terms for typologies used by various linguists, then discuss them briefly. It is to be noted that eminent linguists, past and present, still differ in the terminology they use. For instance, Edward Sapir [LN-34 to LN-36] is thought to have initiated the terms *polysynthetic* and *symbolic* more than 80 years ago. However, the latter term is still seldom used by linguists. It is also to be noted that these terms are not mutually exclusive. For example, an agglutinative language can also be inflectional, the prototypical example of this being Turkish.

Table 5-6:   Summary of *typologies* found in Languages.

- *Agglutinative*
- *Analytic*
- *Inflectional*
- *Monosyllabic*
- *Periphrastic*
- *Polysynthetic*
- *Symbolic*
- *Synthetic*

Chapter 5: Grammar and Grammatical Terms, The Form of Language, Order in Language, and Possible Structure of a Single, Parent Human Language, the "Anti-Nostratic"

5.2.2. DESCRIPTION OF THE VARIOUS TYPOLOGIES

We can now briefly discuss the above *typologies*.

ANALYTIC: In an *analytic* language, words are not inflected at all, i.e., verbs remain completely unconjugated and substantives remain completely undeclined. Thus, in such a language, one could have only the phrases *He kill me, me kill he*. That is to say, the substantives *He* and *me* could never be declined as *him* and *I*, and the verb *kill* could never be conjugated as *kills*. Surprisingly, there are modern languages that retain exactly such form. These are said to be highly analytic. Notably among these are Mandarin and Vietnamese. What meaning Mandarin and Vietnamese cannot convey via inflection, however, they easily indicate via word order, i.e. syntax, and lexical relationships. English is analytic in many respects, since many of its substantives and verbs are not at all or minimally inflected.

MONOSYLLABIC: A *monosyllabic* language would be one in which *all words* are monosyllables. No known world language fits this bill, but, again Mandarin, comes somewhat close: A good part of its vocabulary is monosyllabic.

Although there is a tendency to conflate *monosyllabic* with *analytic*, this is incorrect: All analytic languages are not monosyllabic, and a monosyllabic language, if it existed, would not necessarily be analytic.

INFLECTIONAL has already been defined briefly earlier in this chapter. It implies alteration of a word through a characteristic *affix* (frequently a suffix), to achieve conjugation (of verbs) or declension (of nouns). *Inflection* is used to change the tense, mood, voice, etc. of verbs, and the case (nominative, accusative, dative, etc.) of substantives (nouns).

As an example of inflection, in the modern Italian verbal form *habiamo*, "we have", *hab* is the *verb-stem* indicating the verb "to have" and *-iamo* is the *inflectional ending* indicating the first person plural. Similarly, in the modern Italian nouns *graffito, graffiti*, *graffit* is a *noun-stem* and the inflectional endings *-o* and *-i* indicate singular and plural respectively. Less commonly, the principle of inflection can be extended to the verb-stem or noun-stem used, as in the English *mouse, woman* (singular), *mice, women* (plural) or the German *haus* ("house", singular), *häuser* (plural); Europeans, in 19th century linguistics literature, used to call this *umlaut*. (The reader may note that we have been

Chapter 5: Grammar and Grammatical Terms, The Form of Language, Order in Language, and Possible Structure of a Single, Parent Human Language, the "Anti-Nostratic"

using the terms *verbal-stem* and *noun-stem*, and may be curious as to what they signify. These are different from *verbal-root* and *nominal-root* in the sense that a single verbal-root can give rise to many verbal stems, each conjugated in a different conjugation class. Similarly, a nominal root (or noun-root) can give rise to several noun-stems, each declined differently.)

As yet another example of inflection, in the modern Tamil, *jannaal* designates a window. When we use it in the accusative sense, as in *janallai muuda*, "close the window", the inflection, in the suffix *-ai*, indicates the accusative case. As yet another example, Hindi *aadhaa ghantaa* means "half an hour", in the nominative case; when we say *aadhe ghante me*, "in half an hour", in the locative case, the stems *aadh ghant* are inflected with the ending *-e* to yield the locative case. And as still another example, the modern Maraathi verb-stem *zaa*, "to go", becomes, in the present indicative, *(mii) zaato, (tuu (feminine)) zaate*, "(I) go, you (female) go", where the inflectional endings are *-to* for first person ("I") and *-te* for feminine second person ("you", female). We can cite a myriad of such examples from modern languages, nearly all of which are only *partly* inflectional. The modern Semitic languages such as Arabic are also *partially* inflectional, but again here, there are degrees: They are much more inflectional than the modern European languages.

As a contrast to *partial* inflectional character, the ancient Indo-European languages such as Classical Greek and Sanskrit were *highly,* almost *completely,* inflectional. Indeed, in Sanskrit and Classical Greek, an entire verbal phrase, such as English *that I would know* comprising tense (here, present), mood (here, optative), voice (here, active), and person (here, first person), would be expressed in a single, highly inflected word. In Sanskrit, this would be *jaaniyaam* from the verbal-stem *jnaa* ("to know"). (This is also the case in Turkish, as discussed above, but Turkish is still classified as an agglutinative language, for reasons that will be apparent in the sequel.)

PERIPHRASTIC: Analytical languages may also be called *periphrastic. Periphrastic* implies extensive use of *helping* or *auxiliary* words to achieve what inflection achieves. Italian is somewhat periphrastic. On the other hand, English is a highly periphrastic language. Thus, in the English verbal phrases *I do, I will do, I have done, I had done, I will have done* etc., the words *will, have* and *had* are auxiliary, "helping" words that effect a change of tense to the verb *to do*. They substitute the function of inflectional endings which would have been applied to the stem *do* in languages such as Classical Greek or Sanskrit. In modern Hindi, similarly, we have, with the verb-stem *kar*, "to do", *Main kartaa huun, main karuungaa, maine karaa hai, maine karaa thaa, maine karaa*

Chapter 5: Grammar and Grammatical Terms, The Form of Language, Order in Language, and Possible Structure of a Single, Parent Human Language, the "Anti-Nostratic"

hogaa (the terminal *n*'s indicate nasalization), as the equivalents of the English *I do, I will do, I have done, I had done, I will have done*. These are all again highly periphrastic constructions, with auxiliary words such as *huun, hai, thaa, hogaa*, etc. Yet, importantly, both the English and Hindi constructions above are able to express *all* the different shades of meaning embodied in *I do, I will do, I have done, I had done, I will have done* very well without the need for the use of inflection! It is safe to say that languages spoken by a majority of humans today are periphrastic.

AGGLUTINATIVE: In *agglutinative* languages, there is an *agglutination* of the monosyllables into larger words. An example of agglutination is ancient Sumerian, in which the word *lu-gal*, "king" or "great-man", is constructed from the agglutination of *lu*, "great", with *gal*, "man". In Sumerian, the word *lugal* is also *never* inflected in any way. German likes to compound words, e.g. *Machtwort* ("power word") or *Nachbildung* ("after-picture", i.e. "copy") and, in that sense, it is agglutinative. English also displays an agglutinative character in such words as *babysit* or *eyewash* or *keyboard* or the now somewhat archaic *everyman*. And even Sanskrit, which many classify as the most highly inflected language in the world, there is a whole grammatical class known as *samaasa*, "compounds", i.e. words constructed as agglutinations of other words, although the compound words then do get inflected according to the standard Sanskrit rules of inflection.

The Turkic languages [LAs-20] (e.g. Turkish [LAs-19]) and the Malay languages (e.g. the main Bahasa Malaysia/Indonesia) [LAs-31, LAs-58] are modern agglutinative languages. Linguists also classify the Dravidian languages such as Tamil as agglutinative, although this author feels that in the declension of its substantives, Tamil has much inflectional character [LAi-30, LAi-32 to LAi-35].

Turkish is an example of an agglutinative language which at first gives the appearance of being highly inflectional. This can be seen in the paradigms cited in the **Table** overleaf.

> **Table 5-7 (*overleaf*)**: Some paradigms from Turkish, a language that is considered by most scholars to be agglutinative, illustrating a (supposedly) deceptive, "highly inflectional" nature.

Chapter 5: *Grammar and Grammatical Terms, The Form of Language, Order in Language, and Possible Structure of a Single, Parent Human Language, the "Anti-Nostratic"*

(Table 5-7, cont.)

**TURKISH,
DECLENSION OF *ADAM*, "Man" (a word of Arabic borrowing) and *ODA*,
"Father"**

CASE	*ADAM*	*ODA*
Nominative	adam	oda
Accusative	adam-i	oda-yi
Instrumental	adam-la	oda-ÿla
Dative	adam-a	oda-ya
2nd Dative ("causative")	adam-icin	oda-için
Ablative	adam-dan	oda-dan
Genitive	adam-in	oda-nin
Locative	adam-da	oda-da
Vocative	adam!	baba!

**TURKISH,
FIRST PERSON (ONLY) CONJUGATION OF *SEVNEK*, "TO LOVE"**

CONJU-GATION	MEANING (GLOSS)	TENSE/MOOD
sev-i-yorum	I love, I am loving	Present tense, Indicative Mood
sev-i-yordum	I was loving	Present tense, Narrative Mood
sev-i-yormusum	It is said that I was loving	Present tense, Reportative Mood
sev-i-yorsam	If I am loving	Present Tense, Conditional Mood
sev-er-im	I love	Indefinite tense, Indicative Mood
sev-er-dim	I did love	Indefinite tense, narrative mood
sev-er-misim	It is said that I used to love	Indefinite tense, Reportative Mood
sev-sem	If I be loving	Present tense, Subjunctive Mood, etc.

Chapter 5: Grammar and Grammatical Terms, The Form of Language, Order in Language, and Possible Structure of a Single, Parent Human Language, the "Anti-Nostratic"

We will come back a bit later in this chapter to why Turkish is in fact considered by modern linguists to be an agglutinative language in its verb conjugations and substantive declensions, in contradistinction to, say, Classical Greek or Sanskrit, *in spite of the extensive use of inflections in its verb conjugations*. The reader is requested to bear his/her curiosity for now!

Let us now briefly look at an example of an *extreme case of inflectional character*, of hyperstructure, in a language. This is seen in the Table below, which gives a partial conjugation of the Sanskrit verbal root *wid*. This root, when conjugated in the 2nd conjugation in active voice, has the meaning "to know, understand, discover" (cognates English *wit*, German *wissen*, Latin *video*). When conjugated in the 4th conjugation in middle voice, it has the connotation "to discover/understand oneself", i.e. "to be, exist". However, our interest in this verbal root is in the 6th conjugation, where it is a deponent, i.e. conjugated in both active and middle voices, and has the connotation " to discover, recognize, find". Here, the root takes a nasal infix (which is actually more characteristic of the 7th conjugation, but that is a subject for discussion elsewhere), yielding the stem *vind* (cognates only in Germanic languages, e.g. English *find*, German *finden*).

The conjugation of this stem is given in the **Table** below. This Table also gives the reader an idea of the manner of inflection in a typical *non*-agglutinative language. This will be useful for comparison with inflections in an agglutinative language such as Turkish, as we do in the sequel.

> **Table 5-8 (*appended to end of this chapter due to length*)**: Illustration of extreme inflectional character: Paradigms for conjugation of the Sanskrit verbal root *wid*, in the 2nd, 4th, 6th, 7th and 10th conjugations, in both active and middle voices.
>
> (***See Appendix at the end of this chapter.***)

5.2.3 DIFFERENCES IN INFLECTION IN *AGGLUTINATIVE* VS. *NON-AGGLUTINATIVE* LANGUAGES: SYNTHETIC LANGUAGES

We are now in a position to appreciate the difference between the inflections in a language like Turkish, which is considered agglutinative, and a language like Sanskrit, which is *not* considered. Both languages have a highly inflectional character, as can be seen in the paradigms in the Tables above agglutinative.

As a starting point in our comparison, we note that, in Turkish, the suffixes are *invariably the same* regardless of the root word that the suffix operates on. For example, the suffix in the accusative case for substantives is always *-i*, and is unaffected by the nature of the root word (in the paradigm in the Table, *oda*, "father"). Furthermore, there is no Sandhi (euphonic combination) with the root word, nor is there any change seen in the root word.

That is to say, the Turkish suffixes are a true agglutination, an afterthought added to the root word, and not an integral part of the root word. They do not affect the root word in any way. In contrast, in a truly non-agglutinative inflectional language, the affix (whether infix, prefix or suffix) becomes integrated into the root word, and can change it in many ways.

Rather than illustrating this concept with a language such as Sanskrit, with which the reader may be very unfamiliar, we can use our very own English, which still retains strong inflectional characteristics from its past.

Let us first take the words *hunter* and *painless*. We immediately recognize the inflections, i.e. the suffixes *-er* and *-less* (which are also morphemes). The first suffix converts a verb (*hunt*) into an agent, a noun, and the second converts a noun (*pain*) into an adjective. We note that we can add these suffixes to may similar words of the same category (noun or verb), achieving the same result, e.g. *gatherer* and *shameless*. We also note that the root words (*gather, shame*) are unaffected in any way. So far, rather boring!

However, now let us take the English examples *length, breadth* and *feet*. We immediately recognize that these appear to be derived from the root words *long, broad* and *foot*. The first two root words are adjectives and their derivatives are nouns. The last root word (*foot*) is a singular noun and its derivative is the plural. We can see however that the inflections *-th* are not just applied in blanket fashion, as in Turkish. If they were, we would just get *longth* and *broadth*! There is also a phonological change in the root word, from *long* to *leng-* and *broad* to *bread-*. Furthermore, the inflection can also vary, for euphonic purposes, from just *-th*, as we see in the transformation *high --> height*.

Sapir [LN-34 to LN-36] is first thought to have coined a word for this sort of, Sanskrit- or English-type of inflection. He called it *synthesis*. Languages of this type were then designated **synthetic** languages. Synthesis was also called *fusion* by other linguists. Sapir further qualified the type of synthesis seen in *foot/feet, woman/women* (the latter pronounced with an [i]), *haus/häuser* as *symbolic* fusion, then designated the language in question a **symbolic** language.

5.2.4 POLYSYNTHETIC LANGUAGES

We now come to the final typology that we have still not discussed, ***polysynthetic*** languages. Once again, these are best appreciated by citing examples. As a first example, we will excerpt here an illustration of a polysynthetic language by Vajda [LN-88]:

> Besides its basic, concrete meaning, each ***Navajo*** [Navaho] verb form conveys not only a basic idea such as give, take, have; it must also contain morphemes conveying tense, number of subjects, duration or repetition of action and even the shape of the object for those verbs that take direct objects. The imperative, or command for, is morphologically the most simple verb stem. And yet there are over 20 separate verb suffixes conveying the shape and type of a verb's object. We said that ní means Give, but even in the meaning of a basic command to hand the speaker an object it can never be used as a separate word unless it is attached to a suffix that marks the shape of the object to be given:

Chapter 5: Grammar and Grammatical Terms, The Form of Language, Order in Language, and Possible Structure of a Single, Parent Human Language, the "Anti-Nostratic"

Awéé' shaa ní<u>Lteeh</u>.	*Give me the baby.* (-Lteeh = living)
TL'ooL shaa ní<u>lé</u>.	*Give me the rope.* (-lé = long flexible)
Tó shaa ní<u>kaah</u>.	*Give me the water.* (-kaah = liquid in a container)
Tsin shaa ní<u>ti,i,h</u>.	*Give me the pole.* (-ti,i,h= slender, rigid)
Beeldléí shaa ní<u>Ltsóós</u>.	*Give me the blanket.* (-Ltsóós = flat)
Atsi' shaa ní<u>'aah</u>.	*Give me the meat.* (-'aah = dense bulky object)

Navajo (Navaho) has about 20 such verbal object markers altogether. The same noun might be used in conjunction with more than one verbal marker.

- Naaltsoos, *book* or *paper*
- Naaltsoos shaa ní<u>Ltsóós</u>. *Give me the paper.* (-Ltsóós flat)
- Naaltsoos shaa ní<u>'aah</u>. *Give me the book.* (-'aah = dense bulky object)
- tL'iish, *snake*
- TL'iish shaa ní<u>Lteeh</u>. *Give me the snake.* (living)
- TL'iish shaa ní<u>lé</u>. *Give me the dead snake.* (-lé = long flexible)

In Navaho only a very few root morphemes denoting basic concrete concepts can stand as separate words: <u>shash</u> *bear*, <u>chizh</u> *firewood*, <u>oljéé</u> *moon*. All of the remaining words in Navaho contain special affixes. Thus, most noun roots denoting basic concepts are bound morphemes.

Noun morphemes that denote body parts, family relations, or important objects everyone is expected to possess such as shoes, clothing, etc. cannot be used as separate words but must always be accompanied by a prefix denoting the possessor. Thus, amazingly enough, there is no independent Navaho word to mean *mother* or *father*, *sister* or *brother*, *ear*, *tooth*, or *leg*, or even *shoes* or *bow and arrow*. Navaho can express all these concepts, of course, but not on the level of the simple word. In Navaho, one must use morphologically complex words meaning *someone's mother, someone's father*: For instance: <u>shizhé'é</u> *my father*, <u>nizhé'é</u> *your father*; <u>bizhé'é</u> *his/her father* ; or--at best-- <u>'azhé'é</u> which has the general meaning of *one's, some undetermined person's father*.

Chapter 5: Grammar and Grammatical Terms, The Form of Language, Order in Language, and Possible Structure of a Single, Parent Human Language, the "Anti-Nostratic"

> Conversely, if I want to assert possession over such a person or object that intrinsically is not by own, I say literally *my someone else's:* she'e' 'awoo' *my someone else's tooth.* Shiwoo' means *my tooth* in the sense of a part of my body.

...(5.2)

As a second set of examples, we will cite two examples of verb conjugation from North American (Native American) languages, cited by Sapir [LN-36]:

> The idea expressed in English by the sentence *I came to give it to her* is rendered in **Chinook** by *i-n-i-a-l-u-d-am*. This word—and it is a thoroughly unified word with a clear-cut accent on the first *a*—consists of a radical element, *-d-* "to give," six functionally distinct, if phonetically frail, prefixed elements, and a suffix. Of the prefixes, *i-* indicates recently past time; *n-*, the pronominal subject "I"; *-i-*, the pronominal object "it", *-a-*, the second pronominal object "her"; *-l-*, a prepositional element indicating that the preceding pronominal prefix is to be understood as an indirect object (*-her-to-*, i.e., "to her"); and *–u-*, an element that it is not easy to define satisfactorily but which on the whole, indicates movement away from the speaker. The suffixed *–am* modifies the verbal content in the local sense; it adds to the notion convoyed by the radical element that of "arriving" or "going (or coming) for that particular purpose. It is obvious that in Chinook, as in Hupa, the greater part of the grammatical machinery resides in the prefixes rather than in the suffixes.
>
> A reverse case, one in which the grammatically significant elements cluster, as in Latin, at the end of the word is yielded by Fox, one of the better known Algonkin languages of the Mississippi Valley. We may take the form *eh-kiwi-n-a-m-oth-ati-wa-chi(i)* "then they together kept (him) in flight from them. The radical element here is *kiwi-*, a verb stem indicating the general notion of "indefinite movement round about, here and there." The prefixed element *eh-* is hardly more than an adverbial particle indicating temporal subordination; it may be conveniently rendered as "then." Of the seven suffixes included in this highly wrought word, *-n-* seems to be merely a phonetic element serving to

connect the verb stem with the following –*a*-; -*a*- is a "secondary stem" denoting the idea of "flight, to flee"; -*m*- denotes causality with reference to an animate object; -*o*(*ht*)- indicates activity done for the subject (the so-called "middle" or "medio-passive" voice of Greek): -(*a*)*ti*- is a reciprocal element, "one another"; -*wa-ch*(*i*) is the third person animate plural (-*wa*-, plural; -*chi*, more properly personal) of so-called "conjunctive" forms. The word may be translated more literally (and yet only approximately as to grammatical feeling) as "then they (animate) caused some animate being to wander about in flight form one another of themselves." Eskimo, Nootka, Yana, and other languages have similarly complex arrays of suffixed elements though the functions performed by them and their principles of combination differ widely.

The **Nootka** word *inikw-ihl* "fire in the house" is not as definitely formalized a word as its translation suggest. The radical element *inikw*- "fire" is really as much of a verbal as of a nominal term; it may be rendered now by "fire," now by "burn," according to the syntactic exigencies of the sentence. The derivational element –*ihl* "in the house" does not mitigate this vagueness or generality; *inikw-ihl* is still "fire in the house' or "burn in the house." It may be definitely nominalized or verbalized by the affixing of elements that are exclusively nominal or verbal in force. For example, *inikw-ihl'-i*, with its suffixed article, is a clear-cut nominal form: "the burning in the house, the fire in the house"; *inikw-ihl-ma*, with its indicative suffix, is just as clearly verbal: "it burns in the house." How weak must be the degree of fusion between "fire in the house" and the nominalizing or verbalizing suffix is apparent from the fact that the formally indifferent *inikwihl* is not an abstraction gained by analysis but a full-fledged word, ready for use in the sentence. The nominalizing –'*i* and the indicative –*ma* are not fused form-affixes, they are simply additions of formal import. But we can continue to hold the verbal or nominal nature of *inikwihl* in abeyance long before we reach the –'*i* or –*ma*. We can pluralize it: *inikw-ihl-'minih*; it is still either "fires in the house" or "burn plurally in the house." We can diminutivize this plural: *inikw-ihl-'minih-'is*, "little fires in the house" or "burn plurally and slightly in the house." What if we add the preterit tense suffix –*it*? Is not *inikw-ihl-'minih-'is-it* necessarily a verb; "several small fires were burning in the house"? It is not. It may still be nominalized; *inikwihl'minih'isit-'i* means "the former small fires in the house, the little fires that were once burning in the house." It is not an unambiguous verb until it is given a form that excludes every other possibility, as in the indicative *inikwihl-minih''isit-a* "several small fires were burning in the house." We recognize at once that the elements *–ihl –'minih*, *'is*, and *–it*, quite aside from the relatively concrete or abstract nature of their content and aside, further from the degree of their outer (phonetic) cohesion with the elements that precede them, have a psychological independence that our own affixes never have. They are typically agglutinated elements, though they have no greater external independence, are no more capable of living apart from the radical element to which they are suffixed, and the *–ness* and *goodness* of the *–s* of *books*.

...(5.3)

From the above examples, the reader may then appreciate what a *polysynthetic language* truly is:

In a *polysynthetic language*, the verb is definitely inflected, but the inflection is of such a fundamental, corporeal nature, that the "root", if such is said to exist at all, is fundamentally incorporated into the inflection.

...(5.4)

The number of affixes, i.e. inflections, in a polysynthetic language, is also much *larger* than in a standard inflected language such as Classical Greek or Sanskrit.

A true appreciation of polysynthetic languages is quite humbling for the Classics scholar. For it tells him/her that languages of peoples who were considered "primitive" in 19th century jargon, and which were thus thought by 19th century Classicists to be greatly inferior to the likes of Classical Greek or Sanskrit, express fine nuances of meaning with highly complex inflections which are quite beyond that of the simpler inflections of Greek or Sanskrit!

5.2.5 OTHER CLASSIFICATION METHODS FOR TYPOLOGY

Having now been introduced to the various morphological typologies, we are now in a position to appreciate another, more exacting, and some would say, more scientific, definition of typology, subscribed to by many modern linguists [LN-88 to LN-94, IEu-4]. This is based on the *morpheme-to-word ratio*.

    1)   ***ANALYTIC*** languages have an *average* of **one (1)** morpheme per word. An example would be Mandarin.

    2)   ***SYNTHETIC*** languages have an *average* of **one (1) to three (3)** morphemes per word. Sanskrit or Classical Greek would definitely qualify as synthetic languages. English would barely qualify, having just over one morpheme per word. A highly technical text in English, say a software manual or a chemistry research article, would not qualify, and would be classified as analytic. On the other hand, older English literature, such as Chaucer or Keats or even the (more recent) poems of Samuel Taylor Coleridge, would well qualify.

    3)   ***POLYSYNTHETIC*** languages have an *average* of **three (3)** or more morphemes per word. Navajo and Nootka would qualify well.

5.2.6 COMBINATIONS OF TYPOLOGIES

One of the first things that becomes apparent from the above discussion is that *languages can combine the various typologies.*

For example, a language such as English is predominantly analytic, but retains some inflections, some of them very complex (cf. examples in discussion above) and it has compound words that are agglutinations. It is also apparent that languages may possess more of one characteristic than another. Thus, German is also an agglutinative as well as inflectional language, but it is much more agglutinative than English, since it overwhelmingly prefers compounds (agglutinations) in its vocabulary. Sanskrit is overwhelmingly inflectional, but with some agglutinations (compounds, *samaasa*) used primarily in the literary language. Etc.

Chapter 5: Grammar and Grammatical Terms, The Form of Language, Order in Language, and Possible Structure of a Single, Parent Human Language, the "Anti-Nostratic"

5.3 TRANSFORMATION BETWEEN TYPOLOGIES

5.3.1 SOME EVIDENT PRINCIPLES REGARDING TRANSFORMATION BETWEEN TYPOLOGIES

In order to understand transformations between typologies and how languages can simultaneously acquire different typologies, we need to first lay down some principles, easily established from observation. One of the first of these principles that we see from observation is the following:

> *When peoples speaking quite different languages are suddenly forced to meet, interact and, eventually, amalgamate, then, rather than learning each others' grammatical rules, they arrive at means of mutually intelligible expression, primarily through the use of auxiliary, i.e. helping words. This is especially true if those rules involve complex inflections. They also may tend to lose gender distinctions, since these may be different in different languages. The resulting language then becomes very periphrastic. Modern English is a good example of this.*

...(5.5)

Conversely, when a people is left completely isolated linguistically, *its language will naturally develop a more ordered character over time.*

(As a caveat, we also note that this principle is formulated primarily with a view to the interaction of pre-modern peoples: For example the Germanic tribes interacting with Latin speakers during Roman times, or the Normans with the Anglo-Saxons in the 11th century, or Baantu speakers with Hottentot speakers in medieval times. How it applies to modern interactions, such as people from different language groups communicating with each other in halting English at a scientific meeting, would still be the subject of conjecture.)

The above principle is eminently embodied in modern English: The Old English (Anglo-Saxon) of *Beowulf* (a text thought to be composed around the 5th-6th century BCE but whose surviving manuscripts are from much later), retains a significant degree of the inflectional character of the parent Indo-European [IEu-38 to IEu-41]. On the other hand, modern English is an extreme case of a periphrastic language. The already limited inflectional character of Anglo-Saxon was further eroded, first by Norman (i.e., French) influences post-1066 C.E., then by Scandinavian (mainly Danish) influences through Viking invasions pervading the heart of England such as Yorkshire, then through Keltic influences from the conquest of still-Keltic-speaking peoples in the hinterlands of the British Isles. As a result, nearly all tenses and even moods in English are expressed through auxiliary words, as in the example cited earlier: *I have done, I will do, I had done, I will have done, I ought to do, I might have done*, etc. etc.. English has also eliminated the Anglo-Saxon *gender* of objects.

In English, we can also see how transformations between typologies may occur, and how they may be continuing to occur. For, due to the exigencies of the modern world, especially in the need for modern terminology in fields as varied as the physical sciences, software and finance, English has become far more *agglutinative* today than its inflectional, non-agglutinative origins would have ever indicated. This is in fact one of the great strengths of the English language and perhaps the source of its ability to adapt to modern needs, far greater, one might submit, than, say, French. Thus, the ease of coinage of such words as *pullout, dropdown, brainstorm, brushover* (for computer screen menus) or *backsplash* (for kitchen counters) may be ascribed to their agglutinative nature. None of these words can ever hope to get inflected, other than plural forms for the substantives (e.g. *backsplashes*).

5.3.2 CAVEAT REGARDING TYPOLOGICAL CLASSIFICATION

It is pertinent to end this section of our discussion with the caveat, expressed very cogently by Sapir [LN-34 to LN-36], that *"it is impossible to set up a limited number of types (typologies) that would do full justice to the peculiarities of the thousands of languages and dealects spoken on the surface of the earth."* More relevant quotes from Sapir, from 1921 but still quite valid as of 2005, are given below:

> "There is something irresistible about a method of classification that starts with two poles, exemplified by Chinese and Latin,

> clusters what it conveniently can about these poles, and throws everything else into a "transitional type". Hence has arisen the still popular classification of language into an "isolating" (*analytic*) group, an "agglutinative" group and an "inflective" group. Sometimes the languages of the American Indians are made to struggle along as an uncomfortable "polysynthetic" rearguard to the agglutinative languages.....A language may be both agglutinative and inflective, or inflective and polysynthetic, or even polysynthetic and isolating... Every language can and must express the fundamental syntactic relations even though there is not a single affix to be found in its vocabulary. We conclude that every language is a form language. ...An inflective language, we must insist, may be analytic, synthetic, or polysynthetic."

...(5.6)

We also may note that the example of English as elaborated in the discussion above mirrors the slow transition (a cynic might say "degeneration") of languages such as Latin. Starting from the extreme inflectional character of its Indo-European parent, Latin has retained much inflection. But it also developed a more periphrastic and analytic character in other respects. In this, we see the clear influence of the interaction with other linguistic groups (e.g. Etruscan).

All this then appears to hint that, perhaps, languages appear to become structurally more "disordered" as they interact with other languages. This leads us to the subject of the next section.

Chapter 5: Grammar and Grammatical Terms, The Form of Language, Order in Language, and Possible Structure of a Single, Parent Human Language, the "Anti-Nostratic"

5.4 FORM AND ORDER IN LANGUAGE

THE TENDENCY TOWARDS GREATER ORDER IN LINGUISTIC ISOLATION AND A RULE OF NATURAL ORDERING BORROWED FROM SCIENCE: The simple principle embodied in the discussion above, i.e. that, *left to themselves, things (in our case, languages) will naturally seek greater order*, is actually quite universal and scientific. It is quite pervasive, e.g., in the physical and biological sciences. We can roughly phrase it as the following rule:

> **RULE OF NATURAL ORDERING**
>
> ***Left unperturbed, i.e. to itself, a complete and isolated (closed) system, possessing a sufficient number of variables, will, over sufficient time,** naturally **organize itself towards greater order and superstructure**.*

...(5.7)

This rule, borrowed from observation in science, also has the *opposite* sense of the rule in the *second law of thermodynamics* governing <u>entropy</u>. That rule states that the entropy of a *closed* system continues always to *increase* with time. Entropy is said by physicists to be a measure of disorder, so we might say, on initial glance, that the second law of thermodynamics states that the *disorder* of a closed system continues always to *increase* with time. Thus, on initial examination, our rule appears counter-intuitive to the second law of thermodynamics. However, it is not, and we now explain how here.

The thermodynamics rule primarily governs the macrostate of a system as it is determined by the system's many possible microstates. The classic, lay example that we might remember from our freshman science classes is the mixing of milk and coffee in a cup, or, to give a better example, water and food coloring. If one thoroughly mixes these beforehand, they will never *un*mix. Now the single macrostate of the system is defined by the mixture's temperature, pressure and color, to name a few variables. The microstates determining this single macrostate are defined by the relative location of the molecular

Chapter 5: Grammar and Grammatical Terms, The Form of Language, Order in Language, and Possible Structure of a Single, Parent Human Language, the "Anti-Nostratic"

constituents of the coffee and the milk or water and food coloring, their individual vibrational modes (determining their temperature), etc. The larger the number of possible microstates giving rise to the same macrostate, the larger the entropy of the system, and then, in physicists' jargon, the greater the *disorder* of the system. Since a far greater number of microstates can give rise to a thoroughly mixed (milk + coffee) or (water + food coloring) than to a liquid in which the constituents miraculously remain unmixed, we say that the thoroughly mixed macrostate has a higher entropy, and hence, in physicists' jargon, a greater *disorder,* than any unmixed states. Now although in the physicist's definition, the thoroughly mixed liquid state is more disordered than any unmixed states, in our own lay observation, we would perceive the exact opposite, i.e. that the thoroughly mixed state in fact appears more *organized*, more *ordered* than any unmixed states! Thus, our rule's apparent conflict with the 2nd law of thermodynamics is merely one of perception, of what is disordered or disorganized. The physicist looks solely at the *number* of microstates determining a single macrostate and bases his pronouncement on the degree of disorder of the macrostate on that number only. On the other hand, we look at perhaps a more global, and some would say, more subjective, picture of what is organization and order vs. what is not.

To summarize then, what our rule says is that there is a *natural* tendency towards organization and superstructure in an *unperturbed* system. We can see that our rule is elegantly played out in the natural world, and is seen everywhere in Nature: Whenever a system is left to itself, it tends to organize itself internally, and to develop a superstructure. In the fields of chemistry and materials science, studies of just the last two decades (1985-2005) have produced myriad, biomimetic *"self-assembling"* systems which, when left to themselves, naturally seek greater order and superstructure. Nature is of course full of such self-assembling systems. And perhaps the most eminent example of naturally evolving superstructure amongst natural systems is of course the evolution of life on Earth, culminating, in the animal world, in ourselves, *Homo sapiens*.

Over the last 100 years or so, we have learned, from such fascinating things as self-assembling chemical and biological systems, that this complex system is simply the culmination of a *natural* tendency for greater organization amidst a *complete*, self-contained and externally unperturbed system of, among other constituents, amino acids, nucleic acids, proteins and electrolytes. That the qualifiers *with a <u>sufficient</u> number of variables* and *with <u>sufficient</u> time* are important can be seen from our example: We have myriad variables in a soup of amino acids, proteins, nucleic acids, and electrolytes. (We purposely do not define what comprises "sufficient" here, since that would require a treatment, complete with examples, that would run into chapters.)

Chapter 5: Grammar and Grammatical Terms, The Form of Language, Order in Language, and Possible Structure of a Single, Parent Human Language, the "Anti-Nostratic"

Thus, evolution appears to fit in well with our rule, since *evolution is essentially the creation of highly ordered and functional systems from disordered components*. As one example of the application of our rule to evolution, we might then say that, left to themselves in a closed system (e.g. a lake) with a fixed set of physical parameters (the evolutionary "drivers" or "stresses"), and given a sufficient number of variables (temperature, humidity, variation of concentration, fluid flow) and sufficient time (hundreds of millions of years), a soup of amino acids will naturally evolve into highly ordered nucleic acids. We might think it lucky happenstance that Earth did produce these wonderfully complex nucleic acids, but it is likely that if the experiment were repeated (i.e., if we had the luxury of a few hundred million years to repeat it!), it would quite likely yield the *same product*, i.e. the same nucleic acids, every time. "Co-emergent evolution" has been seen in recent discoveries, e.g. in the identical toxins found in poisonous frogs that evolved independently in totally different environments separated by large distances [GDn-53, GDn-54].

Our above rule is also, incidentally, embodied in the well-known concept of *Rta* of ancient Indian philosophy. *Rta,* is variously defined as "Natural Order", "The Laws of Nature", "The Laws of Physics" "The Order of Nature", or "The Law of Nature That Pervades Everything". It causes natural ordering. It is said by some to give an atheistic bent to that aspect of ancient Indian philosophy, since the concept of a deity or anything supernatural is not required to invoke it [HIi-28 to HIi-39]. Thus, here we appear to be dwelling on the borders of philosophy rather than science or linguistics!

A key qualifier in the above rule is the phrase *left unperturbed*, or, in the case of languages, *left to themselves*. In linguistically relevant terms, this qualifier implies *isolation from the influence of other linguistic groups*, i.e. from other languages. It thus necessarily implies cultural, and ultimately, ethnic isolation. It implies that *when a people is left completely isolated linguistically, its language will naturally develop a more ordered character over time.*

We can then formulate the above-quoted general rule *specifically for languages* as follows:

> **RULE OF NATURAL ORDERING AS APPLIED TO LANGUAGES**
>
> *Left unperturbed from external linguistic influences, a language will naturally tend, over sufficient time, towards greater order, greater organization and superstructure.*

...(5.8)

One would hypothecate that this natural ordering *may* be the fate of all languages if their speakers were left to themselves, without the influence of any other linguistic groups, for an extended period of time, i.e., at least several thousand years. This linguistic isolation in turn, unfortunately also implies the complete ethnic isolation of a people speaking a single language, over a reasonable period of time, perhaps several thousand years.

As we have noted elsewhere in this book, such isolation of a people speaking a single language might have been possible in the temperature climates of Eurasia, stretching from eastern Siberia and northern China through western Europe and south to Anatolia, due to the isolating effects of the last Ice Age. (The Ice Age isolation of peoples in temperature climates, and the associated subject of DNA haplogroups, is dealt with in the chapter on world language families earlier in this book.) It was however very unlikely in the warmer Middle East and Africa, with its constant flux of peoples to and from Africa and the Indian Subcontinent, documented by the archaeological record [GDn-1 to GDn-3, LN-83, LAs-4, LAs-5]. And it is definitely not the state of affairs today. Today, even the all-pervading English language is at the other extreme: In a state of continuous, *hyper-perturbation*.

To visualize how languages may tend naturally towards greater order if left to themselves, let us hypothecate on how modern English, left to itself, might develop an increasingly inflectional character: We might consider that the verbal expressions *I have gone, you have gone, he has gone* might transform, with linguistic isolation, into *gone-*

Chapter 5: Grammar and Grammatical Terms, The Form of Language, Order in Language, and Possible Structure of a Single, Parent Human Language, the "Anti-Nostratic"

have-I, gone-have-you, gone-has-he, and then, ultimately, to *gonavaai, gonavu, gonasi*. With this transformation, the verbal root, *go* has now taken a conjugational augment, *[-n-]*, an infix indicating the perfect tense, *[-a-]* and conjugational endings for the 1st, 2nd and 3rd persons, respectively *[-vi, -vu, -si]*. This is illustrated more systematically in the **Table** below.

Table 5-9: *Hypothetical* formulation of how English, left completely isolated linguistically, might evolve a *highly inflectional* imperfect tense from its present highly *periphrastic* one. (See text for discussion.)

CURRENT IMPERFECT TENSE	HYPOTHETICAL IMPERFECT TENSE	TENSE MARKER	PERSONAL ENDING
I have gone	gone-have-I → ***gon-av-aae***	-av-	-aae
You have gone	gone-have-you → ***gone-av-yu***	-av-	-yu
He has gone	gone-has-he → ***gon-as-ii***	-as-	-ii

Readers familiar with Sanskrit will of course see that the hypothetical formulation in the Table above is *exactly* what happens, *so very transparently,* in Sanskrit: For example, the verbal root *wad (vad)*, "to speak" is conjugated *wadaami, wadasi, wadati*, "I speak, you speak, he/she/it speaks". Now we know that the particle stem *ma* or *me* or *mi* indicates "I" in Sanskrit, and the particle stem *ta* indicates the third person, as seen in the declension of the third person pronoun *tad*. Again, this is illustrated in a more formal manner in the **Table** below.

Table 5-10: Illustration of how the conjugation of the Sanskrit verbal root *wad* (*vad*, to speak) may have developed, in direct analogy to the hypothetical formulation of the English imperfect shown in the previous **Table**. The hyphens in the current Sanskrit are added for clarity. (See text for discussion.)

SANSKRIT, present indicative active

CURRENT	HYPOTHETICAL ORIGIN
wad-aa-mi (I speak)	*mi-wada*, then *wada-mi*, then *wadaa-mi* etc.
wad-a-si (you speak)	*si-wada* from fricatization of *ti-wada*, then *wada-si*, etc.
wad-a-ti (he speaks)	*ti-wada* or *ta-wada*, then *wada-ti*, etc.

SANSKRIT, imperfect active

CURRENT	HYPOTHETICAL ORIGIN (TENSE MARKER "-*a*-")
	(-*a*- originally an auxiliary verb, much like English "have", French *avoir*)
a-wad-a-m (I spoke)	*mi-a-wada*, then *a-wada-mi*, etc.
a-wad-a-s (you spoke)	*si-a-wada* or *sa-a-wada*, then *a-wada-si*, etc.
a-wad-a-t (he spoke)	*ti-a-wada* or *ta-a-wada*, then *a-wada-ti*, etc.

We can then well imagine that, at some point in the evolution of Sanskrit, the verb *wad* might have been conjugated *mi-wada, si-wadi, ta-wada*, as shown in the Table above. The corresponding imperfect tense in Sanskrit is *awadam, awada:(s), awadat*, "I spoke, you spoke, he/she/it has spoke". We can well imagine that this might have initially been *mi-a-wada, si-a-wada, ta-a-wada*, surprisingly close to the imperfect-tense example for English above. In the hypothetical inflectional English example above (*gonavaai, gonavu, gonasi*), the -*n*- infix would then, perhaps, be used to distinguish an "-*n*-

Chapter 5: Grammar and Grammatical Terms, The Form of Language, Order in Language, and Possible Structure of a Single, Parent Human Language, the "Anti-Nostratic"

conjugation". In the evolution of Sanskrit, we can hypothecate an even earlier time, where there were only two numbers, *mi* or *ma* ("I") and *ti* or *ta* ("he/she/it" as well as "you"). As the need to differentiate "he/she/it" from "your" arose as the speakers' intelligence developed, the differentiation of "you" from "he/she/it" was made by fricatizing the *ti/ta* into *si/sa*.

Another observation that appears to emerge from the discussion above is that the more recent evolution of languages, say in the last 3000 years, may be very different from the evolution in earlier times, when human populations interacted less with each other. In this context then, one might conjecture that Turkish appears to be at the transition stage between agglutinative and inflectional. One would also then hasten to add that further transition in Turkish appears now highly unlikely. For we have come to the modern age, where isolated linguistic transition is constrained by globalization. In this respect, the not insignificant influence of Arabic substantives introduced into Turkish (such as *aadam*, "man" or *duniyaa*, "world" or *kitaab*, "book") on inflective suffixes pales by comparison to the influence of this globalization.

Chapter 5: Grammar and Grammatical Terms, The Form of Language, Order in Language, and Possible Structure of a Single, Parent Human Language, the "Anti-Nostratic"

5.5 FAINT HINTS OF THE ORIGINS OF LANGUAGE: UNIVERSAL INFANT PHONEMES, *SELF* AND *NOT-SELF*, THE POSSIBLE STRUCTURE OF PROTO-LANGUAGES, THE *ANTI*-NOSTRATIC

5.5.1 INFANT PHONEMES AND WHAT THEY MAY TELL US OF THE STRUCTURE OF EARLY HUMAN LANGUAGE; THE CONCEPT OF *SELF* AND *NOT-SELF*, TERMS BORROWED FROM IMMUNOLOGY

To advance further in the above discussion on the hypothetical origins of ordering in languages, let us quickly look at the relationships embodied in the Table overleaf. This **Table** attempts to relate the most basic words, such as personal pronouns - which linguists have well established *as likely to change least in languages over time* [LN-84] - among languages with very different origins.

The words listed in the **Table** point towards a clear *bilabial artition* for things identified with oneself ("I, me") or close to oneself and a dental artition for things identified not with oneself.

Chapter 5: Grammar and Grammatical Terms, The Form of Language, Order in Language, and Possible Structure of a Single, Parent Human Language, the "Anti-Nostratic"

Table 5-11: Personal pronouns in unrelated languages or language families, hypothetically showing identification of the *bilabial artitions with "Self"* and the *dental artitions with "Not-Self"*.

"SELF" (I, we, etc.), <u>bilabial</u> artition

Word	Indo-European	Chinese (Mandarin)	Tamil	Turkish
"I", "me" etc.	*ma*	*woa*	---	*ben*

"NOT SELF", "OTHER" (you, he/she/it, they, etc.), <u>dental</u> artition

Word	Indo-European	Chinese (Mandarin)	Tamil	Turkish
"You", "He/She/It"	*sa, ta*	*nii, thaa*	*nii*	*sen*

The two stems, *ma* and *ta*, respectively bilabial and dental, and their phonochromatic variants of the same artition, e.g. *wa,* etc. for *ma*, and *na, sa* etc. for *ta*, can then be hypothecated to belong to a period when language was just developing. Now as we all know, the bilabial *ma* is one of the first sounds learned by an infant, and is then frequently applied to familiar, loving or near objects. (We may note that *Maamaa* and *Paapaa* are utterances first applied to parents in virtually *every* language family of the world, in languages as varied and unrelated as Mandarin, the Indo-European languages, Malay, the Baantu languages and Tamil. Variants such as *haahaa* in Japanese and *Ammaa* in Tamil (both for "mother") can be derived from parent *maa* phones, whilst words such as *Aai* ("mother" in Maraathi) are replacement words that do not negate our hypothesis.) On the other hand, the first sounds applied by infants to something distant or foreign, again in virtually every culture of the world, is the dental sound *ta*, as in an infant's babbling *ta-ta-ta* when addressing a faraway object [LN-72, LN-95 to LN-111]. We also note that infants, in their first phone utterances, do not distinguish between

Chapter 5: Grammar and Grammatical Terms, The Form of Language, Order in Language, and Possible Structure of a Single, Parent Human Language, the "Anti-Nostratic"

voiced and unvoiced, between aspirated and unaspirated [LN-72, LN-95 to LN-111]. Rather, the *ARTITION* **is the critical distinguishing property** *for the infant in his/her phones.*

In the context of the above discussion, we then assign the general *bilabial* category represented by *ma* to **Self**, while the general *dental* category represented by *ta* is assigned to *Not-Self*.

Self and *Not-Self* are of course terms borrowed from immunology, describing, e.g., how bacteria identify (and ultimately react to) *friend* vs. *foe*.

We make the hypothesis that **this Self-/Not-Self dichotomy was one of the first, fundamental, semantic distinctions made by primitive man when language was just developing**. With our example above, appearing to apply to virtually *all* the world's languages, we have identified:

> **SELF AND NOT-SELF IDENTIFICATION IN A PUTATIVE, PRIMITIVE PROTO-LANGUAGE**
>
> ***(Based on First Infant Phonemes)***
>
> *BILABIAL = SELF*
>
> *DENTAL = NOT-SELF*

...(5.9)

We find that these distinctions are actually mirrored in infant phonology across unrelated language families: Extensive studies [LN-72, LN-95 to LN-111] have established that the first three artitions invariably learned across language families (from Sino-Tibetan to Indo-European to Baantu to Dravidian) are the ***bilabial***, the ***dental*** and the ***velar***. (The *glottal* artition may, in infants, be lumped with the velar.) Modern linguists well recognize the limited phones and the *phonemic distinctions* of infants as developing progressively along the lines shown in the Table below:

Chapter 5: Grammar and Grammatical Terms, The Form of Language, Order in Language, and Possible Structure of a Single, Parent Human Language, the "Anti-Nostratic"

Table 5-12: *Progressive development* of the ***phonemic distinctions of infants***, as recognized by modern linguists, from very extensive studies [LN-72, LN-95 to LN-111], providing a possible model for the development of the first language in primitive humans. (*The bold parentheses numeral, e.g. **(1)**, before each phone, indicates the serial number of the phon**eme**.*)

Bilabial ("Self") Phones	Nonlabial ("Not Self") Phones	Total No. of Phonemes
(1) [p], [m]	**(2)** [t], [k]	2

Bilabial Phones	Dental Phones	Velar Phones	Total No. of Phonemes
(1) [p], [m]	**(2)** [t]	**(3)** [k]	3

	Bilabial Phones	Dental Phones	Velar Phones	Total No. of Phonemes
Unvoiced	**(1)** [p]	**(2)** [t]	**(3)** [k]	4
Voiced	**(4)** [b], [m]			

	Bilabial Phones	Dental Phones	Velar Phones	Total No. of Phonemes
Unvoiced	**(1)** [p]	**(2)** [t]	**(3)** [k]	6
Voiced	**(4)** [b], [m]	**(5)** [d]	**(6)** [g]	

(cont. overleaf)

Chapter 5: Grammar and Grammatical Terms, The Form of Language, Order in Language, and Possible Structure of a Single, Parent Human Language, the "Anti-Nostratic"

(Table 5-12, cont. from previous page):

	Bilabial Phones	Dental Phones	Velar Phones	Total No. of Phonemes
Unvoiced	(1) [p]	(2) [t]	(3) [k]	
Voiced	(4) [b]	(5) [d]	(6) [g]	8
Nasal	(7) [m]	(8) [n]		

It is our contention then that, just like the progressive modifications shown in the infant phone Table above, the basic phones of the first human language may have been modified as the language progressed in development, but ***their fundamental linguistic and semantic values would not have changed***.

For example, the dental *ta* may be fricatized to *sa*, and the bilabial *ma* may be made into a semi-vowel *wa*, but the new phones would still have a semantic connotation corresponding to some variation of that for the original phone, in this case, some variant of "self". Thus, crudely speaking and as shown in an earlier Table above, the *woa* ("I") and *thaa* ("he/she/it") of Mandarin may be said to have roots in this bilabial/-dental dichotomy, just as the *ma* and *ta* of Sanskrit do, or the *nii* ("you") of Tamil does, or the *se* ("you") of Turkish does. Or the *ta* of would be fricatized to *sa* or nasalized to *na* with a slight change of meaning: From "that" or "he" to "you", as in Sanskrit *sa*, a fricatization of *ta*, with a corresponding slight change in meaning, and Mandarin *ni*); i.e. the other person, still very much in the *Not-Self* category.

We can cite yet another example of the *bilabial-dental-velar* phonemic and *Self/Not-Self* semantic oppositions in the interrogative vs. demonstrative articles of Sanskrit. This is summarized in the **Table** overleaf.

Chapter 5: Grammar and Grammatical Terms, The Form of Language, Order in Language, and Possible Structure of a Single, Parent Human Language, the "Anti-Nostratic"

Table 5-13: Patterns in initial phones in *interrogative, indefinite, indicative* and *demonstrative* forms of articles, based on the Sanskrit.

TYPE	MEANING	INITIAL PHONE	EXAMPLE	NOTES
Interrogative	"Who?"	[k] (*velar*)	Ka?	All Indo-European interrogatives start with some form of [k] or [kw], even English (*kwaet? → hwaet? → what?*)
Indefinitive	"That which"	[j] (*palatal*)	Ya	Remnants in German (*je*, etc.)
Indicative	"This" generally	[:] (*glottal*)	:Amuum	
Definitive, Unfamiliar	"That" or "this" specifically	[t] (*dental*)	Tad	All I-E definitives start with some variant of [t], e.g. English *this, that*, German *der, dem*, Cl. Greek *ton* etc.
Definitive, Unfamiliar	"That" or "this" specifically, especially when a person	[s] (*forward fricative of dental*)	Sa	
Most Familiar, Immediate		[m] (*bilabial, plosive*)	Me, Mama, etc.	Personal pronouns and words for "mother" have bilabial intial phones in nearly *all* languages of the world
Familiar, Next stage of familiarity		[w] (*bilabial, semi-vowel*)	Wi, Wayam, etc.	As for [m]; other examples: Mandarin *woa* ("I", "me"), English *we*

Chapter 5: Grammar and Grammatical Terms, The Form of Language, Order in Language, and Possible Structure of a Single, Parent Human Language, the "Anti-Nostratic"

As a final note, the reconstruction of a putative single, parent human language using (infant) phonemes, according to the analyses above, may be contrasted with the recent (2011) analysis of phonemes spanning all the world's languages using statistical and evolutionary biology techniques [LN-77(b)]. These were used to arrive at the sweeping conclusion that language originated in southwestern Africa. This has been discussed at some length at the end of Chapter 1 in this book, to which reference is made. As noted therein, while this conclusion may or may not be true, to arrive at it using statistical techniques applied to phonemes across essentially all the world's languages is fraught with error.

5.5.2 OTHER FEATURES OF HYPOTHETICAL EARLY HUMAN LANGUAGES

Two other final features of hypothetical early human languages are worth discussing here:

(1) That the *verb* rather than the substantive is the fundament of language (this was briefly touched upon earlier in this chapter).
(2) The presence of the *dual number*.

…(5.10)

Taking a look at the first feature, in what some would call a "primordial" or "primeval" (Max Müller used the word "primitive"!) [HIi-41, HIi-42] language like Sanskrit, the verb is given fundamental place of importance over the substantive (or the indeclinable or any other grammatical form). This is done so even formally by the grammarians, e.g. in formal Paaninian analysis.

Almost miraculously, for such a complex language, in Sanskrit, *every substantive is derivable from a verbal root*. As an example, even the word *Bhagawaan*, "God" is derived ultimately from the verbal root *bhaj*, "to worship, pray"!. This verb-based derivation is formalized in Paaninian analysis. And conversely, *no* verbal root has origins in a substantive, not even denominative verbs; in that case, the parent nouns are invariably derived from some other verbal roots (denominative verbs are verbs derived from nouns, e.g. the English *to bike* is derived from the noun *bike*). Archaic Chinese is

Chapter 5: Grammar and Grammatical Terms, The Form of Language, Order in Language, and Possible Structure of a Single, Parent Human Language, the "Anti-Nostratic"

also said [SCr-25 to SCr-29] to display some of these features, that is to say, the primacy of the verb over the noun.

Now, as noted at the beginning of this chapter, this seems counterintuitive, since one would envision a primitive human first coming up with sounds (names) for objects, and only then thinking semantically of verbs!

Nevertheless, we find some support for the primacy of the verb over the noun in the now fairly numerous studies of the acquisition of (primarily sign) language by bonobos, chimpanzees and other apes [LN-59 to LN-61]. In spite of the fact that the language is taught to them by humans, who may invariably start with a substantive (e.g. the sign-word for a banana), the apes invariably appear to emphasize the verbs early on!

The second feature of a hypothetical early human language relates to the presence of the *dual number*. In the earliest, relatively isolated human populations living in natural surroundings (e.g., forests or savanna rather than villages), the dual number appeared to develop prominently. This appears to reflect the fact that there was prominent, everyday contact with the things of nature, which all have *two eyes, two hands, two feet*, etc. As human development lead to settled living or prominent interaction with other human populations, the need for the dual number was lost, as everyday contact was more with things such as clay pots, hut walls, mats for sleeping, other humans, etc.

The dual number appears not just in Sanskrit, a language that has come down to us through a unique happenstance of fossilization and where it is perhaps more prominent than in any other world language. It also appears, in traces, in other old languages such as Sumerian, and in the older Chinese languages (as seen in renditions of some passages of the early "bone inscriptions" [SCr-25 to SCr-28]). These traces hint at the fact that the dual number may have been prominent in the ancestors of *all* these ancient languages, and, by extension perhaps, *all* ancient languages, but was lost later because there was no need for it in a more developed human environment. And of course, the dual number survives prominently in a modern language, *Arabic*; indeed, Arabic is the only major modern language still retaining the dual number.

Unfortunately, other than Sanskrit, archaic Chinese and perhaps the earliest Sumerian, our stock of such languages that have been "fossilized" or otherwise unaffected by influences from other linguistic groups, and thus can be used for semantic and linguistic analysis, is very limited. We certainly cannot use a language such as the later Sumerian for this: Although admittedly very ancient, from the earliest record that we have, this language appears to bear traces of extensive contact with other linguistic groups and a consequent severe "watering down" of its original grammatical structure. This would be expected in a location such as the land of Sumer (just south of modern-day Baghdad), with its expected large to and fro transition of people between Africa, the Middle East and the Indian subcontinent.

5.5.3 POSSIBLE FORM OF EARLY HUMAN PROTO-LANGUAGES

Based on the above discussions then, we may hypothecate on the possible progressive development of *one* possible primitive human language (among many), which we may give the interesting moniker *Muulwaak* (Sanskrit "root speech"):

We would envision first a ***very limited number of phonemes***, which would increase in number as human intelligence (and, concomitantly, the language) developed, paralleling the *infant phoneme development* discussed above.

We may then hypothecate that *just as for infants, the **bilabial, dental** and **velar** "phonemes" would perhaps have been the very first three phonemes*. These would initially be undifferentiated by voicing, etc. Thus, for instance, [p], [b] and [m] would be allophones of a single, "*bilabial*" phoneme.

These characteristics of one possible hypothetical primitive human language are elucidated in the Table below. It is to be noted that this is a hypothecation for only *one* possible early human language. Others may have had a different composition, but our hypothesis is that the overall principles, e.g. a limited number of phonemes with the *bilabial* and *dental* "supra-phonemes" being prominent, would have been the same for all early languages.

Chapter 5: *Grammar and Grammatical Terms, The Form of Language, Order in Language, and Possible Structure of a Single, Parent Human Language, the "Anti-Nostratic"*

Table 5-14 *(cont. overleaf)*:   HYPOTHETICAL *CHARACTERISTICS* OF ONE POSSIBLE, *FIRST HUMAN LANGUAGE*, or **Muulwaak**, (see discussion above).

(1)   ONLY THREE (3) INITIAL PHONEMES:

We may call these "*supra-phonemes*": *"bilabial", "dental", "velar"*. These eventually **develop into around eight (8) phonemes** (corresponding to the last table in the depiction of *infant phonemes* above). The number of phonemes then **stays at around 10 to 15** until much further development in the language. (In contrast, most modern languages have between 20 and 50 phonemes.)

(2)   THE DEVELOPMENT OF HUMAN INTELLIGENCE IS THE KEY DRIVER OF THE DEVELOPMENT OF HUMAN LANGUAGE *(SEE CHAPTER 1)*:

Thus, *as this intelligence develops further, the **need for more phonemes***, and thus their number, grows, and the need for further semantic distinctions then also grows. (Again, this may parallel the development of intelligence in infants today.)

(3)   *CLEAR DISTINCTION BETWEEN <u>SELF</u> AND <u>NOT-SELF</u>:*

An initial clear distinction between **Self** and **Not-Self**, with the "bilabial phoneme" initially representing *Self* and the "dental phoneme" initially representing *Not-Self*, is parlayed into the initial vocabulary. (Traces of this may still appear in fundamental words such as personal pronouns, as seen in an earlier Table.)

(Table continued overleaf)

(Table 5-14, cont.)

(4) <u>ARTITION</u> REMAINS THE KEY DISTINGUISHING FEATURE OF PHONEMES:

Artition is fundamental for *semantic connotation*. As the need for more phonemes arises, more variants are created from a single artition, but the artition does not change. For example, the plosive *ta*, of dental arition, may give rise to a fricative *sa* and a nasal *na*, both still of dental arition, with slight semantic variations of the meaning of the parent word beginning with *ta*. These in turn give more varied semantic connotations to words.

(5) THE <u>VERB</u> RATHER THAN THE SUBSTANTIVE APPEARS TO BE SEMANTICALLY DISTINGUISHED FIRST:.

For reasons still not clearly understood but clearly present in an ancient language such as Sanskrit [LAi-11, LAi-12] and appearing to be substantiated in the spontaneous development of sign languages from scratch (Nicaraguan, Arabic sign languages, [LN-56 to LN-58], the *verb* rather than the substantive appears to be semantically distinguished first. Subsequently, it would appear that substantives are derived from verbs, rather than vice versa or independently.

(6) THE <u>DUAL NUMBER</u> DEVELOPS PROMINENTLY:

In the earliest, relatively isolated human populations living in natural surroundings (e.g., forests or savanna rather than villages), the *dual number* develops prominently. This reflects the fact that there is prominent, everyday contact with the things of nature, which all have *two eyes, two hands, two feet,* etc. As human development leads to settled living or prominent interaction with other human populations, the need for the dual number gets lost, as everyday contact is more with things such as clay pots, hut walls, mats for sleeping, other humans, etc.

(Table concluded)

Chapter 5: Grammar and Grammatical Terms, The Form of Language, Order in Language, and Possible Structure of a Single, Parent Human Language, the "Anti-Nostratic"

The informed reader may note that our above development is substantially different from the developments for "***Nostratic***" and other proto-languages of proposed "macro" families, hypothecated by some prominent linguists [LAs-78, LAs-79], and as discussed briefly in the previous chapter. We may thus call our *Mulwaak* an "*anti*-Nostratic"!

Also in relation to the subject of early human language, we may cite the very recent studies of African ethnic groups such as the Ju!huansi and the Hadzabe [GDn-21, LAs-6], where attempts have been made to conflate *ethnic* archaicness with *linguistic* archaicness, in spite of evidence to the contrary. The conclusion drawn from this has been that *clicks*, rather than the bilabial or dental phones represented in the Tables above, were the first phonemes!

We will leave the informed reader to arrive at his/her own comparisons and conclusions and not discuss the ongoing developments in this field further in this book.

5.5.4 CONCOMITANT MONOSYLLABIC AND HIGHLY INFLECTIONAL CHARACTER: IS IT POSSIBLE?

As we will see in the discussion in the following paragraph, languages can have substantial *monosyllabic* character, *yet* be highly, almost extremely, inflectional.

The monosyllabic characteristic appears merely to reflect the evolution of language. We may indeed conjecture that language most likely developed from monosyllabic utterances of primitive *Homo sapiens*. In languages where monosyllabic character appears to be pronounced, such as Sanskrit or Archaic Chinese, it may reflect a high degree of "primeval" character of the language, preserved for us to see through fortunate happenstance. This primeval character may have ensued from independent, isolated development.

The *monosyllabic* yet *highly inflectional* character of Sanskrit is seen from the conjugation of the verbal roots *wad* and *wid* (stem *wind*) presented earlier in this chapter. Sanskrit is almost entirely unique in the world in this regard in possessing this in full force: **Nearly all verbal roots in Sanskrit are monosyllabic**. And since all substantives are derived from verbal roots according to Paaninian analysis, *all Sanskrit words thus have monosyllabic roots.*

Chapter 5: Grammar and Grammatical Terms, The Form of Language, Order in Language, and Possible Structure of a Single, Parent Human Language, the "Anti-Nostratic"

As an example of this derivation of all manner of substantives from *monosyllabic* verbal roots in Sanskrit, let us look momentarily at just a single verbal root: The Sanskrit verb *suu*, "to give birth". This root yields, with the masculine substantive (noun) endings (i.e. inflections) *-nu* and *-ta*, the substantives *suunu* ("son", whence the English, German, Russian etc. cognates), and *suuta* ("son' in the sense of offspring). It also yields, from the feminine substantive endings *-nuu* and *-taa*, *suunuu* and *suutaa*, both meaning "daughter". All these words are lost in the other Indo-European languages. With the infix *-a-* (*"guna"*), we also get, from *suu*, *sawa* (from $s + a + uu + a$), as in *pra-sawa*, "birth", yet another noun from the same verbal root. Thus, we have, from the single verbal root meaning "to give birth," four names (2 each) for sons and daughters, and one noun for the act of birth.

In this fashion, nearly *all* substantives, and through them, even compound words (*samaasa*), can, in Sanskrit, be traced to **monosyllabic** verbal roots. Yet, at the same time, Sanskrit remains the most inflectional language known today. Thus, Sanskrit appears to show that *monosyllabic and inflectional character are not mutually exclusive.*

The Chinese languages are of course another group that have a highly *monosyllabic* character. Yet here again, the decipherment of Archaic Chinese writings from about 300 B.C. E. have revealed some inflectional character as well [SCr-25 to SCr-28], and it has also revealed the presence of gender in verbs, which is absent in nearly all modern Chinese languages today. It is thus not entirely unreasonable to conjecture that the Sino-Tibetan languages also originally reflected evolution in a highly linguistically isolated environment. The subsequent degeneration (metathesis) of the languages to their present state, where many completely lack inflectional character and even gender, might then reflect large movements of Sino-Tibetan peoples starting in pre-historic times and their extensive interaction with other linguistic groups; they apparently eventually dominated these other groups. This movement occurred much before recorded history, so we know nothing of the languages as they were in their full, original form. In contrast, Sanskrit was "fossilized" in India at a time of recorded history, so we have the luxury of being able to observe it, as a living laboratory.

The above discussion appears to imply that all early human languages may have started as *monosyllabic*. However, here again, we must take our hypothecations with a pinch of salt, as it were. Human development has been so varied and the environments that early humans were exposed to were so varied, that it would not be unreasonable to assume that, here and there, an early human language developed differently, perhaps starting out as polysyllables.

5.6 EXERCISES

(1) Why might the *verb* rather than the *substantive* be considered the fundament of language? In your opinion, which is more intuitively the fundament of language?

(2) Enumerate with examples from several languages all attributes of verbs.

(3) Enumerate with examples from several languages all attributes of substantives.

(4) Define and discuss the terms *typology, morpheme* and *morphology.* Define and discuss with examples the terms *agglutinative, inflectional, synthetic* and *polysynthetic.* Identify and discuss the typologies of the following languages: English; Sanskrit; Classical Greek; Turkish; Inuit; Basque; Navajo (Navaho).

(5) Discuss the "Rule of Ordering" as applied to languages and identify its relation to similar rules found in science, if any.

(6) Identify the common stages of development of infant phonemes as found in a majority (in terms of number of speakers) of human languages.

(7) (*Advanced study, after reviewing the Appendix to this chapter, which immediately follows*): Briefly research the ancient Indo-European languages closely related to Sanskrit, *Classical Greek, Latin* and *Avestan,* and identify how many conjugation systems they have for verbs and how they relate to the ten conjugation systems of Sanskrit. Are there any verbal roots in these other languages that may simultaneously be conjugated in different conjugations with slightly different shades of meaning?

CHAPTER 5 APPENDIX (TABLE 5-8). ILLUSTRATION OF EXTREME INFLECTIONAL CHARACTER IN A LANGUAGE: PARADIGMS FOR CONJUGATION OF THE SANSKRIT VERBAL ROOT -wid- (-vid-) IN THE 2nd, 4th, 6th, 7th and 10th CONJUGATIONS

[*Table 5-8* (appended here due to its length)]

TABLE OF CONTENTS

5.A.1 OVERVIEW OF THESE FIVE CONJUGATIONS 313

5.A.2 Conjugation of *wid (vid)* in 2nd conjugation, meaning "to know, to understand, to discoVer" (stem: *wed*) (Cognates English *wit*, German *wissen*, Latin *video*, etc.) 314

5.A.3 CONJUGATION OF *WID (VID)*, IN 4TH CONJUGATION, MEANING "TO BE, TO EXIST, TO DISCOVER OR UNDERSTAND ONESELF" 331

5.A.4 CONJUGATION OF *wid (vid)*, IN 6TH CONJUGATION, MEANING TO "FIND, TO COME TO KNOW, RECOGNIZE, COME TO DISCOVER" 333

Chapter 5 APPENDIX (Table 5-8): Illustration of Extreme Inflectional Character in a Language: Paradigms for Conjugation of the Sanskrit Verbal Root -wid- in the 2nd, 4th, 6th, 7th and 10th Conjugations

5.A.5. CONJUGATION OF *wid*, **IN 7**[TH] **CONJUGATION, MEANING "TO UNDERSTAND"** 338

5.A.6 CONJUGATION OF *wid*, **IN 10**[TH] **CONJUGATION, MEANING " TO TELL, TO COMMUNICATE, TO FEEL"** 340

Chapter 5 APPENDIX (Table 5-8): Illustration of Extreme Inflectional Character in a Language: Paradigms for Conjugation of the Sanskrit Verbal Root -wid- in the 2nd, 4th, 6th, 7th and 10th Conjugations

313

5.A.1 OVERVIEW OF THESE FIVE CONJUGATIONS

Conjugation#	Stem	Meaning	Cognates, If Applicable
2nd, both active and middle voices (but middle voice moribund). #	wed	to know, understand, discover.	English *wit*, German *wissen*, Latin *video/videre* (which initially had a sense "to know, understand", only later "to see").
4th, middle only. #	widya	to discover/-understand oneself; to be, exist.	---
6th, active and middle. #	wind	to find; to discover; to recognize.	English *find*, German *finden*, but almost nowhere else.
7th, middle only (active not used). #	wind	to understand.	
10th, middle only. #	wedaya	to tell, communicate; to feel.	---

 # Note on whether verbs conjugated in active of middle voices for information only. Verbs also conjugated in passive voice, causative, desiderative, intensive, etc.

Chapter 5 APPENDIX (Table 5-8): Illustration of Extreme Inflectional Character in a Language: Paradigms for Conjugation of the Sanskrit Verbal Root -wid- in the 2nd, 4th, 6th, 7th and 10th Conjugations

5.A.2 CONJUGATION OF *wid (vid)* IN 2ND CONJUGATION, MEANING "TO KNOW, TO UNDERSTAND, TO DISCOVER" (STEM: *wed*) (COGNATES ENGLISH *wit*, GERMAN *wissen*, LATIN *video*, ETC.)

PRESENT TENSE, INDICATIVE MOOD

ACTIVE VOICE

	Singular	Dual	Plural
First Person	wed-mi	wid-was	wid-mas
Second Person	wet-si	wit-thas	wit-tha
Third Person	wet-ti	wit-tas	wid-anti

MIDDLE VOICE

	Singular	Dual	Plural
First Person	wid-e	wid-wahe	wid-mahe
Second Person	wit-se	wid-aathe	wid-dhwe
Third Person	wit-te	wid-ate	wid-ate

PASSIVE VOICE

	Singular	Dual	Plural
First Person	wid-ye	wid-yaawahe	wid-yaamahe
Second person	wid-yase	wid-yethe	wid-yadhwe
Third Person	wid-yate	wid-yete	wid-yante

Chapter 5 APPENDIX (Table 5-8): *Illustration of Extreme Inflectional Character in a Language: Paradigms for Conjugation of the Sanskrit Verbal Root -wid- in the 2nd, 4th, 6th, 7th and 10th Conjugations*

IMPERFECT TENSE (augment [-a-])

ACTIVE VOICE

	Singular	Dual	Plural
First Person	a-wed-am	a-wid-wa	a-wid-ma
Second Person	a-wet	a-wit-tam	a-wit-ta
Third Person	a-wet	a-wit-taam	a-wid-an

MIDDLE VOICE

	Singular	Dual	Plural
First Person	a-widi	a-wid-wahi	a-wid-mahi
Second Person	a-wit-thaas	a-wid-aathaam	a-wid-dhwam
Third Person	a-wit-ta	a-wid-aataam	a-wid-ata

PASSIVE VOICE

	Singular	Dual	Plural
First Person	a-wid-ye	a-wid-yaawahi	a-wid-yaamahi
Second Person	a-wid-yathaas	a-wid-yethaam	a-wid-yadhwam
Third Person	a-wid-yata	a-wid-yetaam	a-wid-yanta

Chapter 5 APPENDIX (Table 5-8): Illustration of Extreme Inflectional Character in a Language: Paradigms for Conjugation of the Sanskrit Verbal Root -wid- in the 2nd, 4th, 6th, 7th and 10th Conjugations

OPTATIVE MOOD

ACTIVE VOICE

	Singular	Dual	Plural
First Person	wid-yaam	wid-yaawa	wid-yaama
Second Person	wid-yaas	wid-yaatam	wid-yaata
Third Person	wid-yaat	wid-yaataam	wid-us

MIDDLE VOICE

	Singular	Dual	Plural
First Person	wid-iiya	wid-iiwahi	wid-iimahi
Second Person	wit-iithaas	wid-iiyaathaam	wid-iidhwam
Third Person	wid-iita	wid-iiyaataam	wid-iiran

PASSIVE VOICE

	Singular	Dual	Plural
First Person	wid-yeya	wid-yewahi	wid-yemahi
Second Person	wid-yethaas	wid-yeyaathaam	wid-yedhwam
Third Person	wid-yeta	wid-yeyaataam	wid-yeran

Chapter 5 APPENDIX (Table 5-8): Illustration of Extreme Inflectional Character in a Language: Paradigms for Conjugation of the Sanskrit Verbal Root -wid- in the 2nd, 4th, 6th, 7th and 10th Conjugations

IMPERATIVE MOOD

ACTIVE VOICE

	Singular	Dual	Plural
First Person	wed-aani	wed-aawa	wed-aama
Second Person	wid-dhi	wit-tam	wit-ta
Third Person	wet-tu	wit-taam	wid-antu

MIDDLE VOICE

	Singular	Dual	Plural
First Person	wed-ai	wed-aawahai	wed-aamahai
Second Person	wit-swa	wid-aathaam	wid-dhwam
Third Person	wit-taam	wid-aataam	wid-ataam

PASSIVE VOICE

	Singular	Dual	Plural
First Person	wid-yai	wid-yaawahai	wid-yaamahai
Second Person	wid-yaswa	wid-yethaam	wid-yadhwam
Third Person	wid-yataam	wid-yetaam	wid-yantaam

Chapter 5 APPENDIX (Table 5-8): Illustration of Extreme Inflectional Character in a Language: Paradigms for Conjugation of the Sanskrit Verbal Root -wid- in the 2nd, 4th, 6th, 7th and 10th Conjugations

SIMPLE FUTURE TENSE (infix [-ish-], "to wish to")

ACTIVE VOICE

First Person	wed-ishyaami| wet-syaami	wed-ishyaawas | wet-syaawas	wed-ishyaamas | wet-syaamas
Second Person	wed-ishyasi | wet-syasi	wed-ishyathas | wet-syathas	wed-ishyatha | wet-syatha
Third Person	wed-ishyati | wet-syati	wed-ishyatas | wet-syatas	wed-ishyanti | wet-syanti

MIDDLE VOICE

First Person	wed-ishye| wet-sye	wed-ishyaawahe | wet-syaawahe	wed-ishyaamahe | wet-syaamahe
Second Person	wed-ishyase| wet-syase	wed-ishyethe | wet-syethe	wed-ishyadhwe | wet-syadhwe
Third Person	wed-ishyate| wet-syate	wed-ishyete | wet-syete	wed-ishyante | wet-syante

PERIPHRASTIC FUTURE TENSE

ACTIVE VOICE

	Singular	Dual	Plural
First Person	wed-it-aasmi | wet-t-aasmi	wed-it-aaswa| wet-t-aaswa	wed-it-aasma| wet-t-aasma
Second Person	wed-it-aasi|wet-t-aasi	wed-it-aastha|wet-t-aastha	wed-it-aastha|wet-t-aastha
Third Person	wed-it-aa| wet-t-aa	wed-it-aarau|wet-t-aarau	wed-it-aara|wed-t-aara

Chapter 5 APPENDIX (Table 5-8): Illustration of Extreme Inflectional Character in a Language: Paradigms for Conjugation of the Sanskrit Verbal Root -wid- in the 2nd, 4th, 6th, 7th and 10th Conjugations

PERFECT TENSE

ACTIVE VOICE

	Singular	Dual	Plural
First Person	wed-a	wid-wa	wid-ma
Second Person	wet-tha	wit-thus	wid-a
Third Person	wed-a	wit-tus	wid-us

AORIST TENSE (augment –a-)

ACTIVE VOICE

	Singular	Dual	Plural
First Person	a-wed-isham	a-wedishwa	a-wed-ishma
Second Person	a-wed-iis	a-wedishtam	a-wed-ishta
Third Person	a-wed-iit	a-wedishtaam	a-wed-ishus

MIDDLE VOICE

	Singular	Dual	Plural
First Person	a-wed-ishi	a-wed-ishwahi	a-wed-ishmahi
Second Person	a-wed-ishthaas	a-wed-ishaathaam	a-wed-idhwam
Third Person	a-wed-ishta	a-wed-ishaataam	a-wed-ishata

Chapter 5 APPENDIX (Table 5-8): Illustration of Extreme Inflectional Character in a Language: Paradigms for Conjugation of the Sanskrit Verbal Root -wid- in the 2nd, 4th, 6th, 7th and 10th Conjugations

CAUSATIVE FORM,
"TO CAUSE TO KNOW", "TO MAKE KNOWN", "TO INSTRUCT" ETC.
infix [-aya-]

PRESENT TENSE, INDICATIVE MOOD

ACTIVE VOICE

	Singular	Dual	Plural
First Person	wed-ayaami	wed-ayaawa	wed-ayaama
Second Person	wed-ayasi	wed-ayatha	wed-ayatha
Third Person	wed-ayati	wed-ayata	wed-ayanti

MIDDLE VOICE

	Singular	Dual	Plural
First Person	wed-aye	wed-ayaawahe	wed-ayamahe
Second Person	wed-ayase	wed-ayethe	wed-ayadhwe
Third Person	wed-ayate	wed-ayete	wed-ayante

PASSIVE VOICE

	Singular	Dual	Plural
First Person	wed-ye	wed-yaawahe	wed-yaamahe
Second Person	wed-yase	wed-yethe	wed-yadhwe
Third Person	wed-yate	wed-yete	wed-yante

Chapter 5 APPENDIX (Table 5-8): *Illustration of Extreme Inflectional Character in a Language: Paradigms for Conjugation of the Sanskrit Verbal Root -wid- in the 2nd, 4th, 6th, 7th and 10th Conjugations*

IMPERFECT TENSE (augment -a-)

ACTIVE VOICE

	Singular	Dual	Plural
First Person	a-wed-ayam	a-wed-ayaawa	a-wed-ayaama
Second Person	a-wed-ayas	a-wed-ayatam	a-wed-ayata
Third Person	a-wedayat	a-wed-ayataam	a-wed-ayan

MIDDLE VOICE

	Singular	Dual	Plural
First Person	a-wed-aye	a-wed-ayaawahi	wed-ayaamahi
Second Person	a-wed-ayathaas	a-wed-ayethaam	a-wed-ayadhwam
Third Person	a-wed-ayata	a-wed-ayetaam	a-wed-ayanta

PASSIVE VOICE

	Singular	Dual	Plural
First Person	a-wed-ye	a-wed-yaawahi	a-wed-yaamahi
Second Person	a-wed-yathaas	a-wed-yethaam	a-wed-yadhwam
Third Person	a-wed-yata	a-wed-yetaam	a-wed-yanta

Chapter 5 APPENDIX (Table 5-8): *Illustration of Extreme Inflectional Character in a Language: Paradigms for Conjugation of the Sanskrit Verbal Root -wid- in the 2nd, 4th, 6th, 7th and 10th Conjugations*

OPTATIVE MOOD

ACTIVE VOICE

	Singular	**Dual**	**Plural**
First Person	wed-ayeyam	wed-ayewa	wed-ayema
Second Person	wed-ayes	wed-ayetam	wed-ayeta
Third Person	wed-ayet	wed-ayetaam	wed-ayeyus

MIDDLE VOICE

	Singular	**Dual**	**Plural**
First Person	wed-ayeya	wed-ayewahi	wed-ayemahi
Second Person	wed-ayethaas	wed-ayeyaathaam	wed-ayedhwam
Third Person	wed-ayeta	wed-ayeyaataam	wed-ayeran

PASSIVE VOICE

	Singular	**Dual**	**Plural**
First Person	wed-yeya	wed-yewahi	wed-yemahi
Second Person	wed-yethaas	wed-yeyaathaam	wed-yedhwam
Third Person	wed-yeta	wed-yeyaataam	wed-yeran

Chapter 5 APPENDIX (Table 5-8): Illustration of Extreme Inflectional Character in a Language: Paradigms for Conjugation of the Sanskrit Verbal Root -wid- in the 2nd, 4th, 6th, 7th and 10th Conjugations

IMPERATIVE MOOD

ACTIVE VOICE

	Singular	Dual	Plural
First Person	wed-ayaani	wed-ayaawa	wed-ayaama
Second Person	wed-aya	wed-ayatam	wed-ayata
Third Person	wed-ayatu	wed-ayataam	wed-ayantu

MIDDLE VOICE

	Singular	Dual	Plural
First Person	wed-ayai	wed-ayaawahai	wed-ayaamahai
Second Person	wed-ayaswa	wed-ayethaam	wed-ayadhwam
Third Person	wed-ayataam	wed-ayetaam	wed-ayantaam

PASSIVE VOICE

	Singular	Dual	Plural
First Person	wed-yai	wed-yaawahai	wed-yaamahai
Second Person	wed-yaswa	wed-yethaam	wed-yadhwam
Third Person	wed-ayataam	wedayetaam	wed-ayantaam

Chapter 5 APPENDIX (Table 5-8): Illustration of Extreme Inflectional Character in a Language: Paradigms for Conjugation of the Sanskrit Verbal Root -wid- in the 2nd, 4th, 6th, 7th and 10th Conjugations

SIMPLE FUTURE TENSE (infix –ish-, "to wish to")

ACTIVE VOICE

	Singular	**Dual**	**Plural**
First Person	wed-ay-ish-yaami	wed-ay-ish-yaawas	wed-ay-ishy-yaamas
Second Person	wed-ay-ish-yasi	wed-ay-ish-yathas	wed-ay-ish-yatha
Third Person	wed-ay-ish-yati	wed-ay-ish-yatas	wed-ay-ish-yanti

MIDDLE VOICE

	Singular	**Dual**	**Plural**
First Person	wed-ay-ishye	wed-ay-ishy-aawahe	wed-ay-ishy-aamahe
Second Person	wed-ay-ishy-ase	wed-ay-ishy-ethe	wed-ay-ishy-adhwe
Third Person	wed-ay-ishy-ate	wed-ay-ishy-ete	wed-ay-ishy-ante

PERIPHRASTIC FUTURE TENSE

ACTIVE VOICE

	Singular	**Dual**	**Plural**
First Person	wed-ay-it-aasmi	wed-ay-it-aaswas	wed-ay-it-aasmas
Second Person	wed-ay-it-aasi	wed-ay-it-aasthas	wed-ay-it-aastha
Third Person	wed-ay-it-aa	wed-ay-it-aarau	wed-ay-it-aaras

Chapter 5 APPENDIX (Table 5-8): *Illustration of Extreme Inflectional Character in a Language: Paradigms for Conjugation of the Sanskrit Verbal Root -wid- in the 2nd, 4th, 6th, 7th and 10th Conjugations*

INTENSIVE FORM
"TO KNOW INTENSIVELY OR SERIOUSLY"

PRESENT TENSE, INDICATIVE MOOD

ACTIVE VOICE

	Singular	Dual	Plural
First Person	we-wed-mi | we-wid-iimi	we-wid-wa	we-wid-ma
Second Person	we-wet-si | we-wid-iisi	we-wit-tha	we-wit-tha
Third Person	we-wet-ti | we-wid-iiti	we-wit-ta	we-wid-ati

MIDDLE VOICE

	Singular	Dual	Plural
First Person	we-wid-ye	we-wid-yaawahe	we-wid-yaamahe
Second Person	we-wid-yase	we-wid-yethe	we-wid-yadhwe
Third Person	we-wid-yate	we-wid-yete	we-wid-yante

Chapter 5 APPENDIX (Table 5-8): Illustration of Extreme Inflectional Character in a Language: Paradigms for Conjugation of the Sanskrit Verbal Root -wid- in the 2nd, 4th, 6th, 7th and 10th Conjugations

IMPERFECT TENSE (augment (-a-)

ACTIVE VOICE

	Singular	Dual	Plural
First Person	a-we-wed-am	a-we-wid-wa	a-we-wid-ma
Second Person	a-we-wet| a-we-idiis	a-we-wit-tam	a-we-wit-ta
Third Person	a-we-wet	a-we-wit-taam	a-we-wedus

MIDDLE VOICE

	Singular	Dual	Plural
First Person	a-we-widye	a-we-wid-yaawahi	a-we-wid-yaamahi
Second Person	a-we-wid-yathaas	a-we-wid-yethaam	a-we-wid-yadlhwam
Third Person	a-we-wid-yata	a-we-wid-yetaam	a-we-wid-yanta

Chapter 5 APPENDIX (Table 5-8): Illustration of Extreme Inflectional Character in a Language: Paradigms for Conjugation of the Sanskrit Verbal Root -wid- in the 2nd, 4th, 6th, 7th and 10th Conjugations

OPTATIVE MOOD

ACTIVE VOICE

	Singular	Dual	Plural
First Person	we-wid-yaam	we-wid-yaawa	we-wid-yaama
Second Person	we-wid-yaas	we-wid-yaatam	we-wid-yaata
Third Person	we-wid-yaat	we-wid-yaataam	we-wid-yus

MIDDLE VOICE

	Singular	Dual	Plural
First Person	we-wid-yeya	we-wid-yewahi	we-wid-yemahi
Second Person	we-wid-yethaas	we-wid-yeyaathaam	we-wid-yedhwam
Third Person	we-wid-yeta	we-wid-yeyaatam	we-wid-yeran

Chapter 5 APPENDIX (Table 5-8): Illustration of Extreme Inflectional Character in a Language: Paradigms for Conjugation of the Sanskrit Verbal Root -wid- in the 2nd, 4th, 6th, 7th and 10th Conjugations

IMPERATIVE MOOD

ACTIVE VOICE

	Singular	Dual	Plural
First Person	we-wed-aani	we-wed-aawa	we-wed-aama
Second Person	we-wid-dhi	we-wit-tam	we-wit-ta
Third Person	we-wed-iitu	we-wit-taam	we-wid-atu

MIDDLE VOICE

	Singular	Dual	Plural
First Person	we-wid-yai	we-wid-yaawahai	we-wid-yaamahai
Second Person	we-wid-yaswa	we-wid-yethaam	we-wid-yadhwam
Third Person	we-wid-yataam	we-wid-yetaam	we-wid-yantaam

Chapter 5 APPENDIX (Table 5-8): Illustration of Extreme Inflectional Character in a Language: Paradigms for Conjugation of the Sanskrit Verbal Root -wid- in the 2nd, 4th, 6th, 7th and 10th Conjugations

DESIDERATIVE FORM
" TO WISH TO KNOW"

PRESENT TENSE, INDICATIVE MOOD

ACTIVE VOICE

	Singular	Dual	Plural
First Person	wi-wid-ishaami| wi-wits-aami	wi-widi-shiaawas |wi-wits-aawas	wi-wid-ishaamas| wi-wits-aamas
Second Person	wi-wid-ishasi| wi-wits-asi	wi-wid-ishathas| wi-wits-athas	wi-wid-ishatha| wi-wits-atha
Third Person	wi-wid-ishati| wi-wits-ati	wi-wid-ishatas| wi-wit-satas	wi-wid-ishanti| wi-wits-anti

IMPERFECT TENSE (augment -a-)

ACTIVE VOICE

	Singular	Dual	Plural
First Person	a-wiwidisham| a-wiwitsam	a-wi-widishaawa| a- wiwitsaawa	a-wi-wid-ishaama| a-wi-wits-aama
Second Person	a-wiwidishas| a-wiwitsas	a-wi-widishatam| awi-witsatam	a-wi-wid-ishata| a-wi-wits-ata
Third Person	a-wiwidishat| a-wiwitsat	a-wi-widishataam| a-wi-witsamtaam	a-wi-wi-dishan| a-wi-wits-an

Chapter 5 APPENDIX (Table 5-8): Illustration of Extreme Inflectional Character in a Language: Paradigms for Conjugation of the Sanskrit Verbal Root -wid- in the 2nd, 4th, 6th, 7th and 10th Conjugations

OPTATIVE MOOD

ACTIVE VOICE

	Singular	Dual	Plural
First Person	wi-wid-isheyam| wi-wits-eyam	wi-wid-ishewa| wi-wits-ewa	wi-wid-ishema| wi-wits-ema
Second Person	wi-wid-ishes| wi-wits-ses	wi-wid-ishetam| wi-wits-etam	wi-wid-isheta| wi-wits-eta
Third Person	wi-wid-ishet| wi-wits-et	wi-wid-ishetaam| wi-wi-wits-etaam	we-wid-isheyus| wi-wits-eyus

IMPERATIVE MOOD

ACTIVE VOICE

	Singular	Dual	Plural
First Person	wi-wid-ishani| wi-wits-aani	wi-wid-ishaawa| wi-wits-saawa	wi-wid-ishaama| wi-wits-saama
Second Person	wi-wid-isha| wi-wits-a	wi-wid-ishatam| wi-wits-atam	wi-wid-ish-ata| wi-wits-ata
Third Person	wi-wid-ishatu| wi-wits-atu	wi-wid-ishataam| wi-wits-ataam	wi-wid-ish-antu| wi-wits-antu

PERFECT TENSE (reduplicated)

ACTIVE VOICE

	Singular	Dual	Plural
First Person	wi-wi-wid-isha| wi-wi-wits-a	wi-wid-ishiwa| wi-wits-iwa	wi-wi-wid-ishima| wi-wi-wits-ima
Second Person	wi-wi-wid-ishitha| wi-wi-wits-itha	wi-wi-wid-ishathus| wi-wi-wits-athus	wi-wi-wid-isha| wi-wi-wits-a
Third Person	wi-wi-wid-isha| wi-wi-wits-a	wi-wi-wid-ishatus| wi-wi-wits-atus	wu-wi-wid-ishus| wi-wi-wit-sus

Chapter 5 APPENDIX (Table 5-8): Illustration of Extreme Inflectional Character in a Language: Paradigms for Conjugation of the Sanskrit Verbal Root -wid- in the 2nd, 4th, 6th, 7th and 10th Conjugations

5.A.3 CONJUGATION OF *WID (VID)*, IN 4TH CONJUGATION, MEANING "TO BE, TO EXIST, TO DISCOVER OR UNDERSTAND ONESELF"

PRESENT TENSE, INDICATIVE MOOD

MIDDLE VOICE

	Singular	Dual	Plural
First Person	wid-ye	wid-yaavahe	wid-yaamahe
Second Person	wid-yase	wid-yethe	wit-yadhwe
Third Person	wid-yate	wid-yete	wid-yante

IMPERFECT TENSE (augment (-a-)

MIDDLE VOICE

	Singular	Dual	Plural
First Person	*a-wid-ye*	*a-wid-yaawahi*	*a-wid-yaamahi*
Second Person	*a-wid-yathaas*	*a-wid-yethaam*	*a-wid-yadhwam*
Third Person	*a-wid-yata*	*a-wid-yetaam*	*a-wid-yanta*

OPTATIVE MOOD

MIDDLE VOICE

	Singular	Dual	Plural
First Person	wid-yeya	wid-yewahi	wid-yemahi
Second Person	wid-yethaas	wid-yeyaathaam	wid-yedhwam
Third Person	vid-yeta	vid-yeyaataam	vid-yeran

Chapter 5 APPENDIX (Table 5-8): Illustration of Extreme Inflectional Character in a Language: Paradigms for Conjugation of the Sanskrit Verbal Root -wid- in the 2nd, 4th, 6th, 7th and 10th Conjugations

IMPERATIVE MOOD

MIDDLE VOICE

	Singular	Dual	Plural
First Person	wid-yai	wid-yaawahai	wud-yaamahai
Second Person	wid-yaswa	wid-yethaam	wid-yadhwam
Third Person	wid-yataam	wid-yetaam	wid-yantaam

SIMPLE FUTURE TENSE

MIDDLE VOICE

	Singular	Dual	Plural
First Person	wet-s-ye	wet-s-yaawahe	vet-s-yaamahe
Second Person	wet-s-yase	wet-s-yethe	wet-s-yadhve
Third Person	wet-s-yate	wet-s-yete	wet-s-yante

PERFECT TENSE (reduplicated)

MIDDLE VOICE

	Singular	Dual	Plural
First Person	wi-wid-e	wi-wid-iwahe	wi-wid-imahe
Second Person	wi-wid-ishe	wi-wid-aathe	wi-wid-idhwe
Third Person	wi-wid-e	wi-wid-aate	wi-wid-ire

Chapter 5 APPENDIX (Table 5-8): Illustration of Extreme Inflectional Character in a Language: Paradigms for Conjugation of the Sanskrit Verbal Root -wid- in the 2nd, 4th, 6th, 7th and 10th Conjugations

5.A.4 CONJUGATION OF *wid (vid)*, IN 6TH CONJUGATION, MEANING "TO FIND, TO COME TO KNOW, TO RECOGNIZE, TO COME TO DISCOVER" (COGNATE WITH ENGLISH *find*, GERMAN *finden*)

PRESENT TENSE, INDICATIVE MOOD

ACTIVE VOICE

	Singular	Dual	Plural
First Person	wind-aami	wind-aavas	wind-aamas
Second Person	wind-asi	wind-athas	wind-atha
Third Person	wind-ati	wind-atas	wind-anti

MIDDLE VOICE

	Singular	**Dual**	Plural
First Person	wind-e	wind-aavahe	wind-aamahe
Second Person	wind-ase	wind-ethe	wind-adhve
Third Person	wind-ate	wind-ete	wind-ante

PASSIVE VOICE

	Singular	**Dual**	Plural
First Person	wid-ye	wid-yaavahe	wid-yaamahe
Second Person	wid-yase	wid-yethe	wid-yadhve
Third Person	wid-yate	wid-yete	wid-yante

Chapter 5 APPENDIX (Table 5-8): Illustration of Extreme Inflectional Character in a Language: Paradigms for Conjugation of the Sanskrit Verbal Root -wid- in the 2nd, 4th, 6th, 7th and 10th Conjugations

IMPERFECT TENSE (augment –a-)

ACTIVE VOICE

	Singular	Dual	Plural
First Person	a-wind-am	a-wind-aawa	a-wind-aama
Second Person	a-wind-as	a-wind-atam	a-wind-ata
Third Person	a-wind-at	a-wind-ataam	a-wind-an

MIDDLE VOICE

	Singular	Dual	Plural
First Person	a-wind-e	a-wind-aavahi	a-vind-aamahi
Second Person	a-wind-athaas	a-wind-ethaam	a-wind-adhwam
Third Person	a-wind-ata	a-wind-etaam	a-wind-anta

PASSIVE VOICE

	Singular	Dual	Plural
First Person	a-wid-ye	a-wid-yaawahi	a-wid-yaamahi
Second Person	a-wid-yathaas	a-wid-yethaam	a-wid-yadhwam
Third Person	a-wid-yata	a-wid-yetaam	a-wid-yanta

Chapter 5 APPENDIX (Table 5-8): Illustration of Extreme Inflectional Character in a Language: Paradigms for Conjugation of the Sanskrit Verbal Root -wid- in the 2nd, 4th, 6th, 7th and 10th Conjugations

OPTATIVE MOOD

ACTIVE VOICE

	Singular	**Dual**	**Plural**
First Person	wind-eyam	wind-eva	wind-ema
Second Person	wind-es	wind-etam	wind-eta
Third Person	wind-et	wind-etaam	wind-eyus

MIDDLE VOICE

	Singular	**Dual**	**Plural**
First Person	wind-eya	wind-evahi	wind-emahi
Second Person	wind-ethaas	wind-eyaathaam	wind-edhwam
Third Person	wind-eta	wind-eyaataam	wind-eran

PASSIVE VOICE

	Singular	**Dual**	**Plural**
First Person	wid-yeya	wid-yewahi	wid-yemahi
Second Person	wid-yethaas	wid-yeyaathaam	wid-yedhwam
Third Person	wid-yeta	wid-yeyaataam	wid-yeran

Chapter 5 APPENDIX (Table 5-8): Illustration of Extreme Inflectional Character in a Language: Paradigms for Conjugation of the Sanskrit Verbal Root -wid- in the 2nd, 4th, 6th, 7th and 10th Conjugations

IMPERATIVE MOOD

ACTIVE VOICE

	Singular	Dual	Plural
First Person	wind-aani	wind-aawa	wind-aama
Second Person	wind-a	wind-atam	wind-ata
Third Person	wind-atu	wind-ataam	wind-antu

MIDDLE VOICE

	Singular	Dual	Plural
First Person	wind-ai	wind-aawahai	wind-aamahai
Second Person	wind-aswa	wind-ethaam	wind-adhwam
Third Person	wind-ataam	wind-etaam	wind-antaam

PASSIVE VOICE

	Singular	Dual	Plural
First Person	wid-yai	wid-yaawahai	wid-yaamahai
Second Person	wid-yaswa	wid-yethaam	wid-yadhwam
Third Person	wid-yataam	wid-yetaam	wid-yantaam

SIMPLE FUTURE TENSE

ACTIVE VOICE

	Singular	Dual	Plural
First Person	wet-s-yaami	wet-s-yaavas	wet-s-yaamas
Second Person	wet-s-yasi	wet-s-yathas	wet-s-yatha
Third Person	wet-s-yati	wet-s-yatas	wet-s-yanti

MIDDLE VOICE

	Singular	Dual	Plural
First Person	wet-s-ye	wet-s-yaawahe	wet-s-yaamahe
Second Person	wet-s-yase	wet-s-yethe	wet-s-yadhwe
Third Person	wet-s-yate	wet-syete	wet-s-yante

Chapter 5 APPENDIX (Table 5-8): Illustration of Extreme Inflectional Character in a Language: Paradigms for Conjugation of the Sanskrit Verbal Root -wid- in the 2nd, 4th, 6th, 7th and 10th Conjugations

PERIPHRASTIC FUTURE TENSE

ACTIVE VOICE

	Singular	Dual	Plural
First Person	wett-aasmi	wett-aasvas	wett-aasmas
Second Person	wett-aasi	wett-aasthas	wett-aastha
Third Person	wett-aa	wett-aarau	wett-aaras

PERFECT TENSE (reduplicated)

ACTIVE VOICE

	Singular	Dual	Plural
First Person	wi-wed-a	wi-wid-iva	wi-wid-ima
Second Person	wi-wed-itha	wi-wid-athus	wi-wid-a
Third Person	wi-wed-a	we-wi-datus	wi-wid-us

MIDDLE VOICE

	Singular	Dual	Plural
First Person	*wi-wid-e*	wi-wid-iwahe	wi-wid-imahe
Second Person	wi-wid-ishe	wi-wid-aathe	wi-wid-idhwe
Third Person	wi-wid-e	wi-wid-aate	wi-wid-ire

AORIST TENSE (augment -a-)

ACTIVE VOICE

	Singular	Dual	Plural
First Person	*a-wid-am*	*a-wid-aawa*	*a-wid-aama*
Second Person	*a-wid-as*	*a-wid-atam*	*a-wid-ata*
Third Person	*a-wid-at*	*a-wid-ataam*	*a-wid-an*

Chapter 5 APPENDIX (Table 5-8): Illustration of Extreme Inflectional Character in a Language: Paradigms for Conjugation of the Sanskrit Verbal Root -wid- in the 2nd, 4th, 6th, 7th and 10th Conjugations

5.A.5. CONJUGATION OF *wid*, IN 7TH CONJUGATION, MEANING "TO UNDERSTAND"

PRESENT TENSE, INDICATIVE MOOD

MIDDLE VOICE

	Singular	Dual	Plural
First Person	wind-e	wind-wahe	wind-mahe
Second Person	wint-se	wind-aathe	wind-dhwe
Third Person	wint-te	wind-aate	wind-ate

IMPERFECT TENSE

MIDDLE VOICE

	Singular	Dual	Plural
First Person	a-wind-i	a-wind-wahi	a-wind-mahi
Second Person	a-wint-thaas	a-wind-aathaam	a-wind-dhwam
Third Person	a-wint-ta	a-wind-aataam	a-wind-ata

OPTATIVE MOOD

MIDDLE VOICE

	Singular	Dual	Plural
First Person	wind-iiya	wind-iiwahi	wind-iimahi
Second Person	wind-iithaas	wind-iiyaathaam	wind-iidhwam
Third Person	wind-iita	wind-iiyaataam	wind-iiran

Chapter 5 APPENDIX (Table 5-8): Illustration of Extreme Inflectional Character in a Language: Paradigms for Conjugation of the Sanskrit Verbal Root -wid- in the 2nd, 4th, 6th, 7th and 10th Conjugations

IMPERATIVE MOOD

MIDDLE VOICE

	Singular	Dual	Plural
First Person	winad-ai	winad-aawahai	winad-aamahai
Second Person	wint-sva	wind-aathaam	wind-dhwam
Third Person	wint-taam	wind-aataam	wind-a-taam

SIMPLE FUTURE TENSE

MIDDLE VOICE

	Singular	Dual	Plural
First Person	wet-sye	wet-syaawahe	wet-syaamahe
Second Person	wet-syase	wet-syethe	wet-syadhwe
Third Person	wet-syate	wet-syete	wet-syamte

PERFECT TENSE

MIDDLE VOICE

	Singular	Dual	Plural
First Person	wi-wid-e	wi-wid-iwahe	wi-wid-imahe
Second Person	wi-wid-ishe	wi-wid-aathe	wi-wid-idhwe
Third Person	wi-wid-e	wi-wid-aate	wi-wid-ire

Chapter 5 APPENDIX (Table 5-8): Illustration of Extreme Inflectional Character in a Language: Paradigms for Conjugation of the Sanskrit Verbal Root -wid- in the 2nd, 4th, 6th, 7th and 10th Conjugations

5.A.6 CONJUGATION OF *wid*, IN 10TH CONJUGATION, MEANING " TO TELL, TO COMMUNICATE, TO FEEL"

PRESENT TENSE, INDICATIVE MOOD

MIDDLE VOICE

	Singular	Dual	Plural
First Person	wed-ay-e	wed-ay-aawahe	wed-ay-aamahe
Second Person	wed-ay-ase	wed-ay-ethe	wed-ay-adhve
Third Person	wed-ay-ate	wed-ay-ete	wed-ay-ante

IMPERFECT TENSE (augment - a-)

MIDDLE VOICE

	Singular	Dual	Plural
First Person	a-wed-aye	a-wed-ayaawahi	a-wed-ay-aamahi
Second Person	a-wed-ayathaas	a-wed-ayethaam	a-wed-ay-adhwam
Third Person	a-wed-ayata	a-wed-ay-etaam	a-wed-ay-anta

OPTATIVE MOOD

MIDDLE VOICE

	Singular	Dual	Plural
First Person	wed-ay-eya	wed-ay-ewahi	wed-ay-emahi
Second Person	wed-ay-ethaas	wed-ay-eyaathaam	wed-ay-edhwam
Third Person	wed-ay-eta	wed-ay-aataam	wed-ay-eran

Chapter 5 APPENDIX (Table 5-8): Illustration of Extreme Inflectional Character in a Language: Paradigms for Conjugation of the Sanskrit Verbal Root -wid- in the 2nd, 4th, 6th, 7th and 10th Conjugations

IMPERATIVE MOOD

MIDDLE VOICE

	Singular	Dual	Plural
First Person	wed-ay-ai	wed-ay-awahai	wed-ay-aamahai
Second Person	wed-ay-aswa	wed-ay-ethaam	wed-ay-adhwam
Third Person	wed-ay-ataam	wed-ay-etaam	wed-ay-antaam

SIMPLE FUTURE TENSE (infix -ish-, -is-, "to wish to")

MIDDLE VOICE

	Singular	Dual	Plural
First Person	wed-ay-ishye	wed-ay-ish-yaawahe	wed-ayish-yaamahe
Second Person	wed-ay-ishyase	wed-ayishyethe	wed-ay-ishyadhwe
Third Person	wed-ay-ishyate	wed-ayishyete	wed-ay-ishyante

PERFECT TENSE

MIDDLE VOICE

	Singular	Dual	Plural
First Person	wi-wed-e	wi-wed-iwahe	wi-wed-imahe
Second Person	wi-wed-ishe	wi-wed-aathe	wi-wed-idhwe
Third Person	wi-wed-e	wi-wed-aate	wi-wed-ire

Chapter 5 APPENDIX (Table 5-8): Illustration of Extreme Inflectional Character in a Language: Paradigms for Conjugation of the Sanskrit Verbal Root -wid- in the 2nd, 4th, 6th, 7th and 10th Conjugations

GLOSSARY

OF PHONOLOGICAL, LINGUISTIC AND RELATED TERMS

<u>N.B.</u>: *The definitions herein are abbreviated. For a fuller definition, see the sections in the main text of the book. It is also noted that these definitions do <u>not</u> include grammatical terms, terms relating to the form of language, and any other terms not having a direct phonological connotation.*

**THE FOLLOWING WORDS (a total of 104) ARE DEFINED IN THIS GLOSSARY.
(THE DEFINITIONS FOLLOW THIS LIST OF WORDS.)**

abjad
abugida
affricate
allophone
alveolar
angramaya
apico- (examples apico-alveolar)
approximant
artition
aspirate, aspirated, aspiration
avaigyaanic
bilabial
central
click (egressive, ingressive)
close
close-mid

GLOSSARY

closure
completeness
dental
determinatives
de-voiced
digraph
egressive
ejective
empiricity
epiglottal
featural
flap
forward-fricative
fricative
galatophone
geminate
glottal
glyph
guttural
ictus
ideographic
idiosyncrasy, phonemic, see *phonemic idiosyncrasy*
implosive
infralabio-supradental
ingressive
lateral
liaison
logographic
logophonetic
logosyllabic
maatraic
medio- (example medio-palatal)
medio-palatal
morpheme
morphographic
multigraph
nasal
nonvowel

open
open-mid
orthography
palatal
pharyngeal
phone
phoneme
phonemic condensate
phonemic idiosyncrasy
phonemo-idiosyncratic
phonochromaticity
phonographic
phono-indicative
pictographic
plosive
post-op
pre-op
quasi-phonetic (vs. phonetic)
Rebus (principle)
retroflex
rhoticity
sandhi
semivowel
shibilant
sibilant
sonant
spirant
stop
supralabio-infradental
surd
syllabary
syllabic
tap
tone
toneme
trill
unaspirated
uniphonemographic

GLOSSARY

uniphonographic
unvoiced
uvular
vaigyaanic
velar
voiced
voiceless
vowel
vowel, cardinal
vowel, derivative
vowel, fundamental
vowel, primary

DEFINITIONS OF THE WORDS IN THE ABOVE LIST START HERE:

abjad: A script wherein each glyph represents a single non-vowel. Vowels are either "filled in" by the reader or indicated by diacritics or other markers. Modern Arabic and Hebrew scripts are *abjad's*.

abugida: A script wherein non-vowels and vowels are represented by single glyphs. The addition of a vowel to a non-vowel is further indicated by *maatra's*, i.e. markers or indicators of some sort. All Indian-type or Indian-base scripts, starting from Braahmi, including modern South-East Asian scripts. are *abugida's*. There are some newly invented abugida's as well.

affricate: A combination phone that is composed of a stop followed by a fricative of the same artition. Example: *[t]* (phone) + *[s]* (fricative = *[ts]* (affricate).

allophone: A phone that is one of the two or more phones belonging to a single phoneme. Usually denoted by square brackets (as opposed to slashes, //, for phonemes). Examples: [p] and [ph] are allophones of the English phoneme /p/; [v] and [w] are allophones of the Hindi phoneme /vw/.

alveolar: Relating to the alveolar ridge, the ridge between the upper teeth and the palate in the roof of the mouth. Usually denoting the articulation position (artition) corresponding to this, when the apex of the tongue makes contact with the alveolar ridge.

angramaya: Having a language structure like English, i.e. base language from one language family or sub-family , higher vocabulary from other language families of sub-families. Examples: English, with base language Germanic (sub-family of the Indo-European family), higher vocabulary Romance (Italic) and Greek; Hindi, with base language Indo-European, higher vocabulary from Sanskrit (Indo-European) as well as Arabic (Afro-Asiatic), Faarsi (Indo-European), Turkish (Altaic), etc; Indonesian and Thaai, with base language Austronesian (Indonesian) and Daic (Thaai), higher vocabulary Indo-European (Sanskrit). [From Sanskrit, "English-like".]

apico- Relating to the apex of the tongue, as in *apico-alveolar*, denoting the artition corresponding to the apex of the tongue contacting the alveolar ridge.

approximant: The IPA term used to denote a semi-vowel.

artition: Short for *articulation position*.

aspirate, aspirated, aspiration: Additional expression of the breath, during articulation of a phone.

avaigyaanic: Not *vaigyaanic* (see *vaigyaanic*)

bilabial: Of both lips. As in the articulation of [p].

central: "r"-sound. The breath is expelled or taken in along the *central* portion of the

GLOSSARY

tongue. This can be visualized by holding the tongue in the "r"-articulation position and breathing out and in heavily. The central portion of the tongue will cool with the breath.
click (egressive, ingressive)
close: Jaw closed. Usually referring to articulation of vowels.
close-mid: Jaw partially closed. Usually referring to articulation of vowels.
closure: Closing of the points of articulation. For example, prior to articulation of [p], *closure* of the lips occurs.
completeness: A characteristic of a script representing how completely it is able to address all phones found in all of the world's languages.
de-voiced: See *unvoiced*.
dental: Of the teeth. Usually relating to articulating position. Further bifurcated into *supradental* (upper teeth) and *infradental* (lower teeth). The [t] is a (supra)dental artition.
determinatives: See under *Rebus principle*.
digraph: Having two letters, as in *gh*.
egressive: Relating to expulsion of the breath.
ejective: Articulation of a phone through egress of the breath but with the vocal chords firmly closed as in a glottal stop. Crudely put, "talking with the throat closed". Opposite, in a sense, of an *implosive*, where the breath is taken in rather than let out. Can include fricatives such as [s] and [f] as well. Present and phonemically distinguished in languages such as Georgian and Zulu.
empiricity: Whether there is an ad-hoc, "adapt-as-you-go" nature to way the script represents a language, and whether there are certain empirical rules that must be learned along the way.
epiglottal: See *glottal*.
featural: A characteristic of a script wherein each glyph has markers or indicators indicating the properties of the phone, such as voicing, phonochromaticity and artition. Haangul (Korean) is the prototypical example of a *featural* script.
flap: Light and quick or ("flapping", "tapping"), rather than full closure, of the articulation position. A typical flap is the common "r-sound" of Spanish or Hindi when it is not trilled. Usually synonymous with *tap*.
forward-fricative: The fricative at one articulation position in front of a phone, called the *parent* phone of the forward-fricative. Thus, the forward-fricative of [t] is [s], of [p] is [f], of [k] is [sh]. Usually retains the voicing characteristics of the parent. Thus, the forward-fricative of [p] is [f], but of [b] is [v]; similarly the forward fricative of [k] is [sh], but of [g] is [zh].
fricative: A phone characterized by a partial impediment of the breath and usually by a hissing or frictional sound, as in the phones [s], [sh], [f], [v], etc.
galatophone: A phone that does not exist or is seldom used in a particular language but

which is invariably mistaken for another, usually closely related phone that exists in the language. Thus, e.g., [p] does not exist or is rarely used in most dialects of Arabic. When it is articulated, it is invariably articulated as [b]. Thus, [p] is a galatophone of [b] in Arabic. Similarly, [r] is a galatophone of [l] in Japanese. Each galatophone must always be associated with a parent phone. We then say that the galatophone *"is a galatophone for the parent phone"*. Thus, e.g., in Arabic, "[p] is a galatophone for the parent phone [b]", and in Japanese, "[l] is a galatophone for the parent phone [r]", etc. Galatophones almost always have the same phonemic value as the parent phone. Thus, when an Arabic speaker mistakenly substitutes [p] for [b] in a word, it will not change the meaning of the word, although some Arabic speakers may in fact occasionally pronounce [b] as [p]. Similarly, when a Japanese speaker substitutes [l] for [r] in a word, it will not change the meaning of the word. In a sense, galatophones are *"nonexistent allophones"*. [From Hindi *galti* ("error", of Arabic origin) + *phone*]

geminate: A twin or double phone, almost always non-vowel, usually expressed by a dual letter. Phonemically distinguished in many languages from the corresponding single phone. Thus, e.g., Hindi *pakaa* ("cooked, ripe") vs. *pakkaa* ("sure, certain, permanent, firm, pucca"), where the [kk] is a geminate.

glottal: Of the glottis. Usually relating to articulation position obtained by closure of the glottis, as in the *glottal stop*.

glyph: A character, letter or symbol of a script.

guttural: See *velar*.

IPA: International Phonetic Association. Also used to refer to the alphabet of the association, as in "the letter *a* of the IPA".

ictus: In phonology, relating to stress, "accent", usually used to distinguish a stress accent from a tonal or musical accent.

ideographic: A characteristic of a script wherein each glyph in the script represents a word, an object or an idea. Roughly synonymous with *pictographic*.

idiosyncrasy, phonemic, see *phonemic idiosyncrasy*

implosive: Articulation of a phone through ingress of the breath but with the vocal chords firmly closed as in a glottal stop. Crudely put, "talking with the throat closed". Opposite, in a sense, of an *ejective,* where the breath is let out rather than taken in. Can include fricatives such as [s] and [f] as well. Present and phonemically distinguished in languages such as Georgian and Zulu.

infralabio-supradental: An artition corresponding to contact of the lower lip with the upper teeth, as in [f].

ingressive: Involving intake of the breath.

lateral: "l"-sound. The breath is expelled or taken in along the *lateral* (side) portion of the tongue, usually along the left or right side but not both. This can be visualized by

GLOSSARY

holding the tongue in the "r"-articulation position and breathing out and in heavily. The lateral portion of the tongue will cool with the breath.

liaison: In French, pertaining to euphonic combination of adjacent phones (Sandhi), usually through introduction of additional phones. As in *y + a + il? ---> ya't-il?* ("Is there?).

logographic: A characteristic of a script wherein each glyph represents one word (Cl. Greek *logos*, "word").

logophonetic: A characteristic of a script wherein it is partially *logographic* and partially phonetic.

logosyllabic: A characteristic of a script wherein it is partially *logographic* and partially syllabic.

medio- Relating to the medial portion of the tongue, as in *medio-alveolar*, which denotes the artition corresponding to the middle of the tongue contacting the alveolo-dental position, as in the fricative [s]. This is distinguished from the *apico-dental* fricative [th] (of English *think*).

maatraic: A characteristic of a script of the Indian type, i.e., one that uses *maatraa's* (markers or indicators) for vowels and ligature (close joining together) of adjacent phones, where applicable. All Indian and South-East Asian scripts (except the ancient Nomic Vietnamese and the modern Roman-based ones such as modern Vietnamese and Indonesian/Malay) are *maatraic* scripts.

medio-palatal: Artition having medial portion of tongue contacting the palate. As in the German *ich*, French *agneau*. Distinguished from the *apico-palatal* (also called just *palatal*), as in *Jack*.

morpheme: The Webster's dictionary defines this as "any word or part of a word, as an affix or combining form, that conveys meaning, cannot be further divided into smaller elements conveying meaning, and usually occurs in various contexts with relatively stable meaning." Morphemes can be *free* or *bound*, and example of the latter being the *-ness* in English *happiness*.

morphographic: A characteristic of a script wherein each glyph represents one morpheme.

multigraph: Multiple letters used to represent a phone, as in *ggh*. Rare. Cf. *digraph* (but not *monograph*!)

nasal: In phonology, pertaining to passage (usually egress) of the breath through the nasal passage.

nonvowel: Any phone in which the breath is impeded partially or completely. Thus [p], [w], and [w] are all nonvowels.

open: Jaw open. Usually referring to articulation of vowels.

open-mid: Jaw partially open. Usually referring to articulation of vowels.

GLOSSARY

351

orthography: System of writing or transcription, particularly relating to expression of language.
palatal: Of the palate, usually denoting the artition.
pharyngeal: Of the pharynx. Can denote the artition, but also the mechanism of breath egress or ingress, i.e. related to pharynx air.
phone: Any sound. [From Greek noun ˙⸴≜◁▢, (*phone*), "sound, voice", Sanskrit verb *bhan*, "to speak, to sound".]
phoneme: A phone or set of phones with linguistic value. A phone or set of phones, the replacement of which will change the meaning of a word. Specific to individual languages. In modern Western linguistic practice, denoted by slashes, //. Thus, the phones [r] and [l] of English *root* and *loot* are different phonemes, denoted /r/ and /l/, because substitution of one by the other changes the meaning of a word (from *root* to *loot*). Similarly, the phones [p] and [ph] are different phonemes, /p/ and /ph/, in Hindi, because substitution of one by the other changes the meaning of a word, as in *pal* ("a moment, an instant") vs. *phal* ("fruit"), whereas they are not different phonemes, but rather allophones of the same phoneme, /p/, in English, since articulation of English *put* with or without aspiration does not change the meaning of the word.
phonemic condensate: The result of a combination of different phones to produce a single phoneme. For example, the aspirated and unaspirated stops (plosives) can be combined to yield a single, *aspirated/unaspirated phonemic condensate*, applicable, e.g., in English and Tamil, which do not phonemically distinguish unaspirated from aspirated phones. A sort of opposite to an *allophone,* in the sense that an allophone is a result of breaking up of a phoneme into its phones, whereas a phonemic condensate is the result of combining phones to represent a phoneme in a particular language. Like the phoneme, it is very language-specific. Thus, [p] and [b] can be condensed in many Chinese languages into a single phonemic condensate, but they of course cannot in any Indo-European language. In *Navlipi*, represented sometimes by a *post-op*, and sometimes by digraphs or multigraphs.
phonemic idiosyncrasy: For a definition that does justice, see **PREFACE** and an earlier chapter. **phonemo-idiosyncratic:** A characteristic of a script wherein it addresses phonemic idiosyncrasies found across the world's languages.
phonochromaticity: "Color of the phone", encompassing such phone properties as voicing, aspiration, nasalization, fricatization, clicking, taps, trilling, implosive/ejective articulation, etc.
phonographic: A characteristic of a script wherein it is based on "*phonographs*", i.e. a script in which each *glyph* ("letter", "symbol") represents a *separate phone,* and one strives to assign to each *phone* a separate *glyph.*
phono-indicative: A characteristic of a script wherein each glyph indicates the

GLOSSARY

characteristics or properties of the phone. An example is Haangul.
pictographic: See *ideographic*.
plosive: Phone, prior to the articulation of which full closure of some part of the articulation apparatus is achieved, followed by an explosion of the breath when the phone is articulated. Thus, [p] (closure of the lips), [t] (closure at the apico-alveolar artition), and [k] (closure at the velum) are plosives.
post-op: Post-positional operator, placed *after* the phone on which it operates. As in the *Navlipi* phone *{kh$_o$}* in which *h$_o$* is the post-op for aspiration, operating on the phone [k]. An "opposite" or *pre-op*.
pre-op: Pre-positional operator, placed *before* the phone on which it operates. An "opposite" or *post-op*. *Navlipi* does not use pre-ops.
quasi-phonetic (vs. phonetic): Whether the script has a truly phonetic (i.e., phonological) nature or only a partial (i.e., *quasi-phonetic*) one. There are degrees of quasi-phoneticity, with some scripts as used for certain languages being more or less phonetic than others.
Rebus (principle): A principle of orthography best illustrated by examples: Thus, to write English *treat* we could use a symbol we've come up with for *tree*, say a picture of a tree, and add a mnemonic dot at the end to indicate the final *t* of *treat*. Or to write *God*, we could use some symbol we've already come up with for *got*, with perhaps a little halo marker for the deity. This principle was developed universally in *all* orthographies that were originally ideographic. The little distinguishing markers, such as the halo to turn *got* into *God*, are called *determinatives*.
retroflex: Artition position with the apex of the tongue curled back and touching the palate, as in many Indian plosives.
rhoticity: Term used by the IPA to denote vocalic central phones ("r"-sounds which are vowels).
Sandhi: Term borrowed from Sanskrit grammarians denoting the *euphonic* ("good sounding", *su-bhan*) joining together of two adjacent phones, usually accompanied by a phonological reduction or change of some sort. Denoted sometimes by other terms, e.g. *liaison* in French (as in *a + il = a t'il*, done for euphony). This melding together of adjacent phones occurs naturally in most languages. Thus, in English, we have the following examples of Sandhi: *want + to = wanna; give (let) + me = gimme (lemme); got (did) + you = gotcha (didja),* etc. etc.. Sanskrit Sandhi originated in similar, natural, common usage but then degenerated into rigid grammatical rules that *had* to be followed *every time, without fail*; this would be the equivalent of being told, in English, that *got + you* could *never* be pronounced as *got you*, but *always* had to be changed into *gotcha!* A few Sanskrit Sandhi rules are given elsewhere in this book. [(Sanskrit "union").]
semivowel: A nonvowel derived directly from a vowel, usually by addition of a

fundamental vowel ([a], [i], [u]). Semivowels are never plosives. Examples: [w], [j], from parent vowels [u], [I].

shibilant: A term similar to *sibilant*, denoting a fricative of the [sh], i.e. palatal, variety, e.g. [sh] and [zh]. A subset of sibilants.

sibilant: A fricative with an *"s-sound"*, e.g. [s], [z]. Also includes shibilants.

sonant: See *voiced*.

spirant: See *fricative*.

stop: See *plosive*.

supralabio-infradental: An artition corresponding to contact of the upper lip with the lower teeth.

surd: See *unvoiced*.

syllabary: A script in which one glyph represents one syllable.

syllabic: A *syllabic* script is a *syllabary*, i.e. one in which one glyph represents one syllable.

tap: Nearly synonymous with *flap*, q.v..

tone: The pitch or musical accent or musical value for a phone. Relevant not only to tone languages such as Mandarin or Yoruba, but also "semi-tonal" languages such as Vedic Sanskrit and the oldest Greek and Latin, where the "acute, grave, circumflex" accents were originally musical. One may have high, mid and low tones, but also combinations. One may have rising, following and steady tones.

toneme: A tone with a linguistic value. The tone::toneme relation is analogous to the phone::phoneme relation. (See *phoneme*.) As an example, one may have a high/steady and a high/falling tone in a language, two obviously distinct tones, but they may have the same linguistic value, and thus belong to the same toneme.

trill: Repeated phone, usually but not always relating to a flap. E.g., [rrr] is the trilled version of the flap-[r]. The term trill may also apply to phones other than flaps: For example, the lateral, "giddyap" click, denoted {lʒ} in *Navlipi*, can be trilled, producing a continuous sound.

unaspirated: Without additional breath, usually in reference to articulation of phones.

uniphonemographic: A characteristic of a script wherein one glyph represents one and only one phoneme in the language that the script addresses, and vice versa.

uniphonographic: A characteristic of a script wherein one glyph represents one and only one phone, and vice versa.

unvoiced: Vocal chords do not vibrate, e.g. in [p]. Can be easily visualized by holding two fingers lightly on the vocal chords (Adam's apple in males) and articulating [p] (unvoiced) then [b] (voiced). **uvular:** Artition relating to the uvula.

vaigyaanic: A characteristic of a script wherein it possesses a scientific and systematic phonological organization and presentation in full force.

GLOSSARY

velar: Artition relating to the velum, e.g. in the phones [k], [g]. Also called *guttural*.
voiced: Vocal chords vibrate, e.g. in [b]. Can be easily visualized by holding two fingers lightly on the vocal chords (Adam's apple in males) and articulating [p] (unvoiced) then [b] (voiced). One will feel the vocal chords vibrate.
voiceless: See *unvoiced*.
vowel: A phone for which there is no impediment to the breath during utterance.
vowel, derivative: Any vowel derived from the fundamental vowels such as [a], [i], [u], [vocalic-alveolar-r], [vocalic-alveolar-l].
vowel, cardinal: One of the eight or so vowels designated by Western phonological practice, and also by the IPA, as of fundamental nature, and used to anchor "vowel diagrams".
vowel, fundamental: A vowel having an anchoring *formant frequency* and from which all other non-fundamental vowels can be derived. Some examples are [a], [i], [u], [vocalic-alveolar-r], [vocalic-alveolar-l].
vowel, primary: See *vowel, fundamental*.

LITERATURE CITED

INCLUDING 624 REFERENCES, CITED IN ORDER OF THEIR APPEARANCE IN THE TEXT, BUT WITH ADDITIONAL GROUPING AND SUB-GROUPING TO FACILITATE EASY REFERENCE

THE BIBLIOGRAPHY LISTED HEREIN COMPRISES OVER 600 REFERENCES. A VAST MAJORITY OF THESE ARE IN ENGLISH, BUT THERE ARE A FEW CITATIONS IN OTHER EUROPEAN LANGUAGES, AND THERE ARE OF COURSE CITATIONS TO CLASSICAL WORKS IN THE FIELD IN THEIR ORIGINAL LANGUAGES, E.G. CLASSICAL GREEK AND SANSKRIT.

IT IS ALSO TO BE NOTED THAT THIS BIBLIOGRAPHY ENCOMPASSES *ALL THREE* VOLUMES OF THE *NAVLIPI* SERIES. THUS, IT MAY APPEAR TO THE READER TO HAVE REFERENCES NOT CITED IN ONE OR THE OTHER OF THE VOLUMES THAT HE/SHE IS READING- THIS MUST BE BORNE IN MIND.

EDITORIAL NOTE ON METHOD OF LITERATURE CITATION USED

It may be noted that the literature citations in this book are referenced in a somewhat unique, even quixotic, way, specifically adapted to this work. (Needless to say, this is

LITERATURE CITED

done to make the literature cited easier to peruse by the reader.)

Firstly, they are represented with **square brackets** and with sequential numbers, e.g. "[3]", as used in the physical sciences literature, rather than alphabetically and by year, e.g. "Sapir, E., 1955a", as used in the linguistics or biological sciences literature. The author feels that this method is more concise and less disruptive of the flow of discussion in any passage.

Secondly and more unusually, reference citations are **grouped by category** and then numbered sequentially therein and further sub-grouped, all for the sake of easier reference. The categories used are represented by three letters, the first two of which are caps. For example, we have the categories **GLi, PHo** and **SLa**, respectively representing Linguistics-General, Phonology and relating to Specific Languages (such as Yoruba or Faarsi). Thus, the citations are given as "[GLi-3]" or "[SLa-(4-6)]", etc. Due to this method of numbering, reference citations may turn out *not* to be in order sometimes. For example, a passage an initial chapter may cite references [GLi-1] and [GLi-2] first, but then suddenly jump to reference [PHo-29]. This is certainly very much against the convention even in the physical sciences. However, once again, the author feels that the grouping of references by category makes referring to them (and looking them up, if necessary), much, much more convenient for the reader.

Thirdly, within each category, references are further sub-grouped and given a descriptive title that is highlighted (underlined, italicised and bolded) above the group. Some examples of such descriptive titles are "*Origins of language*", "*Sign language (including Nicaraguan Sign Language, Arabic Sign Language)*" and "*Relating to mathematical and genetics aspects of language*".

As an aside, it may be noted that either an original (in the case of books) or a (single) photocopy or pdf (in the case of journal articles and out-of-copyright works) of *each and every reference* cited is actually in the possession of the author, and it has been thoroughly perused for relevance. Thus, it goes without saying that *only the minimal, relevant literature is cited*, since otherwise the number of references may have run into unworkable thousands.

LITERATURE CITED IS LISTED UNDER EACH OF THE FOLLOWING CATEGORIES IN ORDER AND NUMBERED SEQUENTIALLY WITHIN EACH CATEGORY

LN
(General linguistics, seminal or more significant references)

PHo
(Phonetics)

SCr
(Relating to scripts in general and to other scripts. Also, other scripts not technically part of Prior Art competing with Navlipi. e.g. Maya script. Also orthography.)

LAs
(Relating to specific languages, e.g. to Yoruba or Faarsi, etc., except Indian languages)

LAi
(Relating to Indian languages)

HIh
(Relating to general human history, including migrations, except Indian history)

HIi
(Relating to Indian history)

LITERATURE CITED

IEu
(Relating to Indo-European languages, history, migration, etc.)

GDn
(Relating to genetics, DNA, etc.)

LN
(General linguistics, seminal or more significant references)

Widely consulted references:
LN-1. Aronoff, M.; Rees-Miller, J., *Handbook of Linguistics, The,* Blackwell Publishing, Cambridge, MA (USA), (2006).

LN-2. Grimes, B. F. (Ed.), *Ethnologue: Languages of the World, 13th edn.,* Summer Institute of Linguistics, Dallas (USA), (1996).

General linguistics, including primers:
LN-3. **(a)** Moseley, C. (Co-Editor), *Atlas of the World's Languages* Routledge Publishers, Oxford, U.K. and New York, USA, (1994). **(b)** Asher, R. E.; Simpson, J. M. Y, (Eds.), *Encyclopedia of Language and Linguistics,* Pergamon, Oxford (England) **8,** 4101-9, (1994)

LN-4. Woodard, R.D., *The Atlas of Languages: The Origin and Development of Languages throughout the World,* Quarto, London (England); Facts on File, New York (USA), 162-209, (1996).

LN-5. Schmitt, N. (Ed.), *An introduction to applied linguistics,* Arnold, London (England); Oxford University Press, New York (USA), (2002).

LN-6. Frawley, W.J., *International Encyclopedia of Linguistics: 4-Volume Set,* Oxford University Press, New York, NY (USA), (1 May 2003).

LN-7. Fromkin, V.A., (Ed.), with contributions by: Curtiss, S.; Hayes, B.P.; Hyams, N.; Keating, P.A.; Koopman, H.; Munro, P., Sportiche, D.; Stabler, E.P.; Steriade, D.; Stowell, T.; Szabolsci, *Linguistics, An Introduction to Linguistic Theory,* Blackwell Publishing, Cambridge, MA (USA), (2000), (ISBN: 0-205-42118-0).

LN-8. Crystal, D., *A Dictionary of Linguistics and Phonetics, 5th edition* Blackwell Publishing Ltd, Malden, MA (USA), (2003).

LN-9 Newmeyer, F., *Linguistics: The Cambridge Survey,* Cambridge University Press, Cambridge (England), (1989).

LN-10 Fremantle, A., *A primer of linguistics,* St. Martin's Press, New York (USA), (1974).

LN-11 (a) Radford, A., *Linguistics: an introduction,* Cambridge University Press, Cambridge (England), (1999), (ISBN: 0631226648). **(b)** Gleason, H.A., *An Introduction to Descriptive Linguistics*, Holt, Rinehart and Winston, New York (1961) (ISBN 0030104653 / 9780030104657 / 0-03-010465-3)

LN-12 Akmajian, A., *Linguistics, an introduction to language and communication, 3rd edition,* M.I.T Press, Cambridge, MA (USA), (1990).

LITERATURE CITED

LN-13 O'Grady, W., *Contemporary linguistics: an introduction,* St. Martin's Press, New York (USA), (1989).
LN-14 Newmeyer, F., *Generative Linguistics: A Historical Perspective,* Routledge Press, London, (England), (1997).
LN-15 Todd, L., *An introduction to linguistics,* Longman, Burnt Mill, Harlow, Essex (England); York Press, Beirut (Lebanon), (1987).
LN-16 Matthews, P. H., *Linguistics: a very short introduction,* Oxford University Press, Oxford, (England), (2003).
LN-17 Hudson, G., *Essential Introductory Linguistics,* Blackwell Publishing Ltd, Malden, MA (USA), (2000).
LN-18 Hockett, C.F., *Course in Modern Linguistics,* Macmillan, New York, NY (USA), (1958).
LN-19 Martinet, A. (Ed.), *Elements de Linguistique Generale,* Armand Colin, Paris (France), (1960).
LN-20 Palmer, L.R., *An Introduction to Modern Linguistics,* Macmillan, New York, NY (USA), (1936).
LN-21 Potter, S., *Modern Linguistics,* Bonn University Press, Deutsch (Germany), (1957).
LN-22 Saussure, F. de, *Course in General Linguistics,* Peter Owen, London (England), (1959).
LN-23 Sturtevant, E.H., *An Introduction to Linguistic Science,* Yale University Press, London (England), (1947).
LN-24 Whorf, B.L., *Language, Thought and Reality,* Wiley and M.I.T. Press, Cambridge, MA (USA), (1956).
LN-25 Carroll, J.B., *Study of Language,* Blackwell Publishing, Cambridge, MA (USA), (1953).
LN-26 Hockett, C.F., *Refurbishing Our Foundations: Elementary Linguistics from an Advanced Point of View,* John Benjamins Publishing Co., Philadelphia, PA (USA), (1987).
LN-27 Hockett, C.F.;Greenberg, J. (Eds.), *Universals of Language,* MIT Press, Cambridge, MA (USA), (1963).
LN-28 Jespersen, O., *Language: Its Nature, Development and Origin,* Allen and Unwin, New South Wales (Australia), (1954).
LN-29 Jespersen, O., *Mankind, Nation and Individual,* Allen and Unwin, New South Wales (Australia), (1946).
LN-30 Lord, R., *Comparative Linguistics [Teach Yourself Books],* David McKay Company, Inc., New York, NY (USA), (1971).

Paanini (Panini):
LN-31 Salus, P., *Panini to Postal: a bibliography in the history of linguistics,* Linguistic Research, Edmonton, Alberta (Canada), (1971).

LN-32 Panditraj, M.M.; Shastri, G.; Pande, G.D. (Eds.), *Astadhyayi of Panini, [The Chaukhamba Surbharati Granthamala],* Chaukhambha Sanskrit Prathishthan, Varanasi (India), (2007).

LN-33 Dahiya, Y., *Panini as a Linguist: Ideas and Patterns,* Eastern Book Linkers, Delhi (India), (1995).

Prominent authors in linguistics (e.g. Sapir, Bloomfield, Chomsky):
LN-34 Sapir, E.; Mandelbaum, D.G. (Eds.), *Selected Writings of Edward Sapir in Language, Culture and Personality,* University of California Press, Berkeley, CA (USA), (1949).

LN-35 Sapir, E.; Mandelbaum, D.G. (Eds.), *Culture, Language and Personality, Selected Essays,* University of California Press, Berkley & Lost Angeles, CA, (USA), (1956, rev. ed. 1960).

LN-36 Sapir, E., *Language, An Introduction to the Study of Speech,* Harcourt, Brace & World, Inc., NY (USA), (1949).

LN-37 (a) Bloomfield, L., *An Introduction to the Study of Language,* Kessinger Publishing, LLC., Kila, MT (USA), (1914). **(b)** Bloomfield, L., *Language,* Henry Holt & Company, NY (USA), & London (England), (1933 & 1935).

LN-38 Bolinger, D.L.M.: For a complete bibliography of Prof. Bolinger's works, see the excellent and complete compilation at: http://www.cinestatic.com/bolinger.htm

LN-39 Chomsky, N., *Reflections on Language,* Pantheon, New York (USA), (1975).

LN-40 Chomsky, N., "Linguistics and cognitive science: problems and mysteries", Kasher, A. (Ed).,*The Chomskyan Turn,* Blackwell, Oxford (England), 26-53, (1991).

LN-41 Chomsky, N., *Knowledge of Language: Its Nature, Origin and Use,* Praeger, New York (USA), (1986).

Origins of language:
LN-42 Pinker, S. , *The Language Instinct: How the Mind Creates Language (P.S.),* Harper Perennial Modern Classics, New York, NY (USA), (3rd edition, 2007).

LN-43 (a) Liebermann, P., *Biology and Evolution of Language,* Harvard University Press, Cambridge, MA (USA), (1984). **(b)** Bickerton, D., *Roots of Language,* Karoma, Ann Arbor, MI (USA), (1981).

LN-44 Ruhlen, M., *The Origin of Language: Tracing the Evolution of the Mother Tongue,* Wiley, New York (USA), (1994).

LITERATURE CITED

LN-45 Chandrasekhar, P., State University of New York at Buffalo, meeting of French Language Group, Amherst Campus, (September 1982).
LN-46 Eakin Emily, K.C, "The First Word, The Search for the Origins of Language", *The New Yorker,* (12 August 2007).
LN-47 Newmeyer, F., *Grammatical Theory: Its Limits and Its Possibilities,* University of Chicago Press, Chicago, IL (USA), (1983).
LN-48 Newmeyer, F., *Language Form and Language Function,* M.I.T Press, Cambridge, MA (USA), (2000).
LN-49 Hirsh-Pasek, K.; Golinkoff, R., *The Origins of Grammar: Evidence from Early Language Comprehension,* M.I.T Press, Cambridge, MA (USA), (1996).
LN-50 Trubetzkoy, N.; Liberman, A. (Ed.), *Studies in General Linguistics and Language Structure,* Duke University Press, Durham, NC (USA) and London (England), (2001).
LN-51 Hauser, M.D.; Chomsky, N.; Fitch, W.T., "The Faculty of Language: What Is It, Who Has It, and How Did It Evolve?", *Science,* **298,** 1569-1579, (2002).
LN-52 Seydel, C., "Ancient Roots for an African language?", *Science,* **13:6**, (22 October 2001).
LN-53 Keller, R., *On Language Change: The Invisible Hand in Language,* Routledge, London (England), (1994).
LN-54 JACKENDOFF, R., *FOUNDATIONS OF LANGUAGE: BRAIN, MEANING, GRAMMAR, EVOLUTION*, OXFORD UNIVERSITY PRESS, NEW YORK (USA), (2002).
LN-55 Wade, N., "Early Voices: The Leap to Language", *New York Times Science Times*, F1, (15 July 2003).

Sign language (including Nicaraguan Sign Language, Arabic Sign Language):
LN-56 Senghas, A.; Kita, S.; Ozyurek, A., "Children Creating Core Properties of Language: Evidence from an Emerging Sign Language in Nicaragua", *Science* **305: 5691**,1779-1782, (17 September 2004).
LN-57 Senghas, A., The development of Nicaraguan Sign Language via the language acquisition process, MacLaughlin, D.; McEwen, S., (Eds.), *Proceedings of the 19th Annual Boston University Conference on Language Development,* Cascadilla Press, Somerville, MA (USA), (1995).
LN-58 Sandler, W.; Meir, I.; Padden, C.; Aronoff, M., "The emergence of grammar: Systematic structure in a new language", *Proceedings of the National Academy of Science USA (PNAS),* **102**, 2661-2665, (15 February 2005).
LN-59 "The evolution of language: Gestures of Intent", *The Economist*, 99, (5 May 2007).

LITERATURE CITED

LN-60 Pollick, A.; Waal-Frans, B.M. de, "Ape gestures and language evolution", *Proceedings of the National Academy of Science USA (PNAS)*, **104,** 8184-8189, (8 May 2007).

LN-61 Gardner, R. A.; Gardner, B. T.; Cantfort, T. E. (Eds.), *Teaching Sign Language to Chimpanzees,* State University of New York Press, Albany, NY (USA), (1989).

LN-62 Peperkamp, S.; Mehler, J., "Signed and spoken language: a unique underlying system?" *Language and Speech,* Kingston Press Services, Middlesex (England), 42, 333-46, (1999).

LN-63 Padden, C. A., *Interaction of Morphology and Syntax in American Sign Language,* Garland, New York (USA), (1988).

LN-64 Wilbur, R. B., *American Sign Language: Linguistic and Applied Dimensions,* Little Brown, Boston, MA (USA), (1987).

LN-65 Corballis, M.C., *From Hand to Mouth: The Origins of Language,* Princeton University Press, Princeton, NJ (USA), (2002).

LN-66 Fox, M., *Talking Hands [What Sign Language Reveals About the Mind],* Simon Schuster, New York, NY (USA), (2007), (ISBN: 0-15-648233-9).

LN-67 "The talking cure", *The Economist Technology Quarterly,* (12 March 2005).

LN-68 Newport, E.; Meier, R., The Acquisition of American Sign Language, Slobin, D. (Ed.), *The Crosslinguistic Study of Language Acquisition, The Data*, Erlbaum, Hillsdale, NJ (USA), **1,** (1985).

LN-69 Humphries, T., Padden, C., O'Rourke, T. J., *A Basic Course in American Sign Language, 2nd edn.,* T.J. Publishers, Silver Spring, MD (USA), (1994).

LN- 70 Brentari, D., in: Sign language phonology, Goldsmith, J. (Ed.), *The Handbook of Phonological Theory,* Blackwell, Cambridge, MA (USA), 615-39, (1995).

LAs-71. Corina, D.; Sandler, W., "Phonological structure in sign language", *Phonology* **10:2,** 165-208, (1993).

LN-72 Bowerman, M., "The origins of children's spatial semantic categories: Cognitive vs. linguistic determinants", in: Gumperz, J. J.; Levinson, S.C., (Eds.), *Rethinking Linguistic Relativity,* Cambridge University Press, Cambridge (England), (1991).

Primers and general references containing significant errors:

LN-73 Ohio State University Dept. of Linguistics. Tserdanelis, G.; Wong, W.Y.P. (Eds), *Language Files, Materials for an Introduction to Language & Linguistics (Ninth Ed.),* Ohio State University Press, Columbus, OH (USA), (2004), (ISBN 10: 0-631-19711-7).

LN-74 See pp. 53ff. and pp. 415ff. in Reference LN-73.

LITERATURE CITED

LN-75 Crystal, D., *Linguistics [Second Ed.],* Penguin Group, New York, NY (USA), 415ff, (1985).
LN-76 Parker, F., Riley, K., *Linguistics for Non-Linguistics, A Primer with Exercises,* Pearson Publishing, NY (USA), (2005).

Relating to mathematical and genetic aspects of language, including analysis thereof:
LN-77 (a) Gray, R.; Atkinson, Q.D., "Language-tree divergence times support the Anatolian theory of Indo-European origin", *Nature* **426**, 435-439, (27 November 2003). **(b)** Atkinson, Q.D., "Phonemic Diversity Supports a Serial Founder Effect Model of Language Expansion from Africa. (Analysis of word sounds suggests that language originated once, in central and southern Africa.)", *Science* **332**, 346-349 (15 April 2011).
LN-78 Fodor, I., "The Rate of Linguistic Change: Limits of the Application of Mathematical Methods in Linguistics", *Janua Linguarum, Series Minor* **43**, Mouton, The Hague, (1965).

Historical and extinct languages:
LN-79 Friedrich, J., *Extinct Languages,* Dorset Press, New York, NY, (USA), (1989).
LN-80 (a) Moseley, C., (Editor-in-chief), *UNESCO Atlas of the World's Languages in Danger* (UNESCO Press, 3rd Edition, Paris, 2010- includes online interactive version). **(b)** Moseley, C. (Editor), *Encyclopedia of the World's Endangered Languages*, Routledge Publishers, Oxford, U.K. and New York, USA, (2007). **(c)** Harrison, D., *When Languages Die: The Extinction of the World's Languages and the Erosion of Human Knowledge,* Oxford University Press, New York, NY (USA), (2008).
LN-81 Hitt, J., "Say No More: On a remote island in Patagonia, the last six speakers of Kawesqar struggle to find the right words. What gets lost when a language dies?", *New York Times Magazine*, 52-58 and 100, (29 February 2004).
LN-82 For additional material on languages of the world and extinct languages, see Chapter 2 in Reference LN-1.

Historical and language origins, cont., significant references:
LN-83 Diamond, J.; Bellwood, P., "Farmers and Their Languages: The First Expansions", *Science,* **300,** 597, (2003).

Relating to most common and most unchanging words in languages:
LN-84 Pagel, M.; Atkinson, Q.; Meade, A., "Frequency of word-use predicts rates of lexical evolution throughout Indo-European history", *Nature* **449**, 717-720, (11 October 2007).

Historical and extinct languages, cont.:
LN-85 Joseph, B. D.; Janda, R. D. (Eds.), *Handbook of Historical Linguistics,* Blackwell, Oxford (England), (2000).
LN-86 Jones, C, (Ed.), *Historical Linguistics: Problems and Perspectives,* Longman, New York (USA), 237-78, (1993).
LN-87 Koerner, E. F. K.; Asher, R. E. (Eds.), *Concise History of the Language Sciences: From Sumerians to the Cognitivists,* Pergamon, Oxford (England), (1995).

Morphology, grammar, intonation, etc.:
LN-88 Vajda, E., "Distinguishing referential from grammatical function in morphological typology", *Linguistic Diversity and Language Theories*, University of Colorado, Boulder, CO (USA), (2005).
LN-89 (a) Spencer, A.; Zwicky, A., (Eds.), *Handbook of Morphology,* Blackwell, Oxford (England), (1999). **(b)** Spencer, A., *Morphological Theory,* Blackwell, Oxford (England) and Cambridge, MA (USA), (1991).
LN-90 Hirst, D.; Di Cristo, A., *Intonation Systems. A Survey of Twenty Languages* , Cambridge University Press, London and Cambridge, England (1998).
LN-91 Aronoff, M., *Word Formation in Generative Grammar*, M.I.T. Press, Cambridge, MA (USA), (1976).
LN-92 Fodor, J.A.; Katz, J. (Eds.), *The Structure of Language: Readings in the Philosophy of Language*, Prentice-Hall, Englewood Cliffs, NJ (USA), (1964).
LN-93 Gleason, H.A., *Workbook in Descriptive Linguistics*, Holt, Rinehard and Winston, New York (USA), (1955).
LN-94 Hamp, E.P.; Householder, F.W.; Austerlitz, R. (Eds.), *Readings in Linguistics II*, University of Chicago Press, Chicago, IL (USA), (1966).

Acquisition of language by children, young adults and adults, and language learning:
LN-95 Gee, J. P. "First Language Acquisition as a guide for theories of learning and pedagogy", *Linguistics and Education* **6,** 331-54, (1994).
LN-96 Eimas, P., Speech perception in early infancy, Cohen, L. B.; Salapatek, P. (Eds.), *Infant Perception: From Sensation to Cognition,* Academic Press, New York (USA), (1975).

LITERATURE CITED

LN-97 Eimas, P., The perception and representation of speech by infants, In Morgan, J.; Demuth, K. (Eds.), *Signal to Syntax: Bootstrapping from Speech to Grammar in Early Acquisition,* Lawrence Erlbaum, Mahwah, NJ (USA), 25-39, (1996).

LN-98 Miesel, J. M.; Hyltenstam, K.; Obler, L. K., (Eds.), "Early differentiation of languages in bilingual children", *Bilingualism across the Lifespan,* Cambridge University Press, Cambridge (England), 13-40, (1990).

LN-99 Clark, E., "What's in a word? On a child's acquisition of semantics in his first language", In Moore, T. E. (Ed.), *Cognitive Development and the Acquisition of Language,* Academic Press, New York (USA), (1973).

LN-100 Ingram, D., "Phonological rules in young children", *Journal of Child Language* **1,** 49-64, (1979).

LN-101 Oller, D., The emergence of speech sounds in infancy, Yeni-Komshiam, G.; Kavanagh, J.; Ferguson, C. (Eds.), *Child Phonology,* Academic Press, New York (USA), (1980).

LN-102 Gnanadesikan, A., *Markedness and Faithfulness Constraints in Child Phonology*, University of Massachusetts, Cambridge, MA (USA), (1995).

LN-103 Ingram, D., "Phonological rules in young children", *Journal of Child Language* **1,** 49-64, (1979).

LN-104 Menn, L., "Development of articulatory, phonetic, and phonological capabilities", In Butterworth, B. (Ed.), *Language Production* **Vol. 2**, 3-50, Academic Press, London (England), (1983).

LN-105 *The Economist,* Technology Quarterly, (2 December 2006), p. 20.

LN-106 (a) Pinker, S., *Language Learnability and Language Development*, Harvard University Press, Cambridge, MA (USA), (1996). **(b)** Cairns, H., *The Acquisition of Language,* Pro-Ed, Austin, TX (USA), (1996).

LN-107 Bush, C., "On specifying a system for transcribing consonants in child language: A working paper with examples from American English and Mexican Spanish", Stanford University Child Language Project, Stanford, CA (USA), (1973).

LN-108 MacDaniel, D.; Cairns, H.; Hsu, J., "Binding principles in the grammars of young children", *Language and Acquisition* **1:4,** 121-38, (1990).

LN-109 Kuhl, P.; Williams, K.; Lacerda, F.; Stevens, K.; Lindblom, B., "Linguistic experience alters phonetic perception by 6 months of age", *Science* **255,** 606-8, (1992).

LN-110 Juscyk, P.; Frederici, A.; Wessels, J.; Svenkerud, V.; Jusczyk, A., "Infants' sensitivity to the sound patterns of native language words", *Journal of Memory and Language* **32,** 402-20, (1993).

LN-111 Fernald, A., "Four-month olds prefer to listen to motherese", *Infant Behavior and Development* **8,** 181-95, (1985).

PHo
(Phonetics)

Significant general, all-encompassing books:
PHo-1. O'Connor, J.D., *Phonetics,* Penguin Group, New York, NY (USA), (1973).

General primers, handbooks and manuals:
PHo-2. Hardcastle, W. J.; Laver, J. (Eds.), *The Handbook of Phonetic Sciences,* Blackwell, Oxford (England), (1997).
PHo-3. Ladefoged, P., *A Course in Phonetics, 3rd edition,* Harcourt Brace Jovanovich, New York (USA), (1993).
PHo-4. Ladefoged, P.; Maddieson, I., *The Sounds of the World's Languages,* Blackwell, Oxford (England), (1996).
PHo-5 Ladefoged, P., *Vowels and consonants,* Blackwell Publications, Malden, MA (USA), (2005).
PHo-6 Ladefoged, P., "The Classification of Vowels", *Lingua,* **5** 113-28, (1956).
PHo-7 Roca, I.; Johnson, W., *A Course in Phonology,* Blackwell Publishing Ltd, Malden, MA (USA), (1999).
PHo-8 Pickett, J., *The Sounds of Speech Communication: A Primer of Acoustic Phonetics and Speech Perception,* Pro-Ed, Austin, TX (USA), (1980).
PHo-9 Brosnahan, L. F., *Introduction to Phonetics,* Heffer, Cambridge (England), (1970), (ISBN: 0631201262).
PHo-10 Catford, J.C., *A practical introduction to phonetics, 2nd edition,* Oxford University Press, Oxford, (England), (2001).
PHo-11 Clark, J., *An introduction to phonetics and phonology,* Blackwell, Oxford (England), (1995).
PHo-12 Silverman, D., *A critical introduction to phonology: of sound, mind, and body,* Continuum, London (England), (2006).
PHo-13 Goldsmith, J. (Ed.), *The Handbook of Phonological Theory,* Blackwell Publishing Ltd, Malden, MA (USA), (1996), (ISBN: 063121478X).
PHo-14 Panconcelli-Calzia, G. in: Kaiser, L. (Ed.), *Manual of Phonetics,* North-Holland Publishing Co., Amsterdam (Netherlands), (1957).
PHo-15 Grammont, M.,*Traite de phonetique,* Delagrave, Paris (France), (1933).
PHo-16 Heffner, R.-M.S., *General Phonetics,* University of Wisconsin Press, Madison, WI (USA), (1949).
PHo-17 (a) Kaiser, L., *Manual of Phonetics,* North-Holland Publishing Co., Amsterdam (Netherlands), (1957). *For Cantonese reference, see p. 215 in this; for Nama reference, see p. 85 in this.* **(b)** For Nama, see also:

LITERATURE CITED

http://en.wikipedia.org/wiki/Khoekhoe_language **(c)** For Nama, see also: http://www.omniglot.com/writing/nama.htm

PHo-18 Malmberg, B., *Phonetics,* Dover Publications, Inc., NY (USA), (1963).
PHo-19 Abercrombie, D., *Elements of General Phonetics,* Aldine Publishing Company, Chicago, IL (USA), (1967).
PHo-20 Laver, J., *Principles of Phonetics,* Cambridge University Press, London (England), (1994).

Relating to Khosian (click) languages' phonology:
PHo-21 Traill, A., *Phonetic and Phonological Studies of !Xoo Bushman,* Helmut Buske Verlag, Hamburg (Germany), (1985).
PHo-22 Traill, A., "Agreement Systems in !Xoo", *Limi* **2**, (1974).
PHo-23 Van Reenen, J.F., "Dentition, jaws and palate of the Kalahari Bushman", *Journal of the Dental Association of South Africa* **19**, (1964), (ISBN: 0631222847).
PHo-24 Jakobson, R., "Extra-pulmonic consonants (ejectives, implosives, clicks)", *Quarterly Progress Report,* **90**, (1968), (ISBN: 978-0631214816).
PHo-25 Kagaya, R., "Soundspectrographic analysis of Naron clicks", *Ann. Bull. of the Research Institute of Logopedics and Phoniatrics,* (1984).
PHo-26 Beach, D.M., *Phonetics of the Hottentot Language,* W. Heffer & Sons, Ltd., Cambridge (England), (1938).
PHo-27 Westermann, D.; Ward, I.C., *Practical Phonetics for Students of African Languages,* Oxford University Press, London (England), (1933, 2nd ed.1949).

LITERATURE CITED

SCr
(Relating to scripts in general and to other scripts. Also, other scripts not technically part of Prior Art competing with Navlipi. e.g. Maya script. Also orthography.)

Significant general, all-encompassing works:

SCr-1. (a) Daniels, P.; Bright, W., (Eds.), *(The) World's Writing Systems,* Oxford University Press, Oxford (England), (1996).
(b) (i) Ostler, N., *Empires of the Word: A Language History of the World,* HarperCollins Publishers/Harper Perennial, London, UK and New York, NY, USA (2005). **(ii)** See also: Ostler, N., *The Last Lingua Franca: English Until the Return of Babel,* Walker & Company, New York, NY, USA (2010).
(c) Coulmas, F. (Ed.), *The Blackwell Encyclopedia of Writing Systems*, Blackwell Publishers, Oxford, UK, and Cambridge, MA, USA (1996).
(d) Rogers, H., *Writing Systems: A Linguistic Approach*, Blackwell Publishing, Malden, MA, USA (2005).
(e) Sampson, G., *Writing Systems*, Stanford University Press, Stanford, CA, USA (1985).
(f) Chandrasekhar, P., *NAVLIPI,* U.S. patent application N°. 12/764,094, dated 21 April 2010.

SCr-2. Albright, Robert, W.; Voegelin, C.F. (Eds), "The International Phonetic Alphabet: Its backgrounds and Development", *International J. Am. Linguistics Part III, Publication Seven of the Indiana University Research Center in Anthropology, Folklore, and Linguistics* **24,** (Jan. 1958), (ISBN: 0-521-63751-1).

SCr-3. *Handbook of the International Phonetic Association, A guide to the use of the International Phonetic Alphabet*, International Phonetic Association (IPA), Cambridge University Press, London (England), (2002).

SCr-4 For a very recent example of the continued but ad-hoc addition of glyphs to the IPA alphabet, see, e.g., Erard, M., "With Sound From Africa, the Phonetic Alphabet Expands", *The New York Times*, (13 December 2005).

General books and references:

SCr-5 Coulmas, F., *Writing systems: an introduction to their linguistic analysis,* Cambridge University Press, Cambridge (England), (2003).

SCr-6 Coulmas, F., *The Blackwell Encyclopedia of Writing Systems,* Blackwell, Oxford (England), (1996), (ISBN: 978-0195139778).

LITERATURE CITED

SCr-7 Coulmas, F., *Writing Systems of the World,* Blackwell Publishing, Oxford (England), (1989).
SCr-8 Senner, W. (Ed.), *Origins of Writing,* University of Nebraska Press, Lincoln, NE (USA), 203-37, (1989).
SCr-9 Campbell, G., *Handbook of scripts and alphabets,* Routledge, London (England) and New York (USA), (1997).
SCr-10 Sampson, G., *Writing Systems,* Stanford University Press, Stanford, CA (USA), (1985).
SCr-11 Oates, J. (Ed.), "Early Writing Systems [special issue]", *World Archaeology 17/3,* (1986).
SCr-12 Nakanishi, A., *Writing Systems of the World: Alphabets, Syllabaries, Pictograms,* Tuttle, Rutland, VT (USA), (1980).
SCr-13 Day, L., *Alphabets old & new, 3rd edition,* Omega, London (England), (1988).
SCr-14 Jensen, H., *Sign, Symbol and Script, 3rd edn. Tr. George Unwin,* George Allen and Unwin, London (England); Putnam's New York (USA), (1969).
SCr-15 Gelb, I.J., *A Study of Writing,* University of Chicago Press, Chicago, IL (USA), (1963), (ISBN 13: 978-0197259177).
SCr-16 Fevrier, J., *Histoire de l'ecriture, 2nd ed.,* Payot, Paris (France), (1959).
SCr-17 Gaur, A., *A History of Writing (Rev. Ed),* Crossriver Press, New York (USA), (1992).
SCr-18 Gelb, I.J., *A Study of Writing,* University of Chicago Press, Chicago, IL (USA), (1952).
SCr-19 Diringer, D., *The Alphabet: A Key to the History of Mankind,* Funk and Wagnalls, New York (USA), (1948).
SCr-20 Friedrich, J., *Geschichte der Schrift unter besonderer Berucksichtigung ihrer geistigen Entwicklung,* Heidelberg, Winter (Germany), (1966).

__Primers on extinct scripts:__
SCr-21 Gordon, C.H., *Forgotten Scripts: Their Ongoing Discovery and Decipherment,* Dorset Press, New York, NY (USA), (1982).

__By region- Sumer:__
SCr-22 Thureau-Dangin, F., *Die sumerischen und akkadischen inschriften,* Hinrich, Leipzig (Germany), (1907).

__By region- Egypt:__
SCr-23 Lichtheim, M., *Ancient Egyptian Literature: A Book of Readings 3 vols.,* University of California Press, Berkeley & Los Angeles (USA), (1980).

By region- Semitic to Greek:
SCr-24 Pope, M., *The Story of Archaeological Decipherment: From Egyptian Hieroglyphs to Linear B,* Scribner's, New York (USA), (1975).

By region- Chinese:
SCr-25 Boltz, W., "Early Chinese Writing", *World Archaeology,* **17,** 420-36, (1986).
SCr-26 Gao, M., *Gu wen zi lei bian [Tables of ancient characters],* Zhong hua, Peking (China), (1980).
SCr-27 Sampson, G., "Chinese Script and the Diversity of Writing Systems", *Linguistics,* **32,** 117-32, (1994).
SCr-28 Boltz, W., *Origin and Early Development of the Chinese Writing System [American Oriental Series 78], The,* American Oriental Society, New Haven, CT (USA), (1994).
SCr-29 (a) Chinese Labor Library, *Chinese Characters: Unsimplified, Simplified, plus Pinyin Romantization*, Foreign Languages Press, Beijing (China), (1985). **(b)** See also: *Mandarin for Beginners*, official Chinese Government publication, Beijing (China), (1978), which gives 23 elementary lessons in Mandarin, each including Chinese script, Romanization and word-for-word English translations. The passage shown is taken from Lesson 21, p. 121, of this book. The government printing office that published the book is no longer in existence under its original name, and is not traceable as of 2005.
SCr-30 Victor, H.; Mair, Hung-Kay, Bernard (ed.), "West Eurasian and North African Influences on the Origin of Chinese Writing." In *Contacts between Cultures: Selected papers from the 33rd International Congress of Asian and North African Studies*, Toronto, *Eastern Asia: Literature and Humanities,* Edwin Mellen, Lewiston, NY (USA), **3,** 335-38, (1990).
SCr-31 Cai, X., *Chuanyin kuaizi [Rapid graphs for transmitting sounds],* Hubei Guan Shuju: woodblock. Repr. Beijing: Wenzi Gaige Chubanshe, (1956). California Press, Berkeley & Los Angeles (USA), (1980).

By region- Mesoamerican:
SCr-32 Martinez, R.; Del Carmen, M.; Ceballas, P.O.; Coe, M.; Diehl, R.; Houston, S.D.; Taube, K.; Calderón, A.D., "Oldest Writing in the New World", *Science* **313**, 1610-1614, American Association for the Advancement of Science, Washington, D.C. (USA), (15 September 2006).

LITERATURE CITED

SCr-33 Marcus, J., *Mesoamerican Writing Systems: Propaganda, Myth, and History in Four Ancient Civilizations,* Princeton University Press, Princeton, NJ (USA), (1992).
SCr-34 Saturno, W. et al., "Early Maya Writing at San Bartolo, Guatemala", *Science* **311,** 1281, (2006).
SCr-35 Houston, S., *Maya Glyphs [Reading in the Past],* British Museum, London (England) & University of California Press, Berkeley and Los Angeles, CA (USA), (1989),
SCr-36 Wilford, J.N., "Symbols on the Wall Push Maya Writing Back by Years", *The New York Times,* (10 January 2006).
SCr-37 Wilford, J.N., "Stone Said to Contain Earliest Writing in Western Hemisphere", *The New York Times International,* (15 September 2006).

SCr-38 **(a)** Brinton, D.G., *The ancient phonetic alphabet of Yucatan,* J. Sabin, New York (USA), (1870). **(b)** See also: "Cascajal Block", *Wikipedia,* http://en.wikipedia.org/wiki/Olmec_script#cite_ref-0 .

By region- Semitic to Greek, cont.:
SCr-38 Sass, B., *Studia Alphabetica: On the Origin and Early History of the Northwest Semitic, South Semitic and Greek Alphabets (orbiblicus et orientalis 102).* Universitatsverlag, Freiburg (Switzerland), (1991).
SCr-39 Bernall, M., *On the Transmission of the Alphabet to the Aegean before 1400 B.C. Bulletin of the American Schools of Oriental Research* **267,** 1-19, (1987).
SCr-40 Driver, G.R., *Semitic Writing: From Pictograph to Alphabet, New rev. ed.,* Oxford University Press, London (England), (1976), (ISBN: 978-08543-1180).
SCr-41 "The Decipherment of Minoan and Eteocretan", *Journal of the Royal Asiatic Society,* Cambridge University Press, London (England), 148-158, (1975), (ISBN: 0226286061).
SCr-42 Brice, W.C., *Inscriptions in the Minoan Linear Script of Class A.,* The Societies of Antiquaries, Oxford & London (England), (1961).
SCr-43 Albright, W., *Proto-Sinaitic Inscriptions and Their Decipherment, [Harvard Theological Studies 12),* Harvard University Press, MA (USA), (1999).
SCr-44 Gelb, I.J., *Old Akkadian Writing and Grammar, 2nd ed., Materials for the Assyrian Dictionary,* University of Chicago Press, Chicago, IL (USA), (1961).
SCr-45 *Webster's New Universal Unabridged Dictionary, Deluxe 2nd Edition,* Dorset & Baber, Cleveland, OH (USA), (1983).

By region- Korean/Haangul (Hangul):
SCr-46 For a general overview of Haangul, including its structure, see, e.g.:
http://www.zkorean.com/korean-alphabet-hangul
SCr-47 Kim-Renaud, Y-K. (Ed.), *Korean Writing System: Its History and Structure.* University of Hawaii Press, Honolulu, HI (USA), (1996).
SCr-48 Kim-Renaud Y.-K., (Ed.), *The Korean Alphabet,* University of Hawaii Press, Honolulu, HI (USA), (1997).
SCr-49 Ledyard, G., *Korean Language Reform of 1446: The Origin, Background and Early History of the Korean Alphabet, (Ph.D. dissertation),* University of California, Berkley & Los Angeles, CA (USA), (1966).
SCr-50 Kim, C. W., "On the origin and structure of the Korean script. Inaugural lecture as Chair of Linguistics, University of Illinois, Urbana-Champaign", *Sojourns in Language, Vol. 2. Collected Papers,* Tower Press, 1988, Seoul (South Korea), 721-34, (1980).
SCr-51 For a general overview of the history of Haangul, see, e.g.:
http://www.zkorean.com/hangul/history_of_hangul
SCr-52 For examples of Haangul glyphs suitable for the non-Korean, see, e.g.:
http://www.zkorean.com/hangul/appearance
SCr-53 Hope, E.R., "Letter Shapes in Korean Onmun and Mongol Phagspa Alphabets", *Oriens* **10:1,** 150-59 (1957).
SCr-54 *Mongolian alphabet, Wikipedia,* [http://en.wikipedia.org/wiki/Mongolian_script].

By region- Japanese:
SCr-55 Habein, Y., *History of the Japanese Written Language,* University of Tokyo Press, Tokyo (Japan), (1984).

Related to Pitman, Gregg, Evans and other shorthands:
SCr-56 Abercrombie, D., *Isaac Pitman [: A Pioneer in the Scientific Study of Language],* Pitman and Sons, London (England), (1937).
SCr-57 *Pitman Shorthand,* Sir Isaac Pitman & Sons, Ltd., Toronto (Canada), (1937).
SCr-58 Graham, A., *Handbook of Standard or American Phonography [In Five Parts],* A.J. Graham & Co., NY (USA), (1886).
SCr-59 Gregg, J.; Leslie, L.; Zoubek, C., *Gregg Shorthand Manual Simplified,* McGraw-Hill Book Company, NY (USA), (1949).
SCr-60 Gregg, J. R., *The Basic Principles of Gregg Shorthand,* Gregg, New York (USA), (1923).
SCr-61 Evans, J., *Shorthand,* Barnes & Noble, Inc., New York (USA), (1946).

LITERATURE CITED

By region- North American:
SCr-62 Chiltoskey, Mary U., *Cherokee Words With Pictures,* Cherokee Publishing, Cary, NC (USA), (1972).
SCr-63 Walker, W.; Sarbaugh, J., "The Early History of the Cherokee Syllabary", *Ethnohistory* **40,** 70-94, (1993).
SCr-64 King, D., & Chapman, J., *Sequoyah Legacy [Official Guide to the Sequoyah Birthplace Museum],* Cherokee Publishing, Cary, NC (USA), (1988). See also: "Cascajal Block", *Wikipedia,*
[http://en.wikipedia.org/wiki/Olmec_script#cite_ref-0].

By region- European/Central Asian:
SCr-65 Nersoyan, G., "Why and When of the Armenian Alphabet", *Journal of the Society for Armenian Studies* **2**, 51-71, (1985-86).

By region- Vietnamese, Hmong and related:
SCr-66 For a description of native Vietnamese "alphabets", see, e.g.: Perlez, J., "Deciphering the Code to Vietnam's Old Literary Treasures", *The New York Times International*, (15 June 2006).
SCr-67 (a) Vang, C. K.; Yang, G. Y.; Smalley, W. A., *The Life of Shong Lue Yang: Hmong "Mother of Writing" (Keeb Kwm Soob Lwj Yaj: Hmoob 'Niam Ntawv'), trans.* by Mitt Moua and Yang See *(Southeast Asian Refugee Studies Occasional Papers 9),* University of Minnesota, Center for Urban and Regional Affairs, Minneapolis (USA), (1990). **(b)** See also: **(SCr-46).** Smalley, W. A.; Vang, C. K.; Yang, G. Y., *Mother of Writing: The Origin and Development of a Hmong Messianic Script,* University of Chicago Press, Chicago, IL (USA), (1990).

By region- African:
SCr-68 Whitney, W.D., "On Lepsius's Standard Alphabet", *American Oriental Society* **8**, 335-373, (1866).
SCr-69 Lepsius, R., *Standard Alphabet for Reducing Unwritten Languages and Foreign Graphic Systems to a Uniform Orthography in European Letters, 2nd ed.,* Williams & Norgate. Repr. Amsterdam: J. Benjamins, Amsterdam (Netherlands), (1981), (Original: London (England), (1863)).
SCr-70 (a) "Practical Orthography of the African Languages", *Suppl. To Le Maitre Phonetique,* Oxford University Press, Oxford (England), (1930). **(b)** See also: Bender, M. L.; Bowen J. D.; Cooper, R. C.; Ferguson, C. A. (Eds.) Bender, M. L.; Head, S. W.; Cowley, R., "The Ethiopian Writing System", *Language in Ethiopia,* Oxford University Press, London (England), 120-29, (1976).

SCr-71 Mafundikwa, S., *Afrikan alphabets: the story of writing in Afrika,* Mark Batty, West New York, NJ (USA), (2004).

Related to potential future methods of transcription, including direct brain-to-final-medium:

SCr-72 Bennett, J., "The Curse of Cursive: Penmanship, like hieroglyphics and the IBM Selectric, has lost its purpose. Let's erase it for good", *Newsweek*, 44, (23 February 2009).

SCr-73 "Mind Games: Brain-controlled games and other devices should soon be on sale", *The Economist*, 87-88, (17 March 2007).

SCr-74 Chistovich, L.A., et al, "Temporal processing of peripheral auditory patterns of speech", *The Representation of Speech in the Peripheral Auditory System*, Elsevier Biomedical Press, New York (USA), (1982).

Very significant, original world scripts, created over several millennia to ca. 2005. (Including older European works from ca. 1400 C.E. onwards as well as modern American ones.):

SCr-75 With respect to Indian *Modi*, see, e.g., Pai, P., "Decoding a Forgotten Script Fuels Property Claims", *India Abroad* **14**, March 1996.

SCr-76 Gamkrelidze, T. V., *Alphabetic Writing and the Old Georgian Script. A Typology and Provenance of Alphabetic Writing Systems,* Caravan Books, Delmar, NY (USA), (1994).

SCr-77 *Georgia alphabet, Wikipedia:* http://en.wikipedia.org/wiki/Georgian_alphabet

SCr-78 Harper, K., "Writing in Inuktitut: An Historical Perspective", *Inuktitut,* **53,** 3-35, (1983).

SCr-79 Harper, K., *Current Status of Writing Systems for Inuktitut, Inuinnaqtun and Inuvialuktun,* Northwest Territories Culture and Communications, Yellowknife (Canada), (1992).

SCr-80 Inuktikut Script image taken, with permission, from:
http://en.wikipedia.org/wiki/Image:Inuktitut.png

SCr-81 (a) Tschihold, J., *Die neue Typographie, Ein Handbuch für zeitgemäss Schaffende*, Verlag des Bildungsverbandes der Deutscher Buchdrucker, Berlin, (1928). See also *Typografische Entwurfstechnik*, Akademischer Verlag Dr Fritz Wedekind & Co., Stuttgart (Germany), (1932). **(b)** See also: "Jan Tschichold", *Wikipedia***,** http://en.wikipedia.org/wiki/Jan_Tschichold .

Scr-82 A useful summary of these European and North American contributions can be found in: Albright, R.W., "The International Phonetic Alphabet: Its Backgrounds and Development", *International J. American Linguistics*, **24:1**, i-viii and 1-78,

LITERATURE CITED

published by Indiana University Research Center in Anthropology, Folklore, and Linguistics, (Bloomington, IN, USA) (January 1958).

SCr-83 Hart, J., *Orthology*, William Seres, London, (1569).

SCr-84 Hart, J., *A Methode or Comfortable Beginning for all Unlearned*, Henrie Denham, London (England), (1570).

SCr-85 Robinson, R., *The Art of Pronunciation*, Nicholas Okes, London (England), (1617).

SCr-86 Wilkins, J., *An Essay Towards a Real Character and a Philosophical Language*, John Martin, London (England), (1668).

SCr-87 Mulcaster, R., *Elementarie*, Ed. by E.T. Campagnae, Oxford University Press, London (England), (1925).

SCr-88 Butler, C., *The English Grammar, or the Institution of Letters, Syllables, and Words in the English Tongue*, Ed. by A. Richler in *Neudrucke Frühneunglishcer Grammatiken*, **IV**, Akademie der Wissenschaften, Vienna, (1910).

SCr-89 Holder, W., *Elements of Speech: AN Essay of Inquiry into the Natural Production of Letters with an Appendix concerning Persons Deaf and Dumb*, John Martin, London (England), (1669).

SCr-90 Smith, T., *De Recta et Emendata Linguae Angelicae Scriptione Dialogue*, Ed. by O. Diebel in *Neudrucke Frühneunglishcer Grammatiken,* **VIII**, Akademie der Wissenschaften, Vienna, (1913).

SCr-91 Meigret, L., *Traité Touchant le Commun Usage de l'Ecriture Francoise*, Jeanne de Mernef, Paris (France), (1545).

SCr-92 For Latin shorthands, see, e.g.: Plutarch, "Cato the Younger", *Lives*, Trans. by John Dryden, (ca. 1660).

SCr-93 "Franz Xaver Gabelsberger", *Wikipedia*, http://en.wikipedia.org/wiki/Franz_Xaver_Gabelsberger .

SCr-94 Ellis, A.J., *Alphabet of Nature; or Contributions Towards a more accurate Analysis and Symbolization of Spoken Words, with some Account of the Principle Phonetical Alphabets Hitherto Proposed,* S. Bagster and Sons, London (England), (1845).

SCr-95 Ellis, A.J., "On Glosik", *Trans. of Philol. Soc.*, 93, (1870-1872).

SCr-96 (a) Wintersteen, L.R., *A History of the Deseret Alphabet*, M.A. thesis, Brigham Young University, Provo, UT (USA), 1970). **(b)** For more on the Deseret alphabet, see, e.g.: http://www.utlm.org/images/deseretalphabet_englishequiv.gif .

SCr-97 Bell, Alexander M., *Visible Speech: The Science of Universal Alphabetics; or Self-Interpreting Physiological Letters, for the Writing of All Languages in One Alphabet*, Marshall & Co., London (England), (1867).

LITERATURE CITED

SCr-98 Sweet, H., *A Primer of Phonetics*, 71-72 and 77-78, Clarendon Press, Oxford (UK), (1890). See also: *Collected Papers of Henry Sweet*, Clarendon Press, Oxford (UK), (1913).
SCr-99 Jespersen, O., *The Articulations of Speech Sounds Represented by Means of Analphabetic Symbols*, Elwert, Marburg (Germany), (1889). See also: Jespersen, O., *Phonetische Grundfragen*, Druck and Verlag bon B.G. Teubner, Leipzig and Berlin, (Germany), (1904).
SCr-100 Janvrin, F., "The Atomic Structure of Speech", *Archives Néerlandaises de Phonétique Expérimentale,* **VI**, 101-104, (1931).
SCr-101 Emsley, B. "The First Phonetic Dictionary", *Quarterly Journal of Speech*, **XXVIII**, (1942).
SCr-102 Story, C., *Fonetic Primer, [Offering the Universal Alfabet and the Science of Spelling], The,* Isaac H. Blanchard Company, New York, NY (USA), (1907), (ISBN: 0-340-05895-1).
SCr-103 Johnston, H., *Phonetic Spelling: A proposed Universal Alphabet for the rendering of English, French, German and all other forms of Speech,* Cambridge University Press. London (England), (1913).
SCr-104 Owen, R., *Global Alphabet [A Method of Teaching English to the World],* US Government Printing Office, Washington, D.C. (USA), (1944).
SCr-105 Pike, K., *Phonemics [A Technique for Reducing Languages to Writing],* University of Michigan Press, Ann Arbor, MI (USA), (1947).
SCr-106 Pike, K., *Phonetics [A Critical Analysis of Phonetic Theory and a Technic for the Practical Description of Sounds,* University of Michigan Press, London (England), (1943).
SCr-107 Dalby, D. "A Survey of the Indigenous Scripts of Liberia and Sierra Leone: Vai, Mende, Loma, Kpelle and Bassa", *African Language Studies* **8**, 1-51, (1967). See also: Hendrix, H. (Ed.), *The search for a new alphabet: a literary studies in a changing world: in honor of Douwe Fokkema,* J. Benjamins, Amsterdam (Netherlands) and Philadelphia, PA (USA), (1996).
SCr-108 Nyei, M. B., "A Three Script Literacy among the Vai: Arabic, English and Vai", *Liberian Studies Journal, 9,* 13-22, (1981).
SCr-109 Welmers, W. E., *A Grammar of Vai,* University of California Press, Berkeley & Los Angeles (USA), (1976).
SCr-110 See: http://en.wikipedia.org/wiki/UNIFON . Unifon script image taken, with permission, therefrom.
SCr-111 Shavian or Shaw alphabet, see *Wikipedia*, http://en.wikipedia.org/wiki/Shaw_alphabet .
SCr-112 Ewing, J., *The Columbian alphabet,* Matthias Day, Trenton, NJ (USA), (1798).

LITERATURE CITED

SCr-113 Abulhab, S., "Method and Font for Representing Arabic Characters, and Articles Utilizing Them", *U.S. Patent # US 6,704,116 B1*, 9 March 2004.
SCr-114 (a) For the Fraser script, see, e.g.: http://en.wikipedia.org/wiki/Fraser_alphabet .
(b) See also: http://unicode.org/mail-arch/unicode-ml/y2004-m05/0635.html
SCr-115 For the Pollard script, see, e.g.: http://en.wikipedia.org/wiki/Pollard_script
SCr-116 Noel, R. S., *The Languages of Tolkien's Middle Earth,* Houghton Mifflin, Boston (USA), (1980).
SCr-117 Bloquerst, A.J., *Nouvel abecedaire, ou, Alphabet syllabique,* Philadelphia, PA (USA), (1811).
SCr-118 Wilbur, J., *The grammatical alphabet,* H.C. Southwick, Albany ,NY (USA), (1815).
SCr-119 *Arthur's alphabet,* McLoughlin Bros., New York (USA), (1875).
SCr-120 Greenaway, K., *Kate Greenaway's Alphabet,* Routledge, London (England), (1885).
SCr-121 Weeks, R., *The N.E.A. phonetic alphabet with a review of the Whipple experiments*, The New Era Printing Company, Lancaster, PA (USA), (1912).
SCr-122 Thackeray, W.M., *The Thackeray Alphabet*, Harper & Brothers, New York (USA), (1930).
SCr-123 Herzog, G.; Newman, S.S.; Sapir, E.; Haas, M.; Swadesh, M.; Voegelin, C.F., "Some orthographic recommendations", *American Anthropologist* **36**, 629-31, (1934).
SCr124 Roudet, L., *Eléments de Phonétique Générale*, University Library, Paris (France), (1910).
SCr-125 For Unicode transcriptions of the world's scripts, see, e.g.: Erard, M., "For the World's A B C's, He Makes 1's and 0's: To Call Cyrillic, Chinese or Cherokee to the Screen, Typographer Helps Forge a Digital Lingua Franca", *The New York Times*, G1, (25 September 2003).
SCr-126 References drawn from relevant sections of *Wikipedia*, Where reproduced, reproductions are in accordance with *Wikipedia's* use policy and with all relevant permissions.

***Relating to the AMERICANIST (APA) "phonetic notation" (script)*:**
SCr-127 Powell, J. W. , *Introduction to the Study of Indian languages, with words, phrases, and sentences to be collected*, 2nd Ed., Washington, D.C., USA: U.S. Government Printing Office. (1880).
SCr-128 Boas, F., "Introduction" (pp. 5–83), in Boas, F. (Ed.), *Handbook of American Indian languages.* Bureau of American Ethnology Bulletin, **40**. Washington, D.C., USA. (1911, Reprinted 1966).

SCr-129 American Anthropological Society, *Phonetic transcription of Indian languages: Report of committee of American Anthropological Association.* Smithsonian miscellaneous collections, **66**, 6 (1916). Smithsonian Institution/American Anthropological Society, Washington, D.C., USA.

SCr-130 Bloomfield, L.; Bolling G. M., "What symbols shall we use?" *Language, 3* (2), 123-129 (1927).

SCr-131 Herzog, G. ; Newman, S. S.; Sapir, E. ; Swadesh, M. H. ; Swadesh, M.; Voegelin, Charles F. "Some orthographic recommendations", *American Anthropologist, 36* (4), 629-631 (1934).

SCr-132 *Americanist* script figures reproduced, with permission, from the listings under the following websites:

(a) http://www.associatepublisher.com/e/a/am/americanist_phonetic_notation.htm

(b) http://en.wikipedia.org/wiki/Americanist_phonetic_notation

LITERATURE CITED

LAs
(Relating to specific languages, e.g. to Yoruba or Faarsi, etc., except Indian languages)

General:
LAs-1. Ruhlen, M., *A Guide to the World's Languages, Classification* Stanford University Press, Stanford, CA (USA), **1**, (1987).
LAs-2 *Hammond New Century World Atlas,* Hammond World Atlas, Corp. (Langenscheidt Publishing Group), 22-23, (2000).
LAs-3 *List of countries by populations, Wikipedia:*
[http://en.wikipedia.org/wiki/list_of_countries_by_population].

Related to human migration, archaeology and related subjects:
LAs-4 For a concise summary of human migrations of the last 100,000 years and how they possibly relate to the isolated and unisolated development of languages, see, e.g., the several migration focal points shown in the figures in the following article: Stix, G., "Traces of a Distant Past", *Scientific American*, 56-63, (July 2008).
LAs-5 Ross, M.; Blench, I, R.; Spriggs, M., (Eds.), *Archaeology and Language,* Routledge, London (U.K.) 209-261, (1997).

Related to specific languages, language families or groups- African:
LAs-6 (a) Wade, N., "In Click Languages, an Echo of the Tongues of the Ancients", *The New York Times*, (18 March 2003).
(b) Hahn, C.H.L.; Vedder, H.; Fourie, L., *The native tribes of South West Africa*, Cass Publishing, London, UK (1966).
LAs-7 (a) Sands, B., *Eastern and Southern African Khoisan: Evaluating Claims of Distant Linguistic Relationship,* Koppe, Cologne (Italy), (1998).
(b) Kroenlein, J.G., *Wortschatz der Khoi-Khoin (Namaqua-Hottentotten)/Gesammelt, aufgeschrieben und verdeutscht von J.G. Kroenlein, herausgegeben mit unterstṅtzung der K'nigl. Academie der Wissenschaften*, Dutsche Kolonialgesselschaft/ C. Heymanns Verlag, Berlin, Germany (1889).
LAs-8 Maingard, L.F., "The third bushman language", *African Studies* **17**, 100-115, (1958).
LAs-9 Welmers, W.E., *African Language Structures*, University of California Press, Berkeley, CA (USA), (1973).

LAs-10 Greenberg, J. H., *The Languages of Africa,* Indiana University, Bloomington, IN (USA), and Mouton, The Hague, (1963).
LAs-11 Greenberg, J., "Studies in African Linguistic Classification: IV. Hamito-Semitic *Southwestern Journal of Anthropology, - Article consists of 20 pgs, not accessible online.,* **6,** 47-63, (Spring 1950).
LAs-12 Ladefoged, P., *A Phonetic Study of West African Languages,* Cambridge University Press, London (England), (1964).
LAs-13 Diakonoff, I. M., *Afrasian Languages,* Akademika Nauka, Moscow (Russia), (1988).
LAs-14 Bendor-Samuel, J. (Ed.), *The Niger-Congo Languages,* University Press of America, Lanham, MD (USA), (1989).
LAs-15 Bamgbose, A., Yoruba, Dunstan, E. (Ed.), *Twelve Nigerian Languages: A Handbook on their Sound Systems for Teachers of English,* Longmans Green, London (England), 163-72 (1969).
LAs-16 Bender, M. L., *The Nilo-Saharan Languages: A Comparative Essay, 2nd edn.,* Lincom Europa, Munich (Germany), (1997).
LAs-17 Payne, D., "Maa Language Project: Kenyan Southern Maasai, Samburu", University of Oregon: http://pages.uoregon.edu/maasai/

Related to specific languages, language families or groups- Swedish:
LAs-18 Malmberg, B., "Observations on the Swedish Word Accent", *Haskings Laboratories Report,* (1955).

Related to specific languages, language families or groups- Ural-Altaic:
LAs-19 Attaoullah, F., *Beginner's Turkish,* Hippocrene Books, Inc., New York (USA), (1998), (ISBN: 81-206-1376-7).
LAs-20 Johanson, L.; Csato, E. (Eds.), *The Turkic Languages,* Routledge, London (England), (1998).
LAs-21 *Altaic languages, Wikipedia,* [http://en.wikipedia.org/wiki/Altaic].
LAs-22 Poppe, N., *Introduction to Altaic Linguistics,* Harrassowitz, Wiesbaden (Germany), (1965).
LAs-23 *Ural-Altaic languages, Wikipedia,* [http://en.wikipedia.org/wiki/Ural-Altaic].
LAs-24 Decsy, G. (Ed.), *Ural-Altaische Jahrbucher/Ural-Altaic Yearbook, 56, 1984,* Eurolingua, (1984), (ISBN-10: 0931922178, ISBN-13: 9788-0931922176).
LAs-25 Erdy, M., *The Sumerian, Ural-Altaic, Magyar relationship: a history of research*, Gilgamesh, New York (USA), (1974).
LAs-26 Abondolo, D. (Ed.), *The Uralic Languages,* Routledge, London (England), (1998).

LITERATURE CITED

Related to specific languages, language families or groups-   Altaic/Korean:
LAs-27 Brooke, J., "For Mongolians, E Is for English, and F Is for the Future", *The New York Times,* international pages, (15 February 2005).
LAs-28 Ju Won, K., *Materials of Spoken Manchu,* Seoul National University Press, Seoul (South Korea), (2008), (ISBN: 978-89-521-0947-7).
LAs-29 Lee, I.; Ramsey, R., *Korean Language,* State University of New York Press, Albany, NY (USA), (2000).
LAs-30 Korean National Commission for UNESCO (Ed.), *Korean Language,* Si-sayoung-o-sa Publishers, Inc. Seoul (South Korea), (ISBN: 0-7914-4831-2).

Related to specific languages, language families or groups-   Austronesian/Indonesian:
LAs-31 Robson, S.; Millie, J., *Instant Indonesian [How to Express 1,000 Different Ideas With Just 100 Key Words and Phrases!],* Tuttle Publishing, Boston, MA (USA), (2004).

Related to specific languages, language families or groups- Swaahili (Swahili):
LAs-32 *Swahili, The Rough Guide, Phrasebook,* Rough Guides / Pearson PLC, London (England), (1998).

Related to extinct languages:
LAs-33 "Babel runs backwards", *The Economist,* 62-64, (1 January 2005).

Related to language isolates:
LAs-34 Catford, J.C., "Mountain of the tongues; the languages of the Caucasus", *Ann. Rev. Anthropology* **6**, 283-314, (1997).
LAs-35 Hewitt, B.,"Indigenous Languages of the Caucasus", The, *North West Caucasian Languages,* Caravan Books, Delmar, NY (USA), **2**, (1989).
LAs-36 Foley, W. A., *The Papuan Languages of New Guinea,* Cambridge University Press, Cambridge, (1986).
LAs-37 Dixon, R. M. W., *The Languages of Australia,* Cambridge University Press, Cambridge (England), (1980).
LAs-38 Bonfante, G.; Bonfante, L., *Etruscan Language: An Introduction, The,* Manchester University Press, NY (USA), (1983).
LAs-39 Hewitt, B.G. in collaboration with Z.K. Khiba, *Abkhaz. Lingua Descriptive Studies* **2**, North- Holland, Amsterdam (Netherlands), (1979).

Related to specific languages, language families or groups- Slavic:
LAs-40 Comrie, B.; Greville, G., *Slavonic Languages,* Routledge Press, London, (England), (1993).
LAs-41 Gardiner, S., *Old Church Slavonic: An Elementary Grammar,* Cambridge University Press, London (England), (1984).

Related to specific languages, language families or groups- Romance:
LAs-42 Posner, R., *Romance Languages,* Cambridge University Press, Cambridge (England), (1996).
LAs-43 Harris, M.; Vincent, N. (Eds.), *The Romance Languages,* Routledge, London (England), (1988).

Related to specific languages, language families or groups- Celtic/Scottish/Gaelic:
LAs-44 MacAulay, D., (Ed.), *Celtic Languages,* Cambridge University Press, Cambridge (England), (1993).
LAs-45 Renton, R.W.; MacDonald, J.A., *Scottish Gaelic-English / English-Scottish Gaelic*, Hippocrene Books, Inc., New York (USA), (1994).
LAs-46 Carmody, F.J., "*Is* in Modern Scottish Gaelic", *Word* **1**, 162-87, (1945).
LAs-47 Hamp, E.P., "Morphophonemes of the Keltic mutations, *Language* **27**, 230-47, (1951).

Related to specific languages, language families or groups- Sino-Bodic:
LAs-48 van Driem, G., "Sino-Bodic", *Bulletin of the School of Oriental and African Studies,* University of London, London (England), **60,** 455-88, (1997).

Related to specific languages, language families or groups- Chinese:
LAs-49 French, H.W., "Uniting China to Speak Mandarin, the One Official Language: Easier Said Than Done", *The New York Times International*, p. 4, (10 July 2005).
LAs-50 Chang, N T., "Tones and intonation in the Chengtu dialect", *Phonetica* **2,** 59-85, (1958).

Related to specific languages, language families or groups- Semitic/Afro-Asiatic:
LAs-51 Hetzron, R. (Ed.), *The Semitic Languages,* Routledge, London (England), (1997).
LAs-52 Loprieno, A., *Ancient Egyptian,* Cambridge University Press, Cambridge (England), (1995).
LAs-53 Versteegh, K., *The Arabic Language,* Columbia University Press, New York (USA), (1997).

LITERATURE CITED

LAs-54 Beeston, A.F.L., *Written Arabic*, Cambridge University Press, Cambridge (England), (1968).

LAs-55 Thornton, F.; Nicholson, R.A. (Eds.), *Elementary Arabic, A Grammar,* Asian Ed. Services, New Delhi (India), (2000).

Related to specific languages, language families or groups- Taiwanese
LAs-56 (a) Gluck, C., "Taiwan's aborigines find new voice", *BBC News*: http://news.bbc.co.uk/2/hi/asia-pacific/4649257.stm , (4 July 2005).
(b) Campbell, W., *A dictionary of the Amoy vernacular spoken throughout the prefectures of Chin-chiu, Chiang-chiu and Formosa*, Fukuin Printing Co., Yokohama, Japan (1913, reprint 1965).

Related to specific languages, language families or groups- Hawai'ian:
LAs-57 Hudson, M., *Ruins of Identity,* University of Hawaii Press, Honolulu, (HI), (USA), (1999).

Related to specific languages, language families or groups- Austronesian:
LAs-58 *Austronesian languages, Wikipedia,* [http://en.wikipedia.org/wiki/Austronesia].

Related to specific languages, language families or groups- Japanese:
LAs-59 Tsujimura, N. (Ed.), *The Handbook of Japanese Linguistics,* Blackwell Publishing Ltd, Malden, MA (USA), (1999).
LAs-60 Kuno, S., *The Structure of the Japanese Language,* M.I.T Press, Cambridge, MA (USA), (1973).
LAs-61 Nagase, O., Personal Communication, (2008).

Related to specific languages, language families or groups- Austro-Asiatic:
LAs-62 *Austro-Asiatic Languages, Wikipedia,* [http://en.wikipedia.org/wiki/Austro-Asiatic].

Related to specific languages, language families or groups- North/Meso-American:
LAs-63 Boas, F., Introduction in Boas, F. (Ed.), *Handbook of American Indian Languages, Vol. 1,* Bureau of American Ethnology, Washington (USA), (1911).
LAs-64 Campbell, L., *American Indian Linguistics: The Linguistic History of Native America,* Oxford University Press, New York (USA), (1997).
LAs-65 Hinton, L.; Munro, P. (Eds.), *Studies in American Indian Languages: Description and Theory,* University of California Publications in Linguistics **131** (USA), (1998).

LAs-66 Mithun, M., *The Languages of Native North America,* Cambridge University Press, Cambridge (England), (1999).
LAs-67 Campbell, A., *American Indian Languages,* Oxford University Press, New York, NY (USA), (1997).
LAs-68 Suarez. J. A., *The Mesoamerican Indian Languages,* Cambridge University Press, Cambridge (England), (1983).
LAs-69 Boas, F.; Swanton, J.R., *Siouan: Dakota (Teton and Santee dialects) with remarks on the Ponca and Winnebago*, 875-965, (1911).
LAs-70 (a) Hoogshagen, S.; Hoogshagen, H.H., "Mariano Silva y Aceves" in *Diccionario Mixe de Coatlán, Serie de Vocabularios Indigénas*, **32 SIL**, D.F., Mexico, (1993). **(b)** See also: Wichmann, S., *The Relationship Among the Mixe-Zoquean Languages of Mexico*, University of Utah Press, Salt Lake City, UT (USA), (1995), (ISBN 0-87480-487-6).
LAs-71 Spier, L., "Comparative Vocabularies and Parallel Texts in Two Yuman Languages of Arizona", *University of New Mexico Publications in Anthropology* **2**, University of New Mexico Press, Albuquerque (USA), (1946).
LAs-72 Gowan, G.M., "Mazateco whistle speech", *Language,* (1948).

Related to specific languages, language families or groups- South American:
LAs-73 McQuown, N.A.,"The indigenous languages of Latin America", *American Anthropologist, New Series,* **57:3**, 501-570, (June 1955).
LAs-74 Tax, S., "Aboriginal languages of Latin America", *Current Anthropology* **1**, (1960).
LAs-75 Kaufman, T., "Language history in South America: What we know and how to know more," In Payne, D. L. (Ed.), *Amazonian Linguistics: Studies in Lowland South American Languages,* University of Texas Press, Austin, TX (USA), 13-67, (1990).
LAs-76 Dixon, R. M. W.; Aikhenvald, A., *The Amazonian Languages,* Cambridge University Press, Cambridge (England), (1999).
LAs-77 Elson, B., *Studies in Peruvian Indian Languages: 1,* University of Oklahoma University Press, Norman, OK (USA), (1963).

Related to specific languages, language families or groups- "Nostratic":
LAs-78 Bomhard, A.R., *The Nostratic macrofamily: a study in distant linguistic relationship*, Mouton de Gruyter, Berlin (Germany), (1994).
LAs-79 Illic-Svityc, V. M., *Opyt sravnenija nostraticeskix jazykov, 3 vols.,* Akademika Nauka, Moscow (Russia), (1971-84).

LITERATURE CITED

LAi
(Relating to Indian languages)

<u>Related to Sanskrit and comparative Indo-European grammar, phonology and etymology:</u>

LAi-1 Halder, G., *Languages of India*, National Book Trust, New Delhi (India), (2000).

LAi-2 Misra, S.S., *A Comparative Grammar of Sanskrit, Greek and Hittite,* World Press, Calcutta (India), (1968).

LAi-3 Vasu, S.C., (Ed., Transl.), *Ashtadhyayi of Panini,* Motilal Banarsidass Publishers Pvt Ltd, Delhi (India), (2003).

LAi-4 Apte, V.S., *Practical Sanskrit-English Dictionary [Containing Appendices on Sanskrit Prosody & Important Literary & Geographical Names of Ancient India],* Rev. Ed., Motilal Banarsidass Publishers Pvt Ltd, Delhi (India), (1965, reprint 1985).

LAi-5 Goldman, R.P.; Goldman, S.J.S., *Devavanipravesika: An Introduction to the Sanskrit Language,* University of California at Berkeley Press, Berkeley, CA (USA), (2002).

LAi-6 (a) *RgVeda Padapatha,* Sri Satguru Publications, Indian Books Centre, Delhi (India), (1992). (b) *RgWeda Samhita, Shrimatsaayanaaachaarya-wirachitabhaashyasameta* (RgVeda Samhita, with the Commentary of Saaynaachaarya). Published, in four volumes, by Vaidika Samshodhana Mandala (Vedic Research Institute), Pune, India (1978).

LAi-7 Jha, V.N., *A Linguistic Analysis of the Rgveda-Padapatha, [Sri Garib Dass Oriental Series No. 142, Pre-Paninian Grammatical Traditions (Pt.-1),* Sri Satguru Publications, Delhi (India), (1992), (ISBN: 81-7030-320-6).

LAi-8 Dwivedi, K., *Sanskrit Saahitya Kaa Itihaas [A History of Sanskrit Literature],* Raashtriya Sanskrit Saahitya Kendra (National Center for Sanskrit Literature), (2005).

LAi-9 Aggarwal, H.R.; Foreword by Sarup, L., *A Short History of Sanskrit Literature [Second Rev Ed.],* Munshiram Manoharlal Publishers Pvt Ltd, New Delhi (India), (1963).

LAi-10 Gupta, D. K. (Ed.), *Recent Studies in Sanskrit and Indology [Felicitation Volume],* Ajanta Publications, Delhi (India), (1982).

LAi-11 Gandhi D.N.; Kanade, R.J., *Dhaturupakosa, Sri Garib Das Oriental Series No.89, Compiled for the use of the Sanskrit Students,* Sri Satguru Publications, Delhi (India), (2005).

LAi-12 Yaaska (Author, est. before 1250 B.C.E.); Shaastri S., Sharmaa, S., (Eds.), *Shrimatyaaskamaharshi-Prakaashitam* **Niruktam***, Nighantu-Paathasamupetam*

[Niruktam of Yaaska], Shri Venkateshwara Steam Press, Mumbai (India), (1912), (ISBN: 81-7030-202-1).

Related to the Indus/Harappan script:
LAi-13 Mahadevan, I., Indus Script: Texts, Concordance and Tables [Memoirs of the Archaeologial Survey of India 77], The, Archaeological Survey of India, New Delhi (India), (1977).
LAi-14 Mahadevan, I., "S.R. Rao's Decipherment of the Indus Script", *Indian Historical Review* **8: 1-2,** 58-73, (1982).
LAi-15 (a) Mahadevan, I., "The Indus 'non-script' is a non-issue", *The Hindu*, Sunday Magazine, 3 May 2009. (The Hindu newspaper, Chennai, India) (2009). Viewable at:
  http://www.hindu.com/mag/2009/05/03/stories/2009050350010100.htm
  (b) See also: Mahadevan, I., "MELUHHA AND AGASTYA : ALPHA AND OMEGA OF THE INDUS SCRIPT", Publication of the Indus Research Centre, Roja Muthiah Research Library, Chennai, India (2009).
LAi-16 Archaeological Survey of India, *Corpus of Indus Seals and Inscriptions (Memoirs of the Archaeological Survey of India),* Suomalainen Tiedeakatemia, Mariankatu, Helsinki (Finland), (1987).
LAi-17 Parpola, A., *Deciphering the Indus script,* Cambridge University Press, London (England), (1994).
LAi-18. Mahadevan, I., "Agricultural Terms in the Indus Script", [http://www.harappa.com/arrow/indus-script-terms.html], (27 May 2007).
LAi-19 Kalyanaraman, S., "Inscribed terracotta seal at Vais'ali compared with inscribed stone celt of Sembiyan-kandiyur",
  [http://kalyan96.googlepages.com/vaisaliseal.pdf], (3 May 2006).
LAi-20 Rao, S.R., *Decipherment of the Indus Script,* Asia Publishing House, Bombay (India), (1982).
LAi-21 Jha, N., *Indus Valley Seals Deciphered! Alphabet Writing Originated with the Ancient Hindus, Vedic Glossary on Indus Seals,* Ganga-Kaueri Publishing, Varanasi (India), (1996).
LAi-22 Punekar, S.M., *Mohenjodaro Seals, Read and Identified,* Caxton Publications, Delhi (India), (1984).

LITERATURE CITED

LAi-23 (a) "Vikramkhol (Bikramkhol)", Regarding a possible "missing link" between the Harappan (Indus Valley) and Braahmi (Brahmi) scripts, see the descriptions of the Vikramkhol script, e.g. at:
http://en.wikipedia.org/wiki/Historic_sites_in_Orissa
(b) See also: "Significance of Mayiladuthurai find",
www.hindu.com/2006/05/01/stories/2006050101992000.htm (2006).

Related to Dravidian languages:
LAi-24 McAlpin, D., *Proto-Elamo-Dravidian: The Evidence and Its Implications [Transactions of the Am. Phil. Society, held at Phil. For Promoting Useful Knowledge, Volume 71, Part 3],* Am. Phil. Society, Philadelphia, PA (USA), (1981).
LAi-25 Damerow, P.; Englund, R., "The Proto-Elamite Texts from Tepe Yahya" American School of Prehistoric Research Bulletin, Cambridge University Press, London (England), **39**, (1989).
LAi-26 Amiet, P., "Il y a 5000 ans les Elamites inventaient l'ecriture", *Archeologia* **12**, 20-22, (1966).
LAi-27 (a) Reiner, E., "The Elamite Language", *Altkleinasiatische Sprachen, (Handbuch der Orientalistik, div. 1),* **2**, 54-118, (1969).
(b) Schmitt, R., *Meno-logium Bagistano-Persepolitanum: Studient zu den altpersischen Montasnamen und ihern elamischen Wiedergaben,* Verlag der Österreichischen Akademie der Wissenschaften, Vienna, Austria (2003).
LAi-28 Bush, F., *A Grammar of the Hurrian Language,* Brandeis University, Department of Mediterranean Studies Dissertation, Boston, MA (USA, (1964).
LAi-29 (a) Damerow, P.; Englund, R., *Die Zahlzeichensysteme der Archaischen Texte aus Uruk,* Mann, Berlin, (1987).
(b) Damerow, P.; Englund, R.K., *The proto-Elamite texts from Tepe Yahya*, Harvard University Press, Cambridge, MA, USA (1989).
LAi-30 Krishnamurti, B., *Dravidian Languages,* Cambridge University Press, London (England), (2003).
LAi-31 Steever, S., *Dravidian Languages, (Routledge Language Family Descriptions),* Routledge Press, London, (England), (1998), (ISBN: 81-208-0290-x).
LAi-32 Varadarajan, Prof. M., "Tamil Language - A brief review of its history and features", *[http://www.TamilCanadian.com/].*
LAi-33 Varadarajan, M.; Vralaaru, M., *The History of Tamil Language*, Madras (Chennai), India, (1954).
LAi-34 Iyengar, P.T.S., *History of Tamil from the Earliest Times to 600 A.D.,* Madras (Chennai), India, (1929).

LAi-35 Sastri, S., *Tolkappiyam-Collatikaram*, Annamalai University, Annamalainager (India), (1979).
LAi-36 Visalakshy, P., *The Grantha script,* Dravidian Linguistics Association, Thiruvananthapuram (India), (2003).
LAi-37 Marr, J.R., *The Early Dravidians* in Basham, A.L. (Ed.), *A Cultural History of India*, Oxford University Press, London (England), (1975).
LAi-38 Bray, D., *Brahui Language Introduction and Grammar,* Asian Ed. Services, New Delhi (India), (1986).

Related to Persian scripts:
LAi-39 Stronach, David, Vallat, Francois (Ed.), "On the Genesis of the Old Persian Cuneiform Scripts", In *Contributions a l'histoire d'Iran: Melanges offerts a Jean Perrot,* Editions Recherches sur les Civilisations, Paris (France), 195-203, (1990).
LAi-40 Schmitt, R., *Behistun Inscription of Darius the Great: Old Persian Text (Corpus Inscriptonum Iranicarum),* School of Oriental and African Studies, London (England), (1991).
LAi-41 Hincks, E., *On the Three Kinds of Persepolitan Writing, and on the Babylonian Lapidary Characters" [Transactions of the Royal Irish Academy 21 Polite Literature* H.Gill, Oxford (England), 249-56, (1846).
LAi-42 Hincks, E., *On the First and Second Kinds of Persepolitan Writing" [Transactions of the Royal Irish Academy 21 Polite Literature],* 114-31, (1846).
LAi-43 Windfuhr, G., "Notes on the Old Persian Signs", *Indo-Iranian Journal,* **12/2**, (June 1970).
LAi-44 Rawlinson, H., "The Persian Cuneiform Inscription at Behistun, Deciphered and Translated with a Memoir on Persian Cuneiform Inscriptions in General, and on That of Behistun in Particular:" *J. Royal Asiatic Society* **10**, (1846).

Related to Maraathi (Marathi), Hindi, etc.:
LAi-45. (a) See, e.g., the presentations by D.M. Mirajdar, A. Avachat and R.R. Borade, at *Vishwa Marathi Sahitya Sammelan 2009 (World Marathi Literature Convention)*, 14-196 February 2009, Cupertino, CA (USA). See also: http://wikibin.org/articles/vishwa-marathi-sahitya-sammelan.html.
(b) Jacobi, H., *Ausgewählte Erzählungen in Maharashtri. Zur Einführung in das Studium des Prakrit. Grammatik, Text, Wörterbuch*, S. Hirzel Press, Leipzig, Germany (1886).

LITERATURE CITED

LAi-46 Wiirkar (Virkar), K., *Subodh Maraathi-Ingrajii Shabdakosh [Wirkar, K., Elucidated Maraathi-English Dictionary],* Anmol Pirakaashan, Pune (India), (2005).
LAi-47 Shapiro, M.; Garry, J.; Rubino, C. (Eds.), *Hindi: Facts about the world's languages* in: *An encyclopedia of the world's major languages, past and present,* New England Publishing Associates, Higganum, CT (USA), (2001)
LAi-48 Prasaad (Prasad), K.; Sahaaya (Sahaya), R.; Shriwaastawa (Shrivastava), M. (Compilers), *Brhat Hindi Kosh [Great Hindi Dictionary],* Jnaana Mandal Ltd., Vaaraanasi, (India), (1989).
LAi-49 Harley, A.H., *Colloquial Hindustani,* Kegan Paul, Trench, Trubner and Co. Ltd., London (England), (1944).

Related to Praakrts (Prakrits):
LAi-50 Jain, B.D., *Ardha Magadhi Reader,* Sri Satguru Publications, Delhi (India), (1982).
LAi-51 Doshi, A.B.J., *Praakrta Maargopadeshikaa [Instructor for Praakrit], Trans. Into Hindi by Saadhvii, S. Suwrataajii, Saadhwii Shri Mrgaawatiijii, Saadhwii Shri Shiilawatijii and Shri Wijayawallabhbhasuurajii,* Motilal Banarsidass Publishers Pvt Ltd, Delhi (India), (1968).
LAi-52 Tagare, G.V., *Historical Grammar of Apabrahmsa,* Motilal Banarsidass Publishers Pvt Ltd, Delhi (India), (1987).
LAi-53 Law, B.M., *A History of Pali Literature,* Indica Books, New Delhi (India), (2002).
LAi-54 Kaashyapa (Kashyapa), B.J., *Paali-Mahaa Wyaakarana [Great Paali Grammar],* Motilal Banarsidass Publishers Pvt Ltd, Delhi (India), (1963),
LAi-55 Law Bimala, C.;Geiger, W. *A History of Pali Literature,* Kegan Paul Trench, Trubner & Co., London (England), (2000).
LAi-56 Gupta, K.M., *Linguistic Approach to Meaning in Pali,* Sundeep Prakashan, New Delhi (India), (2006), (ISBN:13 978-0415100236),
LAi-57 Hazra, K.L., *Pali Language and literature: a systematic survey and historical study,* D.K. Printworld, New Delhi (India), (1994).
LAi-58 Oberlies, T., *Pāli: A Grammar of the Language of the Theravāda Tipitaka",* Walter de Gruyter, Berlin (Germany), (2001).

Related to Dravidian languages, cont.:
LAi-59 Chhabra, B., *Expansion of Indo-Aryan Culture during Pallava Rule,* Munshiram Manoharlal Publishers Pvt Ltd, New Delhi (India), (1965).

Related to post-Harappan Indian scripts:

LAi-60 Sivapriyananda, "Brahmi, Kharoshthi, Telugu, Oriya, Kannada, Gurmukhi, Devanagari", *The India Magazine,* 36-45, (August 1982).

LAi-61 Upasak Chandrika, S., *History and Palaeography of Mauryan Brahmi Script,* Nava Nalanda Mahavihara, Nalanda (India), (1960).

LAi-62 Iyer, S. (Ed.), *Studies in Indian Epigraphy: Journal of the Epigraphical Society of India*, **Vol. XI**, Caxton Publishing, Delhi (India), (2008)

LAi-63 Salomon, R., *Indian Epigraphy: A Guide to the Study of Inscriptions in Sanskrit, Prakrit, and Other Indo-Aryan Languages*, Oxford University Press, Oxford (England), (1998). See esp. pp. 34 ff.

LAi-64 Dani, A., *Indian Palaeography, 2nd ed.,* Munshiram Manoharlal Publishers Pvt Ltd, New Delhi, (India), (1986).

Related to South-East Asian and Tibetan scripts:

LAi-65 Coedes, G.; Vella, W. (Eds.), (Trans. Cowing, S.), *The Indianized States of Southeast Asia,* University Press of Hawaii, Honolulu (HI), (1968).

LAi-66 Sarkar, K., *Early Indo-Cambodian Contacts, Literacy and Linguistics,* Visva-Bharati, Santiniketan, West Bengal (India), (1968).

LAi-67 Coedes, G., *The Making of South East Asia,* Routledge & Kegan Paul, London (England), (1966).

LAi-68 Nagaraju, S.; Ramesh K.V. et al, (Eds.), Palaeography of the Earliest Inscriptions of Burma, Thailand, Cambodia and Vietnam, Agam Kala Prakashan, Delhi (India), (Dr. B. Chhabra Felicitation) 67-80, (1984).

LAi-69 de Casparis, J. G., *Indonesian Palaeography (Handbuch der Orientalistik Division 3, Vol. 4, Part I),* Brill, Leiden (Netherlands), (1975).

LAi-70 Huffman, F. E., *Cambodian System of Writing and Beginning Reader,* Yale University Press, New Haven, CT (USA), (1970).

LAi-71 Danwiwat, N., *Thai Writing System,* Buske, Hamburg (Germany), (1987).

LAi-72 Chandra, L., *Indian Scripts in Tibet,* Sharada Rani, New Delhi (India), (1982).

LAi-73 Mair, V., "Cheng Chi'iao's Understanding of Sanskrit: The Concept of Spelling in China (re: Buddhist Influence in E. Asian Scripts), *A Festschrift in Honour of Professor Jao Tsung-I on the Occasion of His Seventy-fifth Anniversary,* Chinese University of Hong Kong, Hong Kong (China), 331-41, (1993).

Related to Western theories of the absence of writing in ancient India:

LAi-74 Farmer, S.; Sproat, R.; Witzel, M., "The Collapse of the Indus-Script Thesis: The Myth of a Literate Harappan Civilization", *Electronic J. Vedic Studies* **11:2** 19-57 (2004).

LITERATURE CITED

LAi-75 See, e.g., some of the postings at http://www.ancientscripts.com/.
LAi-76 See p. xiii in Preface in Deshpande, Madhav, M., *Samskrtasubodhini: A Sanskrit Primer,* University of Michigan Press, Ann Arbor, MI (USA), (2001).
LAi-77 Daniels, Peter; Harrak, Amir (Eds.), "Contacts between Semitic and Indic Scripts", [In *Contacts between Cultures: Selected Papers from the 33rd International Congress of Asian and North African Studies,* Toronto, *West Asia and North Africa* Edwin Mellen, Lewiston, NY (USA), **1**, 146-52, (15-25 August 1990).
LAi-78 Bṻhler, G., "Indische Palaeographic von circa 350 Chr.- circa 1300 P. Chr.", *Grundriss der Indo-arischen Philologie und Alterumkunde,* Trubner, Strassburg (France), **1**, (1896).
LAi-79 Weber, A., "Uber den semitischen Ursprung des indischen Alphabets, *Zeitschrift der Deutschen Morgenlandischen Gesellschaft,* **10**, 389-406, (1856).

Related to Indian viewpoints on writing in ancient India:
LAi-80 Varma, K.C., *Annals of the Bhandarkar Oriental Research Institute, LXI,* Karve Nagar, Pune (India), (1980).
LAi-81 Dandekar, R.N. (Ed.), *Progress of Indic Studies, 1917-1942,* Bhandarkar Oriental Research Institute, Pune (India), (1942). See also: *Vedic Mythological Tracts,* Ajanta Publications, Delhi (India), (1979); *Insights into Hinduism,* Ajanta Publications, Delhi (India), (1979); *Exercises in Indology,* Ajanta Publications, Delhi (India), (1981).
LAi-82 Rao, R.P.N.; Yadav, N.; Vahia, M.N.; Joglekar, H.; Adhikari, R.; Mahadevan, I., "Entropic Evidence for Linguistic Structure in the Indus Script", *Science* DOI: 10.1126/science.11170391, (23 April 2009).

Related to Paanini and "spoken" Sanskrit vs. the literary language:
LAi-83 "Speaking fluency" in Classical (Paaninian, Paninian) Sanskrit merely implies sentence construction and articulation to express ideas, according to the strict grammatical rules of Paaninian Sanskrit. The jury is still out on whether Classical Sanskrit, as it has come down to us today, was truly a spoken language, or merely a refined, literature version of a spoken language. If it is merely the literary language that we have today, then what the spoken language was must be reconstructed. This author is of the opinion that Paanini (Panini) and his predecessor grammarians (of which he cites 63) effectively fossilized Sanskrit, and thus killed any record of earlier, spoken versions. At the time of Paanini, who certainly pre-dates Buddha and Mahaawiira (Mahavir) since there is no mention of anything even remotely related to Buddhism or Jainism in his works,

LITERATURE CITED

Sanskrit was already not a spoken language. Rather, it was like the language found at Boghaz-Koy in Anatolia (see Refs. [HIi-41, HIi-43 to HIi-47]), i.e. an *Apabrahmsa*. It is this author's hypothesis that the earlier, spoken versions of Sanskrit may have contained everyday words alluded to elsewhere in this book, such as *wadra*, *udra* ("water") or the verb *wir* ("to show courage; to contest"), which now appear to be lost forever, as well as familiar forms such as *tuu*, which is used for "you" in just about every Indo-European language, ancient and modern, including ones on the Indian subcontinent, in place of the formalized Paaninian *twam*, i.e. *tu-am*. This spoken Sanskrit may have also retained, in everyday use, grammatical forms such as the pluperfect, a tense which is now fossilized as the "7th aorist" of Classical Sanskrit. Earlier, spoken versions may also have had less formalized and compulsory use of *Sandhi*. Any linguist will admit that Sandhi is a mandatory construct for the literary language derived from natural euphony in the spoken language. In Paaninian Sanskrit, *Sandhi* is *compulsory*. That is much like making it compulsory to *always* pronounce *did you* and *want to* in American English as *didja* and *wanna* -- examples of *Sandhi* in American English.

LITERATURE CITED

HIh
(Relating to general human history, including migrations, except Indian history)

HIh-1. Cavalli-Sforza, L. L.; Cavalli-Sforza, F., *The Great Human Diasporas: The History of Diversity and Evolution,* Addison-Wesley, Reading, MA (USA), (1995).
HIh-2. Teresi, D., *Lost Discoveries: The Ancient Roots of Modern Science - From the Babylonians to the Maya,* Simon Schuster, New York, NY (USA), (2002).
HIh-3. Zohary, D.; Hopf, M., *Domestication of Plants in the Old World, (Re: migration into Mideast), Ed. # 3,* Clarendon Press, Oxford (England), (2000).
HIh-4. Bellwood, P., "Early Agriculturalist Population Diasporas? Farming, Languages, & Genes", *Ann. Rev. Anthropol.* **30,** 181, (2001).
HIh-5 For a concise summary of human migrations of the last 100,000 years, see, e.g.: Stix, G., "Traces of a Distant Past", *Scientific American*, 56-63, (July 2008).
HIh-6. Fleet, K., *The Cambridge History of Turkey*, Cambridge University Press, Cambridge (England), (2009).
HIh-7. Silverman, D. (Contributor), *Ancient Egypt*, Duncan Baird Publishers, London (England), (2003).
HIh-8 Wilford, J.N., "Archaeologists Unearth a War Zone 5,500 Years Old", *The New York Times International*, (16 December 2005).

LITERATURE CITED

395

HIi
(Relating to Indian history)

Recent, seminal references:
HIi-1. "Boring No More, a Trade-Savvy Indus Emerges", *Science* **320**, 1276-1285, (6 June 2008).

Significant references related to archaeology:
HIi-2. Archaeological Survery of India, "Excavations - Dholavira", http://www.asi.nic.in/asi_exca_2007_dholavira.asp .
HIi-3. Archaeological Survery of India, "Excavations- Adichchanallur, An Iron Age Urn Burial Site", http://www.asi.nic.in/asi_exec_adichchanallur.asp ,
HIi-4. Archaeological Survery of India, "Excavations - 2006-2007", http://www.asi.nic.in/asi_exca_2007_sanauli.asp , (2007).
HIi-5. Meadow, R. (Ed.), Harappa Excavations, 1986-1990: A multidisciplinary approach to 3rd millennium urbanism" *Monographs in World Archeology,* Prehistory Press **3**, (December 1991).
HIi-6. Whitehouse, D. (Ed.), *BBC News*, Science/Technology section, *"Earliest writing found"*, http://news.bbc.co.uk/1/hi/science/nature/334517.stm .
HIi-7. *Harappa Excavations 1986-1990: A Multidisciplinary Approach to Third Millennium Urbanism,* Prehistory Press, Madison, WI (USA), (1991).
HIi-8. **(a)** Kenoyer, J.M.; Allchin, R. & B. (Eds.), "Excavations at Harappa 1994-1995: New Perspectives on the Indus Script, Craft Activities, and City Organisation", *South Asian Archaeology 1995,* Oxford & IBH, New Delhi (India), (1997). **(b)** See also: "Mehrgarh", http://en.wikipedia.org/wiki/Mehrgarh .
HIi-9 Bakliwal, P.C.; Grover, A.K., *Rec. Geol. Surv. India,***116**, (1988).

Related to ancient landmarks, cities etc. (e.g. Saraswati river, Dwaarakaa (Dwarka, Dvarka):
HIi-10 (a) Hawthorne, M., "Dvaraka: Behold the Holy City Where Krishna Was Prince", *Hinduism Today, Jan/Feb/March 2008*, pp. 62-66, (2008). **(b)** See also: http://en.wikipedia.org/wiki/Dwarka
HIi-11 Francfort, H.-P., "Evidence for Harrapan Irrigation System in Haryana and Rajasthan", *Eastern Anthropologist* **45**, 87-103, (1992).
HIi-12 For studies and references on the original course and later, sudden drying up of the Saraswati river around 1900 B.C.E., and on the very large number of Harappan sites identified along the Saraswati's bed, and, more notably, some claims that the Saraswati river did not even exist, see, e.g.: **(a)** Bakliwal, P.C.;

LITERATURE CITED

Grover, A.K., "Signature and Migration of Sarasvati River in the Thar Desert, Western India", *Rec. Geol. Survey of India* **116**, 77-86, (1988). **(b)** LANDSAT at http://landsat.gsfc.nasa.gov **(c)** http://india.mapsofindia.com/culture/indian-rivers/saraswati-river.html **(d)** http://en.wikipedia.org/wiki/Sarasvati **(e)** http://en.wikipedia.org/wiki/Out_of_India_theory **(g)** Lawler, A., "News and Analysis: Archaeology In Indus Times, the River Didn't Run Through It", *Science*, **332**, 23 (1 April 2011).

HIi-13 Thappar, B.K., "Kalibangan: A Harappan Metropolis beyond the Indus Valley", *Expedition* **17:2,** 19-33, (1975).

HIi-14 Misra, S.S, *Fresh Light on Indo-European classification and chronology*, Ashutosh Prakashan Sansthan, Varanasi (India), (1980).

HIi-15 Sethna, K.D., *The Problem of Aryan Origins (from an Indian Point of View)*, Aditya Prakashan, Delhi (India), (1992).

HIi-16 Deo, S.; Surynath, K (Eds.), *The Aryan Problem*, Bharatiya Itihasa Sankalana Samiti, Pune (India), (1993).

HIi-17 Misra, S.S., *The Aryan Problem: A Linguistic Approach,* Munshiram Manoharlal Publishers Pvt Ltd, New Delhi (India), (1992).

HIi-18 Gupta, S.P., *The Indus-Saraswati Civilization*, Pratibha Prakashan, Delhi (India), (1996).

HIi-19 Singh, B., *The Vedic Harappans*, Aditya Prakashan, New Delhi (India), (1992).

HIi-20 Asimov, M.S., *Ethnic Problems of the History of Central Asia in the Early Period: Second Millenium B.C. In Greek and English*, Hayka, Moscow (Russia), (1981).

Related to South India:
HIi-21 Kishitar, V.R.R., *Pre-Historic South India*, Madras (Chennai), India, (1951).
HIi-22 Sastri, K.A.N., *A History of South India,* Oxford University Press, New Delhi (India), (2002).
HIi-23 See p.p 52ff., p.p 56ff. in Reference HIi-22.
HIi-24 See p.p. 78-80 in Reference Hii-22.

Related to origins of Tamil:
HIi-25 Gernot, W., *Hurrians*, Aris & Philips, Warminster (UK), (1989). Ltd, Delhi (India), 52ff, 56ff, (2006), (ISBN: 81-208-0164-4).
HIi-26 For ruminations on Tamil origins, see, e.g.: von Furer-Haimendorf, C., *Proc. 37th Indian Science Congress, Poona, 1950*, Part II: Presidential Addresses, 175-180, (1950). Also see: von Furer-Haimendorf, C., *Tamil Culture*, **2**, 127-135, (1953).

LITERATURE CITED

HIi-27 Lawler, A., "Central Asia's Lost Civilization", *Discover Magazine*, (30 November 2006). Available at: http://discovermagazine.com/2006/nov/ancient-towns-excavated-turkmenistan.

Related to ancient Indian theories of creation:
HIi-28:

> *RgWeda (RgVeda, Rig Veda)* **X.190**, **X.129**, widely considered to be the original Hindu creation hymns, upon which all Hindu theories of creation are technically based. In the opinion of many, they appear to convey profound intellectual contemplation on the part of their authors: They apparently come to conclusions coincidentally similar to theories of creation in modern physics, such as the Big Bang. And this is apparently done simply through powers of deduction (i.e. without the body of knowledge of modern physics). And in some cases they even appear to go further than these modern theories. For example, **X.190** posits that the Creator created the Laws of Physics (*Rta, Rita*) ***first*** [*Rtam cha Satyam chaabhiddhaat tapaso adhiajaayata*], and only *then* could the rest of Creation be born. The authors apparently and quite logically deduced that one needed a framework (*Rta*, the Laws of Physics) before one could even begin thinking of things like energy, space, the matter of heavenly bodies, and the other paraphernalia of Creation. It further posits that if a different set of Laws of Physics had been used by the Creator, one would have ended up with a different Universe! This hymn also envisions the concept of Nothingness (that is to say, *NO* matter, *NO* space, *NO* time, etc.) and, like all subsequent Hindu theories of creation, posits that *Existence*, i.e. the Universe as we know it, sprang from *Non-Existence*. (Indeed, in the other hymn (**X.129**, see below), it is said that "there was neither Existence nor Non-Existence" (*na asad aasiit na sad aasit tadaaniim*)!) That is to say, *even non-existence did not exist!* The theories also posit that Creation is recurring (*yathaa puurwam akalpayat*), always followed by Destruction, then Creation, then Destruction, then Creation, etc., with the universe existing in each cycle for tens of billions of years. And again, each cycle of Creation is said to start with an intense point of pure energy (*Tapas*), hauntingly anticipating the mathematical singularity in the origins of the Big Bang, although this is given a spiritual bent by saying that the Creator is responsible for this *Tapas*. More profoundly, **X.190** envisions that Time (*samwatsaras*) is a property that *needs to be created* (i.e. it is not something that we can assume always existed), and it is created *after* Space (*samudraadarnawaadadhi*) is created. **X.190** also gives a spiritual or moral bent to the Creation, saying that Truth (*Satyam*) was created

along with the Laws of Physics (*Rtam*), these being the *two pillars* of this particular Hindu theory of Creation; and of course that a Creator (here surprisingly, male, although in all later Hindu theology God is neuter) *is* responsible for the Creation! **X.129** goes a bit beyond **X.190** in the sense that it postulates that in the Beginning of All Beginnings, there was neither Existence nor Non-Existence (*Naasadaasiinno sadaasiit tadaaniim*)! **X.129** also gives an atheistic bent to the theory of Creation in its last two stanzas (#6, #7), saying "Who truly knows, who can here declare it, whence comes this Creation?...He (the Creator, masculine) alone truly knows, or perhaps even He knows not." (The Creator is here, again, surprisingly, male, although in later, mainstream monistic Hinduism, God is always neuter and may be considered inseparable from (*adwaita*) or separate from (*dwaita*) the Creation, according to two different schools of Indian philosophical thought, denoted *Adwaita* and *Dwaita*.)

Related to ancient Indian philosophy as represented in the Upanishads and other Vedaantic (Vedantic) writings:

HIi-29 (HIi-42a). See, e.g., Limaye, A.V.P.; Vadekar, R.D., *Eighteen Principle Upanisads*, Vaidika Samsodhana Mandala (Vedic Research Institute), Pune (India), (1958).

HIi-30 Gambhīrānanda, S., *Ch*āndogya Upaniṣad: *With the Commentary of Śri Śankarācārya*, Advaita Ashrama, Calcutta (India), 1997.

HIi-31 Chinmayananda, *Discourses on Aitareya Upanisad*, Central Chinmaya Mission Trust, Mumbai (India), (2000).

HIi-32 Chinmayananda, *Discourses on Īśāvāsya Upanisad*, Central Chinmaya Mission Trust, Mumbai (India), (1997).

HIi-33 Chinmayananda, *Discourses on Mandukya Upanishad*, Central Chinmaya Mission Trust, Bombay (India), (1990).

HIi-34 Gambhīrānanda, S., *Taittirīya Upanisad: With the Commentary of Śankarācārya*, Advaita Ashrama Publication Department, Calcutta (India), (1998).

HIi-35 Mādhavānanda, *The Brhadāranyaka Upanisad: With the Commentary of Śankarācārya*, Advaita Ashrama Publication Department, Calcutta (India), (1993).

HIi-36 Chinmayananda, *Discourses on Kathopanisad*, Central Chinmaya Mission Trust, Mumbai (India), (2000).

HIi-37 Swaminathan, C.R., *Kanvasatapathabrahmanam*, **1**, Motilal Banarsidass Publishers Private Limited, New Delhi (India).

HIi-38 See p.p. 224-225, 258-263 in Reference LAi-9.

HIi-39 (a) *Taittiriiya Samhita* **VII.** 4. 8. **(b)** *Tandya Braahmana,* **V.** 9. **(c)** See also: Houben, J.E.B., *The Pravargya Brahmana of the Taittiriya Aranyaka: An Ancient Commentary on the Pravargya Ritual*, Motilal Banarsidass Publishers Private Limited, New Delhi (India), (1991). See also: Bali, S., *Sayana's Upodhata on Taittiriya Samhita and the Rgveda Samhita*, Motilal Banarsidass Publishers Private Limited, New Delhi (India).

Related to F. Max Müller:
HIi-40 (a) See, e.g., *Max Mḧller* http://en.wikipedia.org/wiki/Max_M%C3%BCller . **(b)** See also: http://en.wikipedia.org/wiki/Indo-Aryan_migration .

HIi-41 (a) Müller, F.M., *Lectures on the Science of Language: Delivered at the Royal Institution of Great Britain in April, May, & June 1861, 5th Edition, Revised,* Longmans, Green, and Co., London (England), (1866). **(b)** See also: Müller, F.M., *A History of Ancient Sanskrit Literature: So Far As It Illustrates the Primitive Religion of the Brahmans,* Bhuvaneshwari Ashrama (Allahabad), Asian Educational Services, New Delhi (India), (1993). **(c)** See also: Figulla, H.; Weber, O., *Keilschrifttexte aus Boghazkoi, Vol. 3,* Hinrichs, Liepizig (Germany), (1919).

HIi-42 Van Den Bosch, L., *Friedrich Max Müller: A Life Devoted to the Humanities*, Brill Academic Publishers, Boston, MA (USA), (2002).

Related to the excavations at Boghaz-koy:
HIi-43 Thieme, P., "The 'Aryan Gods' of the Mitanni Treaties", *Journal of the American Oriental Society,* **80,** 301-317, (1960).

HIi-44 Raulwing, P, "Zur etymologischen Beurtelung der Berufsbezeichnung Assussanni des Pferdetrainers Kikkuli von Mittani", ., in Anreiter et al, (Eds), *Man and the Animal World, Studies in Archaeozoology, Archaeology, Anthropology and Paleolinguistics in Memoriam Sandor Bokonyi, Archaeologia Main Series 8, Budapest,* 1-57, (1996).

HIi-45 Kammenhuber, A., *Hippologia hethitica,* Harrassowitz, Wiesbaden (Germany), (1962).

HIi-46 Ekrem, A., *Hattian and Hittite Civilizations*; Publication of the Republic of Turkey; Ministry of Culture, Ankara Publishing, Ankara, (Turkey), (2001), (ISBN: 975-17-2756-1). See also Ref. **HIi-41(c)** above.

HIi-47 Francfort, H.-P., *Eastern Anthropologist,* **45,** 87-103, (1992).

LITERATURE CITED

Relating to Indian viewpoints on ancient Indian history:
HIi-48 Misra, S.S., *New Lights on Indo-European comparative studies.* Varanasi: Manisha Prakashan, Manisha Oriental Research Series, (1975).
HIi-49 Misra, S.S., *The Old-Indo-Aryan, a historical and comparative analysis*, Ashutosh Prakashan Sansthan, Varanasi (India), (1993).
HIi-50 Kak, S., "Archaeoastronomy and Literature", *Current Science* **73**, 624-627, (10 October 1997).
HIi-51 Tripathi, R.S., *History of Ancient India,* Motilal Banarsidass Publishers Pvt Ltd, Delhi (India), (1999), (ISBN: 81-208-0018-4).
HIi-52. Frawley, D., "On the Banks of the Saraswati: The ancient history of India revised," *The Quest*, 22-30, (Autumn 1992).
HIi-53 Jacobi, H., *Indian Antiquary*, **Vol. XXIII**, 154, pp. 85 ff. (1895). Excerpts available at:
http://www.google.com/#hl=en&source=hp&q=Jacobi%2C+H.%2C+Indian+Antiquary%2C+Vol.+XXIII%2C+154&aq=f&aqi=&oq=&fp=2cca7b2e99206b9c

Related to ancient Indian astronomy:
HIi-54 Billard, R., *L'Astronomie Indienne,* Ecole Francaise d'Extreme Orient, Paris (France), (1971).
HIi-55 Thurston, H., *Early Astronomy,* Springer-Verlag, NY (USA), 188, (1994).
HIi-56 Kak, S.C., "The Astronomical Code of the Rigveda", *Puratattva: Bulletin of the Indian Archaeological Society* **25**, 1-20, (1994).

Indian and pro-Indian viewpoints on ancient Indian history, cont.:
HIi-57 Frawley D., *Gods, Sages and Kings: Vedic Secrets of Ancient Civilization*, Passage Press, Salt Lake City, UT (USA), (1991). See also: Feuerstein, G.; Kak, S.; Frawley, D., *In Search of the Cradle of Civilization: New Light on Ancient India*, Motilal Banarsidass Publishers Private Limited, Delhi (India), (2001).
HIi-58 Frawley, D., *The Myth of the Aryan Invasion of India*, Voice of India, New Delhi (India), (1994).
HIi-59 Panconcelli-Calcia, G., *Phonetik als Naturwissenschaft*, Wissentschaftliche Editionsgesellschaft mbH, Berlin, Germany (1948). pp. 51 ff.
HIi-60 Sastry, K., *Vedanga Jyotisa of Lagadha,* Indian National Science Academy, New Delhi (India), (1985).

LITERATURE CITED

Relating to ancient Indian works in engineering and mathematical sciences:

HIi-61 See introduction and discussion of predecessor works in *Natyasastra of Bharatamuni, with the Commentary of Abhinavabharati by Abhinavaguptacarya,* Parimal Publications, Delhi, (India), (1988) (ISBN: 81-7110-002-3). See also: *ibid.*, Vol. 1, Ch.'s 1-7.

HIi-62 *Natya Sastra of Bharatamuni [Raga Nrtya Series No. 2],* (Trans. Into English by a Board of Scholars), Sri Satguru Publications, Delhi (India), (1981), (ISBN: 81-7030-134-3).

HIi-63 Arya, R., *Vaastu, The Indian Art of Placement, Design and Decoration of Homes to Reflect Eternal Spiritual Principles,* Destiny Books, Rochester, VT (USA), (2000), (ISBN: 0-89281-885-9).

HIi-64. Maharaja, Jagadguru Swami Sri Bharati Krsna Tirthaji (Author); Agrawala, V.S. (Ed.), *Vedic Mathematics,* Motilal Banarsidass Publishers Pvt, (2006).

HIi-65 See, e.g., the references in: Mukhopadhyaya, G., *Surgical Instruments of the Hindus: A Comparative Study of the Surgical Instruments of the Greek, Roman, Arab and the Modern European Surgeons, with 396 Illustrations in 82 Plates,* R.K. Naahar & Co., New Delhi (India), (1977).

HIi-66 Sankalia, H.D., *Prehistoric and Historic Archaeology of Gujarat,* Munshiram Manoharlal Publishers Pvt Ltd, New Delhi (India), (1987), (ISBN: 81-215-0049-4).

Relating to ancient Indian works on politics and law:

HIi-66 Gairola, S.V. (Ed.), *Arthasastra of Kautilya and The Canakya Sutra [The Vidyabhawan Sanskrit Granthamala],* Chowkhamba Vidyabhawan, Varanasi (No. India), (1984).

HIi-67 Rangarajan, L.N., *The Arthashastra, [Kautilya],* Penguin Group, New York, NY (USA), (1992).

HIi-68 Bhatt, R., *Manusmrti [The Vrajajivan Pracyabharati Granthamala],* Chaukhamba Sanskrit Prathishthan, Delhi (India), (Reprint edition 1987).

Relating to ancient Indian works on philosophy:

HIi-69 See, e.g., Dutt, M.N.; Shastri, J.K.L. (Eds.), *Agni Mahapuranam, Sanskrit Text, English Translation and Index of Verses (Vol. 1),* Parimal Publications, Delhi (India), (2001), (ISBN: 81-7110-192-3).

LITERATURE CITED

IEu
(Relating to Indo-European languages, history, migration, etc.)

Relating to Indo-European linguistics:

IEu-1 Bopp, Franz, *A Comparative Grammar of the Sanscrit, Zend, Greek, Latin, Lithuanian, Gothic, German, & Sclavonic Languages,* (Translated into English from the German by Lt. Eastwick), Elibron Classics, Bibliobazaar, Charleston, SC (USA), (ISBN 1-4021-5370-8). (Originally published 1862; several reprints through 2006.) (1862)

IEu-2 Brugmann, K., *Kurze Vergleichende Grammatik der Indogermanischen Sprachen*, Karl J. Tubner, Strassburg (Strassbourg, Strasbourg, France), (1904).

IEu-3 Brugmann, K. (Trans. from the German by Wright, J.), *Elements of The Comparative Grammar of the Indo-Germanic Languages,* B. Westermann & Co., NY (USA), Reprint by Kessinger Publishing Legacy Reprints, (1888).

IEu-4 Osthoff, H.; Brugmann, K., *Morphologische Untersuchungen auf dem Gebiete der indogermanischen Sprachen,* S. Hirzel, Leipzig (Germany), (1878).

IEu-5 Pokorny, J., *Indogermanisches Etymologisches Woerterbuch*, Edition of French and European Publications, Paris (France), (1969).

IEu-6 Szemerenyi, O.J.L., *Introduction to Indo-European Linguistics [Translated from Einfuhrung in die vergleichende Sprachwissenschaft],* Oxford University Press, Oxford (England), (1999).

IEu-7 Lehmann, W., (Ed.), *A Reader in 19th Century Historical Indo-European Linguistics,* Indiana University Press, Bloomington, IN (USA), (1967).

IEu-8 Lehmann, W.P., *Theoretical Bases of Indo-European Linguistics,* Routledge Press, London (England), (1999).

IEu-9 Lehmann, W.P., *Proto-Indo-European syntax*, University of Texas Press, Austin, TX (USA), (1974).

IEu-10 Beekes, R., *Comparative Indo-European Linguistics,* John Benjamins Publishing Co., Amsterdam (Netherlands), (1959).

IEu-11 Rix, Hulmet, et al, *Lexicon der Indogermanischen Verben,* John Benjamins Publishing Co., Amsterdam (Netherlands), (1998).

IEu-12 Gamkrelidze, T. V.; Ivanov; V.V., *Indo-European and the Indo-Europeans, A Reconstruction & Historical Analysis of a Proto-Language and a Proto-Culture, Parts I & II, The Text,* Mouton de Gruyter, Berlin (Germany), (1995).

IEu-13 (a) von Schlegel, F., *The Philosophy of Life and Philosophy of Language in a Course of Lectures*, H.G. Bohn, London (England), (1847). **(b)** See also: "Out of India theory", http://en.wikipedia.org/wiki/Out_of_India_theory .

LITERATURE CITED

IEu-14 Kaul, R.K., *Studies in William Jones: An Interpreter of Oriental Literature*, South Asia Books, New Delhi (India), (1996).

Relating to "Proto-Indo-European" derivations:
IEu-15 (a) Mackey, Jake, Dept. of Classics, Princeton University, private communication, (2007).
(b) Sen, S.K.; Hamp, E.P., in *Encyclopedia of Indo-European Culture* , 503 (1997).
(c) Sen, S.K., "Proto-Indo-European, a Multiangular View", *J. Indo-European Studies,* **22**, 67-90 (1994).
(d) Sampson, G., "A reconstructed specimen of PIE", at:
http://www.grsampson.net/Q_PIE.html
(e) See, e.g., http://en.wikipedia.org/wiki/The_king_and_the_god and http://simple.wikipedia.org/wiki/Proto-Indo-European_language

Relating to Indo-European linguistics, cont.:
IEu-16 Gimbutas, M.; Robbins Dexter, M.; Jones-Bley, K. (Eds.), *The Kurgan Culture and the Indo-Europeanization of Europe: Selected Articles From 1952 to 1993*, Institute for the Study of Man, Washington, D.C. (USA), (1997).

Relating to Germanic/Gothic:
IEu-17 Konig, E.; Van der Auwera, J. (Eds.), *The Germanic Languages,* Routledge, London (England), (1994).
IEu-18 Prokosch, E., *A Comparative Germanic Grammar*, University of Pennsylvania Linguistic Society of America, Philadelphia, PA (USA), (1939).
IEu-19 Wright, J., *Grammar of the Gothic Language*, Clarendon Press, Oxford (England), (1910).
IEu-20 Brauner, W., *Althochdeutsche Grammatik*, Henry Holt and Co., New York (USA), (1967).
IEu-21 Ellis, J., *An Elementary Old High German Grammar, Descriptive and Comparative*, Clarendon Press, Oxford (England), (1953).

Relating to Avestan:
IEu-23 Beekes, R., *A Grammar of Gatha-Avestan,* E.J. Brill, Leiden (Netherlands), (1988).
IEu-24 *[http://www.avesta.org/avesta.html], http://www.fas.harvard.edu/~iranian/,* (2008).

LITERATURE CITED

IEu-25 Jackson, A.V. W., *An Avesta Grammar in comparison with Sanskrit,* Wissenschaftliche Buchgesellschaft, Darmstadt (Germany) (1968).
IEu-26 Schmitt, R., *Altpersisch*. In *Compendium Linguarum Iranicarum,* Reichert, Wiesbaden (Germany), 56-85, (1989).
IEu-27 Geldner, K. F., *Avesta, the Sacred Book of the Parsis. 3 vols,* Kohlhammer, Stuttgart (Germany), (1896).
IEu-28 Hoffman, K. Avestan language, *Encyclopedia Iranica,* **3:1,** 47-62, (1988).

Relating to Classical and Homeric Greek:
IEu-29 Morwood, J., *Oxford Grammar of Classical Greek,* Oxford University Press, New York (USA), (2001).
IEu-30 Cunliffe, R., *Lexicon of the Homeric Dialect,* University of Oklahoma University Press, Norman, OK (USA), (1963).
IEu-31 Smyth, H., *Greek Grammar,* Harvard University Press, MA (USA), (1984).
IEu-32 Liddell, H.G.; Scott, R., *Greek-English Lexicon,* Oxford University Press, London (England), (1996).
IEu-33 Liddell, H.G.; Scott, R., *Intermediate Greek-English Lexicon,* Oxford University Press, London (England), (1995).

Relating to Russian:
IEu-34 Brown, N., *Russian Course,* Penguin Group, New York, NY (USA), (1996).
IEu-35 Cubberley, P., *Russian: A Linguistic Introduction,* Cambridge University Press, London (England), (2002).
IEu-36 Fairbanks, G.; Leed, R., *Basic Conversational Russian,* Holt, Rinehart & Winston, New York (USA), (1964).
IEu-37 Unbegaun, B.O., *Russian Grammar*, Oxford University Press, Oxford (England), (1957).

Relating to Anglo-Saxon (Old English), Including Effects on Modern English:
IEu-38 Sweet, H., *Sweet's Anglo-Saxon Primer*, Rev. by Norman Davis, Clarendon Press, Oxford (England), (1882).
IEu-39 Quirk, R.; Wrenn, C.L., *An Old English Grammar, Methuen,* London (England), (1957).
IEu-40 Moore, S.; Knott, T.A., *The Elements of Old English, 10th Edition*, Rev. by James R. Hulbert, George Wahr Publishing Co., Ann Arbor, MI (USA), (1955).
IEu-41 Bright, J.W., *Bright's Anglo-Saxon Reader,* Henry Holt and Co., New York (USA), (1959).

IEu-42 Jones, C., *An Introduction to Middle English*, Holt, Rinehart and Winston, New York (USA), (1972).

IEu-43 Jones, D., *An Outline of English Phonetics, 1ˢᵗ Edition*, W. Heffer and Sons, Cambridge, MA (USA), (1918).

Relating to Latin, Including Effects on Modern Romance Languages:

IEu-44 Palmer, L.R., *The Latin Language*, University of Oklahoma Press, Norman, OK (USA), (1988). Palmer notes in this book: "We have now examined the evidence bearing on the prehistory of the Latin language and come to the tentative conclusion that the proto-Latins were an IE tribe originating in central Europe which entered Italy towards the end of the second millennium B.C.. Arriving in Latium about the tenth century B.C., they settled Latium in scattered rural communitities (or populi) which combined in loose confederations. Rome itself originated in a synoecismus of *cremating* Latin and inhuming Sabine folk."

IEu-45 Verner, K., "Eine Ausnahme der ersten Lautverschiebung", *Z. fur vergleichende Sprachforschung,* **23**, 97-130, (1877).

IEu-46 Wheelock, F., *Latin, An Introductory Course Based on Ancient Authors [College Outline Series],* Barnes & Noble, Inc., NY (USA), (1963).

IEu-47 Greenough, J.B. et al, *Allen and Greenough's New Latin Grammar,* Focus Publishing, Newburyport, MA (USA), (2001).

IEu-48 (a) Bennett, C., *New Latin Grammar,* Bolchazy-Carducci Publishers, Mundelein, IL (USA), (1998). (England), (1998). **(b)** Lewis, C.T., *Elementary Latin Dictionary,* Oxford University Press, London, (1998).

IEu-49 Caso, A., *The Kaso English to Italian Dictionary: With a Proposed One-to-One Relationship of Italian Graphemes (letters) and Phonemes (Sounds)*, Branden Books, Wellesley, MA, USA (2004) (ISBN 0-8283-2082-9).

Relating to Hittite:

IEu-50 Sturtevant, E., *A Comparative Grammar of the Hittite Language,* Linguistics Society of America, MD (USA), (1933).

IEu-51 Held, W.H.; Schmalstieg, W.R.; Gertz, J.E., *Beginning Hittite,* Slavica Publishers, Inc., (Indiana University Press), Bloomington, IN (USA), (1988).

LITERATURE CITED

GDn
(Relating to genetics, DNA, etc.)

General Genetics/DNA:
GDn-1. Cavalli-Sforza, L.L.; Menozzi, P.; Piazza, A., *The History and Geography of Human Genes,* Princeton University Press, Princeton, NJ (USA), (1994).
GDn-2 Wells, S., *Journey of Man: A Genetic Odyssey,* Princeton University Press, Princeton, NJ (USA), (2002).
GDn-3 Hedrick, P.; Waits, P., "What ancient DNA tells us", *Heredity* **94,** 463-4, (May 2005).
GDn-4 Ely, B., "How do researchers trace mitochondrial DNA over the centuries?", *Scientific American,* (January 2007).
GDn-5 Borman, S., "Mapping Human Genetic Variation", Genomics, *Chemical & Engineering News, [http://www.cen-online.org],* February 21 (2005); See also one of the original references cited in this article: Hinds, D.A., et al., *Science,* **307,** 1072-1079, (2005).
GDn-6 Henry, C. M., "Looking for Answers in Ancient DNA", *C&EN,* (29 March 2004).
GDn-7 Williamson, S.; Hubisz, M.; Clark, A.; Payseur, B.; Bustamante, C.; Nielsen, R., "Localizing Recent Adaptive Evolution in the Human Genome", *Public Library of Science (PLoS) Genetics,* **6,** e90, (3 June 2007).
GDn-8 Barreiro, L.; Laval, G.; Quach, H.; Patin, E.; Quintana-Murci, L., "Natural selection has driven population differentiation in modern humans", *Nat Genet* **40:3**, 340-345, (3 February 2008).
GDn-9 Knight, A.; Underhill, P.; Mortensen, H.; Zhivotovsky, L.; Lin, A.; Henn, B.; Louis, D.; Ruhlen, M.; Mountain, J., "African Y Chromosome and mtDNA Divergence Provides Insight into the History of Click Languages", *Current Biology* **31** 464-473, (18 March 2003).
GDn-10 Voight, B.; Kudaravalli, S.; Wen, W.; Pritchard, J., "A Map of Recent Positive Selection in the Human Genome", *Public Library of Science (PLoS) Biology* **4**, (2006).
GDn-11 Wade, N., "Still Evolving, Human Genes Tell New Story", *New York*, (7 March 2006).

Relating to the FOXP2 gene:
GDn-12 Itzhaki, J., "The FoxP2 story. A Tale of genes, language and human origins", http://genome.wellcome.ac.uk/doc_wtd020797.html (2003).

GDn-13 Enard, W.; Przeworski, M.; Fisher, S.; Lai Cecilia, S.L.; Wiebe, V.; Kitano, T.; Monaco, A.; Paabo, S., "Molecular evolution of FOXP2, a gene involved in speech and language", *Natur,* **418,** 869-872, (22 August 2002).

GDn-14 Lai, C; Fisher. S.; Hurst, J.; Levy, E.; Hodgson, S.; Fox, M.; Jeremiah, S.; Povey, S.; Jamison, D.; Green, E.; Vargha-Khadem, F.; Monaco, A. (Eds.), "The SPCH1 region on human 7q31: genomic characterization of the critical interval and localization of translocations associated with speech and language disorder". *Am J Hum Genet* **67,** 357-68, (2000).

GDn-15 Vargha-Khadem, F.; Gadian, DG; Copp, A.; Mishkin, M.; "FOXP2 and the neuroanatomy of speech and language", *Nature Reviews Neuroscience,* **6,** 131-137, (2005).

GDn-16 Haesler, S.; Rochefort, C.; Georgi, B; Licznerski, P.; Osten, P.; Scharff, C., "Incomplete and Inaccurate Vocal Imitation after Knockdown on FoxP2 in Songbird Basal Ganglia Nucleus Area X", *Public Library of Science (PLoS) Biology* **5,** e321, (2007).

General Genetics/DNA, cont.:

GDn-17 Macaulay, V.; Hill, C.; Achilli, A.; Rengo, C.; Clarke, D.; Meehan, W.; Blackburn, J.; Semino, O.; Scozzari, R.; Cruciani, F.; Taha A.; Shaari Norazila; Kassim, R.; Joseph, M.; Ismail, P.; Zainuddin, Z.; Goodwin, W.; Bulbeck, D.; Bandelt, H.; Oppenheimer, S.; Torroni, A.; Richards, M., "Single, Rapid Coastal Settlement of Asia Revealed by Analysis of Complete Mitochondrial Genomes" *Science* **308,** 1034-1036, (13 May 2005).

GDn-18 Melton, T. et al., "Genetic Evidence for the Proto-Austronesian Homeland in Asia: mtDNA and Nuclear DNA Variation in Taiwanese Aboriginal Tribes", *Am. J. Hum. Genet* **63,** 1807-1823, (1998).

Relating to littoral migration of ancient H. sapiens from Africa:

GDn-19 Oppenheimer, S.; Richards, M., "Slow Boat to Melanesia", *Nature,* **410** 166, (2001).

GDn-20 Shang, H.; Tong, H.; Zhang, S.; Chen, F.; Trinkaus, E., "An early modern human from Tianyuan Cave, Zhoukoudian, China", *Proceedings of the National Academy of Science USA (PNAS),* **104,** 6573-6578, (17 April, 2007).

GDn-21 Wilford, J., "Kenya Fossils Challenge Linear Evolution to Homo Sapiens", *The New York Times*, (9 August 2007).

GDn-22 Fuku, N.; Nishigaki, Y.; Tanaka, M., "Human mitochondrial genome polymorphism database (mtSNP)", *Tanpakushitsu Kakusan Koso,* **50,** 1753-8, (2005).

LITERATURE CITED

GDn-23 Horai, S. et al., "mtDNA polymorphism in East Asian Populations, with special reference to the peopling of Japan", *Am. J. Hum. Genet.* **59,** 579, (1996).

General Genetics/DNA, cont.:
GDn-24 "Initial sequence of the chimpanzee genome and comparison with the human genome", *Nature* **437,** 69-87, (1 September 2005).

Relating to DNA-based ancestry determinations of Dravidians and Aaryans (Aryans):
GDn-25 Barnabas, S.; Apte, R.V.; Suresh, C.G., "Ancestry and interrelationships of the Indians and their relationship with other world populations: A study based on Mitochondiral DNA Polymorphisms", *Ann Hum Genet* **60,** 409-422, (September 1996).
GDn-26 Barnabas S., Shouche Y., Suresh C.G., "High-Resolution mtDNA Studies of the Indian Population: Implications for Palaeolithic Settlement of the Indian Subcontinent", *Ann Hum Genet.,* **70,** 42-58, (January 2006).
GDn-27 Barnabas S., Joshi B., Suresh GC., "Indian-Asian relationship: mtDNA reveals more," *Naturwissenschaften,* **87,** 180-3, (April 2000).
GDn-28 Barnabas S., Apte R.V., Suresh CG., "Human evolution: the study of the Indian mitochondrial DNA.", *Naturwissenschaften* **83,** 28-9, (January 1996).
GDn-29 Bamshad et al., "Genetic evidence on the origins of Indian caste populations", *Genome Research,* **11,** 994-1004, (2001).
GDn-30 Kivisild et al., "The Genetic Heritage of the Earliest Settlers Persist Both in Indian Tribal and Caste Populations", *Am. J. Human Genet,* (2003).
GDn-31 Mukherjee et al., "High-resolution analysis of Y-chromosomal polymorphisms reveals signatures of population movements from central Asia and West Asia to India", *J. Genetics* **80,** 125-135, (December 2001).
GDn-32 Anjana, S.; Swarkar, S.; Audesh, B.; Awadesh, P.; Ramesh, B., "Genetic among five different population groups in India reflecting a Y-chromosome gene flow.", *J.Hum Genet,* **50,** 49-51, (2005).
GDn-33 Sengupta, Sanghamitra et al., "Polarity and Temporality of High-Resolution Y-Chromosome Distributions in India Identify Both Indigenous and Exogenous Expansions and Reveal Minor Genetic Influence of Central Asian Pastoralists", *Am. J. Human Genet* **78,** 202-221, (2006).

Newer (1985-2009) references relating to DNA-based ancestry of peoples of the Indian subcontinent:
GDn-34 Sharma, S., et al., "The Indian origin of paternal haplogroup R1a1[*] substantiates the autochthonous origin of Brahmins and the caste system ", *J. Human*

Genetics **54**, 47–55 (2009); *doi:10.1038/jhg.2008.2;* (published online 9 January 2009*)*

GDn-35 Sharma, S., et al., "The Autochthonous Origin and a Tribal Link of Indian Brahmins: Evaluation Through Molecular Genetic Markers", Paper # 1344/T presented at the 57th Annual Meeting of The American Society of Human Genetics, October 23–27, 2007 • San Diego, CA, USA.

GDn-36 Sahoo, S., et al., "A prehistory of Indian Y chromosomes: Evaluating demic diffusion scenarios", *Proceedings of the National Academy of Sciences* 103 (4): 843–848, doi:10.1073/pnas.0507714103. (Published online January 13, 2006).

Related to DNA-based ancestry of Japanese:

GDn-37 Omoto, K.; Saito, N., "Genetic origins of the modern Japanese: A partial support for the dual structure hypothesis", *Am. J. Phys. Anthropology* **102**, 437, (1997).

General Genetics/DNA, cont.:

GDn-38 Bromham L., and Penny, D., "The Modern Molecular Clock", *Nature Reviews Genetics,* **4**, 216, (March 2003).

GDn-39 Fitch David, H.A., "Lecture Notes: Deviations From the Null Hypotheses: Finite populations sizes and genetic drift, mutation and gene flow"*:* *http://www.nyu.edu/projects/fitch/courses/evolution/html/genetic_drift.html* (1997).

Relating to the R1a and R1b haplogroups:

GDn-40 (a) Re the haplogroup R1a, see, e.g.: *Haplogroup R1a (Y-DNA), Wikipedia,* http://en.wikipedia.org/wiki/Haplogroup_R1a_%28Y-DNA%29 **(b)** Re the haplogroup R1b, see, e.g.: *Haplogroup R1b (Y-DNA), Wikipedia,* http://en.wikipedia.org/wiki/Haplogroup_R1b_(Y-DNA)].

Related to DNA-based ancestry of Europeans:

GDn-41 Arnaiz-Villena, A.; Gomez-Casado, E.; Martinez-Laso, J., "Population genetic relationships between Mediterranean populations determined by HLA allele distribution and a historic perspective" Hypothesis article, *Tissue Antigens,* **60**, 111, (August 2002).

GDn-42 (a) Cinnioglu, C. et al., "Excavating Y-chromosome Haplotype strata in Anatolia", *Hum Genet,* 114, 127-48, (2004).

GDn-43 Maliarchuk, BA.; Czarny, J., "African DNA lineages in mitochondrial gene pool of Europeans", *Mol Biol (Mosk),* 39, 806-12, (2005).

GDn-44 (a) Semino et al., "The Genetic Legacy of Paleolithic Homo sapiens sapiens in Extant Europeans: A Y Chromosome Perspective", *Science,* **290**, 1155-59,

LITERATURE CITED

(2000). **(b)** See also: Passarino et. al., "Different genetic components in the Norwegian population revealed by the analysis of mtDNA and Y chromosome polymorphisms", *Eur. J. Hum. Genet,* **10,** 521-9, (2002).

GDn-45 Achilli, A.; Rengo, C.; Battaglia. V.; Pala, M.; Olivieri, A.; Fornarion, S.; Magri, C.; Scozzari, R.; Babudri, N.; Santachiara-Benerecetti, A.; Bandelt, H.; Semino, O.;Torroni, A., "Saami and Berbers--an unexpected mitochondrial DNA link", *Am J Hum Genet* **76,** 883-6, (May 2005).

GDn-46 Ammerman, A.; Pinhasi, R.; Banffy, E., "Ancient DNA from the first European farmers in 7500-year-old Neolithic sites", *Science,* **312,** 1875, (2006).

GDn-47 Wells, S., "The Eurasian Heartland: A continental perspective on Y-chromosome diversity", *Proceedings of the National Academy of Science USA (PNAS),* **98,** 10244-10249, (28 August 2001).

GDn-48 Oppenheimer, S., *Origins of the British: A Genetic Detective Story*, Basic Books, New York (USA), (2006), (ISBN-10: 0786718900, ISBN-13: 978-0786718900).

GDn-49 Wade, N., "A United Kingdom? DNA Suggests the Possibility", *The New York Times*, (6 March 2007).

Selected "racist" and "anti-racist" references and articles:

GDn-50 Lewontin, R., *The Triple Helix*, Harvard University Press, Cambridge, MA (USA), (2000). See also: Lewontin, R.; Singh, R.S.; Uyenoyama, M., *The Evolution of Population Biology*, Cambridge University Press, Cambridge (England), (2004).

GDn-51 Wade, N, "In the Genome Race, the Sequel is Personal", *The New York Times Science*, (4 September 2007).

GDn-52 Leroi, A., "A Family Tree in Every Gene", *The New York Times Op-Ed,* (14 March 2005).

Related to convergent evolution:

GDn-53 Angier, N., "Independently, Two Frogs Blaze the Same Venomous Path", *The New York Times*, (9 August 2005).

GDn-54 Clark, V.; Raxworthy, C.; Rakotomalala, V.; Sierwald, P.; Fisher, B., "Convergent evolution of chemical defense in poison frogs and arthropod prey between Madagascar and the Neotropics", *Proceedings of the National Academy of Science USA (PNAS)*, **102,** 11517-11622, (16 August 2005).

Related to DNA-based ancestry of Europeans, cont.:
GDn-55 "Cowabunga: Tuscan cattle shed light on where the Etruscans came to Italy from", *The Economist*, 82, (17 February 2007).

GDn-56 Wade, N., "DNA Boosts Herodotus' Account of Etruscans as Migrants to Italy", *The New York Times,* F3, (3 April 2007).

Newer (post-2005) research or publications proposing new theories counter to older genetic theories:
GDn-57 Grine, F.E.; Bailey, R.M.; Harvati, K.; Nathan, R.P.; Morris, A.G.; Henderson, G.M.; Ribot, I.; Pike, A.W.G., "Late Pleistocene Human Skull from Hofmeyr, South Africa, and Modern Origins", *Science* **315,** 226-229 (12 January 2007).

GDn-58 Zielinski, S., "Interview: Fred Spoor", *Smithsonian Magazine,* (October 2007).

GDn-59 Reich, D., "The HLA-DRB1 shared epitope is associated with susceptibility to rheumatoid arthritis in African Americans through European genetic mixture", *Bioinfobank*, [http://lib.bioinfo.pl/auid:1635956], (31 January 2008).

GDn-60 Wang, S.; Ray, N.; Rojas, W.; Parra, M.V.; Bedoya, G. et al, "Geographic Patterns of Genome Admixture in Latin American Mestizos", *[http://www.plosgenetics.org]*, (2008).

GDn-61 Bush, E.; Lahn Bruce, T., "The Evolution of Word Composition in Metazoan Promoter Sequence", *Public Library of Science (PloS)* **2,** e150, (November 2006).

Related to mitochondrial-DNA:
GDn-62 Anderson, S.; Bankier, A.T.; Barrell, B.G.; de Bruijn, M.H.; Coulson, A.R.; Drouin, J.; Eperon, I.C.; Nierlich, D.P.; Roe, B.A.; Sanger, F.; Schreier, P.H.; Smith, A.J.; Staden, R.; Young, I.G., " Sequence and organization of the human mitochondrial genome", *Nature* **290: 5806**, 457–465, (9 April 1981).

Newer (post-2005) research or publications proposing new theories counter to older genetic theories, cont.:
GDn-63 "Convergent adaptation of human lactase persistence in Africa and Europe", *Nature Genetics* **39,** 31-40, (10 December 2006).

GDn-64 Wade, N., "Lactose Tolerance in East Africa Points to Recent Evolution", *The New York Times International*, A15, (11 December 2006).

GDn-65 Re the seminal work of Dmitri K. Belyaev in this regard, see, e.g.: Wade, N., "Nice Rats, Nasty Rats: Maybe It's All In the Genes", *The New York Times, Science Times section,* (25 July 2006).

GDn-66 Malhi, R.S., et al., "Native American mtDNA Prehistory in the American Southwest", *Am. J. Phys. Anthropol.* **120,** 108, (2003).

LITERATURE CITED

Newer (1985-2009) references relating to DNA-based ancestry of peoples of the Indian subcontinent, cont.:
GDn-67 Indian Genome Variation Consortium, "Genetic landscape of the people of India: a canvas for disease gene exploration", *J. Genet.*, **87**. 3-20 (2008).
GDn-68 Zerjal, T. et al., "Y-chromosomal insights into the genetic impact of the caste system in India", *Hum. Genet.* **121**, 137–144 (2007).
GDn-69 Basu, A. et al. "Ethnic India: a genomic view, with special reference to peopling and structure", *Genome Res.* **13**, 2277–2290 (2003).
GDn-70 David Reich, D.; Thangaraj, K.; Patterson, N.; Price, A.L.; Singh, L., "Reconstructing Indian population history", *Nature*, **461**, 489-495 (2009).

Relating to the tree line during the peak of the last Ice Age ("Last Glacial Maximum", LGM):
GDn-71 See, e.g., http://en.wikipedia.org/wiki/File:Last_glacial_vegetation_map.png

INDEX

*A detailed Index is provided below.
This however does <u>not</u> include an author index.*

(NOTE: For all terms, see also definition and explanation in the GLOSSARY.)

!**Xhosan,** *see* **Khoisan**
!**Xo Bushman,** *absence of alveolar ridge in speakers of,* 12
!**Xo Bushman,** *articulation of,* 12

Aaryans, *in relation to Dravidians in India,* 185 *ff.*
Abjad, *definition of,* 64 *ff.* , 73
Abugida, *definition of,* 64 *ff.* , 73
Accent, ictus (stress), *see* **Accent, stress**
Accent, musical (tone), 43 *ff.*; *see also* **Tone**
Accent, pitch, 43 *ff. see also* **Tone**
Accent, stress, 43, 45 *ff.*
Afro-Asiatic, *language family, discussion,* 172 *ff.*
Afro-Asiatic, *language family, tree diagrams,* 142-143
Agglutinative languages, 280 *ff.*, 286
Akkadian, 224
Albanian, *language family, discussion,* 161
Aleut, 212
Algonquian-Ritwan, 211
Allophone, 99 *ff.*
Allotone, 101 *ff.*
Alphabet, *definition of,* 55 *ff.*, 73 *ff.*
Al-Sayyid Bedouin Sign Language (ASBSL), 6
Altaic and Japanese, *language family, discussion,* 178 *ff.*
Altaic and Japanese, *language family, tree diagrams,* 145
Altaic, *language family,* 178 *ff.*
Amharic, 172

Andaman Islands, *languages of,* 228-229
Andean *(language),* 216 *ff.*
Angramaya ("English-like") *character, of various languages,* 233-240
Angramaya ("English-like"), 233-240
Angramaya ("English-like"), *definition,* 234
Angramaya *nature, of various languages, discussion of,* 234-240
Anti-Nostratic, *see* **Nostratic**
Apabrahmsa, 155
Arabic, 172
Arabic, Old, 224
Ardha-Maagadhi, 154
Armenian, *language family, discussion,* 160
Articulation position, *see* **Artition**
Artition, 3, 10, 13, 14-41, 92 *ff.*
Artition, *discretization of, see* **Discretization**
Artition, *figure of human vocal tract,* 11, 12
Artition, *total number (15), in NAVLIPI, Table,* 92-93
Aryans, *see* **Aaryans**
Aspiration, 37 *ff.*
Assyrian *(language),* 224
Athabaskian, 212
Atlantic (African language), 169-170
Australian, 218, 230
Austro-Asiatic, *language family, discussion,* 203 *ff.*
Austronesian, *language family, discussion,* 174-177
Austronesian, *language family, tree diagrams,* 144
Avaigyaanic, *definition,* see **Vaigyaanic**
Avestan, 224
Aymara, 211, 216 *ff.*
Azeri, 179-181
Aztec, 213

Baanglaa, *see under* **Indo-European**
Baantu, *see* **Niger-Congo**
Babylonian *(language),* 224
Bactria-Margiana Archaeological Complex (BMAC), 199
Bahasa Indonesia, *see* **Indonesian**
Bahasa Malaysia, *see* **Malay**

INDEX

Balinese, 176
Balto-Slavic, *language family, discussion,* 159 *ff.*
Balto-Slavic, *language family, tree diagrams,* 134
Bantu, *see* **Baantu, Niger-Congo**
Basque, 218, 229, 230
Bengali, *see* **Baanglaa**
Benué-Congo, 169-170
Berber, 172-173
Bodo, 168
Bonobos, *language of, see* **Gesture language**
Braahmi (script), 156, 201-202
Brahmi, *see* **Braahmi**
Burashaski, 228, 231
Burmese, 168

Caddoan, 212
Cantonese, 167
Carib *(language)*, 212, 216
Caribbean, *language families of, discussion,* 211 *ff.*
Caste, *in India, in relation to ethnic and DNA constitution,* 186
Caucasian *(languages),* 228
Caucasian, *language family, discussion,* 218
Central America, *language families of, discussion,* 211 *ff.*
Central, *definition of,* 22-23
Chadic, 173
Cherokee script, 72
Chibchan, 212, 216
Chinese languages, *discussion,* 165-167
Chinese languages, ancient, *possible inflectional character of,* 227
Chinese script (ancient), 57-62
Chinook, *discussion of polysynthetic character of,* 283-284
Chroneme, 101 *ff.*
Chukotko-Kamchatkan, 218, 231
Chumashan, 212
Church Slavonic, *see* **Slavonic**
Classical Greek, *see* **Greek**
Click languages, 210; *see also* **Khoisan, !Xo Bushman**
Click languages, *articulation of,* 12; *see also* **!Xo Bushman**

INDEX

Click, 40 *ff.*
Closure, 36 *ff.*
Color *(human), in relation to language, discussion of,* 248-256
Compensation, 25
Completeness, *definition,* 67-70, 73-76
Consonant*, in relation to definition of vowel and non-vowel,* 17
Coorgi, see **Tulu**
Coptic, 224
Cushitic, 173

Daic, *language family, discussion,* 205 *ff.*
Dari, 157
Demotic (script), 173
Determinatives, 63 *ff.*
Diacritics, 77-80
Dialect, *definition,* 147 *ff.*
Dialect, *vs. language,* 147 *ff.*
Diphthong, 29-31
Discretization, *continuous,* 15
Discretization, *intermediate,* 15
Discretization, *of artition,* 15, 90 *ff.*
Discretization, *of phonological variables,* 25
DNA studies, *accuracy of, genetic drift in relation to* 183
DNA studies, *genetic data based on, see* **Genetic data**
DNA studies, *in relation to language origins,* 181-193
Dogri, 156
Dravidian, *ethnic group, geographic origins, discussion,* 181
Dravidian, *language family, discussion,* 181 *ff.* ; *see also* **Tamil, Elamite, Braahui**
Dravidian, *language family, tree diagrams,* 146
Dravidians, *map of potential geographical interactions with Aaryans (Aryans),* 193-197
Dravidians, *theory of possible westward migration from putative homeland in India,* 200
Egyptian *(language),* 173, 224

Ejective, 41 *ff.*
Elamite, 146, 181
Elamite, *relation to Tamil, see* **Tamil**
Empiricity, *definition,* 67-70, 73-76
English, *Angramaya character,* 234-240

English-like languages, *see* **Angramaya**
Equations, *vowel, see* **Vowel equations**
Eskimo (Esquimaux), 212
Estonian, 208
Ethnicity, *in relation to language, discussion of,* 248-256
Etruscan, 219, 225, 228, 230
Ewe, 169-170
Extinct languages, *see* **Languages, extinct**
Extinct or moribund languages, *see* **Languages, extinct**

Featural, *definition of,* 55 *ff.,* 65 ff., 73 *ff.*
Finnish, 178 *ff.*, 208
Finno-Ugric, 178 *ff.*
Flap, 39 *ff.*
Formant frequencies, *of fundamental vowels,* 28-29
Formosan, 174-175
Forward Fricative, 96 *ff.*
Forward Fricative, *examples of,* 97
Forward Fricative, *linguistic significance of,* 97-98
FOXP2 *(gene), in relation to language,* 5, 7
Fricatization, 38 *ff.*
Fujienese, 166
Fulfulde, 169-170

Gaandhaari, 154
Gaelic, Old, 223-224
Galatophone, 102-105
Galatophone, *examples of,* 105
Gan *(Chinese language),* 167
Genetic dating, *in relation to linguistic analysis,* 256-257; *see also* **DNA studies**
Genetic drift, *see* **DNA studies**
Georgian, 218
German, *words of Germanic origin in, comparison with English,* 235
Germanic (East, West, North), 223
Germanic, *language family, discussion,* 161
Germanic, *language family, tree diagram,* 137
Gesture language, *of bonobos,* 6
Gestures in language, 6, 7

Glide, 34
Glyph, *definition of,* 55 *ff.,* 73 *ff.*
Gothic, *see* **Germanic**
Grammar, *see* **Grammatical**
Grammatical terms, *in linguistic literature,* 263 *ff.*
Greek *(language, all phases, incl. Classical, Homeric, Mycenaean, Modern),* 221-222
Greek, *language family, tree diagram,* 132
Guarani, 216 *ff.*

Haangul script, 71
Hakka *(Chinese language),* 166
Hamitic, *see* **Afro-Asiatic**
Hamito-Semitic, *see* **Afro-Asiatic**
Hangul, *see* **Haangul**
Haplogroup, I, 229-230
Haplogroup, R1a *("Aaryan haplogroup"), discussion,* 185 *ff.* 229
Haplogroup, R1a *("Aaryan haplogroup"), prevalence today in peoples of Afghanistan, Tajikistan, Kyrgystan, Turkmenistan,* 186
Haplogroup, R2a, 229-230
Haplotype, *see* **Haplogroup**
Harappan *(language), see* **Dravidian**
Harappan script (ancient), *see* **Indian script (ancient)**
Harappan, *earliest developments, see* **Mehrgarh**
Hausa, 172-173
Hawai'ian, 175-177
Hebrew, 172
Hieroglyphics (script), 173
Hindi/Urdu, *Angramaya character,* 234-240
Hindi/Urdu, *words of Arabic and Faarsi origin in,* 239-240
Hiragana, 66, 70, 180
Hittite, 219
Hmong, 209
Hmong-Mien, *language family, discussion,* 209
Hokkien-Taiwanese, *see* **Minnan**
Homeric Greek, *see* **Greek**
Human speech, *see* **Speech, human**
Hunanese *(Chinese language), see* **Xiang**
Hungarian, *see* **Maagyaar**

INDEX

Hurrian, 189, 200

Ice Age, last (LGM), *in relation to Aaryans (Aryans) and Dravidians*, 187 *ff.*
Ice Age, last (LGM), *in relation to development of parent Indo-European language,* 187 *ff.*
Ictus accent, *see* **Accent**
Ideographic, *definition of,* 56 *ff.*
Ideo-phonograpic, *definition of,* 64 *ff.*
Igbo, 169-170
Ijo, 169-170
Implosive, 41 *ff.*
India, *aboriginal peoples of,* 183-184
Indian script (ancient), 57-62
Indian, *language family, discussion,* 152 ff.
Indian, *language family, tree diagrams,* 131 ff.
Indic, *see* **Indian**
Indo-European, *language family, discussion,* 150 *ff.*
Indo-European, *language family, number of speakers of, approx.,* 152
Indo-European, *language family, tree diagrams,* 130-137
Indo-European, *putative parent language, development of, in relation to last Ice Age (LGM),* 187 *ff.*
Indo-Germanic, *see* **Indo-European**
Indonesian, 175-176
Indus Valley, *see* **Harappan**
Infant phonemes, *see* **Phonemes, infant**
Intelligence, *human, language in relation to,* 4, 5, 8
International Phonetic Association (IPA), *alphabet of,* 16
IPA, *see* **International Phonetic Association (IPA)**
Iraanian, *language family, discussion,* 157 *ff.*
Iraanian, *language family, tree diagrams,* 132
Iraanians, *in relation to Indo-Europeans, DNA studies of,* 186-187
Iranian, *see* **Iraanian**
Irish (Old), 223-224
Iroquoian, 212
Isolates, language, *see* **Language isolates**
Italic, *language family, tree diagram,* 136

Japanese syllabary, 66, 70, 180

Japanese, 178 *ff.* ; *see also* **Altaic and Japanese**
Japanese, *language family, see* **Altaic and Japanese**
Javanese, 176
Jaw position, *as used by NAVLIPI,* 20, 26, 89 *ff.*
Je, 216 *ff.*
Jiangxese *(Chinese language), see* **Gan**

Kadai, 205
Kamchatkan, 231
Kam-Sui, 205
Kannada, 201-202
Karesan, 212
Kashmiri script, 157
Kassite, 189
Katakana (Katagana), 66, 70, 180
Kawesqar, 230
Kazhak, 179-181
Kejia, *see* **Hakka**
Keltic, 223-224
Keltic, *language family, discussion,* 162-163
Keltic, *language family, tree diagrams,* 135
Khaasi, 203 *ff.*
Khmer, 203 *ff.*
Khoisan, *language family, discussion,* 210
Kirghiz (Kirghyz), 179-181
Kordofanian, 169-170
Korean, 178-181
Kuurgi, see **Tulu**

Ladhak, 168
Language families, *world, map of distribution of,* 126
Language families, *world, tree diagrams of,* 123 *ff.*
Language isolates, *summary,* 125
Language, form of, 273-290
Language, *origins of, theories,* 4
Language, parent *(putative original human language(s)), possible form of,* 297-303, 303-309
Language, *rule of natural ordering in,* 290-296

Language, typologies, *list of,* 274
Language, typology, 273-290
Language, typology, *combinations of,* 286
Language, typology, *transformation of,* 287
Language, *vs. dialect,* 147 *ff.*
Languages, extinct or moribund, *ancient, of significance,* 219 *ff.* ; *see also under individual languages or language families*
Languages, *in world, number of, in 2005 CE,* 117
Lao, 205
Lateral, *definition of,* 22-23
Latin, *(language, all phases, incl. Old and medieval),* 222-223
Line position, *use in orthography,* 77-80, 82 *ff.*
Lip position, *as used by NAVLIPI,* 20, 26, 89 *ff.*
Liquid, 34
Logographic, *definition of,* 56 *ff.*
Logophonetic, *definition of,* 64 *ff.*
Logosyllabic, *definition of,* 64 *ff.*
Luwian, 219
Lydian, 219

Maagadhi, 154
Maagyaar, 178 *ff.,* 208
Maanchu, 179-181
Maatraic, *definition of,* 65 *ff.*
Macro-Ge, 216 *ff.*
Macro-language families, *see* **Nostratic**
Magadhi, *see* **Maagadhi**
Magyar, *see* **Maagyaar**
Mahaarashtri (Old Maraathi), 154
Malagasy, 176
Malay, 175-176
Malayaalam, 201-202
Malayalam, *see* **Malayaalam**
Malayo-Polynesian, *see* **Austronesian**
Manchu, *see* **Maanchu**
Maori, 175-177
Masaai, 207
Masai, *see* **Masaai**

Mayan, 212
Mehrgarh *(earliest Harappan semi-urban development),* 182
Mende, 169-170
Miao-Yao, *see* **Hmong-Mien**
Miinaa, 169-170
Min *(Chinese language), see* **Minnan, Minbei**
Minbei, *see* **Fujienese**
Minnan*(Chinese language),* 167
Miwok-Costanoan, 212
Mixe-Zoque, 212
Mixteco, 211, 216 *ff.*
Modern Greek, *see* **Greek**
Mongolian, 178-181
Mongolic, *language family,* 179-181
Mon-Khmer, 203 *ff.*
Moribund languages, *see under* **Languages**
Multigraphs, 77-80, 82 *ff.*
Munda, *see* **Mundaa**
Mundaa, 203 *ff.*
Musical accent, *see* **Accent; Tone**
Muskogean, 212
Myanmari, *see* **Burmese**
Mycenaean Greek, *see* **Greek**

Na-Dene, 212
Nahuatl, 213
Nama, 210
Nasalization, 37 *ff.*
Navajo (Navaho), 212
Navajo (Navaho), *discussion of polysynthetic character of,* 281 *ff.*
Negrito, 183
Nicaraguan Sign Language (NSL), 5
Nicobar Islands, *languages of,* 228-229
Niger-Congo, *language family, discussion,* 169 *ff.*
Niger-Congo, *language family, tree diagram,* 140
Nilo-Saharan, *language family, discussion,* 207
Nonvowel, *classification of,* 35 *ff.*
Nonvowel, *definition of,* 18 *ff.*

Non-vowels, *approximate total number of, in human speech,* 91
Nootka, *discussion of polysynthetic character of,* 284-285
North America, *language families of, discussion,* 211 *ff.*
Nostratic, 232
Not-Self, *see* **Self**
Noun, *see* **Substantive**
Nubian, *see* **Kordofanian**

Objectives, *of NAVLIPI Vol. II,* xxiii - xxv, 3
Oceania, *languages of,* 228-230
Olmec, 212
Organization, systematic, *of scripts, definition,* 67-70, 73-76
Organs, *for human speech, see* **Speech, human**
Origins of language, *theories, see* **Language,** *origins*
Orominga, 173
Orthography, *definition of,* 55 *ff.,* 73 *ff.*
Orthography, *tools for, modern,* 77 *ff.*
Orthography, *tools for, modern, summary of,* 84
Oto-Manguean, 213
Outlet, *for language,* 4

Paarsi, *see* **Avestan**
Pahaadi, 156
Paisaachi, 154
Pakhto, *see* **Pushtu**
Pakhtun, , *see* **Pushtu**
Panini, *see* **Paanini**
Panoan, 216 *ff.*
Papua-New Guinea, *languages of,* 228-230
Parent language, *see* **Language, parent**
Parsi, *see* **Avestan**
Pashto, , *see* **Pushtu**
Persian script (ancient), 66
Persian, *see* **Iraanian**
Phagspa (script), 180
Phoenician *(language),* 224
Phone, *definition,* 10
Phoneme, 99 *ff.*

INDEX

424

Phonemes, infant, *in relation to origin and development of language,* 297 *ff.*
Phonemic condensate, 3, 106 *ff.*
Phonemic condensate, *classification of,* 109
Phonemic condensate, *common types,* 108
Phonemic condensate, *examples,* 109
Phonemo-ideosyncratic, *definition,* 67-70, 73-76
Phonetic complements, 63 *ff.*
Phonetic shifts, *between language families,* 241 *ff.* ; *rules,* 245-247
Phonetic, *definition,* 67-70, 73-76
Phonochromaticity, 3, 42 *ff.*, 89 *ff.*, 92 *ff.*
Phonochrome, 89 *ff.*
Phonochrome, *total number (35), in NAVLIPI, Table,* 92-94
Phono-graphic, *definition of,* 64 *ff.*
Phono-indicative, *definition of,* 66
Phonological terms, *miscellaneous,* 111
Phonological variable, 25, 89 *ff.*
Phonology, *definition,* 10
p-**Italic,** *see* **Latin**
Pitch accent, *see* **Accent**
p-**Keltic,** *see* **Keltic**
Plosive, 36 *ff.*
Polynesian languages, *see* **Austronesian**
Polysynthetic languages, 281 *ff.*, 285, 286
Post-op(s), 77 *ff.* , 83 *ff.*
Post-positional operators, *see* **Post-op**
Praakrt, 155
Prakrit, *see* **Praakrt**
Pre-op(s), 77 *ff.* , 83 *ff.*
Pre-positional operators, *see* **Pre-op**
Pushtu, 157, 202
Pushtuun, *see* **Pushtu**

q-**Italic,** *see* **Latin**
q-**Keltic,** *see* **Keltic**
Quasi-phonetic, *definition,* 67-70, 73-76
Quechua, 211, 216 *ff.*
Quechuamaran, 216 *ff.*

INDEX

425

R1a haplogroup, *see* **Haplogroup**
Race, *in relation to language, discussion of,* 248-256
Rebus principle, 63 *ff.*
Rhoticity, 34
Rita *(Rule of natural order, laws of Nature), see* **Language**
Romaani, 156
Romance, *language family and languages, discussion,*162; *see also under* **Latin, Indo-European**
Rta *(Rule of natural order, laws of Nature), see* **Language**

Saami, 208
Sandhi, 29
Sanskrit, *(language, all phases, incl. Vedic, Classical ("Paaninian")),* 220-221
Sanskrit, *conjugation of verbal root -wid- in, in 2nd, 4th, 6th, 7th and 10th conjugations,* 313-341
Santhali, 203 *ff.*
Sauraseni, 154
Script, *definition of,* 55 *ff.,* 73 *ff.*
Self and Not-Self *(immunological terms), as applied to language,* 297-303
Seminole, 213
Semitic, *see* **Afro-Asiatic**
Semivowel, *definition,* 32
Semivowels, *in relation to vowels,* 32-33
Shaarada (Kashmiri) script, *see* **Kashmiri**
Shanghainese, *see* **Wu**
Shibilant, 38 *ff.*
Sibilant, 38 *ff.*
Sign language, Al-Sayyid Bedouin, *see* **Al-Sayyid Bedouin Sign Language (ASBSL)**
Sign language, *general,* 8
Sign language, Nicaraguan, *see* **Nicaraguan Sign Language (NSL)**
Single Nucleotide Polymorphism (SNP), *see* **Haplogroup**
Sino-Tibetan, *language family, discussion,* 164 *ff.*
Sino-Tibetan, *language family, tree diagrams,* 139-140
Siouan, 213
Slavonic (Old), 223
Slavonic, Church, *see* **Slavonic**
Sonant, 36 *ff.*
South America, *language families of, discussion,* 216 *ff.*

Speech, human, *organs for, figure,* 11, 12
Spirant, 38 *ff.*
Stop, 36 *ff.*
Stress accent, *see* **Accent**
Substantive, *attributes of (number, gender, case, others),* 272 *ff.*
Sumerian script (ancient), 57-62
Sumerian, 224-225, 228
Sumerian, *possible inflectional character of,* 225
Supra-language families*, see* **Nostratic**
Surd, 36 *ff.*
Susian, 200
Swaahili, 169-170
Swahili, *see* **Swaahili**
Syllabary, 62
Syllabic, *definition of,* 56 *ff.*
Synthetic languages, 280 *ff.,* 286
Systematic organization, *of scripts, see* **Organization, systematic**

Tagalog, 175-176
Tahitian, 175-177
Tai, 205
Taino/Arawakian, 211, 216
Taiwan, *Austronesian languages of,* 174-175
Tamil, *relation to "Proto-Dravidian",* 188 *ff.*
Tamil, *relation to Elamite,* 188 *ff.*
Tamil, *relation to Elamite, comparative Table of cognate words,* 190-191
Tap, 39 *ff.*
Telaguu, *see* **Telugu**
Telugu, 201-202
Thai script, 71
Thai, 205
Thigh slapping, *as expression of language,* 4
Tibetan, 168
Tibeto-Burman, *language family, discussion,* 168 *ff.*
Ticuanan, 216 *ff.*
Tokhaarian, 224
Tokharian, *see* **Tokhaarian**
Tone, 43 *ff.*

INDEX

427

Toneme, 101 *ff.*
Tones, *Cantonese,* 44
Tones, fundamental, *definition of,* 44
Tones, *Mandarin,* 44
Tones, significant, *definition of,* 44
Tones, *Yoruba,* 44
Tongue articulation position, *as used by NAVLIPI,* 21-24, 26, 89 *ff.*
Transcription, *definition of,* 55 *ff.,* 73 *ff.*
Transformed letters (glyphs), 78 *ff.* ; *of the IPA,* 78
Transformed letters (glyphs), *of NAVLIPI,* 79
Trill, 40 *ff.*
Trojan, Troy, 219
Tulu, 156, 201-202
Tungusic, *language family,* 179-181
Tupian, 216 *ff.*
Turkic, *language family,* 179-181
Turkish script, 72
Turkish, 179-181
Turkish, *conjugation of verbs in,* 278 *ff.*
Turkish, *declension of nouns in,* 278

Uighur, 179-181
Uni-phonemographic, *definition,* 67-70, 73-76
Uni-phonographic, *definition,* 67-70, 73-76
Unvoiced, 35 *ff.*
Ural-Altaic, *language family*, 178 *ff.*
Uralic, *language family*, 178 *ff.*
Uralic, *language family, discussion,* 208
Uto, 213
Uvular nasal phone, *articulation of,* 12
Uyghur, *see* **Uighur**
Uzbek, 179-181

Vai script, 171
Vaigyaanic, *definition,* 67-70, 73-76
Variable, dependent, *see* **Phonological variable**
Variable, phonological, *see* **Phonological variable**
Vedic Sanskrit, *see* **Sanskrit**

Verb, *as fundament of language,* 264 ff.
Verb, *attributes (number, gender, tense, mood, voice, others), Table,* 267-271
Verb, *attributes (person, number, gender, tense, mood, voice, others),* 264 ff.
Verb, *conjugation, animation,* 265 ff.
Vietnamese script, *modern, diacritics in,* 80 ff.
Vietnamese, 203 ff.
Voiced, 35 ff.
Voicing, *see* **Voiced**
Vowel equations, 30-31
Vowel, cardinal, *see* **Vowel, fundamental**
Vowel, *classification of,* 19 ff. , 31 ff.
Vowel, *definition of,* 17 ff.
Vowel, fundamental, 27-29
Vowel, fundamental, *formant frequencies of, see* **Formant frequencies**
Vowel, *generation of,* 26 ff.
Vowel, *length of,* **24-25**
Vowels, *approximate total number of, in human speech,* 91

Wakashan, 213
wid (vid), *(Sanskrit verbal root), see* **Sanskrit**
World language families, *see* **Language**
World languages, *see* **Languages**
Writing, *origins of,* 56 ff.
Writing, *tools for, see* **Orthography**
Wu *(Chinese language),* 167

Xiang *(Chinese language),* 167

Yoruba, 169-170
Yue *(Chinese language), see* **Cantonese**
Yuman, 212, 213

Zhejiangese, *see* **Wu**
Zoroastrian, *see* **Avestan**
Zulu, 169-170
Zuni, 212, 231

ABOUT THE AUTHOR

Education, Experience, Positions Held

Prasanna Chandrasekhar was born on 17 October 1957 in Mumbai, India. He received his B.Sc. (Honors) in Chemistry from the University of Delhi, Delhi, India in 1978, his M.S. in Inorganic Chemistry/X-Ray-Crystallography from Concordia University, Montréal, Canada in 1980, and his Ph.D. in Electro-analytical Chemistry from the State University of New York at Buffalo, Buffalo, NY, USA in 1984. He was a postdoctoral associate at the Department of Chemistry and Materials Science Center, Cornell University, Ithaca, NY, USA in 1984-5, and a Senior Research Scientist at Honeywell, Inc. in Minneapolis, MN, USA and Horsham, PA, USA from 1985-1987. From 1987-1992, he was Manager of Electrochemical Programs at Gumbs Associates, Inc., East Brunswick, NJ, USA. He founded Ashwin-Ushas Corporation, a small U.S. defense contractor (*see* http://www.ashwin-ushas.com), in October 1992, and has been President and CEO there since.

Current Scientific Interests and Work

Dr. Chandrasekhar's current scientific research interests and active research include conducting polymers, electrochemistry, materials science, solar energy, space sciences, bio-remediation, remediation of hazardous medical wastes and analytical microbiology.

Publications

Dr. Chandrasekhar is the author of over 90 peer-reviewed scientific papers. He has also authored several chapters in textbooks, and is the sole author of the widely acclaimed (non-edited) textbook *Conducting Polymers: Fundamentals and Applications. A Practical Approach* (Kluwer Academic Publishers/Springer Verlag, Boston, USA and Dordrecht, The Netherlands, 1999, ISBN 0-7923-8564-0); this is still used in graduate courses throughout the world. A current publication list is available on request.

ABOUT THE AUTHOR

LANGUAGE, PHONOLOGY, LINGUISTICS:
Work and Experience in These and Related Fields

While he had no formal training in the linguistics or related fields, a highly multi-lingual and multi-cultural environment during early childhood sparked a strong interest in these fields early on for Dr. Chandrasekhar. This was nurtured with active self-study of major languages and ancient literature, as well as linguistics, phonology, comparative philology and related subjects.

Dr. Chandrasekhar has *reading, writing and speaking fluency* in: English, French, German, Hindi/Urdu, Maraathii (Marathi), Tamil, and Classical and Vedic Sanskrit**.

He has *reading ability* in: Spanish, Italian, Portuguese, Romanian, Classical Greek, Anglo-Saxon (Old English), Nepaali (Nepali), and several other languages.

Dr. Chandrasekhar also has a basic, *"100-word street vocabulary"*, without reading or writing ability, in several other languages, as varied as Egyptian Arabic, Dutch and Mandarin common speech (*Putonghua*).

He also has a very strong grounding in English (including Old and Middle English) literature, in Sanskrit (including Vedic) literature, and in the grammar of Indo-European, Dravidian, and several other language families.

Dr. Chandrasekhar taught a non-credit course in Elementary Sanskrit and Dewanaagari Script to students of Latin and Greek in the Classics Department of Princeton University, Princeton, NJ, USA, in the Spring semester of 1989. He taught a similar course in 2005-6 to Indian-American children at a local Hindu temple (Sri Guruvayoorappan Temple, Marlboro, NJ) in New Jersey, USA.

Dr. Chandrasekhar is also currently working on a Sanskrit Primer especially targeted to students of Classics (Greek, Latin). This will use the *Navlipi* script, along with Dewanaagari, Roman and Greek transcriptions.

**[See footnote, Ref. [LAi-83], regarding "speaking fluency" in Sanskrit, and a discussion of whether what we know as Sanskrit today is merely a literary language, thanks to Paanini (Panini) and others, and, if so, what the spoken language might have been like.]*

www.ingramcontent.com/pod-product-compliance
Lightning Source LLC
Chambersburg PA
CBHW060308240426
43661CB00059B/2690